DIDYMUS THE BLIND
AND THE ALEXANDRIAN CHRISTIAN
RECEPTION OF PHILO

STUDIA PHILONICA MONOGRAPHS

General Editor
Thomas H. Tobin, S. J.

Number 8

DIDYMUS THE BLIND
AND THE ALEXANDRIAN CHRISTIAN
RECEPTION OF PHILO

by
Justin M. Rogers

 PRESS

Atlanta

Copyright © 2017 by Justin M. Rogers

All rights reserved. No part of this work may be reproduced or transmitted in any form or by any means, electronic or mechanical, including photocopying and recording, or by means of any information storage or retrieval system, except as may be expressly permitted by the 1976 Copyright Act or in writing from the publisher. Requests for permission should be addressed in writing to the Rights and Permissions Office, SBL Press, 825 Houston Mill Road, Atlanta, GA 30329 USA.

Library of Congress Cataloging-in-Publication Control Number: 2017952398

Printed on acid-free paper.

STUDIA PHILONICA MONOGRAPHS
STUDIES IN HELLENISTIC JUDAISM

Editor

Thomas H. Tobin, S.J.

Advisory Board

Ellen Birnbaum, Cambridge, MA
Jacques Cazeaux, CNRS, University of Lyon
Lester Grabbe, University of Hull
Annewies van den Hoek, Harvard University
Pieter W. van der Horst, Zeist, The Netherlands
Alan Mendelson, Hamilton, Canada
Robert Radice, Sacred Heart University, Milan
Jean Riaud, Catholic University, Angers
James R. Royse, Claremont, CA
David T. Runia, University of Melbourne
Gregory E. Sterling, Yale Divinity School
David Winston, Berkeley

The Studia Philonica Monographs series accepts monographs in the area of Hellenistic Judaism, with special emphasis on Philo and his Umwelt. Proposals for books in this series should be sent to the Editor: Prof. Thomas H. Tobin, S.J., Theology Department, Loyola University Chicago, 1032 W. Sheridan Road, Chicago IL 60660-1537, U.S.A; Email: ttobin@luc.edu.

CONTENTS

List of Abbreviations xi

INTRODUCTION

The Life of Didymus the Blind 1
The Importance of Didymus the Blind 4
Didymus as an Author 6
The Plan for This Work 9

1
DIDYMUS AND THE ALEXANDRIAN SCHOLASTIC HERITAGE

Introduction 10
Philo's Connection with the Alexandrian Scholastic Tradition 10
The Place of Didymus the Blind within the Alexandrian School 17
Didymus as Student and Teacher within the Alexandrian School 20

2
PHILO'S ACCEPTANCE INTO ALEXANDRIAN CHRISTIANITY

Introduction 25
Clement of Alexandria 26
Origen 31
After Origen 34
    Pseudo-Justin 35
    Arius 37
    Athanasius 38
    Eusebius 39
Conclusion 47

viii CONTENTS

3
THE USE OF SOURCES IN CHRISTIAN COMMENTARIES

Introduction 49
Plagiarism and Named References in Ancient Literature 50
Why Refer to Predecessors? 53
Conclusion 57

4
THE JEWISH SOURCES OF DIDYMUS IN THE TURA COMMENTARIES

Introduction 59
The Jewish Sources of Didymus (Excluding Philo) 61
    The Book of the Covenant 61
    The Ascension of Isaiah 63
    The Apocalypse of Elijah 65
    Josephus 67
    Jewish Tradition 71
    Aquila, Symmachus and Theodotion 72
Conclusion 74

5
DIRECT REFERENCES TO PHILO IN THE TURA COMMENTARIES

Introduction 75
The Commentary on Zechariah 76
The Commentary on Ecclesiastes 78
The Commentary on Genesis 81
    (1) *Comm. Gen.* 118.24–119.2: *On Cain and Abel, the Order of Their Births* 82
    (2) *Comm. Gen.* 119.2–10: *On Cain and Abel as Conditions of the Soul* 85
    (3) *Comm. Gen.* 119.11–23: *On Cain and Abel and Their Occupations* 87
    (4) *Comm. Gen.* 139.10–14: *On the Posterity of Cain* 93
    (5) *Comm. Gen.* 147.15–18: *On Adam and Seth* 95
    (6) *Comm. Gen.* 234.31–236.21: *On Sarah and Hagar* 97

Conclusion 117

6
BORROWINGS FROM PHILO: ETYMOLOGY

Introduction 119
Didymus and the Semantics of Biblical Language 119
Etymology and Biblical Interpretation 122
Etymology as a Means of Biblical Interpretation 126
    Etymology in Philo 127
    Etymology in Origen 130
    Etymology in Didymus the Blind 133
Conclusion 142

7
BORROWINGS FROM PHILO: ARITHMOLOGY

Introduction 143
Arithmology in Hellenistic-Jewish Interpretation 144
    Arithmology in Philo 147
    The Philonic View of Arithmology 148
Arithmology in Origen 150
Arithmology in Didymus the Blind 154
    The Methodology of Didymus's Arithmology 156

8
PHILONIC BORROWINGS:
GENERAL EXEGETICAL AND PHILOSOPHICAL THEMES

Introduction 165
The Philonic Impact on Didymus's Doctrine of the Preexistence
    of Souls 165
    Origen on the Preexistence of Souls 166
    Philo on the Preexistence of Souls 169
    Didymus on the Preexistence of Souls 171

CONTENTS

The Philonic Impact on Didymus's Doctrine of Virtue 177
    The Philonic Impact on Didymus' Doctrine of Prepassions and
    Passions 177
    Philo on Prepassion 178
    Origen on Prepassion 179
    Didymus on Prepassion.. 180
The Philonic Impact on Didymus's Doctrine of Ethical Progress
    and the Stages of Virtue 183
    Didymus on Virtue 186
The Philonic Impact on Didymus's Doctrine of the Divine Powers 190
    Didymus on the Divine Powers... 195
Further Areas of Philonic Influence on Didymus's Interpretation
    of the Genesis Creation Account... 199
    Human Hegemony over Animal Creation 199
    Creation in the Image of God 203
Conclusion 208

9
REVIEW AND CONCLUSION

Review and Conclusion 209
Bibliography... 212
Indices 239

LIST OF ABBREVIATIONS

AB	The Anchor Bible
ABRL	Anchor Bible Reference Library
AGJU	Arbeiten zur Geschichte des antike Judentums und des Urchristentums
AJEC	Ancient Judaism and Early Christianity
ALGHJ	Arbeiten zur Literatur und Geschichte des Hellenistischen Judentums
ANRW	*Aufstieg und Niedergang des römischen Welt*
BETL	Bibliotheca Ephemeridum Theologicarum Lovaniensium
BIB	*Biblica*
BICS	Bulletin for the Institute of Classical Studies
BJS	Brown Judaic Studies
CBQ	*Catholic Biblical Quarterly*
CBQMS	Catholic Biblical Quarterly Monograph Series
COMES	Civitatum Orbis Mediterranei Studia
CP	*Classical Philology*
CPJ	*Corpus Papyrorum Judaicarum*. Edited by Victor A. Tcherikover. 3 vols. Cambridge: Harvard University Press, 1957–1964.
CQ	*Classical Quarterly*
CRINT	Compendia Rerum Iudaicarum ad Novum Testamentum
CSCO	Corpus Scriptorum Christianorum Orientalium. Edited by Jean Baptiste Chabot et al. Paris, 1903.
DMOA	Documenta et Monumenta Orientis Antiqui
FC	Fathers of the Church
FRLANT	Forschungen zur Religion und Literatur des Alten und Neuen Testaments
GCS	Die griechischen christlichen Schriftsteller der ersten [drei] Jahrhunderte
GRBS	*Greek, Roman, and Byzantine Studies*
Hen	*Henoch*
HOS	Handbook of Oriental Studies
HTR	*Harvard Theological Review*
HUT	Hermeneutische Untersuchungen zur Theologie
NTS	*New Testament Studies*
JAC	*Jahrbuch für Antike und Christentum*
JBL	*Journal of Biblical Literature*
JECS	*Journal of Early Christian Studies*
JEH	*Journal of Ecclesiastical History*

JHI	*Journal of the History of Ideas*
JHS	*Journal of Hellenic Studies*
JJS	*Journal of Jewish Studies*
JQR	*Jewish Quarterly Review*
JSJ	*Journal for the Study of Judaism*
JSJSup	Journal for the Study of Judaism Supplements
JTS	*Journal of Theological Studies*
Klio	*Klio: Beiträge zur Alten Geschichte*
LCL	Loeb Classical Library
LSJ	Liddell, Henry George, Robert Scott, Henry Stuart Jones. *A Greek-English Lexicon*. 9th ed. with revised supplement. Oxford: Clarendon, 1996
LXX	Septuagint
MT	Masoretic Hebrew Text
NAWG	*Nachrichten (von) der Akademie der Wissenschaften in Göttingen*
NRSV	New Revised Standard Version
OCD	*Oxford Classical Dictionary*
OECS	Oxford Early Christian Studies
PACS	Philo of Alexandria Commentary Series
PCW	*Philonis Alexandrini opera quae supersunt.* Edited by Leopold Cohn, Paul Wendland, and Siegried Reiter. 6 vols. Berlin: De Gruyter, 1896–1915.
PG	Patrologia Graeca
PhA	Philosophia Antiqua
PLCL	Philo in Ten Volumes (and Two Supplementary Volumes). Translated by Frederick H. Colson, George H. Whitaker (and Ralph Marcus). 12 vols. Loeb Classical Library. Cambridge: Harvard University Press, 1929–1962.
PO	Patrologia Orientalis
PRE	*Pauly's Real-Encyclopedia der classischen Altertumswissenschaft.* New edition by George Wissowa and Wilhelm Kroll. 50 vols. In 84 parts. Stuttgart: Metzler and Druckenmüller, 1894–1980.
PTA	Papyrologische Texte und Abhandlungen
PTS	Patristische Texte und Studien
RB	*Revue Biblique*
RevScRel	*Revue des sciences religieuses*
RHE	*Revue d'histoire ecclésiastique*
RHPR	*Revue d'histoire et de philosophie religieuses*
RHR	*Revue d'histoire des religions*

RSPT	*Revue des sciences philosophiques et théologiques*
RSR	*Recherches de science religieuse*
RSV	Revised Standard Version
SBLSP	Society of Biblical Literature Seminar Papers
SC	Sources chretiennes
SCH	Studies in Church History
SCO	Studi classici e orientali
SEAug	Studia Ephemeridis Augustinianum
Sem	*Semitica*
StPatr	Studia Patristica
SPhiloM	Studia Philonica Monographs
SPhiloA	*Studia Philonica Annual*
SPhilo	*Studia Philonica*
STAC	Studien und Texte zu Antike und Christentum
SVF	*Stoicorum Veterum Fragmenta*
TLG	Thesaurus Linguae Graecae
TK	Texte und Kommentare
TSAJ	Texte und Studien zum Antike Judentum
TU	Texte und Untersuchungen
TUGAL	Texte und Untersuchungen zur Geschichte der altchristlichen Literatur
VC	*Vigiliae Christianae*
VCSup	Vigiliae Christianae Supplements
VTSup	Vetus Testamentum Supplements
WUNT	Wissenschaftliche Untersuchungen zum Neuen Testament
ZAC	*Zeitschrift für Antikes Christentum/Journal of Ancient Christianity*
ZAW	*Zeitschrift für alttestamentliche Wissenschaft*
ZKG	*Zeitschrift für Kirchengeschichte*
ZPE	*Zeitschrift für Papyrologie und Epigraphik*

INTRODUCTION

Didymus the Blind was famous in his own day. Unfortunately, within a century of his death, he had fallen victim to the charge of Origenism. His work *On the Holy Spirit* continued to circulate thanks to the Latin translation of Jerome, but his exegetical comments lived on mostly in the catenae. An accidental discovery in 1941, however, yielded approximately 2000 papyrus pages representing commentaries on Gen, Job, Psa, Ecc, and Zech, along with other works.[1] Although these commentaries represent only a fraction of Didymus's exegetical output,[2] they provide us with the largest corpus of biblical exegesis in Greek from a single Christian author.[3]

The Life of Didymus the Blind

The life of Didymus spanned nearly the entire fourth century CE. He was born in Egypt and probably never left there, serving as a theological instructor in one of the desert monasteries outside of Alexandria.[4] Despite

---

1. The Tura papyri were found when the British were clearing an area south of Cairo for the storing of munitions. The story of their discovery has been reported in several publications (e.g., Henri-Charles Puech, "Les nouveaux écrits d'Origène et de Didyme découverts à Toura," *RHPR* 31 [1951]: 293–329; Louis Doutreleau, "Que Savons-nous aujourd'hui des Papyrus de Toura?," *RSR* 43 [1955]: 161–76; Ludwig Koenen and W. Müller-Wiener, "Zu den Papyri aus dem Arsenios Kloster bei Tura," *ZPE* 2 [1968]: 41–63). Some Didymean papyri on Psa remain unpublished, although Brigham Young University professors are in the process of editing them (for photographs of the papyri online, see http://contentdm.lib.byu.edu/cdm/compoundobject/collection/Didymus Papyri/id/58). For an introduction to the collection at BYU, see Dave Nielsen, "The History, Provenance, and Importance of BYU's Didymus Papyri" (online: http://scholarsarchive.byu.edu/cgi/viewcontent.cgi?article=1083&context=studentpub).

2. Didymus makes reference to a host of other works, including commentaries on Exod, Lev, Prov, Song, Isa, Jer, Dan, Hos, Matt, Luke, John, Acts, Rom, 2 Cor, Gal, Eph, Heb, the Catholic Epistles, and Rev (see Louis Doutreleau, *Didyme l'Aveugle: Sur Zacharie*, vol. 1 [SC 83; Paris: Cerf, 1962], 17–19).

3. The commentaries on Gen and Zech were published in the *Sources Chrétiennes* series, and those on Job, Psa, and Ecc appeared in the *Papyrologische Texte und Abhandlungen* series. Thankfully, these editions were not only carefully edited, but translations (in either French or German) were added along with brief explanatory notes. To date, only two of the commentaries have been translated into English, both by the late Robert C. Hill (*Didymus the Blind: Commentary on Zechariah* [FC 111; Washington, D.C.: Catholic University of America Press, 2006]; *Didymus the Blind: Commentary on Genesis* [FC 132; Washington, D.C.: Catholic University of America Press, 2016]).

4. Much has been made about the fact that Rufinus refers to Didymus as a teacher (*doctor*) rather than a director (*magister*) of the famed catechetical school of Alexandria

the desert solitude, it was a volatile time to be a Christian in Egypt. Sociological and ecclesiastical conflict was on the rise, and the political situation of the empire was in transition.[5] But Didymus's interests seem to be almost entirely ecclesiastical. As an ally of Athanasius, he fought early Arianism and Eunomianism, then turned to fight Manicheanism and, later in life, was himself involved in the Origenist controversy.[6] He was also an early hero of monasticism, and entertained the famed Antony.[7] As a teacher, he exerted an exegetical influence on some of the most important figures in the early church, including Eastern figures such as Evagrius Ponticus and Palladius and Western figures such as Rufinus and Jerome. So who was this mysterious teacher who became such a dominant figure in fourth century Egypt?

For biographical details of Didymus's life, we are entirely dependent on his students. We possess three major biographical sources that date within a generation of Didymus's death, but they disagree on the dates of his death and hence his birth. Jerome states that Didymus was already more than eighty-three years old when he composed his *Vir. ill.*, which, as he informs us, was completed "in the fourteenth year of Theodotion," or 392/393 CE. So, according to Jerome, Didymus was born in or before 310 CE.[8] But Palladius, who moved to Alexandria in ca. 388 CE, claims to have visited Didymus four times in a ten-year span. Since Palladius reports that

---

(see the discussion in Richard A. Layton, *Didymus the Blind and His Circle in Late-Antique Alexandria* [Urbana, IL: University of Illinois Press, 2004], 15–18). The relevant testimony reads, *ita brevi deo docente in tantam divinarum humanarumque rerum eruditionem ac scientiam venit, ut scholae ecclesiasticae doctor exsisteret, Athanasio episcopo ceterisque sapientibus in ecclesia dei viris admodum probatus* (*H.E.* 11.7). Older generations of scholars (e.g., Leipoldt, Bardy) were content to trust the ancient biographers (e.g., Philip of Side and Sozomen) in placing Didymus as head of the catechetical school in Alexandria. But newer generations (e.g., Prinzivalli, Layton) have suggested that he never occupied this role.

5. See, for example, Christopher Haas, "Hellenism and Opposition to Christianity in Alexandria," in *Ancient Alexandria between Egypt and Greece*, ed. W.V. Harris and Giovanni Ruffini (Columbia Studies in the Classical Tradition 26; Leiden: Brill, 2004), 217–29.

6. In the Tura commentaries, Didymus never mentions Origen or the controversy surrounding him. However, in fragments of other works the name of Origen does appear. In an interpretation of 1 Cor 16:17–18, Didymus says, οὕτω καὶ ὁ Ὠριγένης δοξάζει τὸ πνεῦμα πλείω τι ἔχειν τῆς ψυχῆς ἐν ἀρετῇ, εἰ καὶ πνεῦμα καὶ ἡ ψυχή (*Fr. 1 Cor. ad loc.*).

7. Antony is reported to have said of Didymus, *nihil te, offendat, O Didyme, quod carnalibus oculis videris orbatus, desunt enim tibi illi oculi, quos mures et muscae et lacerate habent; sed laetare, quia habes oculos, quos angeli habent, e quibus deus videtur, per quos tibi magnum scientiae lumen accenditur* (Rufinus, *H.E.* 11.7; cf. Jerome, *Epist.* 68.2).

8. *Vir. ill.* 1, 135. On Didymus's life, see *Vir. ill.* 109.

Didymus died at eighty-five years of age, his death should be placed around 398 CE, and hence his birth at ca. 313 CE.⁹

Despite the minor confusion about the dates of his life, the blindness of Didymus is a feature about which all of the ancient sources agree. Apparently, Didymus was not born blind, but became so at a very young age due to an accident or a disease.¹⁰ Palladius states that Didymus had suffered his handicap prior to his learning of the alphabet, and thus had to rely totally on memory for his education.¹¹ Sozomen, who depends on earlier sources, imagines the learning of Didymus to be more concrete, reporting the blind student learned the alphabet by running his fingers across a deeply-etched wooden tablet of the alphabet, as though an ancient form of Braille.¹²

However he obtained his early education, it is clear that Didymus was a gifted student and, in adulthood, acquired a reputation for his erudition that extended far beyond his native land. Rufinus imagines him confounding philosophers who approach him with questions.¹³ Even acknowledging that Rufinus's portrait is idealized, the fact that such fourth-century scholars as Rufinus, Jerome, Evagrius Ponticus, Palladius, and probably Gregory of Nazianzus refer to him confirms the reputation he enjoyed in the catholic church of his time.¹⁴

---

9. *Hist. Laus.* 4.1. Palladius himself was accused of Origenism at the Council of the Oak in 403, according to Photius (*Lex.* 59).

10. Palladius seems to have the better information, claiming, οὗτος ἀπὸ ὀμμάτων ὑπῆρχεν, ὡς αὐτός μοι διηγήσατο, τετραέτης τὰς ὄψεις ἀποβαλών (*Hist. Laus.* 4.1). In his *Chron.* Jerome places the blindness of Didymus slightly later, at age five (*Chron.* 246e to the year 372 CE [GCS 24, *Eusebius Werke* VII/1, ed. R. Helm]). In *Vir. ill.* 109, however, Jerome is more ambiguous, stating that the accident occurred "when he was still quite young" (*a parva aetate*, *Vir. ill.* 109). Socrates informs us that a disease took his eyesight: οὗτος κομιδῇ νέος ὢν καὶ τὰ πρῶτα τῶν γραμμάτων στοιχεῖα μαθὼν τῷ τῆς ὀφθαλμίας περιέπεσε πάθει καὶ κακῶς διατεθεὶς τὸ ὁρατικὸν ἀπέβαλεν (*H.E.* 4.25).

11. *Hist. Laus.* 4.1; Socrates informs us that he was in the process of learning the alphabet when he suffered his blindness (*H.E.* 4.25).

12. Sozomen, *H.E.* 3.15.2: Λέγεται δὲ τοὺς χαρακτῆρας τῶν γραμμάτων σανίδι καταχαραγέντας εἰς βάθος ἐκμαθεῖν τοῖς δακτύλοις ἐφαπτόμενος.... Jerome does not include this detail but refers to his elementary learning as *tantum miraculum* (*Vir. ill.* 109).

13. *H.E.* 11.7

14. For Gregory of Nazianzus's acquaintance with Didymus, see John A. McGuckin, *St. Gregory of Nazianzus: An Intellectual Biography* (Crestwood, N.Y.: SVS Press, 2001), 44–45.

The Importance of Didymus the Blind

Didymus the Blind is important in a number of ways. First, Didymus was the last great representative of what modern scholars identify as "Alexandrian" biblical interpretation. Second, he lived during the beginnings of Egyptian monasticism, and exerted an influence on the famous Antony. Third, he receives glowing endorsements from Evagrius Ponticus, Rufinus, Jerome, and Palladius, who personally knew him, studied under him and occasionally requested works from him. Fourth, the work of Robert Hill has shown that Didymus served as a conduit between the Alexandrians and the Antiochenes,[15] a link that may prove promising for those who wish to emphasize the positive dialogue between the schools of thought.

Indeed, the legend and legacy of Didymus appear to have been great. Jerome commemorates him on three occasions as *videns* ("the seeing"),[16] which suggests that the familiar epithet of *caecus* ("the blind") was already being applied to Didymus during his own lifetime.[17] In one case Jerome speaks of studying under Didymus, noting "I thank him for many things. What I did not know I learned; what I knew ... I did not lose."[18] Sozomen states, "Many people came to Alexandria because of his fame, some to hear him and others merely to visit him,"[19] and later, "he was in high demand by men from the whole church."[20] The historian Socrates places Didymus alongside the famed Cappadocian fathers Basil the Great and Gregory of Nazianzus.[21] The entire Christian tradition would remember Didymus both

---

15. On the influence of Didymus among the Antiochenes, see Robert C. Hill, *Reading the Old Testament in Antioch* (The Bible in Ancient Christianity 5; Leiden: Brill, 2005), 8–9, 22, 29, 33, 40–41, 76, 95, 146. Most of Hill's examples are based on *Comm. Zach.*, which is understandable since he was about to issue a translation of the work (see note 3 above).

16. Prologue to his *Comm. Gal.*; see also the prologues to his translations of Origen's *Hom. Jer.* and *Hom. Ezek.* Jerome would later attempt to separate himself from Didymus, however, in the wake of the first Origenist controversy.

17. Pierre Nautin dates Jerome's commentaries on Philemon, Galatians, Ephesians, and Titus between June/July and early Autumn of 386 CE. See "La date des commentaires de Jérôme sur les épîtres pauliniennes," *RHE* 74 (1979): 5–12. Other scholars are not so specific, being content to date the four commentaries between 386 and 388 CE. See Alfred Friedl, "St. Jerome's Dissertation on the Letter to Philemon," in *Philemon in Perspective: Interpreting a Pauline Letter* (ed. D. Francois Tolmie; Berlin: De Gruyter, 2010), 289–316, 289.

18. *Epist.* 84.3: *In multis ei gratias ago. Quod nescivi, didici; quod sciebam ... non perdidi.*

19. *H.E.* 3.15.3: καὶ πολλοὶ κατὰ κλέος τοῦ ἀνδρὸς εἰς Ἀλεξάνδρειαν παρεγέγοντο, οἱ μὲν αὐτοῦ ἀκουσόμενοι, οἱ δὲ ἱστορήσαντες μόνον.

20. *H.E.*, 3.15.4: Τοῖς δὲ ἀπὸ τῆς καθόλου ἐκκλεσίας περισπούδαστος ἦν.

21. *H.E.* 4.25.

in his own time and shortly thereafter, almost universally expressing an admiration for his exegetical talent and Nicene orthodoxy.²²

But the influence of Didymus on subsequent biblical scholarship would be relatively short-lived. Despite his dedication to the Nicene ideal, Didymus was committed, although not uncritically,²³ to the controversial Origen.²⁴ Because of his acceptance and propagation of characteristic Origenist teachings, church history would cast a dark shadow on Didymus.²⁵ Toward the end of his life, the so-called Origenist controversy was already gaining steam, and after his death, in around 398 CE, many tried to break allegiance with Didymus.²⁶ His writings were formally condemned

---

22. The most famous work of Didymus in the Catholic tradition is his *De spirito sancto*. This work attempts to explain the Holy Spirit as a hypostasis alongside the Father and the Son, and was translated into Latin by Jerome at the request of Pope Damasus in ca. 384 CE (see the preface to the Latin translation of *De spirito sancto* and *Epist.* 36.4 of Jerome to Damasus). It is supposed by some modern scholars that Didymus coined the phrase τρεῖς ὑποστάσεις, μία οὐσία (see John Chapman, "Didymus," in *The Catholic Encyclopedia* 4:784 [1908]). Didymus, however, wrote other dogmatic works. His *De trinitate* is a work which appeared orthodox to Jerome (*Ruf.* 2.16). He also wrote *De dogmatibus* and *contra Arianos*, which may be one book or two. Quasten identifies both with books 4 and 5 of the *contra Eunomium*, a work traditionally attributed to Basil rather than Didymus (e.g., *Patrology* 3:88, 210). Jerome reports that Didymus had indeed refuted Eunomius in *Vir. ill.* 120, but whether one can connect the *contra Eunomium* 4–5 with Didymus at all remains doubtful. Recently, Mark DelCogliano has argued that Basil was influenced by Didymus's *De trinitate* in his composition of *contra Eunomium* and, even if Didymus himself did not author books 4–5 of that work, the Didymean tenor of those sections, as well as the whole of books 1–3, remains evident (*JTS* 61 [2010]: 644–58). The position of Hayes is different; see Walter M. Hayes, "Didymus the Blind is the author of Adversus Eunomium IV/V," StPatr 17 (1982): 1108–14.

23. Emanuela Prinzivalli remarks that "the literary production of Didymus appears to be that which is the most balanced in juxtaposing faithfulness to Origen's teaching with a re-thinking of this very teaching" (*Origeniana Decima: Origen as Writer* [ed. Sylwia Kaczmarek and Henryk Pietras; Leuven: Peeters, 2011], 779). Prinzivalli's statement can serve as a corrective to Manlio Simonetti's overly optimistic suggestion that we can use Didymus's *Comm. Gen.* to reconstruct Origen's lost commentary on Gen (*Biblical Interpretation in the Early Church: An Introduction to Patristic Exegesis* [trans. John A. Hughes; Edinburgh: T&T Clark, 1994], 78).

24. Didymus reportedly wrote a commentary on Origen's *Princ.* (Jerome, *Ruf.* 2.16; Socrates, *H.E.* 4.25.7).

25. Didymus, for example, held the notion that souls pre-exist, one of the more controversial of Origen's teachings by the end of Didymus's own life (*Comm. Gen.* 106.10ff. [on Gen 3:21]; *Comm. Job* 56.16–58.16).

26. Jerome, who had been a disciple of Didymus and a translator of at least two of his works (the *Comm. Zach.* and *Did. Spir.*), later rejected him for his Origenism (his *Ruf.* 1.6 is representative where he deems Didymus *Origenis apertissimus propugnator*), a point on which Rufinus keenly attacked his rival (note his *Apol. Hier.* 2.28 where he recalls Jerome's former praises of Didymus as *videns* and *propheta* and *apostolicos vir*).

a century and a half later, along with those of Origen, at the ecclesiastical Council of Constantinople in 553.[27]

Didymus as an Author

The literary output of Didymus is remarkable. Among Alexandrian biblical scholars only Origen is credited with writing more works. And Didymus was certainly not limited to one area of interest. We will discuss the role of Didymus as a biblical exegete, but we should not neglect his other literary efforts. Didymus was a controversialist, personally associated with Athanasius.[28] We know he defended the Trinity against the Arians and Eunomius[29] and wrote a treatise *On the Holy Spirit*, which now exists in Jerome's Latin translation.[30] He regarded "the godless doctrines of the Arians, Manicheans and Eunomius" as having "sprung up like weeds"[31] and did what he could to refute them.[32]

Didymus also shows an interest in philosophy, authoring treatises *On the Soul*, *On Incorporeals*, *On Philosophy*, and *On the Virtues*. All of these treatises,

---

27. For a discussion of the early history of the controversy see Emanuela Prinzivalli, *Magister Ecclesiae: Il Dibattito su Origene fra III e IV Siecolo* (Studia Ephemeridis Augustinianum 82; Rome: Institutum Patristicum Augustinianum, 2002). For the events leading to the condemnation of the Origenists at the fifth ecumenical council see Franz Diekamp, *Die origenischen Streitigkeiten im sechsten Jahrhundert und das fünfte allgemeine Concil* (Münster: Aschendorff, 1899), 131. Diekamp places the date of the official condemnation in March or April, 553. For the roles of Rufinus and Jerome and their circles in the controversy, see Elizabeth A. Clark, *The Origenist Controversy: The Cultural Construction of an Early Christian Debate* (Princeton: Princeton University Press, 1992).

28. Rufinus, *Hist. eccl.* 2.7; Palladius *Hist. Laus.* 4.4.

29. There has been controversy over the authorship of both *Trin.*, attributed to Didymus, and books 4–5 of the *Contra Eunomium*, which has been passed down as a work of Gregory of Nyssa (for the authorship of Didymus's alleged Trinitarian writings see Alasdair Heron, "Studies in the Trinitarian Writings of Didymus the Blind: his Authorship of the Adversus Eunomium IV–V" [Ph.D. diss., Tübingen, 1972]).

30. On the Christology of Didymus, see Michael Ghattas, *Die Christologie Didymos' den Blinden von Alexandria in den Schriften von Tura: Zur Entwicklung der alexandrinischen Theologie des 4. Jahrhunderts* (Studien zur Orientalischen Kirchengeschichte 7; Münster: Lit, 2002). *De spiritu sancto* now exists in a convenient English translation (see Mark DelCogliano, Andrew Radde-Gallwitz, and Lewis Ayres, *Works on the Holy Spirit: Athanasius the Great and Didymus the Blind* [Popular Patristics Series 43; Yonkers, N.Y.: SVS Press, 2011]).

31. *Comm. Eccl.* 302.13: παρεφύη δόγματα ἀσεβῆ τὰ Ἀρειανῶν καὶ Μανιχαίων, τὰ Ἐ[ὐ]ομίου.

32. On Didymus and the Manicheans, see Byard Bennett, "Didymus the Blind's Knowledge of Manichaeism," in *The Light and the Darkness: Studies in Manichaeism and its World* (ed. Paul Mirecki and Jason Beduhn; Leiden: Brill, 2001), 38–67.

although probably rich in Philonic influence, have been lost.³³ Didymus probably never studied philosophy formally, however. Richard Layton goes so far as to suggest that Didymus's philosophy was already mediated by Christian scholasticism, and that he probably never "advanced beyond the preliminary grammatical instruction to the study of rhetoric."³⁴ Still, he remains an important source on Aristotelianism as well as the Christian engagement with Porphyry.³⁵

We have testimony, either from Didymus himself or from his admirers, of no less than twenty-five commentaries on biblical books. Some books were given focused attention, such as Isaiah (two works), but it is doubtful whether most of these commentaries were ever completed. Of the preserved commentaries from Tura, only Zech and Ecc were treated *in toto*.³⁶ Obviously, these shorter biblical books made completion attainable. Gen and Job, by contrast, were likely never completed,³⁷ and although Jerome says that Didymus wrote commentaries on every Psalm,³⁸ there is no other indication that the *Comm. Ps.* was finished.

As an exegete, Didymus shows a penchant for allegorical interpretation, but not to the neglect of the letter. The so-called *defectus litterae* is not as prominent in Didymus as it was in Origen or Philo, and often he extracts maximum utility from the literal meaning.³⁹ Of course, there are the usual

---

33. Philo himself wrote a treatise *On Virtues*, which is mostly preserved (see the discussion in Walter T. Wilson, *Philo of Alexandria On Virtues: Introduction, Translation and Commentary* [PACS 3; Leiden: Brill, 2011], 10–15).

34. Layton, *Didymus the Blind*, 137.

35. On Didymus and Aristotelianism see David T. Runia, "Festugière Revisited: Aristotle in the Greek Patres," *VC* 43 (1989): 1–34. On Didymus and Porphyry see Philip Sellew, "Achilles or Christ? Porphyry and Didymus in Debate over Allegorical Interpretation," *HTR* 82 (1989): 79–100, and Pier Franco Beatrice, "Didyme l'Aveugle et la tradition de l'allégorie," in *Origeniana Sexta: Origène et la Bible/Origen and the Bible* [ed. Gilles Dorival and Alain Boulluec; Leuven: Leuven University Press, 1995], 579–90.

36. This is not to say we actually possess the full treatments. The manuscripts are lacunose at several points.

37. It is possible that at least Gen was never intended to be completed. David Runia observes that Didymus's commentary stops in chapter 17, almost precisely the span of Philo's Allegorical Commentary (*Philo in Early Christian Literature: A Survey* [CRINT 3.3; Assen: Van Gorcum; Minneapolis: Fortress, 1993], 200).

38. *Vir. ill.* 109.

39. For the so-called *opheleia*-criterion in biblical exegesis see Manlio Simonetti, *Lettera e/o allegoria: un contributo alla storia dell'esegesi patristica* (Studia Ephemeridis Augustinianum 23; Rome: Institutum Patristicum Augustinianum, 1985), 79, 146–47. As this relates to Didymus, see Simonetti, "Lettera e allegoria nell'esegesi veterotestamentaria di Didimo," *Vetera Christianorum* 20 (1983): 341–89, 356.

dismisals of anthropomorphic and anthropopathic texts.[40] But in general, Didymus seeks to investigate all levels of potential meaning. This leads to a consistent feature of his exegesis. Didymus generally begins with the most obvious level of interpretation (the literal) and progresses to the most obscure (the allegorical).[41] The *Comm. Gen.* is the most rigid in this regard, although the other Tura commentaries follow the same basic approach.[42]

The point of this interpretive methodology is to lead the reader in his spiritual progress toward virtue, or Christ.[43] Sometimes Didymus expresses this goal in the Platonic sense of ὁμοίωσις θεῷ,[44] and sometimes he Christianizes the formula.[45] Still, the goal is to contemplate God "as he is."[46] The commentaries of Didymus presuppose the Bible to be the fundamental means to achieve the goal of divine contemplation.[47] By focusing on each verse or set of verses, Didymus systematically walks through the biblical text, allowing scripture to be its own best interpreter.[48] Any source

---

40. See Roland Marcin Pancerz, "Didimo il Cieco e gli anthropomorfismi biblici," in *Origeniana Decima*, 751–63.

41. It has been suggested that Porphyry composed different commentaries adapted to the level of student sophistication (H. J. Blumenthal, *Aristotle and Neoplatonism in Late Antiquity: Interpretations of the De anima* [Ithaca, N.Y.: Cornell University Press, 1996], 22). Didymus seeks to accomplish a similar goal in a single work.

42. See e.g., *Comm. Gen.* 102.9–12; 139.4–14; 226.24. On the basic notion of two senses in scripture, as it relates to Didymus, see Jo Tigcheler, *Didyme l'Aveugle et l'exégèse allégorique: Étude sémantique de quelques termes exégétiques importants de son commentaire sur Zacharie* (Graecitas Christianorum Primaeva 6; Nijmegen: Dekker & Van de Vegt, 1977). On the allegorical method of Didymus in general, the work of Wolfgang Bienert is still basic, "*Allegoria*" *und* "*Anagoge*" *bei Didymos dem Blinden von Alexandria* (PTS 13; Berlin: de Gruyter, 1972).

43. See Placid Solari, "Christ as Virtue in Didymus the Blind," in *Purity of Heart in Early Ascetic and Monastic Literature: Essays in Honor of Juana Raasch*, ed. Harriet A. Luckman and Linda Kulzer [Collegeville, Minn: Liturgical, 1999], 67–88).

44. E.g., *Comm. Eccl.* 99.6–7. The terminology is taken from Plato's *Theaetetus* 176b. For a discussion of the ὁμοίωσις formula in an Alexandrian Christian context, see Salvatore R. C. Lilla, *Clement of Alexandria: A Study in Christian Platonism and Gnosticism* (Oxford Theological Monographs; Oxford: Oxford University Press, 1971), 60–117.

45. Knowledge of the Trinity is a prerequisite (*Comm. Job* 288.14–22).

46. E.g., *Comm. Eccl.* 238.26.

47. David Hay argues that the goal of Philo's Allegorical Commentary was exactly the same ("Philo of Alexandria," in *Justification and Variegated Nomism* [ed. Donald A. Carson, Peter T. O'Brien and Mark A. Seifrid; Grand Rapids: Baker Academic, 2001], 1:357–80, 365).

48. This of course reminds us of Origen's interpretive methodology (on Origen as commentator, see Christoph Markschies, "Origenes und die Kommentierung des paulinischen Römerbriefs," in *Commentaries–Kommentare* [ed. Glenn W. Most; Aporemata: Kritische Studien zur Philologiegeschichte 4; Göttigen: Vandenhoeck and Ruprecht, 1999], 66–94, and Lorenzo Perrone, "Continuité et innovation dans les commentaires d'Origène: Un essai de comparaison entre le *Commentaire sur Jean* et le *Commentaire sur*

of information that assists him in explicating the biblical text is fair game. This includes both Christian and non-Christian sources, and it is in this context that we shall investigate his use of Philo of Alexandria.

The Plan for This Work

The explicit mention of Philo in Didymus the Blind is curious. Although Didymus, as most ancient authors, did not generally name his sources, Philo's name appears nine times in the Tura commentaries. In fact, Philo is named in Didymus more than any other non-biblical author. This becomes more curious when we recognize that Didymus names Origen only once, the author assumed by modern scholars to be his most influential source.[49] Didymus's infrequent mention of Origen has been attributed to the growing Origenist controversy,[50] but Didymus shows no clear awareness of it, and Philo himself was cited in this controversy as a corrupting force in Origen's thought.[51] So Philo ought to have been as scandalous to some as Origen himself.

So we must first establish in this study that Philo was already an authority entrenched in Didymus's tradition of biblical exegesis. The first two chapters are, consequently, overviews of Didymus's Alexandrian heritage and the role that Philo played in that tradition. Then we shall go on to show how Didymus utilizes and cites his sources. We do this by setting Didymus in the ancient Christian commentary tradition of source citation and then by comparing his usage of Jewish sources in general to his named citations of Philo. This covers chapters 3–5. Finally, we discuss specific examples of interpretive methodology shared among the two authors, such as etymology and arithmology, as well as common exegetical themes. We discuss this material in chapters 6–8. The purpose of this work is to show that, while Clement and Origen can *sometimes* be regarded as mediators of Philonic thought for Didymus, it is clear also that Didymus knew Philo directly and utilized him as a trusted exegetical source.

Matthieu," in *Le Commentaire entre tradition et innovation* [ed. Marie-Odile Goulet-Cazé; Bibliotèque d'histoire de la philosophie; Paris: J. Vrin, 2000], 183–97.

49. See Pierre Nautin, *Didyme l'Aveugle: Sur la Genèse* (SC 233; Paris: Cerf, 1976), 1:22.
50. See Runia, *Philo in Early Christian Literature*, 201.
51. See Theodore of Mopsuestia, "Treatise against the Allegorists," in Frederick G. McLeod, *Theodore of Mopsuestia* (The Early Church Fathers; New York: Routledge, 2010), 75–79.

1

DIDYMUS AND THE ALEXANDRIAN SCHOLASTIC HERITAGE

Introduction

The Alexandrian school is the ancient Christian scholastic institution about which we are best informed. Eusebius claimed that the school existed from ancient times, although evidence for this claim is scant. At times, the school appears to have been a private institution under a vibrant personal director. At other times, the school was the more official "catechetical school" sponsored by the Alexandrian church.[1] Didymus stands in this scholastic heritage, as does Philo of Alexandria. Didymus is a scholar, utilizing the work of earlier exegetes within his tradition. Therefore, it is necessary to discuss how both the works and ideas of Philo might have reached Didymus and how they became invested with such exegetical authority.

Philo's Connection with the Alexandrian Scholastic Tradition

The beginnings of Alexandrian Christianity remain obscure.[2] The Eusebian notion that the Therapeutae are the first Christians in Egypt tells us more of Eusebius's knowledge of Philo than of early Egyptian Christianity.[3] Also, the Markan mission to Egypt in general and to Alexandria in particular, while possibly historical, cannot even be confirmed by Eusebius, who cites the information as hearsay: "This [Mark], they claim, was the first

---

1. According to Gustave Bardy, the school first became institutionalized with Origen in 202 CE. During his time, the school developed two tiers of instruction, Origen taking the more advanced students and his pupil Heraclas the elementary ones ("Pour l' histoire de l'école d'Alexandrie," *Vivre et Penser* 2 [1942]: 80–109). This position is taken up by Attila Jakab, who portrays Heraclas as a betrayer of Origen, ultimately allying with the Bishop Demetrius to oust Origen (*Ecclesia alexandrina: Evolution sociale et institutionnelle du christianisme alexandrine* [Wien: Lang, 2001], 226).

2. On Egyptian Christianity before Clement see, for example, C. Wilfred Griggs, *Early Egyptian Christianity from Its Origins to 451 CE* (Leiden: Brill, 2000), 13–43.

3. *Hist. eccl.* 2.16–17. For an analysis, see Sabrina Inowlocki, Eusebius of Caesarea's *Interpretatio Christiana* of Philo's *De vita contemplativa*," *VC* 97 (2004): 305–28.

to preach the Gospel in Egypt, after being sent there, and the first to establish churches in Alexandria itself."[4]

It is equally unclear to what extent the synagogual structure of the vibrant Jewish community at the time of Philo translated into the early Christian community in Egypt.[5] By the time of Pantaenus and Clement the church of Alexandria appears to have lost any significant Jewish presence. The ethnic transition probably occurred in the aftermath of the diaspora revolt of 115–117 CE during which time the Jewish community appears to have suffered tremendous decline.[6]

It might be imagined that the Christians simply adapted the existing structure of the Jewish community, including its schools. Whatever schools of scriptural learning existed among the Jews of Alexandria, if they existed at all, probably disappeared during the years following the diaspora revolt. If such schools were connected with the synagogues in Alexandria,[7] they would have been affected even earlier by the pogrom of 38 CE,[8] and probably also by the turmoil of 66 CE.[9] Most scholars prefer to locate Philo's teaching in the synagogues, at least partially.[10] If Gregory Sterling is

---

4. *Hist. eccl.* 2.16.1 (trans. mine). The Greek reads, Τοῦτον δὲ Μάρκον πρῶτόν φασιν ἐπὶ τῆς Αἰγύπτου στειλάμενον, τὸ εὐαγγέλιον, ὃ δὴ καὶ συνεγράψατο, κηρῦξαι, ἐκκλησίας τε πρῶτον ἐπ' αὐτῆς Ἀλεξανδρείας συστήσασθαι.

5. Philo numbers the Jewish community of his time at one million people, although it is generally agreed that the number, as ancient population estimates in general, is exaggerated (*Flacc.* 43). On synagogual worship in Philo see Jutta Leonhardt, *Jewish Worship in Philo of Alexandria* (Texts and Studies in Ancient Judaism 84; Tübingen: Mohr Siebeck, 2001), 74–95.

6. See Victor A. Tcherikover, "The Decline of the Jewish Diaspora in Egypt in the Roman Period," *JJS* 14 (1963): 1–32. Christopher Haas, however, cautions such conclusions based on the scanty evidence we possess (see *Alexandria in Late Antiquity: Topography and Social Conflict* [Baltimore: Johns Hopkins, 1997], 412, n. 46).

7. Philo uses several designations for synagogues, the most common of which is προσευχή (also συναγωγή [*Post.* 67; *Somn.* 2.127; *Legat.* 311]; ἱερός περίβολος [*Flacc.* 48]). Philo is the only ancient author to describe synagogues as διδασκαλεῖα (*Mos.* 2.216; *Spec.* 2.62; Lee I. Levine, *The Ancient Synagogue: The First Thousand Years* [2nd ed.; New Haven: Yale University Press, 2005], 90). It is doubtful, however, that Philo wishes us to see the synagogue as a διδασκαλεῖον in a formal sense.

8. Philo repeatedly emphasizes antagonism toward the synagogue as a key factor in the conflict (e.g., *Legat.* 132–39; 311–13; *Flacc.* 45–52).

9. Josephus, *J.W.* 2.489–97; 7.369. On the events in Alexandria see Joseph Mélèze Modrzejewski, *The Jews of Egypt from Rameses II to Emperor Hadrian* (trans. Robert Cornman; Philadelphia: Jewish Publication Society, 1997), 187–90.

10. E.g., Valentin Nikiprowetzky, *Le Commentaire de l'Écriture chez Philon d'Alexandrie* (Leiden: Brill, 1977), 178–79. Wolfson suggests that Philo taught in synagogual schools on days other than the Sabbath (Harry Austryn Wolfson, *Philo: Foundations of Religious Philosophy in Judaism, Christianity, and Islam* [Cambridge: Harvard University Press, 1948], 1:79. A grand pre-Philonic scholastic tradition as imagined a hundred years ago by Bousset has

correct, however, in suggesting that Philo operated a private school,[11] it is possible that his school, through successors, could have survived the ethnic hostilities in the city. If such a school contained a library of the works of Philo and others, we would then possess a concrete basis for understanding how Clement of Alexandria might have inherited the Philonic corpus.[12]

Only one source suggests a direct continuity between Philo and the Christian school of Alexandria. Written in the late sixth century CE, the *Cause of the Foundation of the Schools* is an account of, *inter alia*, the early Christian school of Alexandria.[13] The Syriac Father Barhadbeshabba states that the Alexandrian school of Christian interpretation was actually founded by Philo Judaeus.[14] After describing the zeal with which the Alexandrian school studies the scriptures, Barhadbeshabba writes, "The

---

not found wide acceptance (Wilhelm Bousset, *Jüdisch-Christlicher Schulbetrieb in Alexandria und Rom* [Göttingen: Vandenhoek & Ruprecht, 1915]). It is still generally agreed, however, that "while Philo was probably associated with a synagogue, his writings [or at least the Allegorical Commentary] were probably used in a synagogue-school where Philo taught the higher vision of scripture to a select group of initiates whose ears were purified" (R. Alan Culpepper, *The Johannine School: An Evaluation of the Johannine-School Hypothesis Based on an Investigation of the Nature of Ancient Schools* [SBL Dissertation Series 26; Missoula, Mont.: Scholars Press, 1975], 211).

11. This school, as Gregory Sterling proposes, would have housed Philo's own writings as well as those of other Jewish authors. The library then eventually fell into Christian hands, thus explaining the use of such sources in Clement of Alexandria ("'The School of Sacred Laws': The Social Setting of Philo's Treatises," *VC* 53 [1999]: 148–64).

12. Sterling addresses this possibility, theorizing that either a Christian student in the school made arrangements to copy Philo's works, or a leader of the school converted to Christianity ("The School," 163). Following Sterling, Royse suggests that Philo's works were housed in the private library of this school, and hence were unpublished (James R. Royse, "Did Philo Publish His Works?," *SPhiloA* 25 [2013)]: 75–100, 99). Annewies van den Hoek agrees that a physical Christian school with a library is responsible for the preservation of Philo's writings ("The 'Catechetical' School of Early Christian Alexandria and Its Philonic Heritage," *HTR* 90 [1997]: 59–87).

13. On the date of this text see Adam H. Becker, *Sources for the Study of the School of Nisibis* (Liverpool: Liverpool University Press, 2008), 86–93. A translation of our document can be found on pp. 94–160.

14. Barhadbeshabba introduces himself as "the chief of the *baduqe* of the holy School of the town of Nisibis," and later styles himself "presbyter and *mepashqana*" (in his *Historia ecclesiastica*; see Arthur Vööbus, *History of the School of Nisibis* [Leuven: Peeters, 1965], 280–82). Barhadbeshabba wrote three works that can be classified as historical in nature. The first is known as the "History of the holy fathers, persecuted for the reason of truth," or by its shorter title, "(*Historia*) *ecclesiastica*." He also wrote a work entitled "Cause of followers of Mar Diodor." There are apparently two Barhadbeshabbas contemporary with one another (see Becker, *Sources*, 11–16).

administrator and [chief] interpreter of this school was Philo the Jew who founded it."[15]

Admittedly, our author is a representative of the School of Nisibis and therefore is heavily influenced by the "Antiochene" tradition. Theodore of Mopsuestia had already associated Origen with Philo in his *Treatise against the Allegorists*.[16] Theodore writes, "As regards these questions [of allegorical interpretations], since the illustrious Mar Origen did not find anyone who could teach him about what is true in the divine Scriptures, he turned to Philo to serve as his guide for interpreting allegories, in order to shamelessly change everything written there according to this [method of] interpretation."[17] Theodore wishes to identify Origen's intentional corruption of pure Christian hermeneutics by having him seek out a Jewish teacher for his allegorical method. The implication, which Barhadbeshabba apparently takes over, is that Alexandrian scholasticism is a corruption that begins with Philo.

For historical purposes Barhadbsabba's account is of little value. If we are right about Barhadbeshabba's source, then his motive is purely polemical. Had there been any evidence of a direct succession from Philo to early Alexandrian Christianity, it is unimaginable that Eusebius of Caesarea would have omitted it. Eusebius in fact begins his documentation of the school's history in ca. 180 CE with Pantaenus.[18] If we take the list of Philip of Side into consideration, we can go a little farther back, to Athenagoras.[19] But Philip is almost certainly mistaken. First, Athenagoras is associated with Alexandria only in Philip, the traditional association with Athens being more likely.[20] Further, it is generally agreed that the list of Philip is unreliable.[21] This leaves us with the account of Eusebius.

---

15. Trans. mine (PO 4.4.18, 375, 112). See the discussion in David T. Runia, *Philo in Early Christian Literature* (Assen: Van Gorcum; Minneapolis: Fortress, 1993), 269–71, and Sterling, "The School," 148.

16. Vööbus states that so many of Theodore's works were translated into Syriac that "before the death of Theodore in 428 almost all of his literary legacy had been made available to the Syrians" (*History*, 19). It can be thus be assumed that Barhadbeshabba is aware of Theodore's hostilities.

17. Translation, Frederick G. McLeod, *Theodore of Mopsuestia* (The Early Church Fathers; New York: Routledge, 2010), 78. The Syriac translation (the Greek is lost) can be found in Lucas Von Rompay, *Théodore de Mopsueste: Fragments syriaques du Commentaire des Psaumes (Psaume 118 et Psaumes 138–148)* (CSCO 190; Leuven: Peeters, 1982).

18. Although Pantaenus is mentioned in Clement (*Ecl.* 56.2), very little is revealed of him. The Eusebian account is a mixture of history and legend (*Hist. eccl.* 5.10–11).

19. Τοῦ διδασκαλείου ἐν Ἀλεξανδρείᾳ Ἀθηναγόρας πρῶπος ἡγήσατο (PG 39:238).

20. On the security of the Athenian connection of Athenagoras, see David Rankin, *Athenagoras: Philosopher and Theologian* (London: Ashgate: 2009), 5–10. Bernard Pouderon has defended the authenticity of Philip's note that Athenagoras was a resident of

Eusebius states, "At that time a man very famous for his learning named Pantaenus had charge of the life of the faithful in Alexandria, for from ancient custom a school of sacred learning existed among them."[22] The phrase "from ancient custom" (ἐξ ἀρχαίου ἔθους) is surprisingly vague, for Eusebius had a list (whether accurate or not) of the bishops of Alexandria, dating back to the beginnings of the church there.[23] Many modern scholars assume Eusebius simply lacked a comparative list of scholarchs, and the gloss "from ancient custom" is inaccurate.[24] But others, following the lead of Walter Bauer, have suggested that Pantaenus succeeded gnostic teachers in the catechetical school.[25] This scenario assumes that Eusebius had ancient information about the institution but chose to omit it for

---

Alexandria ("Athénagore chef d'école. A propos du témoignage de Philippe de Side," StPatr 26 [1993]: 167–76).

21. Gustave Bardy asserts of the list of Philip as a whole, "semblent [the names of directors] y avoir été introduits pour donner l'illusion d'une continuité glorieuse et pour assurer à la métropole de la Pamphylie la gloire d'avoir recueilli l'héritage d'Alexandrie" ("Pour l' histoire," 109). Pouderon likewise doubts that Athenagoras was the founder of the famous Alexandrian school: "si l'on peut attribuer à l'apologiste la direction d'une école privée christianisante, il est plus difficile de lui imputer la création du didascalée alexandrin" (*D'Athènes à Alexandrie: études sur Athénagore et les origines de la philosophie chrétienne* [Leuven: Peeters, 1997]), 175.

22. *Hist. eccl.* 5.10.1, trans. Lake, LCL. The Greek reads, Ἡγεῖτο δὲ τηνικαῦτα τῆς τῶν πιστῶν αὐτόθι διατριβῆς ἀνὴρ κατὰ παιδείαν ἐπιδοξότατος, ὄνομα αὐτῷ Πάνταινος, ἐξ ἀρχαίου ἔθους διδασκαλείου τῶν ἱερῶν λόγων παρ' αὐτοῖς συνεστῶτος.

23. See the following references for a succession of Alexandrian bishops up to the time of Pantaenus: *Hist. eccl.* 2.24; 3.21; 4.1; 4.4; 4.5.5; 4.11.6; 4.19; 4.20; 5.9, taking us from 62 CE to 182 CE. This material, it is generally agreed, was taken from Julius Africanus (see Robert Lee Williams, *Bishop Lists: Formation of Apostolic Succession of Bishops in Ecclesiastical Crises* [Piscataway, NJ: Gorgias, 2005], 143–59).

24. Since the work of Bardy, scholars have questioned the accuracy of Eusebius's portrait of the school in general (Gustave Bardy, "Aux origins de l'école d'Alexandrie," *RevScRel* 27. [1937]: 64–90; "Pour l'histoire," 80–109; M. Hornschuh, "Das Leben des Origenes und die Entstehung der alexandrinischen Schule," *ZKG* 71 [1960]: 1–25; Clemens Scholten, "Die alexandrinische Katechetenschule," *JAC* 38 [1995]: 16–37). More recent attempts have been made to rescue at least some of Eusebius's reliability (e.g., Dietmar Wyrwa, "Religiöses Lernen im zweiten Jahrhundert und die Anfänge der alexandrinischen Katechetenschule," in *Religiöses Lernen in der biblischen, frühjüdischen und frühchristlichen Überlieferung* (ed. Beate Ego and Helmut Merkel; WUNT 180; Tübingen: Mohr Siebeck, 2005), 271–305.

25. On the gnostic character of Egyptian Christianity before Clement, see Walter Bauer, *Orthodoxy and Heresy in Earliest Christianity* (ed. Robert A. Kraft and Gerhard Krodel; Philadelphia: Fortress, 1971), 44–60. On the notion that Pantaenus succeeded gnostic teachers, see Colin H. Roberts, *Manuscript, Society and Belief in Early Christian Egypt* (Schweich Lectures on Biblical Archaeology; Oxford: Oxford University Press, 1985). A more reserved verdict can be found in Birger Pearson, *Gnosticism, Judaism and Egyptian Christianity* (Philadelphia: Fortress, 1990), 194–213.

apologetic reasons.[26] We know that the famous gnostics Basilides and Valentinus spent time in Alexandria, and both acquired a large following.[27] We also know that Clement generally avoids the term διδασκαλεῖον, and it has been suggested he does so because of the term's heretical implications.[28] It is not improbable that such men, later to be considered heretics,[29] could ascend to the leadership of an ecclesiastical school.[30] If heretical teachers held such a post for any length of time, however, it is difficult to imagine that our sources would reflect no memory of it.

As far as the antiquity of the Alexandrian school is concerned, we can only theorize. We have no unambiguous evidence that Alexandrian Judaism promoted schools, and the New Testament gives no clear indication of any traditional scholastic activity.[31] Jerome, who probably depends on Eusebius here, saw a continuity of thought between the Therapeutae described in Philo and the Alexandrian διδασκαλεῖον, but neither he nor Eusebius ties Philo formally to the development of the early Christian community of Alexandria.[32] A number of modern scholars have observed that the survival of the Philonic library among the Alexandrian Christians

---

26. Van den Hoek notes that Irenaeus connects *doctrina*, the equivalent of διδασκαλεῖον, with Valentinus, Marcion, and Tatian (*Haer.* 1.11.1; 1.24.7; 2.31.1; 1.27.1–2; 1.28.1; "The 'Catechetical' School," 63), potentially lending linguistic support to the scholastic heresy theory.

27. For a convenient survey of these men and their influence see Pearson, *Ancient Gnosticism* (Philadelphia: Fortress, 2007), 134–44 (Basilides) and 145–89 (Valentinus).

28. This is the suggestion of van den Hoek ("The 'Catechetical' School," 74).

29. The famous thesis of Moritz Friedländer was that Gnosticism originated prior to the advent of Christianity in the antinomian circles of Alexandrian Judaism (*Der vorchristliche jüdische Gnosticismus* [Göttingen: Vandenhoek & Ruprecht, 1898]). For a critique see Birger Pearson, *Gnosticism, Judaism and Egyptian Christianity* (Philadelphia: Fortress, 1990), 10–28.

30. Tertullian informs us that Valentinus was considered for bishop of Rome (*Val.* 4).

31. Sterling believes that commentary writing can be considered a scholastic activity ("Philo's School: The Social Setting of Ancient Commentaries," in *Sophisten im Hellenismus und Kaiserzeit: Orte, Methoden und Personen der Bildungsvermittlung* [ed. Beatrice Wyss; STAC; Tübingen: Mohr Siebeck]; "Philo's School: The Social Setting of Ancient Commentaries," in Sophisten im Hellenismus und Kaiserzeit: Orte, Methoden und Personen der Bildungsvermittlung [ed. Beatrice Wyss, Rainer Hirsch-Leupold, Solmeng-Jonas Hirschi; STAC 101; Tübingen: Mohr Siebeck, 2017], 123–42]. If he is correct, Philo's commentaries may actually provide us with a concrete basis for the scholastic context of his activity. Even so, there is no way to establish a link between Philo's possible scholasticism and that of the early church.

32. Jerome writes in *Vir. ill. 36, Pantaenus, Stoicae sectae philosophus, iuxta quamdam veterem in Alexandria consuetudinem, ubi a Marco evangelista semper ecclesiastici fuere doctores....*" On Eusebius's highly suggestive presentation, see Justin Rogers, "Origen in the Likeness of Philo: Eusebius of Caesarea's Portrait of the Model Scholar," *Studies in Christian-Jewish Relations* 12 (2017): 1–13.

provides at least some basis for an organic link, but when this link was forged is impossible to know.³³ Josephus is the earliest figure to have certainly used Philo,³⁴ but we have to wait almost one hundred years until the next example, Clement of Alexandria. How did Josephus access the Philonic works? Did Philo publish his works? Did his family, students, or community publish them?³⁵ Despite the historical ambiguities, the survival of the Philonic corpus is the single tangible link connecting Alexandrian Judaism with the scholastic tradition of Alexandrian Christianity.³⁶

The Place of Didymus the Blind within the Alexandrian School

We possess no reliable information about a Christian scholastic institution in Alexandria prior to Pantaenus. But our sources all agree that some school appears to have existed in some sense from the time of Pantaenus until at least the time of Didymus the Blind.³⁷ Most modern scholarship has been devoted either to the origins of the school or to the first three figures associated with the school (Pantaenus, Clement, and Origen).³⁸ This

---

33. Dominique Barthélemy formulated, "Il est donc très vraisemblable que ce fut au didascalée d'Alexandrie, sous Pantène ou sous Clément, que l'oeuvre de Philon, ou du moins ce que l'on en put regrouper, fut sauvée de l'abandon où les juifs hellénophones la laissaient. C'est là que le savant juif renié par son peuple fut promu père de l'Église et que dut être constituée la collection-archétype d'où dérivèrent d'un côté les papyri de Coptos et d'Oxyrhynque, de l'autre les papyri apportés à Césarée par Origène" ("Est-ce Hoshaya Rabba qui censura le «Commentaire Allégorique»?," in *Philon d'Alexandrie: Colloques nationaux du centre national de la recherche scientifique, Lyons, 11–15 Septembre 1966* [Paris: Centre National de la recherche scientifique, 1967], 45–78, 60). See also Runia, *Philo in Early Christian Literature*, 22. But Sterling rejects Barthélemy's conclusion ("School of Sacred Laws," 161–62).

34. See most recently Gregory Sterling, "Did Josephus Know the Writings of Philo?," *SPhiloA* 25 (2013): 101–13.

35. James Royse argues that Philo did not publish his works ("Did Philo Publish His Works?," *SPhiloA* 25 [2013]: 75–100) against Gregory Sterling, who suggests that he did intend them to circulate ("Recherché or Representative? What Is the Relationship between Philo's Treatises and Greek-Speaking Judaism?," *SPhiloA* 11 [1999]: 1–30).

36. See Van den Hoek, "The 'Catechetical' School," 81–85, and Sterling "School of Sacred Laws," 160–63.

37. The final name in the list of Philip of Side is Rodon, the student and apparent successor of Didymus. He, according to Philip, "moved the school [διατριβή] to Sidon at the time of Theodosian the great, with whom Philip himself studied" (ὃς καὶ μετήγαγε ... τὴν διατριβὴν ἐν τῇ αὐτῇ πόλει τῇ Σιδῇ κατὰ τοὺς χρόνους τοῦ μεγάλου Θεοδοσίου· τούτῳ Ῥόδωνι λέγει μαθητεῦσαι ὁ Φίλιππος; PG 39:229).

38. Bardy, "Pour l'histoire de l'Ecole d'Alexandrie," devotes only seven of twenty-nine pages to the period after Origen. A notable exception is the fine essay of Emanuela Prinzivalli, "Le metamorfosi della scuola alessandrina da Eracala a Didimo il Cieco," in *Origeniana Octava*, ed. Lorenzo Perrone [Leuven: Peeters, 2003], 911–37.

restricted focus is due to the fact that the sources become less detailed and, according to the modern assessment, less reliable after the time of Origen.

We have already discussed the skepticism with which scholars view Philip of Side, but even Eusebius has been judged as unreliable for the history of the school in the third and fourth centuries CE.[39] Scholars generally feel that Eusebius is motivated to connect the school with the bishop in order to lend legitimacy to the institution. This stress leads him to invent scholarchs when he has no reliable information. Surely it is not a coincidence that Heraclas (*Hist. eccl.* 6.19.13), Dionysius (6.29.4), and Achillas (7.32.30) move from the position of scholarch to bishop of Alexandria. This looks too good to be true. However, Emanuela Prinzivalli has offered a welcome reassessment of the historical record. She argues that the modern skepticism toward Eusebius is unwarranted.

First, the existence of the scholastic institution through the third century is confirmed by different and independent sources.[40] Second, Eusebius did not create an artificial succession for the "filling out" of the school's history, as scholars argue, since he leaves a gap between Dionysius and Achillas.[41] Third, a closer examination of Eusebius reveals that he does not always connect the school so closely with the bishop. At times the connection is much looser.[42] Prinzivalli has convincingly demonstrated that, at least from the ancient point of view, the school continued to exist throughout the third and fourth centuries CE.

Eusebius, however, does not take us as far as Didymus the Blind, whose appointment in the school occurs after the death of the Caesarean. The ancient sources seem to disagree about whether Didymus was officially the scholarch of the catechetical school in Alexandria. Philip of Side and Sozomen clearly believe that he was.[43] However, modern scholars have

---

39. Prinzivalli writes, "Lo scetticismo ... pare attualmente la modalità di ricezione più diffusa della notizia di Eusebio" ("Le metamorfosi," 913).

40. "Le metamorfosi," 913–14.

41. "Le metamorfosi," 915. Incidentally, Prinzivalli does not believe that lack of information indicates cessation of scholastic activity ("Le metamorfosi," 925).

42. Prinzivalli believes this "loosening" of episcopate and school occurred during the tenure of Dionysius. She writes, "l'episcopato di Diongini abbia segnato una scolta nei rapporti con il didaskaleion, nel senso di un allentamento dei rapporti fra le due entità" ("Le metamorfosi," 925).

43. At the beginning of his discussion on Didymus, Sozomen states, Ὑπὸ δὲ τοῦτον τὸν χρόνον καὶ Δίδυμος ὁ ἐκκλησιαστικὸς συγγραφεὺς διέπρεπε, προϊστάμενος ἐν Ἀλεξανδρείᾳ τοῦ διδασκαλείου τῶν ἱερῶν μαθημάτων. Ἐν τούτῳ δὲ καὶ παντοδαπὴ σοφία ᾤκει, ποιηταί τε καὶ ῥήτορες, ἀστρονομία τε καὶ γεωμετρία καὶ ἀριθμοὶ καὶ δέξαι φιλοσόφων (*H.E.* 3.15.1). Philip of Side includes Didymus in his list of Alexandrian scholarchs (PG 39:229).

focused on the testimony of Rufinus, the earliest historian to inform us of Didymus's scholastic role.[44]

In his description of Didymus's rise, Rufinus states, "Thus in a short time, with God as his teacher, he arrived at such expert knowledge of things divine and human that he became the master of the church school, having won the high esteem of Bishop Athanasius and the other wise men in God's church."[45] Older generations of scholars took Rufinus to mean the renowned apologist Athanasius himself appointed Didymus as head of the famed Alexandrian catechetical school (e.g., Leipoldt, Bardy, Bienert). This seems to be the most natural reading of the passage. Recently, however, scholars have called attention to the fact that Rufinus refers to Didymus only as a *doctor* and does not use the term *magisterium*, his usual translation for the office of catechetical director.[46] Therefore, according to Richard Layton, all one may conclude from Rufinus is that Didymus was a teacher of some reputation in Christian Alexandria.[47] We can agree with Layton that the term *doctor* for "catechetical director" is not typical of Rufinus's vocabulary. But against Layton we may cite the ancient church

---

44. Older generations of scholars accepted that Didymus was head of the school but disagree as to when he received his position. Johannes Leipoldt tentatively dates his accession to ca. 362 CE (*Didymus der Blinde* [Texte und Untersuchungen zur geschichte der altchristlichen literatur 29; Leipzig: Hinrichs, 1905], 6, n. 2). Leipoldt references Guerike who places the assumption of his responsibility much earlier, at ca. 340. C. Andresen guesses ca. 371 (see Wolfgang Bienert, *Allegoria und Anagoge bei Didymos dem Blinden von Alexandria* [Berlin: de Gruyter 1972], 5–6, n. 5).

45. *H.E.* 11.7. Trans. Philip R. Amidon, *The Church History of Rufinus of Aquileia: Books 10 and 11* (New York: Oxford University Press, 1997), 69. The Latin reads, *ita brevi deo docente in tantam divinarum humanarumque rerum eruditionem ac scientiam venit, ut scholae ecclesiasticae doctor exsisteret, Athanasio episcopo ceterisque sapientibus in ecclesia dei viris admodum probatus*. Rufinus knew Didymus and studied under him for a total of eight years (*Apol. Hier.* 2.15: *Ceterum iste, qui in tota vita sua non totos triginta dies Alexandriae, ubi erat Didymus, commoratus est, per totos pene libellos suos longe lateque se iactat Didymi videntis esse discipulum, et* καθηγητήν *in Scripturis sanctis habuisse Didymum. Et omnis ista iactantia in uno mense quaesita est. Ego, qui sex annis Dei causa demoratus sum, et iterum, post intervallum aliquod, aliis duobus, ubi erat Didymus, de quo tu solo te iactas* ...).

46. See Richard A. Layton, *Didymus the Blind and His Circle in Late-Antique Alexandria* (Urbana, Ill.: University of Illinois Press, 2004), 15–6, and Emanuela Prinzivalli, *Didimo il Cieco: Lezioni sui Salmi. Il* Commento ai Salmi *scoperto a Tura* (Milan: Paoline, 2005), 16–17.

47. See also the remarks of J. B. Bennet, "The Origin of Evil: Didymus the Blind's Contra Manichaeos and Its Debt to Origen's Theology and Exegesis" (Ph.D. diss.; Univ. of St. Michael's College, 1997), 16–17, and Emanuela Prinzivalli, *Didimo il Cieco e l'interpretazione dei Salmi* (Quaderni di studi e materiali di storia delle religioni; Rome: Japadre, 1988), 9, both of whom Layton cites. Prinzivalli's subsequent work seems to concur with Layton's presentation as well (see *Didimo il Cieco e l'interpretazione dei Salmi*, 17).

historians, who understood the role of Didymus to be precisely that of catechetical director.

Layton explains, "Sozomen's designation of Didymus as the director of the school is untrustworthy, an amplification of Rufinus's biographical notice made from dubious testimony."[48] A few lines earlier, Layton had stated that Sozomen "based this promotion [to head of the school] on evidence he garnered from another source, the *Universal History* of Philip of Side." It makes little difference for our purposes whether Didymus was merely a "teacher" or whether we accept the testimony of Philip and Sozomen that he was the catechetical "director." Didymus was without question the most famous figure affiliated with the Alexandrian school in the fourth century CE, and its fame continued to spread on the basis of his reputation.

Another interesting point that emerges from the Rufinus quote is the way in which Didymus received his position as head of the school, he "having won the high esteem of Bishop Athanasius and the other wise men in God's church." The idea that Athanasius was personally involved in the appointment of Didymus is found nowhere else among the ancient historians, and Layton is skeptical about the reliability of the comment. He writes, "… the possibility cannot be excluded that Rufinus has simply embroidered his teacher's resume."[49] A few lines later Layton continues, "the 'full approval' bestowed upon Didymus by Athanasius could deflect the accusations faced by Rufinus."[50] In other words, since (1) Rufinus regarded Didymus as a respected teacher and (2) both Didymus and Rufinus were coming under the criticism of being Origenists, then (3) the latter posited Athanasius, whose orthodoxy was not in question, as the seal of Didymus's orthodoxy, which by implication certifies Rufinus himself.

Speaking historically, Athanasius's role in the appointment of Didymus is a curious point. Athanasius spent little time in Alexandria,[51] and the previous history of the Alexandrian episcopate reveals that it was not the custom of bishops to be personally involved in appointing the heads of the catechetical school.[52] But it seems odd, in my judgment, that Athanasius

---

48. Layton, *Didymus the Blind*, 16.
49. Layton, *Didymus the Blind*, 16.
50. Layton, *Didymus the Blind*, 16. On the potential controversy into which Rufinus could have been drawn for his allegiance to Didymus, see 16–18.
51. Johannes Quasten states, "Five times he was banished from his episcopal see and spent more than seventeen years in exile" (*Patrology*, Vol. 3: *The Golden Age of Patristic Literature*, Utrecht: Spectrum, 1963), 20.
52. For example, in the case of Clement, Eusebius states, Πάνταινον δὲ Κλήμης διαδεξάμενος (*Hist. eccl.* 6.6.1). In Origen's case, "some of the pagans" (τινες ἀπὸ τῶν ἐθνῶν) banded

would be mentioned in the context of approving a common "teacher," as Layton maintains. So either Rufinus introduces Athanasius to enhance his presentation of Didymus as catechetical director, as Philip and Sozomen understood him, or Rufinus overplays the role of Athanasius to defend Didymus's orthodoxy, as Layton states. It would be more in line with ancient custom to imagine that Didymus acceded to the post and Athanasius approved the appointment. Approval from such a distinguished figure might have been necessary because of Didymus's handicap. As Prinzivalli observes, "a blind teacher, in order to function, needs help of every kind as well as a sure means of sustenance."[53] Athanasius, as a respected friend, would have been in a perfect position to secure Didymus in the post, and to ensure his theological and exegetical work could continue. Ultimately, however, we cannot be certain of the reliability of Rufinus's details.

Didymus as Student and Teacher within the Alexandrian School

Since antiquity, the city of Alexandria was famous for its schools. Ptolemy I (305–282 BCE) fostered this reputation by attempting to attract certain prominent disciples of Aristotle to Egypt.[54] The same Ptolemy also instituted the "museum," a religious and academic community which promoted teaching and discipleship.[55] In the museum Ptolemy II (282–229 BCE) established the great library.[56] This establishment attracted countless scholars throughout the Hellenistic period and has become a cultural icon for the city of Alexandria.

Another establishment, more relevant for the age of Didymus the Blind in fourth century Alexandria, is the Serapeum. Ptolemy I reportedly introduced the worship of Serapis to Alexandria, and the deity appears to have

---

together to encourage him toward the position of instructor (*Hist. eccl.* 6.3.1–3). Origen, in turn, left (καταλείπω) the position to Heraclas when he was banished from Alexandria (*Hist. eccl.* 6.26; Jerome, *Vir. ill.* 54.4). These examples are sufficient to indicate that the bishop of Alexandria normally played no major role in selecting the scholarch. Rather, the position was normally inherited, as in the philosophical schools, by the existing head naming or appointing his successor.

53. *Didimo il Cieco*, 18 ("un maestro cieco, per poter operare, ha bisogno di aiuti di ogni tipo e di un sostentamento assicurato").

54. See Rudolf Pfeiffer, *History of Classical Scholarship from the Beginnings to the End of the Hellenistic Age* (Oxford: Clarendon, 1968), 95–96. Demetrius of Phaelerum actually comes to Alexandria at the request of the king.

55. This institution was not philosophical in its orientation, however (Pfeiffer, *History*, 97–98).

56. Eusebius, *Hist. eccl.* 5.8.11.

been popular there for several centuries.⁵⁷ The Serapeum also featured a library, known as the "daughter library," that would have attracted a number of scholars and teachers in late antiquity.⁵⁸ After the probable destruction of the museum and its library in 272 CE, the Serapeum became the largest and most important center of learning in the city.⁵⁹ It is here that we find Theon and his famous daughter Hypatia studying and teaching.⁶⁰ The Serapeum was eventually destroyed by Christians following a series of riots.⁶¹ The death of Hypatia in 415 CE marks the end of any "school" environment in which Christians and Pagans would have joined together in learning the Classics.⁶²

Richard Layton has initiated the discussion regarding the ecclesiastical education of Didymus the Blind. He believes that Didymus's education was not traditional, but entirely ecclesiastical.⁶³ He states in summary, "The indirect evidence gleaned from the commentaries suggests that Didymus was himself a product of such a scholastic venture, a local Christian academy that imitated the elite rhetorical and philosophical academies."⁶⁴ This statement seems to contradict a claim Layton makes earlier when he

---

57. Tacitus, *Hist.* 4.83–84; Plutarch, *Is Os.* 361F. On a comparison between these two accounts, see Benjamin W. Hicks, "Roman *Religio* as a Framework at Tacitus' *Histories* 4.83–84," *Journal of Ancient History* 1 (2013): 70–82.

58. See Epiphanius, *De mens. et pond.* 11. See Edward J. Watts, *City and School in Late Antique Athens and Alexandria* (Berkeley: University of California Press, 2006), 150.

59. See Watts, *City and School,* 150–51.

60. For a survey of the relevant data regarding academic life in fourth century Alexandria, see Watts, *City and School,* 187–203.

61. Rufinus, *Hist.* 11.23. The Christians had uncovered an ancient temple and images of Mithras, which they mockingly paraded through the streets of Alexandria. The pagans retaliated by launching an attack against the Christians only to retreat to the Serapeum. Eventually they were granted imperial amnesty and vacated the Serapeum. The Christians then entered and destroyed the complex in 391 CE (on these events in Alexandria in general see Johannes Hahn, *Gewalt und religiöser Konflikt: Studien zu den Auseinandersetzungen zwischen Christen, Heiden und Juden im Osten des Römischen Reiches (von Konstantin bis Theodosius II.)* (KLIO ns 8; Berlin: de Gruyter, 2004), 15–120. On the Serapeum specifically, see Johannes Hahn, "The Conversion of the Cult Statues: The Destruction of the Serapeum 392 A.D. and the Transformation of Alexandria into the 'Christ-Loving' City," in *From Temple to Church: Destruction and Renewal of Local Cultic Topography in Late Antiquity* (ed. Ulrich Gotter, Stephen Emmel, and Johannes Hahn; Leiden: Brill, 2008), 335–65.

62. For the social conflict in the city during the fourth and fifth centuries see Christopher Haas, *Alexandria in Late Antiquity: Topography and Social Conflict* (Baltimore: Johns Hopkins University Press, 1997), 278–330.

63. Layton, *Didymus the Blind,* 135–43.

64. Layton, *Didymus the Blind,* 160.

appears to doubt whether Didymus "advanced beyond the preliminary grammatical instruction to the study of rhetoric."[65]

I find Layton's thesis interesting, but ultimately unconvicing. First, Didymus never describes his education. So how can we determine that an education in the traditional curriculum was distinctively administered in an ecclesiastical setting? That Didymus's "philosophical training came to him already imprinted with a Christian ideology" cannot be substantiated.[66] Didymus utilized secular learning, as did Philo, Clement, and Origen before him, as a handmaiden to theology. His infrequent citation of classical authors is not surprising, for he cites no source with great frequency, with the exception of the Bible. This makes Didymus no different from most late antique Christian commentators. We need not think his disability would hinder him, for blindness was not a deterrant to receiving an education.[67] In contrast to Layton's theory also stand the ancient biographers, who report that Didymus received the standard secular education.

Of Didymus's primary education, only Sozomen bothers to inform us, relating, "It is said that he learned the letters of the alphabet by means of tablets in which they were engraved, and which he felt with his fingers; and that he made himself acquainted with syllables and words by the force of attention and memory, and by listening attentively to the sounds."[68] This description is remarkable, and it is difficult to imagine why Sozomen would have invented it. Still, it is unclear why Didymus would need to feel the letters since he would never have needed to script them with his own hand. Our biographical sources are in agreement with the evidence implicit in the Tura commentaries that Didymus advanced to an education in gram-

---

65. Layton, *Didymus the Blind*, 137.
66. Ibid.
67. Martha L. Rose has convincingly demonstrated that blindness and visual impairment was not viewed with the same stigma that is often attached to it in the modern world (*The Staff of Oedpius: Transforming Disability in Ancient Greece* [Ann Arbor: University of Michigan Press, 2003], 79–94). For attitudes toward blindness in Roman times see Lisa Trentin, "Exploring Visual Impairment in Ancient Rome," in *Disabilities in Roman Antiquity: Disparite Bodies, A capite, ad calcem* (ed. Christian Laes, C.F. Goodey, and M. Lynn Rose; Mnemosune Supplements: History and Archaeology of Classical Antiquity 356; Leiden: Brill, 2013), 89–114. To my knowledge no study exists specifically on visually impaired students in ancient education.
68. *H.E.* 3.15.2 (trans. Chester D. Hartranft, *NPNF*² 2.294). The Greek reads, λέγεται δὲ τοὺς χαρακτῆρας τῶν γραμμάτων σανίδι καταχαραγέντας εἰς βάθος ἐκμαθεῖν τοῖς δακτύλοις ἐφαπτόμενος, συλλαβὰς δὲ καὶ ὀνόματα καὶ τὰ ἄλλα ἐφεξῆς καταλήψει νοῦ καὶ συνεχεῖ ἀκροάσει καὶ ἀναμνήσει τῶν ἀκοῇ θηρωμένων.

mar, rhetoric and philosophy. His knowledge of Aristotle is particularly striking, Alexandria being a center for Aristotelianism at the time.[69]

Even allowing for the expected exaggerations of the biographers, the exceptional quality of Didymus's mind and the superiority of his work ethic stand out. Rufinus tells us that 'he was so well trained in the other disciplines ... that no philosopher could ever defeat or reduce him to silence by proposing any question from these [intellectual] arts; no sooner did he hear his answers than he was convinced that he was an expert in the discipline in question.'[70] Such a knowledge of philosophy could have been self-guided, although it is more likely that Didymus was classically trained in rhetoric and philosophy.

Whatever Didymus may have missed in school, however, he made up with his legendary work ethic:

> But when as usual sleep had overtaken the readers after their nocturnal work, Didymus, believing that the silence was not given for repose or idleness, would recall everything that he had received like a clean animal chewing its cud, and would retrace in his mind and memory what he had earlier understood from the reading of the books which the others had run through, so that he seemed not so much to have heard what had been read as to have copied it out on the pages of his mind.[71]

Didymus's prodigious memory allowed him almost total recall of the Bible, most notably the Solomonic works, which included, in his mind, the Wisdom of Solomon.[72] In the spirit of Origen, Didymus believed scripture to be its own best interpreter and overwhelmingly appeals to parallel passages from both Testaments to explicate its meaning.

Despite his primary appeals to the scriptures, Didymus does not hesitate to refer to many other sources. We shall discuss these in chapters 3 and 4 of the present work. At this point, let us note that the full range of

---

69. See Layton, *Didymus the Blind*, 28–29, 137–41, and David T. Runia, "Festugière Revisited: Aristotle in the Greek Patres," *VC* 43 (1989): 1–34.

70. *Hist.* 11.7; trans. Amidon, *Church History*, 69. The Latin reads, *in ceteris ... disciplinis ita esset paratus, ut nullus umquam philosoforum aliqua ex his artibus proponens optinere eum vel concludere quiverit, sed statim ut responsiones eius acciperet, magistrum eum etiam illius, de qua proposuisset, crederet disciplinae.*

71. *Hist.* 11.7; trans. Amidon, *Church History*, 69. The Latin reads, *cum vero post lucubrationis laborem somnus, ut fieri solet, legentibus advenisset, Didymus silentium illud non ad quietem vel otium datum ducens tamquam mundum animal ruminans cibum quem ceperat ex integro revocabat et ea, quae dudum percurrentibus aliis ex librorum lectione cognoverat, memoria et animo retexebat, ut non tam audisse quae lecta fuerant quam descripsisse mentis suae paginis videretur.*

72. Didymus apparently believed Wis was indeed authored by Solomon (e.g., *Comm. Zach.* 293.24).

Didymus's education is on display, both in references to classical and contemporary pagan thinkers, to Jewish literature of the past and contemporary midrashic "traditions," and to the entire spectrum of Christian belief, including those Didymus considers heretical as well as those he considers orthodox. Clearly, Didymus could not have received knowledge of these sources entirely in school (whether classical or Christian), but his monastic setting allowed him to learn continuously throughout his life.

Didymus's own teaching techniques are seen mostly clearly in the commentaries on Psalms and Ecclesiastes. These two works are rough lecture transcripts, allowing us a rare peek inside a Christian classroom.[73] They feature the teacher's responses to student questions, and even student interruptions of the instruction.[74] These excurses from the subject at hand are frequently marked by the mysterious term επερ, which occurs over three hundred times in the two commentaries.

The commentaries on Gen, Job, and Zech, by contrast, are more polished, each following a rigid tripartite structure of (1) the biblical lemma (ranging from as little as a word to several verses), (2) the literal interpretation, and finally, (3) the allegorical interpretation.[75] While these commentaries may have had their origin in a scholastic setting, they have been subsequently edited for publication. On the whole, the Tura commentaries reflect an active cohort of students interested in the higher study of the scriptures. No trace of the catechumens Didymus might have taught at other points in his life are to be found in the Tura commentaries. Rather, these works probably offer us as much insight as possible into the advanced classes that Rufinus and Jerome would have attended when visiting the famous Alexandrian scholar.

---

73. See Anne Browning Nelson, "The Classroom of Didymus the Blind" (Ph.D. diss., The University of Michigan, 1995), 8–27. Earlier scholars had identified the oral scholastic nature of these texts (see Aloys Kehl, *Der Psalmenkommentar von Tura, Quaternio IX* [Wissenschaftliche Abhandlungen der Arbeitsgemeinschaft für Forschung des Landes Nordrhein-Westfalen: Sonderreihe, Papyrologica Coloniensia, vol. 1; Köln & Opladen: Westdeutscher, 1964], 25–28; Gerhard Binder and Leo Liesenborghs, *Didymos der Blinde: Kommentar zum Ecclesiastes (Tura-Papyrus), Teil I.1: Kommentar zu Eccl. Kap. 1, 1–2, 14* [Papyrologische Texte und Abhandlungen 25; Bonn: Habelt, 1979], x–xiii). For a more recent treatment, see Layton, *Didymus the Blind*, 13–35.

74. On the student questions in the commentaries on Ps and Eccl see Nelson, 28–50.

75. We cannot distinguish the publishable quality of the commentaries by date. Although dating the Tura writings remains problematic, the works on Gen and Job are probably the earliest (360s), with Ps and Eccl following (370s) and finally the work on Zech, requested by Jerome in 386 CE, and probably completed shortly thereafter (see Layton, *Didymus the Blind*, 6–7). Prinzivalli is content to follow this general scheme (*Didimo il Cieco: Lezioni sui Salmi*, 26).

2

PHILO'S ACCEPTANCE INTO ALEXANDRIAN CHRISTIANITY

Introduction

David Runia's survey of *Philo in Early Christian Literature* illustrates, *inter alia*, that Philo was an accepted authority in Alexandrian Christianity, chiefly in Clement, Origen, and Didymus.[1] Each of these three authors found in Philo a predecessor to their respective intellectual goals. Clement, much like Philo for Judaism, was attempting to define the Christian system in light of Hellenic intellectual categories, that is, to show what Jerusalem had to do with Athens.[2] In this enterprise, he certainly drew inspiration from Jewish predecessors, namely, Aristobulus and Philo, the latter of whom had worked out a partial synthesis with the "Hebrew" system.[3] The result is a Christian philosophy that would have been intellectually more palatable to the broader culture of Alexandrian Hellenism than the general Palestinian *Weltschauung* represented in the New Testament.[4]

---

1. *Philo in Early Christian Literature: A Survey* (CRINT 3; Assen: Van Gorcum; Philadelphia: Fortress, 1993), 119–211. Investigation into the influence of Philo on other figures, such as Valentinus, Arius, and Athanasius would likely yield fruit, but as yet remains largely uncultivated.

2. On this aspect of patristic thought in general, see Christian Gnilka, *ΧΡΗΣΙΣ, Die Methode der Kirchenväter im Umgang mit der antiken Kultur*. Vol. 1: *Der Begriff des "Rechten Gebrauchs"* (Basel: Schwabe, 1984), referenced in Eric Osborn, *Clement of Alexandria* (Cambridge: Cambridge University Press, 2005), 27, n. 93, from whom I also borrow the analogy to Tertullian's famous question, *Quid Athenae Hierosolymis?* (*Praescr.* 7). Philo and Aristobulus are explicitly associated with the Mosaic philosophy in Clement, *Strom.* 1.15.72.

3. David Runia briefly treats Clement's reference to Aristobulus as a "Peripatetic" in his "Why Does Clement of Alexandria Call Philo 'The Pythagorean?,'" *VC* 49 (1995): 1–22, 8–10. On Clement and Philo see Annewies van den Hoek, *Clement of Alexandria and His Use of Philo in the* Stromateis*: An Early Christian Reshaping of a Jewish Model* (VCSup 3; Leiden: Brill, 1988). To this work should be added J. C. M. van Winden, "Quotations from Philo in Clement of Alexandria's *Protrepticus*," *VC* 32 (1978): 208–13; Andrew Dinan, "The Mystery of Play: Clement of Alexandria's Appropriation of Philo in the *Paedagogus* (1.5.21.3–22.1)," *SPhiloA* 19 (2007): 59–80; Andrew Dinan, "Another Citation of Philo in Clement of Alexandria's *Protrepticus* (10,93,1–2)," *VC* 64 (2010): 435–44.

4. Henry Chadwick's caution should still be noted: "Clement is not simply producing a hellenized Christianity precisely parallel to Philo's Hellenized Judaism" (*Early Christianity and the Classical Tradition* [Oxford: Clarendon, 1966], 142). Clement is distinctively

Origen and Didymus, in contrast to Clement, did not aim to be grand systematizers, but to be scriptural exegetes.[5] Their interest lay chiefly in how to understand the text of scripture by means of Hellenic hermeneutical methods and to express their explanations by means of Greek rhetorical tropes.[6] In this enterprise they found a predecessor in Philo, who was also, above all else, an interpreter of scripture.[7] For Alexandrian interpreters of the Bible, therefore, Philo served a useful purpose.

In this chapter we shall survey the use of Philo in the Alexandrian Christian tradition, starting with Clement, the first Christian author who certainly had a knowledge of Philo. This survey will demonstrate that Philo was indeed "in the tradition" of Alexandrian interpretation well before the time of Didymus. And we hope also to demonstrate that Didymus was very much a traditional Alexandrian interpreter, and thus both utilized and respected the tradition of exegesis which included Philo.

Clement of Alexandria

The Alexandrian tradition prior to Clement offers us no hard evidence for the Christian use of Philo.[8] Valentinus indeed shares methodological similarities with Philo, especially in the field of arithmology, but he puts them to a different use.[9] When we reach Clement of Alexandria, however, we encounter an author who was thoroughly acquainted with our Jewish scholar. In the indices to the GCS volumes of Clement, Otto Stählin lists

---

Christian and his location of Christ (rather than Moses) as the locus of wisdom suggests a significant difference between the intellectual presuppositions of the two thinkers.

5. Thanks to the work of a number of scholars, including R. P. C. Hanson, Marguerite Harl, Hermann Vogt, and Manlio Simonetti, Origen is now viewed primarily as an exegete (see the survey in Gilles Dorival, "Origen," in *The New Cambridge History of the Bible: From the Beginnings to 600* (ed. James Carleton Paget and Joachim Schaper; Cambridge: Cambridge University Press, 2013], 605–28, 605).

6. The classic work on Origen's application of rhetoric is Bernard Neuschäfer, *Origenes als Philologe* (2 vols.; Schweizerische Beiträge zur Altertumswissenschaft 18.1–2; Basel: Friedrich Reinhardt, 1987).

7. The majority of Philonists now recognize this fundamental point, thanks in large measure to the work of Valentin Nikiprowetzky, *Le commentaire de l'ecriture chez Philon d'Alexandrie: Son caractere et sa portee, observations philologiques* (ALGHJ; Leiden: Brill, 1977).

8. Philo's influence on this period in Alexandrian Christianity deserves far more attention, but no explicit references to Philo exist. For a survey see Runia, *Philo in Early Christian Literature*, 123–31.

9. Joel Kalvesmaki does not view Philo as a prominent influence in Valentian arithmology (see *The Theology of Arithmetic: Number Symbolism in Platonism and Early Christianity* [Hellenic Studies 59; Cambridge: Center for Hellenic Studies, 2013], 27–83).

around 340 references to at least 31 of Philo's works.[10] Of the treatises known to us, only the *Aet.* (which Eusebius also neglects to mention in his catalogue) and the historical works, *Flacc.* and *Legat.*, are missing.[11] No less than 279 references to Philo can be located in the *Strom.* alone, and these serve as the basis for Annewies Van den Hoek's important study, *Clement of Alexandria and His Use of Philo in the* Stromateis.[12]

While a few important cautions should be noted in how we speak of Philo's influence on Clement,[13] scholars universally accept the prominent role Philo plays in Clement's thought.[14] This is remarkable when we consider that Clement mentions the name of Philo only four times in his works and often in contexts that are unimportant to his broader intellectual program.[15] Further, it is curious that all four named references are

---

10. Stählin places a question mark beside the sole reference he traces to Philo's *Hypothetica*.

11. *Hist. eccl.* 2.18. On Eusebius's catalogue of Philo's writings, see Andrew Carriker, *The Library of Eusebius of Caesarea* (Leiden: Brill, 2003), 164–77.

12. Van den Hoek says that Clement uses Philo over 300 times in the *Strom.* (*Clement of Alexandria*, 20), but in a later article states that he is found 279 times ("Techniques of Quotation in Clement of Alexandria: A View of Ancient Literary Working Methods," *VC* 50 [1996]: 223–43, 231). This is not Van den Hoek's discrepancy but is due to Stählin's updated count in the indices to his translation in the *Bibliothek der Kirchenväter* series (see Van den Hoek, "Techniques," 240).

13. See especially the work of Eric Osborn, beginning with his review of Van den Hoek's work in *JTS* 41 (1990): 653–56; "Philo and Clement," *Prudentia* 19 (1987): 35–49; "Philo and Clement: Citation and Influence," in *Lebendige Überlieferung: Prozesse der Annäherung und Auslegung; Festschrift für Hermann-Josef Vogt zum 60. Geburtstag*, ed. Nabil el-Khoury (Beirut: Rückert; Ostfildern: Schwaben, 1992), 228–43; "Philo and Clement: Quiet Conversion and Noetic Exegesis" *SPhiloA* 10 (1998): 108–24; *Clement of Alexandria*, 81–106. Osborn does not deny that Clement knew Philo, of course, but prefers to speak of "use" rather than "influence." He writes, "Now I wish to suggest that the question of influence has always been the wrong question. The influence of Philo on Clement is secondary to the use which Clement makes of Philo" ("Philo and Clement: Quiet Conversion," 109).

14. David T. Runia states, "As Father Van Winden and Annewies Van den Hoek have amply shown, there can be absolutely no doubt that Clement had copies of Philo's works on his desk when writing the *Protrepticus* and the *Stromateis*" ("Clement of Alexandria and the Philonic Doctrine of the Divine Power(s)," *VC* 58 [2004]: 256–76, 256–57). In addition to the work of Van den Hoek and Runia, see Piotr Ashwin-Siejkowski, *Clement of Alexandria: A Project of Christian Perfection* (Edinburgh: T&T Clark: 2008), 30–31, 40–61; Mireille Hadas-Lebel, *Philo of Alexandria: A Thinker in the Jewish Diaspora*, trans. Robyn Fréchet (SPhA 7; Leiden: Brill, 2012), 206–8.

15. Osborn has renewed the earlier point made by Claude Mondésert that Philo is used by Clement on points that are incidental rather than foundational ("Philo and Clement: Quite Conversion," 109, referencing *Clément d'Alexandrie, Introduction à l'étude de sa pensée religieuse à partir de l'écriture* [Paris: Aubier, 1944], 183).

concentrated in the first two books of the *Strom.*[16] Why Clement fails to cite Philo by name more than he does is, of course, impossible to know. Osborn proposes at least three reasons:[17] (1) What we regard as Philonic in Clement actually was part of a larger tradition not exclusive to Philo. This was the suggestion of Wilhelm Bousset in his carefully presented, but highly speculative, study on the *Jüdische-christlicher Schulbetrieb in Alexandria und Rom.*[18] (2) Clement's debates with the Marcionites required a harmonization of the Old and New Testaments, which was accomplished by means of [Philonic] allegory. But the Marcionites also opposed anything "Jewish." This led Clement to utilize Philo without mentioning his name often. (3) Clement felt, as did Justin Martyr, that any good argument should be Christian property. Thus Clement felt justified in extracting and reappropriating what he found beneficial in Philo. If these reasons are deemed legitimate, however, one wonders why Clement cites Philo by name at all.

Van den Hoek takes a slightly different approach, paradoxically proposing that Clement's lack of named references to Philo actually proves that he was more intimately influenced by him.[19] Citation of Philo's name hardly seemed necessary to Clement because he had so thoroughly read and utilized him. Perhaps even Clement's readers could recognize his Philonic references without needing a citation. Add to this Clement's routine failure to acknowledge his intellectual debts regardless of the source, and we come to understand the relative scarcity of Philo's name assures us that Clement viewed Philo no differently than any other author he may have consulted.[20]

A special matter of curiosity, however, lies in why Clement, on two occasions, cites Philo as "the Pythagorean."[21] David Runia suggests that the epithet is intended to associate Philo with Platonic philosophy, which was widely understood at the time of Clement to be a continuation of Pythagorean philosophy.[22] This point is strengthened by the fact that Clement also refers to Aristobulus curiously as "the Peripatetic."[23] He clearly felt the need to connect these thinkers explicitly with Hellenistic schools of

---

16. *Strom.* 1.31.1; 1.72.4; 1.151.2; 2.100.3.
17. Osborn, "Philo and Clement," *Prudentia* 19 (1987): 35–49.
18. The subtitle is *Literarische Untersuchungen zu Philo und Clemens von Alexandria, Justin und Irenäus* (FRLANT 23; Göttingen: Vandenhoek & Ruprecht, 1915).
19. "Techniques of Quotation," 233.
20. Van den Hoek, "Techniques of Quotation," 232–33.
21. *Strom.* 1.72.4; 2.100.3.
22. "Why Does Clement Call Philo 'the Pythagorean?'" *VC* 49 (1995): 1–22.
23. *Strom.* 5.14.97.7.

thought rather than making their connection with Judaism explicit. Jennifer Otto summarizes regarding Philo, "Clement connects the proper exegesis of the Mosaic writings with Pythagorean pedagogical and exegetical methods. Although Philo is employed by Clement as an expert in the Jewish scriptures, his expertise has a decidedly Pythagorean character."[24]

The greater and more profitable question is why Clement uses Philo at all. Eric Osborn theorizes that Clement uses Philo, on the one hand, to reach the Jews and, on the other, to reach the Marcionites. "He sought to show the Jews a way from Old Testament scriptures to Christ and to show the Marcionites a way from Christ to Old Testament scriptures."[25] The focus on Clement's goal of conversion indeed opens new avenues for his use of sources in general and may indeed illuminate an apologetic application of Philo that has been overlooked, but in my judgment does not capture the essence of the issue. Clement drank far too deeply from the Philonic well for us to reduce him to a missionary seeking converts. As with any good teacher, the student learns the intellectual system of his master so well that he becomes a critic, adopting, adapting, and challenging the hypotheses as they have been taught.[26] As a result, the student refines and enhances his own intellectual system. David Runia summarizes what must have been the role Philo played in Clement's thought: "Philo did not teach Clement Platonism, but rather how to connect his Platonism to biblical thought, and specifically to biblical exegesis, above all through the use of allegory."[27]

Turning to Clement's use of Philo specifically, let us note only the work of Annewies Van den Hoek. She has identified at least four major areas of Philonic influence: (1) Hagar and Sarah; (2) the Moses story; (3) the law and virtues; and (4) the temple, priestly vestments, and high priest. These four "blocks" are based on a sequential reading of the *Stromateis* and form the essence of Van den Hoek's monograph. From here she turns to shorter passages and isolated references to Philo. The result is that Clement is found to have used Philo thoroughly in the books he wrote while at Alexandria.[28] However, the last three *Stromateis* and the works written after

---

24. David Runia, "Philo, Judaeus? A Re-evaluation of Why Clement Calls Philo 'the Pythagorean,'" *SPhiloA* 25 (2013): 115–38.

25. Osborn, "Philo and Clement: Quiet Conversion," 109. In his earlier review of Van den Hoek, Osborn answers the question of why Clement used Philo as follows: "He was fishing for converts and Philo could help to catch Marcionites, Gnostics, and Jews. Further, he had an eclectic mind and he found Philo interesting" (*JTS* 41 [1990]: 655).

26. A similar point is made by Osborn, *Clement of Alexandria*, 105.

27. Runia, *Philo in Early Christian Literature*, 155.

28. Van den Hoek, *Clement*, 197–210.

Clement left the city contain much less Philonic material.²⁹ One may conclude on this basis that Clement had access to a library in Alexandria in which Philo's works could be found but did not incorporate them into his travel library. Still, the availability of Philo in Alexandria must lead us to hypothesize that Philo enjoyed a literary reputation among the Christians prior to Clement's time.

Didymus was certainly aware of Clement, for he mentions his name. In an interesting context for Didymus's view of the Christian apocrypha, he states that "Clement says many things [*vacat*]. For he has proven out of his reading, remembering and understanding many things that some have added foreign elements to foreign books, and some even compiled whole treatises. For this reason our teaching rejects the reading of apocrypha since many things are falsified therein."³⁰ Didymus goes on to mention the Gospels of Thomas and of Peter as specific examples of falsified apocrypha.

We can thus see that Didymus was aware of Clement, but there is as of yet no study detailing the potential areas of Clement's influence on Didymus. Based on a cursory reading of the Tura commentaries, it is my impression that Didymus did not utilize Clement often in the composition of his exegetical works. To cite but one example, the editorial notes of Pierre Nautin in the *Comm. Gen.* abound with references to Philo and Origen, but Clement's name appears only twice. This is perhaps because Didymus was a utilitarian, turning to previous exegetes for his own exegetical work. Philo and Origen were more useful, therefore, because they both provided running comments on many of the very scriptural texts on which Didymus was working. Clement is part of Didymus's Christian education but does not seem to be part of his typical exegetical repertoire.

---

29. "The books that Clement wrote in Alexandria show that he had access to the majority of the Philonic treatises. In the last three *Strom.* and in the other works written after leaving the city, however, the number of citations from Philo drops off considerably" (Van den Hoek, "The 'Catechetical' School of Early Christian Alexandria and Its Philonic Heritage," *HTR* 90 [1997]: 59–87, 87). This is not just a Philonic phenomenon. Van den Hoek has also shown that Clement's citations of Prov drops considerably during the post-Alexandrian period of his life (see "Clement of Alexandria and the Book of Proverbs," in *Clement's Biblical Exegesis: Proceedings of the Second Colloquium on Clement of Alexandria* [ed. Veronika Černušková, Judith L. Kovacs, and Jana Plátová; VCSup 139; Leiden: Brill, 2016], 197–216).

30. *Comm. Eccl.* 7.34–8.5. The Greek reads, ὁ Κλήμης γοῦν πολλὰ λέγει ερ.[...] βιβλία ψευδεπίγραφα παρέστησεν | διὰ π[ο]λλῶν· πολλὰ γὰρ καὶ ἀναγν[ο]ὺς καὶ μνημονεύων ὁ ἀνὴρ καὶ ἐπιστάμενος ἔδειξεν | ὅτι προσέθηκαν βιβλίοις ἀλλ[οτ]ρ[ίοις τ]ι[ν]ὲς ἀλλόκοτ{τ}ά τινα, ἔνιοι δὲ καὶ ὅλους λόγους συν|τάξαντες ἀνέγραψαν. διὰ τοῦτο γοῦν καὶ ὁ ἡμέτερος λόγος ἀπαγορεύει τὴν ἀνάγνωσιν | τῶν ἀποκρύφων, ἐπεὶ πολλὰ ἐ[ψευ]δογραφήθη (trans. mine).

Origen

The second great exegetical mind of Alexandrian Christianity is Origen. Origen worked within a rich exegetical tradition and indeed refers to previous sources on a number of occasions.[31] Many studies have documented the exegetical influences on Origen, especially Platonism and Gnosticism.[32] The same can be said in more recent decades about contemporary Judaism.[33] But no monograph devoted exclusively to Origen and Philo has yet appeared.[34] Runia offers several reasons for the deficiency:

---

31. E.g., *Hom. Gen.* 5.5; *Hom. Judic.* 8.4; *Hom. Jer.* 11.3. Joseph W. Trigg regards the four most important influences of Origen to be "the ecclesiastical tradition, Gnosticism, Platonism, and the works of Philo" (*Origen: The Bible and Philosophy in the Third-Century Church* [London: SCM, 1983], 59).

32. For the influence of Greek philosophy and especially of Platonism, see Richard Berchman, *From Philo to Origen: Middle Platonism in Transition* (Chico, Calif.: Scholar's, 1984); Henry Chadwick, *Early Christian Thought and the Classical Tradition* (2nd ed.; Oxford: Oxford University Press, 1984), 95–123; "Christian Platonism in Origen and Augustine," in *Origeniana Tertia: The Third International Colloquium for Origen Studies* (ed. R.P.C. Hanson and Henri Crouzel; Roma: Edizioni dell'Ateneo, 1985), 217–30; Ilaria Ramelli, "Origen, Patristic Philosophy, and Christian Platonism: Re-thinking the Christianisation of Hellenism," *VC* 63 (2009): 217–63. For criticism of the cavalier citation of Platonism, see Mark Edwards, *Origen Against Plato* (Ashgate Studies in Philosophy and Theology in Late Antiquity; Aldershot: Ashgate, 2002). For the influence of (or reaction to) Gnosticism, especially of the Valentinian variety, see Gilles Quispel, "Origen and the Valentinian Gnosis," *VC* 28 (1974): 29–42; Alan B. Scott, "Opposition and Concession: Origen's Relationship to Valentinianism," in *Origeniana Quinta: Papers of the 5th International Origen Congress* (ed. Robert J. Daly; BETL 105; Leuven: Peeters, 1992), 79–84; Holger Strutwolf, *Gnosis als System: Zur Rezeption der valentinianischen Gnosis bei Origenes* (Göttingen: Vandenhoek & Ruprecht, 1993).

33. See Gustave Bardy, "Les traditions juives dans l'œuvre d'Origène," *RB* 34 (1925): 217–52; Nicholas R. M. De Lange, *Origen and the Jews: Studies in Jewish-Christian Relations in Third-Century Palestine* (Cambridge: Cambridge University Press, 1976); Paul M. Blowers, "Origen, the Rabbis, and the Bible: Toward a Picture of Judaism and Christianity in Third-Century Caesarea," in *Origen of Alexandria: His World and His Legacy* (ed. Charles Kannengiesser and William L. Petersen; Notre Dame: University of Notre Dame Press, 1988), 96–116; John A. McGuckin, "Origen on the Jews," in *Christianity and Judaism* (ed. Diana Wood; SCH 29; Oxford: Oxford University Press, 1992), 1–13; Anna Tzvetkova-Glaser, *Pentateuchauslegung bei Origenes und den frühen Rabbinen* (Early Christianity in the Context of Antiquity 7; Frankfurt am Main: Peter Lang, 2010).

34. Only surveys now exist. See Runia, *Philo in Early Christian Literature*, 157–83; Runia, "Philo of Alexandria," in *The Westminster Handbook to Origen* (ed. John A. McGuckin; Louisville: Westminster John Knox, 2004), 169–71; Annewies Van den Hoek, "Philo and Origen: A Descriptive Catalogue of Their Relationship," *SPhiloA* 12 (2000): 44–121; Van den Hoek, "Assessing Philo's Influence in Christian Alexandria: The Case of Origen," in *Shem in the Tents of Japheth: Essays on the Encounter of Judaism and Hellenism* (ed. James L. Kugel; JSJSup 74; Leiden: Brill, 2002), 223–39; Hans Georg Thümmel, "Philon und Origenes," *Origeniana Octava* (ed. Lorenzo Perrone; Leuven: Leuven University Press, 2003), 1:275–86; Ilaria Ramelli, "Philo as Origen's Declared Model: Allegorical and

(1) Origen's works are more voluminous and diverse than Clement's; (2) The complex textual tradition that stands behind Origen's works as we now have them raises questions of reliability; (3) Many of Origen's works exist only in Latin translation, making comparison with the Greek of Philo rather difficult; (4) Adequate indices, comparable to those of the GCS volumes of Clement's works, do not exist for Origen.[35]

The first three of these hurdles still block the path, but the fourth has been partially cleared with the publication of Annewies Van den Hoek's foundational catalogue of possible references to Philo in the works of Origen.[36] She did not, however, include Origen's *Comm. Rom.*, which does furnish a few additional parallels.[37] Nevertheless, Van den Hoek demonstrates well that Origen is influenced by Philo, especially in his exegetical work on the Old Testament. The rating system employed (A–D) also assists the researcher in determining the most promising points of influence, and hence helps to prioritize the list of parallels. But if one wishes to locate a host of named references to Philo in Origen, he or she will be disappointed.

Origen refers to Philo by name even less than Clement. Only three times in Origen's extant writings does the name of Philo occur.[38] Origen, like Clement, is not in the habit of naming his sources, so the fact that he rarely mentions Philo may well be meaningless. It is perhaps more intriguing to note the anonymous references to Philo in Origen. On no less than twenty occasions Origen refers to Philo as his predecessor.[39] Philo is variously referred to as "someone before us" (τις τῶν πρὸ ἡμῶν),[40] "one of the ancients" (τῶν παλαιῶν τις),[41] "some" (τινες),[42] and the like.[43] These

---

Historical Exegesis of Scripture," *Studies in Christian-Jewish Relations* 7 (2012): 1–17. A lengthier summary, although largely dependent upon the work of Runia and Van den Hoek, is offered by Justin M. Rogers, "Origen's Use of Philo Judeaus," in *The Oxford Handbook of Origen* (ed. Ronald Heine and Katherine Jo Torjesen; Oxford: Oxford University Press, forthcoming).

35. Runia, *Philo in Early Christian Literature*, 158–59.
36. Van den Hoek, "Philo and Origen." See also her "Assessing Philo's Influence."
37. *Comm. Rom.* 2.13.19; 3.2.9; 3.6.4 (see Rogers, "Origen's Use of Philo").
38. See *Cels.* 4.51; 6.21; *Comm. Matt.* 15.3.
39. In his earlier work, Runia had located "12 or 13" references (*Philo in Early Christian Literature*, 161). Thanks to the work of Van den Hoek, that number has swelled to "more than twenty" (see David T. Runia, "Philo in the Patristic Tradition: A List of Direct References," 272).
40. E.g., *Comm. Matt.* 10.22.
41. E.g., *Sel. Lev.* 8.6.
42. E.g., *Comm. Jo.* 6.25.

introductory tags demonstrate, as Runia notes, that Origen "saw his own activity very much as part of an exegetical tradition, which clearly goes back at least as far as Philo."[44] This point is underscored by the fact that even Clement is referred to by Origen as a predecessor—exactly the same designation that Philo receives.[45]

Turning our attention now to Origen's use of Philo, we can locate references across the Origenian corpus. Philo is referred to by name twice in the *Cels.*[46] and anonymously as a "predecessor" twice more.[47] In the biblical commentaries Philo's name occurs only once,[48] but he is called a "predecessor" around twenty times.[49] The homilies, likewise, feature anonymous references to Philo, with the greatest concentration being in the *Hom. Ex.* and the *Hom. Num.*, respectively.[50]

The dispersion of Philonic references teaches us at least two lessons. First, Origen felt free to broadcast his use of Philonic material in any medium, and second, Origen usually did not have Philo "on his desk," as has been argued for Clement.[51] Origen is willing to engage Philo's proposals, to modify them or even to disagree with them. He clearly not only read Philo but had wrestled with his exegetical and philosophical solutions. Perhaps this is the key insight to show how thoroughly "Philonic" Origen was. If we could observe uncritical and clear references to Philo in Origen, we might think Philo was nothing more than a reference tool. But the Philo left in Origen's writings has often been chipped and mangled, leaving us with the impression that Philo was the stone upon which Origen's own exegetical sensibilities were sharpened.

Origen's debt to Philo lies overwhelmingly in the realm of biblical exegesis. Van den Hoek calculates that 78 percent of Origen's borrowings from Philo fit into the category of biblical interpretation, either in general

---

43. Van den Hoek has suggested that Origen refers to Philo in the singular (τις) when he accepts the Philonic interpretation, and in the plural (τινες) when he rejects it ("Philo and Origen," 61).

44. Runia, *Philo in Early Christian Literature*, 163.

45. See Origen, *Comm. Matt.* 14.2; *Comm. Rom.* 1.1. On Origen's use of Clement, see Annewies Van den Hoek, "Origen and the Intellectual Heritage of Alexandria: Continuity or Disjunction?," in *Origeniana Quinta*, 40–50.

46. *Cels.* 4.51 and 6.21.

47. *Cels.* 5.55 and 7.20.

48. *Comm. Matt.* 15.3.

49. Anonymous references include *Sel. Gen.* 2:2; 16:4–5; 40:20; *Comm. Matt.* 10.22; 17.17; *Fr. Matt.* 25:30; *Comm. Jo.* 6.217; *Comm. Rom.* 2.13.19; 2.6.4; 3.2.9.

50. *Hom. Gen.* 14.3; *Hom. Exod.* 2.1–2; 8.2; 9.4; 13.3 *Fr. Exod.* 12:22; *Hom. Lev.* 8.6; *Hom. Num.* 9.5; 22.4; 26.4; *Hom. Jes. Nav.* 16.1; *Hom. Jer.* 14.5.

51. Runia, "Clement of Alexandria," 256–57.

or in particular, while the remaining 22 percent relates to philosophical and theological themes.⁵² Perhaps this is an important key in unlocking the secret of how Philo Judaeus became Philo Christianus. Had Philo been used primarily as a source of Hebrew history or of Judaism at the time of Jesus, as Josephus was, he never would have been "converted."⁵³ As it is, Philo's biblical exegesis rarely contrasts with early Christian doctrine, and his allegorism is specifically at odds with the Christian construal of "Jewish" interpretation as biblical literalism.⁵⁴ The fathers could also locate "Christian" doctrines in Philo, such as the Logos as "a second god" (*QG* 2.62). Since Philo is responsible (even as a Jew) for distinctively Christian interpretations, his conversion to Christianity was relatively easy to invent.⁵⁵

Virtually every modern essay on Didymus begins with the assumption of Origenian influence. So it is hardly necessary for us to demonstrate specific cases. We are more concerned here with Origen as a mediator of Philo. As we shall see in chapter eight, Origen continues to assert his influence on Didymus, but Didymus does not seem to know Philo only through Origen. At times, Didymus returns to Philonic positions in opposition to Origen; at other times, he sharpens Origen's positions by utilizing Philonic allegories, etymologies, and arithmologies. These we shall discuss more fully in chapters 6 and 7.

After Origen

Approximately sixty years separates the death of Origen from the birth of Didymus the Blind. This period of time is not one about which we are well-

---

52. Van den Hoek, "Assessing Philo's Influence," 238.

53. Philo is sometimes paired with Josephus as a historical source. Anatolius, bishop of Alexandria, cites Philo, Josephus, and other Hellenistic Jewish authors to calculate the date of Easter (cited in Eusebius, *Hist. eccl.* 7.32.16). The *Cohortatio ad Graecos* follows a similar practice, citing Philo alongside Josephus on three occasions (10B; 11B; 14C).

54. Early Christian polemic seized upon "body" metaphors to indict Jews both for their ceremonial observance and for their literal interpretation of the Bible (see Susanna Drake, *Slandering the Jew: Sexuality and Difference in Early Christian Texts* [Philadelphia: University of Pennsylvania Press, 2013]). While Philo advocates a literal observance of the Mosaic law (e.g., *Migr.* 89–93), the point, to my knowledge, is never emphasized in early Christian texts. The Fathers who used Philo apparently ignored his literal observance of the law, and those who resisted him do not mention it.

55. I leave aside here other factors that contributed to the "conversion," such as Philo's praise of the Therapeutae, taken by Eusebius and subsequent Christians to be the first Christian community in Egypt (*Hist. eccl.* 2.16–17). See now Justin M. Rogers, "Origen in the Likeness of Philo: Eusebius of Caesarea's Porait of the Model Scholar," *Studies in Christian-Jewish Relations* 11 (2017): 1–13.

informed. Eusebius, our best source on the period, is sporadic, but he does yield a little information about Philo's importance. To Eusebius's occasional references can be added the three works of Pseudo-Justin and the writings of Arius and Athanasius. I exclude other authors in the "Origenist" tradition, such as Ambrose and the Cappadocian fathers, because these sources do not, it seems to me, have any great influence on the thought of Didymus the Blind.

Pseudo-Justin

Three works are transmitted in manuscripts of Justin Martyr that do not belong to him but likely date from the fourth century CE: the *Cohortatio ad Graecos*, the *De Monarchia*, and the *Oratio ad Graecos*. In the longest of these writings, the *Cohortatio*, the name of Philo occurs three times, alongside that of Josephus.[56] References to Jewish authors, however, are not plentiful, and the traditional Greek authors are used much more frequently. This is understandable, considering the audience of the work.

In the first of these references, Pseudo-Justin is marshalling evidence for the antiquity of Moses, referring to the Greek authors Hellanicus, Philochorus, Castor, Thallus, and Alexander Polyhistor. He then cites "the wisest historiographers of the Jews, Philo and Josephus."[57] In the second reference on the same topic the two historians are again cited by name, referred to once more as "historiographers."[58] Neither of these citations adds much to our assessment of Pseudo-Justin's knowledge of Philo. It seems that he is simply seeking non-Christian testimony in confirmation of "Christian" claims. Whether these are pagan or Jewish sources matters little to his apologetic program.

In the third reference to Philo Pseudo-Justin is discussing the Septuagint, reporting the legends about its accuracy and the circumstances of its translation. He anticipates objections, insisting that "this information is not mythical, nor fabricated," but that he had personally seen the cells in which the translators labored and had spoken with locals about the accuracy of his information. For additional confirmation he refers to "the

---

56. *Coh.* 9.2; 10.1; 13.4. For the text I have used the edition of Miroslav Marcovich, *Pseudo-Iustinus: Cohortatio ad Graecos, De monarchia, Oratio ad Graecos* (PTS 32; Berlin: de Gruyter, 1990). See also the translation and commentary of Christoph Riedweg, *Ps.-Justin (Markell von Ankyra?), Ad Graecos De Vera Religione: Einleitung und Kommentar* (Schweizerische Beiträge zur Altertumswissenschaft 25; Basel: Reinhardt, 1994).

57. *Coh.* 9:2: οἱ σοφώτατοι Φίλων τε καὶ Ἰώσηπος, οἱ τὰ κατὰ Ἰουδαίους ἱστορήσαντες.

58. *Coh.* 10:1: οἱ σοφώτατοι τῶν ἱστοριογράφων ... Φίλων τε καὶ Ἰώσηπος ... τὰς Ἰουδαίων ἱστοροῦντες πράξεις.

wise and venerable historiographers Philo and Josephus."[59] Again, Pseudo-Justin's motive for citing the two authors is simply to confirm his information.

Beyond these direct references there are many other Philonic parallels, but none of them are precise enough to evaluate Pseudo-Justin's familiarity with actual Philonic texts.[60] Christoph Riedweg concludes Pseudo-Justin has read none of the Philonic writings directly, except for *Mos.*[61] Indeed, this explains why the author terms Philo a "historiographer" and places him alongside Josephus.[62]

As far as *Mos.* is concerned, Pseudo-Justin apparently adopts Philo's description of Abraham as a Χαλδαῖος[63] and also follows his account of the translation of the LXX.[64] Furthermore, the author discusses the namelessness of God along similar lines as Philo, claiming that Plato learned his doctrine in Egypt.[65] This discussion is quite lengthy, culminating in a quotation from Plato's *Timaeus*, after which the author suggests Plato meant the same by τὸ ὄν that Moses meant by ὁ ὤν.[66] Finally, the author refers to the doctrine of double creation, which he claims that Plato received from Moses directly. However, the description of the double creation is similar to Philo's exegesis in *Opif.*[67] It would appear that our author has used Philo, without mentioning him explicitly, as a source for the Platonic theory of creation he provides.[68] Many of the ideas that he attributes to Plato specifically are presented with a Philonic coloring. The thought world of the *Cohortatio* most certainly has been influenced by Philo, but it is impossible to point to anything more than a generic influence.

---

59. *Coh.* 13:4: ἃ καὶ παρ' ἑτέρων ἔξεστιν ὑμῖν μανθάνειν, καὶ μάλιστα παρ' αὐτῶν τῶν περὶ τούτων ἱστορησάντων σοφῶν καὶ δοκίμων ἀνδρῶν, Φίλωνός τε καὶ Ἰωσήπου καὶ ἑτέρων πλειόνων.

60. On the use of Philo in the *Cohortatio*, see Riedweg, *Ps.-Justin* 1:145–47.

61. *Ps.-Justin*, 1:146.

62. Riedweg argues that the *Mos.* can be understood as a ἱστορία (*loc. cit.*).

63. *Mos.* 1.5

64. See *Coh.* 13.1–4, apparently borrowing from Philo, *Mos.* 2.29–40. Pseudo-Justin does not follow Philo exactly. There are several details that the author of the *Cohortatio* adds, which are not found in Josephus either (see Runia, *Philo in Early Christian Literature*, 186, n. 11).

65. See *Coh.* 21.2, apparently borrowing from Philo, *Mos.* 1.75 (see Runia, *Philo in Early Christian Literature*, 186; Riedweg, *Ps.-Justin* 1:146–47).

66. *Coh.* 22.2. The same point is made by Eusebius, *Praep. ev.* 11.9.5.

67. See Runia, *Philo in Early Christian Literature*, 187–88; Riedweg, *Ps.-Justin*, 1:147.

68. Riedweg's index lists over 120 potential references to Philo (2:684–85).

Arius

Arguably, the most controversial figure in fourth century Christianity is Arius of Alexandria. He famously taught that the Son, as Logos or Wisdom, was a product (γέννημα) of the unitary Father.[69] The Father is unknowable in his essence not only to humans, but also to the Son. Such subordinationism was unacceptable to many Christians, not only in Alexandria, but in the Greek world as a whole. Any exegete who even remotely resembled Arius (such as Origen) was instantly viewed with suspicion, and was eventually condemned as a heretic.

A number of studies on Arius before the 1970s tended to paint him with the verdict of history. He was the arch-heretic who corrupted a once pure faith. More recently, however, several scholars have preferred to view Arius from the perspective of his intellectual milieu. This approach features an implied sympathy for Arius and his followers as *Alexandrian* thinkers.[70] The result has been a partial re-evaluation of Arius.[71]

A number of scholars who have pursued the Alexandrian intellectual background of Arius have discussed Philonic influence on him. Raoul Mortley, for example, states, "Philo is in fact the father of Arianism."[72] He is led to such a strong declaration by Philo's doctrine of God's unknowability. Mortley took his cue from the work of Harry Austryn Wolfson, who painted Philo as the father of all Christian thought. For Wolfson, the orthodox and heretical traditions simply understood Philo differently. When it comes to the Philonic influence on Arius, Wolfson argues that Arius, like Philo, attempted to establish the "absolute unity" of God prior to the birth of the Logos.[73] Arius, like Philo, taught that the Logos was generated *ex nihilo* from the essence of God, and was thus inferior to

---

69. A number of studies detail the thought of Arius and his influence. For a summary see the classic works of Robert C. Gregg and Dennis E. Groh, *Early Arianism: A View of Salvation* (Philadelphia: Fortress, 1981), and R. P. C. Hanson, *The Search for the Christian Doctrine of God* (Edinburgh: T&T Clark, 1988), and more recently, Lewis Ayres, *Nicaea and its Legacy* (Oxford: Oxford University Press, 2004).

70. See Rowan Williams, *Arius: Heresy and Tradition* (rev. ed.; Grand Rapids: Eerdmans, 2003), who devotes a significant part of the book to the cultural and theological background of Arius. Hanson features "the antecedents of Arius" in his work, *The Search for the Christian Doctrine of God*, but attributes to Philo hardly any influence.

71. Timothy D. Barnes, for example, argues that Arius's ideals were not original to him, but were part of the fabric of Alexandrian Christian thought (*Constantine and Eusebius* [Cambridge: Harvard, 1981], 202–4).

72. Raoul Mortley, *Connaissance religieuse et herméneutique chez Clément d'Alexandrie* (Leiden: Brill, 1973), 9–10 (qtd. in Runia, *Philo in Early Christian Literature*, 190).

73. Harry Austryn Wolfson, *The Philosophy of the Church Fathers: Faith, Trinity, Incarnation* (3rd ed.; Cambridge: Harvard 1970), 585.

God.[74] The obvious difference between Philo and Arius is that the latter, being a Christian, identified the created Logos with the pre-existent Christ."[75]

Few scholars would be as positive as Wolfson and Mortley on the influence of Philo on Arius. Williams is more reserved. He writes that "Philo mapped out the ground for the Alexandrian theological tradition to build on" and that Arius fits "firmly within that tradition."[76] So Philo and his Christian successors laid the theological foundation for Arius to build upon. Nevertheless, Williams acknowledges three more direct areas of similarity between Philo and Arius: (1) an interest in divine freedom and grace; (2) the Logos as the mediator of divine gifts; and (3) knowing *that* God is from his gifts as opposed to knowing *who* he is in his essence.[77]

For Williams, Arius solves a problem of Alexandrian Christian theology inherited from the Philonic tradition: how can the Logos, as mediator of the creation and therefore existent for the sake of creation, subsist as man in the flesh? Since the works of Arius have not survived, we can never be certain of the totality of Philo's influence. However, if Williams is right that the language and categories of thought by which Alexandrian Christians described God were Philonic, the entire Christological controversy in Alexandria would be set up, at least philosophically, by Philo. Williams views Arius to be following the Philonic tradition he had received, while others in the fourth century were content to break away from it. Arius, in an ironic twist, is actually a more traditional Alexandrian than the "orthodox" leaders who condemned him.

Athanasius

Athanasius was one of the earliest and most important opponents of Arius and Arianism. He is especially important for our purposes since he was personally acquainted with Didymus and reportedly exercised a profound influence on his career.[78] However, Athanasius cannot be located as the conduit through which Philo flowed to Didymus the Blind. We have very little reason, based on his extant writings, to think Athanasius directly

---

74. Wolfson, *The Philosophy of the Church Fathers*, 293–94, 585–86.
75. Wolfson, *The Philosophy of the Church Fathers*, 586; Runia, *Philo in Early Christian Literature*, 191.
76. Williams, *Arius*, 123.
77. Williams, *Arius*, 122.
78. Rufinus reports that Athanasius made Didymus "teacher" in the catechetical school of Alexandria (*Hist.* 11.7; see chapter 1 above).

utilized Philo at all. Still, similarities in thought and theology are promising, whether directly taken from Philo or not.

No study yet exists on the potential parallels between Philo and Athanasius outside of Runia's brief survey.[79] One starting point, cited by Runia, is the article of Cornelia De Vogel,[80] who suggests that Athanasius regularly appeals to Philonic illustrations to discuss the relationship between the Father and the Son. For example, Athanasius illustrates the Son as an "effulgence" (ἀπαύγασμα) and as rays of light emanating from the One God, images likely borrowed from Philo.[81] Athanasius also adapts Philo's illustration of the divine architect in his creation theology.[82] If Williams is right about Arius, Athanasius could be borrowing this language from the Alexandrian tradition or even from Arius himself, and not from Philo directly. Athanasius was a controversialist who despised Jews no less than the Arians.[83] It would not be surprising if he in fact conscientiously attempted to discard whatever Philonism he may have known, even if he could not escape it entirely. Nor would it be surprising if he utilized the language of the Arians to refute them. In either case, it demonstrates that Philonic images are very much in the mind of Athanasius.

Eusebius

Eusebius of Caesarea is different from the authors treated to this point. He was an "Alexandrian" only in terms of his commitment to Origen. Whatever time he may have spent in Egypt did not leave a discernible impact on his thought. Eusebius gained access to Philo's works by means of the library of Pamphilus, which was itself an expansion of the library of Origen.[84] This library, within which was included most of Philo's works,

---

79. Runia, *Philo in Early Christian Literature*, 194–96.
80. Cornelia De Vogel, "Platonism and Christianity: A Mere Antagonism or a Profound Common Ground?," *VC* 39 (1985): 1–62.
81. E.g., Philo, *Opif.* 146 (of the λόγος θεῖος); *Spec.* 4.123 ("of the blessed and triply blessed effulgence of nature," τῆς μακαρίας καὶ τρισμακαρίας φύσεως ἀπαύγασμα). Athanasius, *C. Ar.* 2.31–36; 3.3–4, 13; 4.4.10.
82. Philo, *Opif.* 17, 20–25; Athanasius, *C. Ar.* 2.79 (noted by De Vogel, "Platonism," 12–13).
83. See David T. Runia, "Philo and the Early Christian Fathers," in *The Cambridge Companion to Philo* (ed. Adam Kamesar; Cambridge: Cambridge University Press, 2009), 210–30, 218.
84. See David T. Runia, "Caesarea Maritima and the Survival of Hellenistic-Jewish Literature," in *Caesarea Maritima: A Retrospective After Two Millennia* (ed. A. Raban and K.G. Holum; DMOA 21 [Leiden: Brill], 1996), 476–95. The conclusions of Runia are accepted in Andrew Carriker, *The Library of Eusebius of Caesarea* (Leiden: Brill, 2003).

Origen brought to Caesarea when he left Alexandria in 232 CE.[85] Eusebius is rare among ancient authors in that he betrays a thorough knowledge of virtually the entire Philonic corpus.[86] It is not surprising, then, that Eusebius mentions Philo by name more than any other patristic author.

In the *Chron.* of Eusebius Philo is mentioned four times in three contexts. The first merely amounts to Philo being called "a well-educated man."[87] The other references are to events recorded in Philo's historical writings. In the first, Eusebius mentions the prefect Sejanus, who attempted to destroy the Jewish nation. In connection with the activity of Sejanus, Eusebius cites book two of Philo's *Legat.*, which is now lost.[88] The second reference is to Philo's *Flacc.*[89] Eusebius explains that the prefect Flaccus, acting with the consent of the Alexandrian people, polluted the synagogues of the Jews with idols. For this reason Philo "himself undertook the Embassy to Gaius." The third reference in the *Chron.* is to both Philo and Josephus, who attest that Gaius set statues in Jewish synagogues throughout the Roman world.[90] Very little can be ascertained from the limited comments of the *Chronicon* beyond the fact that Eusebius regards Philo as a learned authority for Jewish history. As a witness to the events Eusebius was narrating, Philo, just as Josephus, was a trusted primary source.

The *Hist. eccl.* of Eusebius was a landmark document of Christian antiquity. Eusebius here attempts to trace the church to its earliest times, and to highlight the sources helpful in his purpose. In book 2, Philo receives a thorough treatment as an eyewitness to early Egyptian Christianity.[91] About

---

85. I follow the chronology of Pierre Nautin, *Origène: Sa vie et son oeuvre* (Christianisme antique 1; Paris: Beauchesne, 1977).

86. The majority of the Philonic works no longer extant today were likely unknown to Eusebius as well, as Dominique Barthélemy suggests ("Est-ce Hoshaya Rabba qui censura le 'Commentaire Allegorique?,'" in *Philon d'Alexandrie*, 45–78, 59, n. 9). Fragments have been identified of several lost works, including the περὶ ἀριθμῶν (for an Armenian fragment, see Abraham Terian, "A Philonic Fragment on the Decad," in *Nourished with Peace: Studies in Hellenistic Judaism in Memory of Samuel Sandmel* (ed. Frederick E. Greenspahn et al.; Chico, Calif.: Scholars Press, 1984), 173–82, and for Latin fragments see Françoise Petit, *L'ancienne version latine des Questions sur la Genèse de Philon d'Alexandrie* (TU 113–14; Berlin: Akademie Verlag, 1973).

87. This text is in the Armenian translation of the *Chronicon*, in a section not extant in Jerome's Latin edition (see Runia, *Philo in Early Christian Literature*, 215–216).

88. *Chron.* 176d to the year 34 CE. Eusebius states elsewhere that Philo had written five books about Jews at the time of Gaius (*Hist. eccl.* 2.5.1). On Eusebius's use of *Legat.*, see Sabrina Inowlocki, "The Reception of Philo's *Legatio ad Gaium* in Eusebius of Caesarea's Works," *SPhiloA* 16 (2004): 30–49.

89. *Chron.* 177e to the year 38 CE.

90. *Chron.* 178e to the year 39 CE.

91. On Eusebius's presentation of Philo in the *Hist. eccl.*, see Jorg Ulrich, *Euseb und die Juden: Studien zur Rolle der Juden in der Theologie des Eusebius von Caesarea* (PTS 149; Berlin:

Philo's life, Eusebius furnishes little that we could not extract from Philo's own works and from the brief notice in Josephus.⁹² The one noteworthy piece of information, which Eusebius introduces with the expression λόγος ἔχει ("as the story goes"),⁹³ is that Philo "encountered Peter" in Rome (εἰς ὁμιλίαν ... Πέτρῳ).⁹⁴ Eusebius obviously anticipated objections to the report because he goes on to say, "And this would not be unlikely," citing as evidence Philo's account of the Therapeutae, whom he considers to be Christians. So Eusebius wishes his readers to think that Philo's meeting with Peter is authentic because Philo praised the first Christians in Egypt, which is itself an identification Eusebius feels obligated to defend.⁹⁵

In *Hist. eccl.* 2.4.2–3 Eusebius relates of Philo:

> In his reign [Gaius Caligula] Philo became generally known as a man of the greatest distinction, not only among our own people but also among those of heathen education. He was a Hebrew by racial descent but inferior to none of the magnates in authority in Alexandria. The extent and quality of the labour he bestowed on the theological learning of his race is in fact patent to all, and it is not necessary to say anything of his position in philosophy and the liberal studies of the heathen world since he is related to have surpassed all his contemporaries, especially in his zeal for the study of Plato and Pythagoras.⁹⁶

---

de Gruyter, 1999), 88–100, and now Rogers, "Origen in the Likeness of Philo," which much material in this section repeats.

92. The only information Josephus offers is found in *Ant.* 18.259: "Philo, the leader of the Jewish embassy [to Gaius Caligula], a man esteemed in all things, brother of Alexander the Alabarch, and not inexperienced in philosophy." For a comparison between Eusebius's and Josephus's biographical notes on Philo, see David J. DeVore, "Eusebius' Un-Josephan History: Two Portraits of Philo of Alexandria and the Sources of Ecclesiastical Historiography," StPatr 66 (2013): 161–79.

93. This citation formula has been analyzed by Carriker, *The Library*, 63–68, who observes that the phrase normally, although not always, introduces a written source in Eusebius. B. Gustafsson states that Eusebius generally uses oral sources only for material closer to his own time (i.e., from book 6 onward) ("Eusebius' Principles in Handling His Sources, as Found in His *Church History*, Books I–VII," StPatr 24 [1961]: 429–441, 436). The source may have been Clement of Alexandria, as David Runia seems to suggest, since he is quoted immediately before this point in the narrative (*Philo in Early Christian Literature: A Survey* [CRINT 3.3; Assen: Van Gorcum; Minneapolis: Fortress, 1993], 7).

94. *Hist. eccl.* 2.17.1.

95. The account is a piece of carefully constructed rhetoric aiming at persuasion, and clearly anticipating objection (see Sabrina Inowlocki, "Eusebius of Caesarea's 'Interpretatio Christiana' of Philo's *De vita contemplativa*," HTR 97 [2004]: 305–28).

96. *Hist. eccl.* 2.4.2–3 (trans. Lake, LCL). The Greek reads, Κατὰ δὴ τοῦτον Φίλων ἐγνωρίζετο πλείστοις, ἀνὴρ οὐ μόνον τῶν ἡμετέρων, ἀλλὰ καὶ τῶν ἀπὸ τῆς ἔξωθεν ὁρμωμένων παιδείας ἐπισημότατος. τὸ μὲν οὖν γένος ἀνέκαθεν Ἑβραῖος ἦν, τῶν δ' ἐπ' Ἀλεξανδρείας ἐν τέλει διαφανῶν οὐδενὸς χείρων, περὶ δὲ τὰ θεῖα καὶ πάτρια μαθήματα ὅσον τε καὶ ὁπηλίκον εἰσενήνεκται πόνον, ἔργῳ πᾶσι δῆλος, καὶ περὶ τὰ φιλόσοφα δὲ καὶ ἐλευθέρια τῆς ἔξωθεν παιδείας οἷός τις ἦν, οὐδὲν δεῖ λέγειν,

These lines represent the highest praise. Although a Hebrew,[97] Philo was a famous citizen of Alexandria respected among both Christians and pagans.[98] Furthermore, he was the best philosopher of his time (a time that included the twelve apostles!). Eusebius cites the two philosophers whose names were most respected in his day, and thus is not attempting to reflect historical reality.[99] Eusebius is exaggerating the quality of his source for his own historical purposes, for Philo will be cited as the earliest eyewitness to Egyptian Christianity.

A little later Eusebius says of Philo, "Moreover, from his very accurate description of the life of our ascetics it will be plain that he not only knew but welcomed, reverenced, and recognized the divine mission of the apostolic men of his day, who were, it appears, of Hebrew origin, and thus still preserved most of the ancient customs in a strictly Jewish manner."[100] The terminology Eusebius employs is evocative. Especially the terms "reverenced" (ἐκθειάζω) and "recognized the divine mission" (σεμνύνω) carry specialized senses deserving analysis.

The former term means "to deify" and is often used negatively of idols, ideas and creatures worshipped among the pagans.[101] The term can be used, however, of reverence or admiration, especially of non-Christians toward the Christian life. For instance, Clement, after citing a number of texts to demonstrate that "Christian" virtue is valued among the Greeks,

---

ὅτε μάλιστα τὴν κατὰ Πλάτωνα καὶ Πυθαγόραν ἐζηλωκὼς ἀγωγήν, διενεγκεῖν ἅπαντας τοὺς καθ' ἑαυτὸν ἱστορεῖται.

97. On the terms "Hebrew" and "Jew" in Eusebius as they relate to Philo and Josephus see Sabrina Inowlocki, *Eusebius and the Jewish Authors: His Citation Technique in an Apologetic Context* (AGAJU 64; Leiden: Brill, 2006), 105–38. She concludes that both authors are called "Jews" and "Hebrews" in different contexts, although the term "Hebrew" is the more honorable of the two, and in the apologetic writings, the term "Hebrew" is used of Jewish authors only when Eusebius "intends to connect them to Christianity" (121).

98. Josephus, by comparison, is called "most noted [ἐπισημότατος] of the historians among the Hebrews" (1.5.3).

99. Alain Petit shows that Philo's "Pythagoreanism" cannot be typical, if he was Pythagorean at all ("Philon et le pythagorisme: un usage problématique," in *Philon d'Alexandrie et le langage de la philosophie* [ed. Carlos Lévy; Monothéismes et Philosophie; Turnhout: Brepols, 1998], 471–82).

100. *Hist. eccl.* 2.17.2 (trans. Lake, LCL). The Greek reads, ἀλλὰ καὶ τὸν βίον τῶν παρ' ἡμῖν ἀσκητῶν ὡς ἔνι μάλιστα ἀκριβέστατα ἱστορῶν, γένοιτ' ἂν ἔκδηλος οὐκ εἰδὼς μόνον, ἀλλὰ καὶ ἀποδεχόμενος ἐκθειάζων τε καὶ σεμνύνων τοὺς κατ' αὐτὸν ἀποστολικοὺς ἄνδρας, ἐξ Ἑβραίων, ὡς ἔοικε, γεγονότας ταύτῃ τε ἰουδαϊκώτερον τῶν παλαιῶν ἔτι τὰ πλεῖστα διατηροῦντας ἐθῶν.

101. See G. W. H. Lampe, *A Patristic Greek Lexicon*, s.v. "ἐκθειάζω," and the word study in Norman Russell, *The Doctrine of Deification in the Greek Patristic Tradition* (Oxford: Oxford University Press, 2005), 341–42, although the latter does not mention Eusebius's usage.

concludes, "You see how even the Greeks deify [ἐκθειάζω] the gnostic life, although not knowing how it must be understood."[102] The author of the *Cohortatio*, in giving his account of the translation of the Septuagint, portrays Ptolemy II Philadelphus marveling at the work, and calling the translators θεοφιλεῖς ἄνδρες, and "deifying [ἐκθειάζω] the books."[103] Certainly neither of these authors wished to express deification literally, as did the Neo-Platonists for whom the term becomes equivalent to the ethical ideal of ὁμοίωσις θεῷ.[104] But the strong metaphor elevates those occasional non-Christians who recognized distinctively "Christian" (anachronistically applied) truths. Philo falls right in line with such a tradition.

The second term, σεμνύνω, again reminds us of divination, for the term often means "to honor as divine."[105] In Eusebius, though, the term most often indicates "irreverent boasting." This context is one of the few occasions in which the term is positive in Eusebius. Kirsopp Lake is correct to translate Philo "recognized the divine mission" of the first Egyptian Christians. Like Josephus, who recognized the greatness of John the Baptizer and Jesus,[106] Philo met Peter in Rome, and subsequently "became a hearer" (ἐπακροασαμένος) of the Therapeutae.[107]

A little later the Therapeutae are acknowledged to be "from the Hebrews" (ἐξ Ἑβραίων) and "were still rather Jewish [ἰουδαϊκώτερον] in their preservation of most of the ancient customs."[108] According to Sabrina Inowlocki, the comparative adjective ἰουδαϊκώτερον in the *Hist. eccl.* elsewhere describes "Christian groups willing to keep Jewish law, such as the Ebionites,[109] or those willing to interpret the scriptures as the Jews do, like the schismatic Nepos."[110] The Therapeutae, then, are identified as *Jewish* Christians, while their informant, Philo, is allowed to remain only a

---

102. *Strom.* 5.11.69.
103. *Cohort.* 14.B.
104. See Plato's *Theaet.* 176B, and its interpretation in Porphyry (*Marc.* 17) and Proclus (e.g., *El. Theol.* 129, 135, 153). For the Platonic theme see Charles P. Bigger, *Participation: A Platonic Inquiry* (Baton Rouge, La.: Louisiana State University Press, 1968). For the theme of ὁμοίωσις in patristic thought see Norman Russell, *The Doctrine of Deification*, 121–40 (on Clement).
105. Lampe, *A Patristic Greek Lexicon*, s.v. "σεμνύνω."
106. Josephus, *Ant.* 18.63 (Jesus); 18.116–117 (John). On Eusebius's discussions, see *Hist. eccl.* 1.11.3–9.
107. *Hist. eccl.* 2.17.12: "This seems to have been said by a man who had listened to their expositions of the sacred scriptures" (ταῦτα μὲν οὖν ἔοικεν εἰρῆσθαι τῷ ἀνδρὶ τὰς ἱερὰς ἐξηγουμένων αὐτῶν ἐπακροασαμένῳ γραφάς).
108. ἰουδαϊκώτερον τῶν παλαιῶν ἔτι τὰ πλεῖστα διατηροῦντας ἐθῶν (*Hist. eccl.* 2.17.2).
109. *Hist. eccl.* 6.17.1.
110. *Hist. eccl.* 7.24.1; "Eusebius of Caesarea's 'Interpretatio Christiana,'" 312.

Hebrew.[111] Eusebius does not convert Philo to Christianity, but it is not difficult to understand how later Christian tradition comes to see him as one of their own. Philo not only knew the Apostle Peter, but he left an admiring eyewitness account of early Egyptian "Christianity."

When we turn to the apologetic works of Eusebius we find a much more extensive use of Philo. The *Dem. ev.* contains only two explicit references to Philo,[112] but the *Praep. ev.* provides us with the densest use of Philonic material in any patristic work. In addition to Runia's surveys, we now possess Sabrina Inowlocki's *Eusebius and the Jewish Authors*, which includes thorough discussions of Philo's role in the apologetic works of Eusebius.

Turning to the *Preparation for the Gospel*, we find the name of Philo in ten different passages,[113] and nine separate Philonic texts are quoted a total of twenty times.[114] Quotations range from brief excerpts to extensive blocks of material. It is from these citations that we derive our only quotations from the *Hypoth.* of Philo and the only substantial Greek fragments of Philo's *Prov.*[115] Eusebius is an essential link in the preservation of the Philonic text, but his quotations are not always as precise as we wish them to be.

Inowlocki shows that Eusebius is willing to manipulate his quotations, sometimes contradicting the author's original meaning in the process.[116] Philo is not exempt from such treatment.[117] For example, in *Praep. ev.* 7.13.3, Eusebius quotes Philo's *Agr.* 51 as follows: "All these things God, their shepherd and king, leads in accordance with justice, he setting over

---

111. By way of comparison it should be noted that the entire Jerusalem church before the time of Hadrian "consisted of Hebrews" (*Hist. eccl.* 4.5.2). Eusebius thus may have an apologetic motive in linking the "original" Jerusalem church with the Alexandrian Therapeutae, to lend credibility to the latter's Christian identity.

112. *Dem. ev.* 8.2.123; 390.5.

113. *Praep. ev.* 1.9.20; 7.12.14–13.7; 7.17.4–18.3; 7.20.9–21.5; 8.15.11–7.21; 8.10.19–12.20; 8.12.21–14.72; 11.14.10–15.7; 11.23.12–24.12; 13.18.12–16 (the list is borrowed from Runia, "Philo in the Patristic Tradition," 278–79).

114. *Praep. ev.* 7.13.1–2; 7.13.3; 7.13.4–6; 7.18.1–2; 7.21.1–4; 8.6.1–7.20; 8.11.1–18; 8.12.1–19; 8.13.1–6; 8.14.1; 8.14.2–42; 8.14.43–72; 11.15.1; 11.15.2–4; 11.5–6; 11.24.1–6; 11.24.7–10; 11.24.11–12; 13.18.12–15; 13.18.16.

115. Of *Prov.* There are a few "short fragments in the *Sacra Parallela*" (Jenny Morris, "The Jewish Philosopher Philo," in Emil Schürer, *The History of the Jewish People in the Age of Jesus Christ* [rev. and ed. Geza Vermes, Fergus Millar, and Martin Goodman; Edinburgh: T&T Clark, 1987], 3:865). Of the *Hypoth.* Morris says only that "knowledge of this treatise rests almost entirely" on Eusebius's quotations (3:866).

116. *Eusebius and the Jewish Authors*, 191–93. This suggestion runs counter to what generations of scholarship have assumed; namely, that Eusebius is faithful in his quotations. Inowlocki draws her caution partially from Marguerite Harl, *Philon d'Alexandrie: Quis rerum divinarum heres sit* (Les œuvres de Philon d'Alexandrie 15; Paris: Éditions du Cerf, 1966), 158–59.

117. Inowlocki, *Eusebius and the Jewish Authors*, 195–206.

them as a Law his true *Logos*, his first-born son, who will receive care of the sacred flock like some minister of the Great king."[118] The reading κατὰ δίκην καὶ νόμον in the Philonic text is altered to κατὰ δίκην, νόμον.[119] The omission of the καί allows Eusebius to turn the Logos of the Philonic text into a universal law in accord with earlier Christian theology. But it creates a much different sense than Philo's original statement. Philo is plundered for the sake of Eusebian apologetic.

Eusebius can also remove statements in Philo that sound too polytheistic. He removes a Homeric citation in *Praep. ev.* 13.18.15 identifying Zeus as "the father of the gods and of mankind").[120] He also removes the term θεῶν from his citation of *Spec.* 1.20, yielding the sense that "God is the father of intelligible and sensible things" rather than of "intelligible and sensible gods," as Philo has it.[121] Eusebius was obviously uncomfortable with Philo's apparent deification of the stars. These are just a few examples, but they teach us to be cautious when handling Eusebian citations. He, as most ancient authors, does not always quote as carefully as we would like, and we cannot ignore apologetic or theological editing of the quotations even when they are attributed.[122]

Intentional alterations of the Philonic text, however, are not always apologetically motivated. Often Eusebius merely cuts a portion he does not wish to quote without altering the essential meaning.[123] Nevertheless, for Eusebius, altering a quotation cannot be separated from his overall apologetic aim. Philo is a predecessor, and he must thus bring Philo into conformity with his own system of thought. As a Hebrew, Philo can be cited as representative of an ancient tradition predating, and thus superior to, the Greeks, and as an early admirer of Christianity can be portrayed as a predecessor of Eusebius himself.[124] Philo is Eusebius's greatest proof for

---

118. Trans. mine. The Greek reads, Ταῦτα δὴ πάντα ὁ ποιμὴν καὶ βασιλεὺς θεὸς ἄγει κατὰ δίκην, νόμον προστησάμενος τὸν ὀρθὸν αὐτοῦ λόγον καὶ πρωτόγονον υἱόν, ὃς τὴν ἐπιμέλειαν τῆς ἱερᾶς ταύτης ἀγέλης οἷά τις μεγάλου βασιλέως ὕπαρχος, διαδέξεται.

119. Inowlocki is incorrect in stating that Cohn and [*sic*] Wendland (Wendland alone was editor of the volume in question) opted to follow the Eusebian reading (*Eusebius and the Jewish Authors*, 197; see PCW 2:106 where the text indeed is κατὰ δίκην καὶ νόμον).

120. Philo, *Prov.* 2.3 (the Eusebian omission is noted by Colson as well [PLCL 9:461]).

121. See *Praep. ev.* 13.18.16.

122. As a comparison, Philo himself can alter his Platonic citations for theological reasons (David T. Runia, "The Text of the Platonic Citations in Philo of Alexandria," in *Studies in Plato and the Platonic Tradition: Essays Presented to John Whittaker*, ed. Mark Joyal [Aldershot: Ashgate, 1997], 261–91).

123. See examples and discussion in Inowlocki, *Eusebius and the Jewish Authors*, 157–67.

124. Eusebius regards Josephus and Philo as "relatives" (οἰκεῖοι) of the Jews, distancing them from contemporary communities in Caesarea who might stand in hostility to the church (*Praep. ev.* 8.10.19).

separating within Judaism allegorists from literalists,[125] or as Jean Pépin interpreted it, diaspora Jews from Palestinian ones.[126]

Philo does not fit the [Palestinian] Jewish mold, either as a philosopher or as an exegete. For example, Origen states explicitly that the Jews rejected the association of the Logos with the son of God,[127] but Philo clearly expresses the connection.[128] Philo can thus be cited along with Aristobulus as a proponent of the Second Cause among the Hebrews,[129] Aristobulus in the form of Sophia and Philo in the form of the Logos.[130] This allows Eusebius to condemn implicitly contemporary "Jews" who pervert the ancient "Hebrew" wisdom pristinely preserved in the Hellenistic Jewish authors.

Philo also functions apologetically as an heir of the Hebrew tradition from which Plato drew and according to which Plato can be corrected. The theme of Plato's dependence on the Hebraic tradition is lifted directly from the Hellenistic Jewish apologists themselves.[131] By the time of Eusebius, the Christian assumption that Plato learned his wisdom from the

---

125. See esp. *Praep. ev.* 8.10.18.

126. Jean Pépin, *Mythe et Allégorie: Les origins grecques et les contestations judéo-chétiennes* (2nd ed.; Paris: Études augustiniennes, 1976), 221–44.

127. *Cels.* 2.31. In this text, Origen accuses Celsus of misquoting a Jewish author as believing the Logos can be described as the son of God. Chadwick wonders if Celsus was aware of Hellenistic-Jewish speculation, citing Philo as representative (*Origen Contra Celsum*, 93 n. 3). Barthélemy refers to this very passage, believing Eusebius depends on Origen here, and suggesting the latter may have assembled Philonic testimonia which Eusebius utilized ("Qui censura le Commentaire allégorique?" 67–68).

128. E.g., *Agr.* 51; *Conf.* 146; *Somn.* 1.215. The bibliography on Philo's Logos doctrine is massive. The most extensive discussion remains that of Harry Austryn Wolfson, *Philo: Foundations of Religious Philosophy in Judaism, Christianity and Islam* (Cambridge, Mass.: Harvard University Press, 1947), 1:226–89. For a more recent discussion of the Logos as the son of God see Baudouin Decharneux, "Le Logos premier-né de Dieu dans l'œuvre de Philon d'Alexandrie," in *Le paradigme de la filiation* (ed. Jean Gayon, Jean-Jacques Wunenburger; Paris: Éditions l'Harmattan, 1995), 361–69. On the relationship between the Logos of Philo and that of the prologue to the Fourth Gospel, see Thomas H. Tobin, "The Prologue of John and Hellenistic Jewish Speculation," *CBQ* 52 (1990): 252–69; Masanobu Endo, *Creation and Christology: A Study on the Johannine Prologue in the Light of Early Jewish Accounts* (WUNT 2:149; Tübingen: Mohr Siebeck, 2002); Harold W. Attridge, "Philo and John: Two Riffs on one Logos," *SPhiloA* 17 (2005): 103–117.

129. *Praep. ev.* 7.13.6.

130. David Winston reports that Philo's logos doctrine (and supposed Trinitarian theology) was central to his Christian reception well into the Middle Ages (*Logos and Mystical Theology in Philo of Alexandria* [Cincinnati: Hebrew Union College Press, 1985], 10). Eusebius was a central player in passing along this aspect of Philo's thought.

131. E.g., Aristobulus fragment 3 (*apud* Eusebius, *Praep. ev.* 13.12.1–2); Josephus, *C. Ap.* 2.256–57.

Hebrews had become a topos in Christian apologetic.[132] So Eusebius feels that Philo can be enlisted in his own effort to work out a Platonic *Quellensforschung*.[133] In *Praep. ev.*, for example, Eusebius can cite Philo as proof that Plato borrowed his doctrine of the Second Cause from the Hebrews.[134] But Philo can also be used to correct Plato's deification of astral bodies.[135] In one case Plato has stuck to his sources, and in another has departed from them.

There are other potential areas of Philonic influence on Eusebius. Philo is used to prove man's role in creation as *imago dei*, a Philonic theme likely mediated by Origen.[136] In addition, Eusebius's role as an exegete has only recently come to be appreciated.[137] It is clear that Philo was known to Eusebius, of course, but no full scale investigation has been conducted on Eusebius's use of Philo in his biblical exegesis.[138] We know that Philo exerted a powerful influence on Eusebius, and much work remains to discover just how pervasive this influence actually was.

Conclusion

From the preceding survey it is clear that Philo was well-established in Alexandrian Christianity. He was received as a trusted philosopher, exegete, and historian. No Christian author surveyed in this chapter seems to have adopted him uncritically, but he was a trusted traditional source for each. It seems that most of the major Christian authors in the Alexandrian tradition had at least some acquaintance with Philo, and most

---

132. The theme is taken over first by Justin Martyr (e.g., *1 Apol.* 44.8), and is repeated in Origen (e.g., *Cels.* 6.19) and Clement (e g., *Strom.* 1.165–66) (on this theme as it relates to Justin Martyr, see Arthur J. Droge, *Homer or Moses? Early Christian Interpretations of the History of Culture* [HUT 26; Tübingen: Mohr Siebeck, 1989], 59–65).

133. As a parallel, note that Simplicius can cite [Pseudo-]Archytas, whom he locates within the Pythagorean tradition, to correct Aristotle on the grounds that Pythagoras was the teacher of Plato who was the teacher of Aristotle (Ilsetraut Hadot, "Le Commentaire philosophique continu dans l'antiquité," *Antiquité Tardive* 5 (1997): 169–76, 171–72.

134. *Praep. ev.* 11.16.1–2.

135. *Praep. ev.* 13.18.12–16.

136. See Eusebius *Praep. ev.* 8.18; on the theme in Origen see Henri Crouzel, *Théologie de l'image de Dieu chez Origène* (Théologie 34; Paris: Aubier-Montaigne, 1956). This theme turns up again in Didymus the Blind (see chapter 5).

137. See, e.g., Michael J. Hollerich, *Eusebius of Caesarea's* Commentary on Isaiah: *Christian Exegesis in the Age of Constantine* (OECS; Oxford: Oxford University Press, 1999).

138. However, see Sébastien Morlet, "L'Écriture image des vertus: la transformation d'un theme philoniene dans l'apologétique d'Eusèbe de Césarée," StPatr 42 (2006): 187–92.

used him to their advantage. His exegetical method was the opposite of what the Fathers regarded as "Jewish" interpretation, and his praise of the Therapeutae put him at the threshold of Christian conversion. By the time of Didymus the Jew Philo could be cited in Christian commentaries without a hint of embarrassment. Although it is impossible to reconstruct with precision the library to which Didymus the Blind (or his assistants) had access, his copious use of Philo proves that, despite the move of Origen's library to Caesarea, Philo's works did not disappear from Alexandria.

3

THE USE OF SOURCES IN CHRISTIAN COMMENTARIES

Introduction

The use of sources is central to scholarship itself, for every new production is a reaction to, and perhaps *against*, a tradition of received influences. Commentaries especially aim to tap a particular tradition, beginning with the source text itself.[1] The commentary works in dialogue with the author of the source text, while also acknowledging, explicitly or implicitly, the earlier hermeneutical tradition. The very existence of commentaries implies the need to refresh the tradition in the author's own day in order to render both the source text and the tradition maximally beneficial to the contemporary intellectual community. Therefore, commentators primarily seek to instruct, and allying oneself with respected figures of the past is an effective way of earning authority for one's instruction.

Referring to predecessors is the easiest way to locate oneself within a particular tradition. The principal factor is the authority of the commentator to speak for the tradition.[2] Since the commentary preserves, defends, or occasionally corrects the tradition, the authority of the commentator is paramount to its didactic purposes.[3] Ineke Sluiter writes, "The commentator thereby becomes part of a living didactic tradition originating with the source text, and he benefits from the social significance attached to tradition."[4] Source citation is simply an effective means of broadcasting one's knowledge of the tradition to which he or she belongs.

---

1. On tradition and its importance in passing down wisdom in the schools, see Eduard Stemplinger, *Der Plagiat in der Griechischen Literatur* (Leizig: Teubner, 1912), 88–102.
2. For a general introduction to the ancient philosophical commentary, see Ilsetraut Hadot, "Der fortlaufende philosophische Kommentar," in *Der Kommentar in Antike und Mittelalter: Beiträge zu seiner Erforschung* (ed. Wilhelm Geerlings and Christian Schulze; Clavis Commentariorum Antiquitatis et Medii Aevi 2; Leiden: Brill, 2002), 183–99, and Han Baltussen, "From Polemic to Exegesis: The Ancient Philosophical Commentary," *Poetics Today* 28 (2007): 247–81.
3. The commentator effectively seeks to defend or maintain authority, usually of the source text, but sometimes of his own interpretations (Glenn W. Most, "Preface," in *Commentaries–Kommentare*, ed. Glenn W. Most [Aporemata: Kritische Studien zur Philologiegeschichte 4; Göttingen: Vandenhoeck and Ruprecht, 1999], VII–XV).
4. Ineke Sluiter, "Commentaries and the Didactic Tradition," in *Commentaries–Kommentare*, 173–205, 173.

CHAPTER 3

Plagiarism and Named References in Ancient Literature

The scholastic nature of the commentary invites quotations from and references to the tradition. Commentators were expected to take over the arguments of their predecessors, and were not required to name their sources. Nevertheless, the accusation of plagiarism could serve as a libel against ancient authors. Pliny the Elder boasts of his immense research in preparing his *Natural History* and then states:

> You will find it proof of this irritation of mine that in these volumes I preface the names of my authorities. However, I feel it is courteous and indicative of a natural modesty to acknowledge the sources that have assisted one's work, and not to do as most of the sources I have mentioned. For in comparing these authors I have discovered that some of the supposedly most reliable and modern writers have copied verbatim the older authors without naming them.[5]

Pliny goes on to except Virgil, Cicero, and Plato from this disparagement, but blatantly accuses most of his other sources as follows: "For it is truly the mark of a guilty soul and bad character to prefer being caught in a theft than to returning what is borrowed, especially when one profits off the use!"[6]

We may leave aside the question of whether Pliny is consistent with his own high standards (indeed, he is not).[7] However, his words provide important commentary on what ancient authors and their audiences could expect. First, it is clear that excessive name-dropping could be poorly received, for it offends the enjoyment of reading. Pliny indeed apologizes for naming his sources too often, although his claim to have read two thousand volumes and one hundred separate authors implies that he could have named predecessors far more frequently.[8] It is unimaginable that Pliny would acknowledge every debt, as his audience is aware. But

---

5. Pliny, *Nat.* praef. 21–22 (trans. mine). The Latin reads, *argumentum huius stomachi mei habebis quod in his voluminibus auctorum nomina praetexui. est enim benignum, ut arbitror, et plenum ingenui pudoris fateri per quos profeceris, non ut plerique ex iis, quos attigi, fecerunt. scito enim conferentem auctores me deprehendisse a iuratissimis ex proximis veteres transcriptos ad verbum neque nominatos.*

6. Pliny, *Nat.* praef 23 (trans. mine). The Latin reads, *obnoxii profecto animi et infelicis ingenii est deprehendi in furto malle quam mutuum reddere, cum praesertim sors fiat ex usura.*

7. E.g., Pliny's treatment of Theophrastus; see G.E.R. Lloyd, *Science, Folklore and Ideology: Studies in the Life Sciences in Ancient Greece* (Cambridge: Cambridge University Press, 1983), 141–49. On ancient authors not living up to their grand claims, see Kenneth Quandt, "Αἱ γὰρ τῶν ἐναντίων εἰσίν: Philosophical Program and Expository Practice in Aristotle," *Classical Antiquity* 2 (1983): 279–98.

8. *Hist. nat.* Praef. 17.

Pliny's words also show that excessive cribbing would be poorly received. His criticism of unattributed quotations as "theft" indicates that the audience can be expected to condemn verbal plagiarism.[9] Indeed Cicero says explicitly the difference between "borrowing" (*sumo*) and "theft" (*surripio*) is the acknowledgment of one's literary debts.[10]

Perhaps the standard applied to unattributed quotations explains why most ancient authors do not quote verbatim, but prefer to paraphrase.[11] When an author does quote verbatim he is expected to cite his source. Paraphrasing allows the author more wiggle room. He may mention the name of his source (and perhaps this is preferred), but may be excused if he chooses not to do so. Within the commentary tradition specifically, individual personalities were not exalted as a rule, but their comments were blended into the tradition. Entire exegetical works can exist without a single author being mentioned by name.

Cyril of Alexandria, for example, who lived a generation after Didymus, never cites predecessors by name, but regularly acknowledges that his work is not original.[12] An example might be cited from the preface to his *Commentary on Isaiah*:

> I know, of course, that a number of previous writers have already dealt with these matters and have produced long treatises on them. These are perfectly adequate, in my opinion. It is therefore not ignoble to appeal to diffidence as a motive for not adding to them and to allow oneself to be persuaded to remain silent, on the grounds that one has nothing new to add to what has already been said by others, but instead would only be repeating the same points and running through the same spiritual themes.[13]

---

9. Roman law did not recognize intellectual property, and specifically stipulates whatever is on a page belongs to the owner of the page "since letters are inferior to the papyrus or parchment" (*quia litterae cartulis siue membranis cedunt*) (Gaius 2.77). On ancient views of plagiarism, see Scott McGill, *Plagiarism in Latin Literature* (Cambridge: Cambridge University Press, 2012).

10. *Brut.* 76 (see McGill, *Plagiarism*, 2).

11. Even the language of explicit quotation should not be taken too seriously. Lloyd writes, "The fundamental point is that when a Greek writer tells us what one of his predecessors 'says,' *phési*, this has often to be taken not as a record of what that predecessor wrote, let alone of words that he spoke, but rather in the sense of what he meant or could be represented as meaning" ("Quotation in Greco-Roman Contexts," 143).

12. See Hannah Miller, "Cyril of Alexandria's Treatment of Sources in His Commentary on the Twelve Prophets," StPatr 68 (2013): 85–93.

13. *Comm. Isa.* Praef. (trans. Norman Russell, *Cyril of Alexandria* [Early Church Fathers; London: Routledge, 2000], 71–72). The Greek reads, Οἶδα μὲν οὖν ὅτι φθάσαντές τινες προγεγράφασιν εἰς ταῦτα, καὶ μακροὺς ἡμῖν περὶ αὐτῶν ἐποιήσαντο λόγους· ἀπόχρη δὲ οἶμαι τουτὶ, καὶ

Anonymity, then, is part of the Christian commentary tradition. It could be assumed the audience is capable of identifying the tradition without feeling obligated to trace every argument back to its original source. Name-dropping, therefore, can be significant, for it highlights the commentator's desire to draw explicit attention to a particular figure, usually to reinforce a point the commentator has already established, and thereby to lend support to his own argument.[14]

But we should not assume that Christian commentators were unconcerned with the potential allegation of plagiarism. In the preface to his *Commentary on the Song of Songs* Theodore of Mopsuestia states rather emphatically,

> We beg our readers not to accuse us of theft if someone should happen to find that something in our interpretations has been said in the Fathers. We freely admit that our own commentary has its origin in their works. So it is not theft, but our paternal heritage that is responsible. What we have received from them we include, and what we discover ourselves we add. We limit what others have said for the sake of space, but elaborate on things that require more attention.[15]

Theodore freely acknowledges his work falls within a tradition, and thus he is obliged to acknowledge predecessors. But he also expresses that he will not always name his sources, even when he might be influenced by them.

So, based on the examples we have seen, it seems ancient audiences were content for authors to admit a vague awareness of predecessors, without requiring them to cite each source by name. Often a brief note in a work's preface was regarded as sufficient to satisfy the audience that comments were not plagiarized, but conscientiously derived from an intellectual tradition.[16]

πρός γε τὸ δεῖν ἑτέροις ὄκνου πρόφασιν οὐκ ἀγεννῆ παρασχεῖν, ἀναπεῖσαί τε σιωπῆσαι ἑλέσθαι μᾶλλον, οἷς ἕτεροι προειρήκασιν ἐπειπεῖν καινὸν μὲν οὐδέν, ταυτοεπεῖν δὲ μᾶλλον, καὶ διὰ τῶν αὐτῶν ἰέναι θεωρημάτων.

14. See Han Baltussen, *Philosophy and Exegesis in Simplicius: The Methodology of a Commentator* [London: Bloomsbury, 2008], 42–46).

15. *Comm. Song* praef. The Greek reads, τοσοῦτον τοὺς ἐντευξομένους παρακαλέσαντες, μὴ κλοπὴν ἡμῶν κατηγορεῖν, εἴ τι τοῖς πατράσιν εἰρημένον ἐν ταῖς ἡμετέραις εὕροιεν ἑρμηνείαις. Ὁμολογοῦμεν γὰρ καὶ ἡμεῖς παρ'ἐκείνων τὰς ἀφορμὰς εὑρηκέναι τῆς σαφηνείας· ἔστι δὲ τὸ τοιοῦτον οὐ κλοπή, ἀλλὰ κληρονομία πατρῷα. Καὶ τὰ μὲν παρ'ἐκείνων εἰληφότες τίθεμεν, τὰ δὲ αὐτοὶ ἐπεξευρόντες προστίθεμεν. Καὶ τὰ μέν, ὡς διὰ πλάτους εἰρημένα τισίν, συντέμνομεν· τὰ δὲ ἐπεξεργασίας δεόμενα διευρύνομεν.

16. On the composition of prefaces, see Jaap Mansfeld, *Prolegomena: Questions to be Settled Before the Study of an Author, or a Text* (PhA 61; Leiden: Brill, 1994).

Why Refer to Predecessors?

If a vague statement of familiarity with the tradition was sufficient, why do ancient commentators name sources at all? None of the rhetorical or stylistic handbooks discuss the nature and importance of source citation, with the exception of Quintilian. He advises young students as follows:

> Finally, let us trust the great orators, who use the works of the early poets either to support their cases or to adorn their eloquence. Particularly in Cicero, but often also in Asinius and others nearest to their times, we find inserted lines from Ennius, Accius, Pacuvius, Lucilius, Terence, Caecilius, and others, producing great charm not only from the learning shown but from the pleasure given by allowing the audience to relax from the asperities of the courtroom in the delights of poetry. There is considerable practical advantage in this also, because orators adduce the sentiments of the poets as a kind of evidence to support their own positions.[17]

From the preceding passage we learn that great rhetoricians always sprinkle their oratory with Classical poetry. They do so for two primary reasons: (1) to substantiate their cases (*ad fidem causarum*), and (2) to adorn their speeches with eloquence (*ad ornamentum eloquentiae*). The latter will lend credibility to the speaker, both as the audience is impressed with his learning and as the listeners are allowed a mental excursion from forensic rhetoric. The former reason allows the orator to call the poets to witness in favor of his case, giving the impression that what is being proposed to the audience was already accepted long ago.

Neither of these reasons, however, requires an explicit citation of the author or authors referenced. Nor in fact do these reasons prevent paraphrase, which can be considered a form of quotation in antiquity.[18] Indeed, all contemporary readers should note that source citation and explicit quotation is a modern invention and cannot be a standard imposed on ancient authors.[19] The above-cited rules set forth by Quintillian

---

17. *Inst.* 1.8.10–12 (trans. Russell, LCL). The Latin reads, *denique credamus summis oratoribus, qui veterum poemata vel ad fidem causarum vel ad ornamentum eloquentiae adsumunt. nam praecipue quidem apud Ciceronem frequenter tamen apud Asinium etiam et ceteros, qui sunt proximi, videmus Enni, Acci, Pacuvi, Lucili, Terenti, Caecili et aliorum inseri versus summa non eruditionis modo gratia sed etiam iucunditatis, cum poeticis voluptatibus aures a forensi asperitate respirent. quibus accedit non mediocris utilitas, cum sententiis eorum velut quibusdam testimoniis quae proposuere confirment.*

18. William C. Helmbold and Edward N. O'Neil, *Plutarch's Quotations* (American Philological Association Monographs 19; Baltimore: American Philological Association, 1959), viii. The same expectations for named references need not apply to paraphrase, however.

19. For the most recent summary of this topic see Wilfried Nippel, *Fußnoten, Zitate, Plagiate: Wissenschaftsgeschichtliche Streifzüge* (Karl-Christ-Preis für Alte Geschichte 1; Heidelberg: Verlag Antike, 2014).

apply explicitly to rhetoric, and although rhetoric certainly influences exegesis, the traditional nature of the commentary implies other reasons for source citation.[20] Thus, Quintillian's rules do not entirely explain source citation in Christian commentaries.

Origen, for example, sometimes cites predecessors only to disagree with them. On one occasion, he references Philo both by name and by work (the *Quod deterius*), in conjunction with the *Sentences of Sextus*, for the view that "it is better to be made a eunuch than to rabidly pursue unlawful intercourses."[21] He then argues against these sources on the authority of Jesus that spiritual castration (the meaning Jesus intended in Matt 19:12) is more virtuous.[22] One might term this the polemical motivation for citation. The purpose of name-dropping here is to identify the cited interpretations as outliers to the tradition,[23] views that must be rejected on the authority of an impeccable figure *within* the tradition.[24]

The polemical motivation, however, is rare. Generally, quotations are utilized either to demonstrate a case (usually, although not always, followed by commentary further unpacking the demonstration), to validate a case already made (to justify the commentator's point), or to clarify an obscure point in the text (often merely a lexical gloss).[25] These three motivations are generally observable in the case of Didymus's source citations.

When Didymus cites Philo without additional comment, referring the reader to him to complete his or her understanding of the anagogical meaning,[26] he is using Philo to demonstrate a case (without necessarily making it himself). The purpose here presumably is to acknowledge a trusted voice within the tradition, which the student ought to consult. One could theorize that the original classroom setting of Didymus's commentaries might be responsible for this feature, but Didymus cites no other

---

20. The influence of rhetorical analysis is apparent in Origen's exegesis (see Bernard Neuschäfer, *Origenes als Philologe* (2 vols.; Schweizerische Beiträge zur Altertumswissenschaft 18.1–2; Basel: Friedrich Reinhardt, 1987), and among the Antiochenes (see Christoph Schäublin, *Untersuchungen zu Methode und Herkunft der antiochenischen Exegese* [Theophania 23; Cologne-Bonn: Hanstein, 1974]).

21. Origen refers to Philo, *Det.* 176 and *Sent.* 13, 273.

22. *Comm. Matt.* 15.3 (trans. mine).

23. By comparison, Van den Hoek notes Clement's tendency to quote his "gnostic" opponents more frequently than the authors with whom he is in greater agreement ("Techniques of Quotation," 237).

24. In the reception history of Matt 19:12 the rigorist interpretations cited by Origen seem to have disappeared without a trace (see Daniel F. Caner, "The Practice and Prohibition of Self-Castration in Early Christianity," *VC* 51 [1997]: 396–415).

25. See Baltussen, *Simplicius*, 66.

26. *Comm. Gen.* 139.10–14; 147.15–18.

author in this way in his writings. Apparently, to Didymus, Philo occupies a place within the Alexandrian tradition unlike any other biblical exegete.

Of course, Didymus stands apart from many ancient Christian authors by choosing to name his sources at all.[27] We have already seen that Cyril of Alexandria, for example, a generation after Didymus, never names sources. While "name dropping" might be considered impolite "because the educated audience was supposed to know their classics,"[28] we cannot assume that Alexandrian Christian students could identify Philo as readily as Homer, Plato, or the Bible. This reasoning applies especially to Origen's association of Philo with the anonymous "someone" (τις) referenced over twenty times. Are his readers supposed to recognize this "someone" is Philo? Perhaps it is better to think that Philo's interpretations were more familiar than his name.[29] This takes us back to the concept of authorized "tradition" in the commentary genre. Philo can be that "someone" integrated already into the inherited tradition of Christian exegesis.

But we should not assume that anonymous references are unimportant. In fact, anonymous references may actually serve a pedagogical purpose in late antique commentaries, for they establish credibility for the author without biasing the reader. Name-dropping could sway the audience toward or away from a certain position before the author has opportunity to reasonably affirm his own position. Harold Tarrant says of Proclus's commentaries, "Naming names encouraged a predisposition to consider an interpretation favourably or unfavourably, as pedestrian or as inspired depending on whether the interpreter was more like Atticus or Iamblichus, instead of getting the student to consider each on its merits."[30] Referencing anonymously allows the reader to consider the argument rather than the stature of the authority who made it.

---

27. It should be noted that the frequency of named citations differs drastically in the preserved commentary tradition. Edward Watts contrasts the practices of Olympiodorus's commentary on the *Gorgias*, which rarely names sources, with the Aristotelian commentaries of Simplicius, which include copious source citations ("Translating the Personal Aspect of Late Platonism in the Commentary Tradition," in *Interpreting the Bible and Aristotle in Late Antiquity: The Alexandrian Commentary Tradition between Rome and Baghdad* [ed. Josef Lössel and John W. Watt; London: Ashgate, 2011], 137–50, 144–45).

28. Annewies Van den Hoek, "Techniques of Quotation in Clement of Alexandria," *VC* 50 (1996): 223–43, 229.

29. On Origen's use of sources (usually anonymously), see Lorenzo Perrone, "*Origenes pro domo sua*: Self-Quotations and the (Re)construction of a Literary Œuvre," in *Origeniana Decima* (ed. Sylwia Kaczmarek and Henryk Pietras; Leuven: Peeters, 2011), 3–38.

30. Harold Tarrant, "Must Commentators Know Their Sources? Proclus *in Timaeum* and Numenius," in *Philosophy, Science and Exegesis in Greek, Arabic and Latin Commentaries* (ed. Peter Adamson, Han Baltussen and M. W. F. Stone; BICS Supplement 83.1; London: Institute of Classical Studies, 2004), 1:175–90, 176.

This element is especially important when we consider that Christian and Platonist commentaries in late antiquity aimed not only at intellectual development, but at spiritual progress as well.[31] The Neoplatonist commentaries, as well as those of Origen and especially Didymus the Blind, conscientiously aim to promote ethical progress. The act of writing commentaries is viewed to be a spiritual exercise that elevates the mind of both the author and the audience.[32] The spiritual aims of the authors are often made plain in the prefaces or epilogues to the commentaries.[33] So the student who reads these works is also involved in a spiritual act, promoting his own ethical progress for the stimulation of the mind. The result is that the commentary is an open dialogue with God, complete with prayers for assistance and calls for inspiration.

Just before addressing the beginning line of the Gospel of John, Origen writes, "Let us now ask God to work with us through Christ in the Holy Spirit to explain the mystical meaning stored up like a treasure in the words."[34] It cannot be determined to what extend this call to inspiration is literal since similar elements can be detected in late antique prologues in general.[35] But it communicates the sacred nature of writing and, by

---

31. For the Neoplatonists, see H. D. Saffrey, "Quelques aspects de la spiritualité des philosophes néoplatoniciens de Jamblique à Proclus et Damascius," *RSPT* 68 (1984): 169–82. This feature of Christian commentary writing in the Alexandrian tradition is discussed in Blossom Stefaniw, "Reading Revelation: Allegorical Exegesis in Late Antique Alexandria," *RHR* 224 (2007): 231–51, and Stefaniw, *Mind, Text and Commentary: Noetic Exegesis in Origen of Alexandria, Didymus the Blind and Evagrius Ponticus* (Early Christianity in the Context of Antiquity 6; Frankfurt: Lang, 2010), 221–97.

32. For this aspect of commentary writing in general see Pierre Hadot, "Théologie, exégèse, revelation, écriture, dans la philosophie grecque," in *Les règles de l'interprétation* (ed. Michel Tardieu; Paris: Cerf, 1987), 13–34. For Proclus as representative, see Michael Erler, "Interpretieren als Gottesdienst: Proklos' Hymnen vor dem Hintergrund seines Kratyloskommentars," in *Proclus et son influence: Actes du colloque de Neuchâtel juin 1985* (ed. Gilbert Boss and Gerhard Seel; Zürich: GMB Éditions du Grand Midi, 1987), 179–217.

33. For a comprehensive treatment see Matthias Skeb, *Exegese und Lebensform: die Proömien der antiken griechischen Bibelkommentare* (Clavis commentariorum, Antiquitatis et Medii Aevi 5; Leiden: Brill, 2007).

34. *Comm. Jo.* 1.89; trans. Ronald E. Heine, *Origen: Commentary on the Gospel According to John Books 1–10* (FC 80; Washington, D.C.: The Catholic University of America Press, 1989), 51. The Greek reads, Ἤδη δὲ θεὸν αἰτώμεθα συνεργῆσαι διὰ Χριστοῦ ἡμῖν ἐν ἁγίῳ πνεύματι πρὸς ἀνάπτυξιν τοῦ ἐν ταῖς λέξεσιν ἐναποτεθησαυρισμένου μυστικοῦ νοῦ.

35. See Alfons Fürst, "Origen: Exegesis and Philosophy in Early Christian Alexandria," in *Interpreting the Bible and Aristotle*, 13–32, 16–25. On Origen's commentary prologues, see Ilsetraut Hadot, "Les introductions aux commentaires exégétiques chez les auteurs néoplatoniciens et les auteurs chrétiens," in *Les règles de l'interpretation*, 99–122; Neuschäfer, *Origenes als Philologe*, 57–84; Ronald E. Heine, "The Introduction to Origen's *Commentary on John* Compared with the Introductions to the Ancient Philosophical

extension, reading the commentary. At the beginning of book three of the *Comm. Zach.*, Didymus offers a prayer to God before citing the lemma to be interpreted (Zech 8:16–17): "This gift will be ours, too, as a result of unceasing prayer by those offering it for us, the gift of wisdom and 'a message by the opening of the mouth' [Eph 6:19], so that we may faultlessly and properly interpret the following verses of the prophet before us, beginning at this point."[36]

If the goal of these commentaries is to promote intellectual growth and thereby ethical progress, then citing the names of learned authorities can detract from the purpose of the genre. If the reader respects a Numenius or even a Philo as an established authority, then attaching the name to an interpretation settles the debate before it is ever conducted. In a scholastic setting, such as that of Didymus, perhaps this tool is useful. Students are not there to debate, but to be indoctrinated. Citing Philo is sufficient evidence to establish a point and move the lesson forward. Conversely, citing a name only to disagree with a certain author, as we observed in Origen's citation of Philo above, serves to dethrone the respected authority, and to substitute the authority of the commentator (or teacher) himself. Both of these methods are effective educational tools, although utilized for different purposes. This is perhaps the reason why Didymus mentions Philo so much more often than other commentators.

Conclusion

We have attempted to survey thus far the personality of Didymus the Blind and his place within the Alexandrian tradition of biblical exegesis. We have also aimed to set the context for his use of sources by briefly considering source citation in the ancient world, especially as it relates to the commentary genre. It is clear that Didymus views himself as continuing a long line of traditional biblical exegesis, which includes a number of authors, both Christian and, in the case of Philo, Jewish. Didymus conforms in many ways to previous exegetes both in his methods and in his presuppositions, and he utilizes the work of his predecessors to reinforce

---

Commentaries on Aristotle," in *Origeniana Sexta* (ed. Gilles Dorival and Allain le Boulleuc; BETL 118; Leuven: Leuven University Press, 1995), 3–12.

36. *Comm. Zach.* 182.23–26; trans. Robert C. Hill, *Didymus the Blind: Commentary on Zechariah* (FC 111; Washington, D.C.: The Catholic University of America Press, 2006), 187. The Greek reads, Ὑπάρξεται ἡ δωρεὰ αὕτη καὶ ἡμῖν διὰ ἀδιάλειπτον εὐχὴν τῶν ἀναπεμπόντων ὑπὲρ ἡμῶν, σοφία καὶ «λόγος ἐν ἀνοίξει τοῦ στόματος», ὥστ' ἀμέμπτως καὶ ὡς δεῖ ἐκλαβεῖν τὰ ἑξῆς τοῦ ἐκκειμένου προφήτου, ἀρχόμενα ἐνθένδε.

his own interpretations. As we move toward the more specific goal of fleshing out the extent to which Didymus uses Philo, it will be helpful to examine his use of other Jewish sources in order to demonstrate the exceptional way in which Philo stands apart from them.

4

THE JEWISH SOURCES OF DIDYMUS IN THE TURA COMMENTARIES

Introduction

Primarily, early Christians quote the Bible, but regular citations of the Classics and Hellenistic Jewish authors are found as well. Didymus the Blind adds to these traditional references a number of citations of Christian sources before him, both of the "orthodox" and the "heretical" variety. Didymus in fact cites over sixty nonbiblical sources by name in the Tura commentaries. Of pagan sources, he mentions no less than twenty, including Homer,[1] Democritus,[2] Isocrates,[3] Epicurus,[4] Protagoras,[5] the Platonist(s),[6] Aristotle,[7] the Stoics,[8] Galen,[9] the Pythagoreans,[10] the Delphic oracle,[11] and the philosopher Porphyry five times.[12] Of Christian sources, he mentions the Apostolic Fathers,[13] Clement of Alexandria,[14] the Acts of John,[15] the Hermetic corpus,[16] and many heretical sources. Strangely, Didymus by comparison rarely mentions "orthodox" sources, preferring instead to name the "heterodox," which he does over thirty times.[17]

---

1. He cites Homer as ὁ ποιητής, *Comm. Eccl.* 354.27
2. *Comm. Eccl.* 209.27.
3. *Comm. Eccl.* 42.28.
4. *Comm. Eccl.* 24.7; 209.27.
5. *Comm. Ps.* 222.20.
6. *Comm. Eccl.* 22.20.
7. *Comm. Ps.* 77.8; *Comm. Eccl.* 69.12; 90.25; 116.14.
8. *Comm. Gen.* 137.12; 185.16; *Comm. Ps.* 53.23; *Comm. Eccl.* 235.15.
9. *Comm. Ps.* 157.10–11.
10. *Comm. Eccl.* 79.26.
11. *Comm. Eccl.* 238.7–27; *Comm. Ps.* 226.16
12. *Comm. Job* 280.23; *Comm. Ps.* 308.14; *Comm. Eccl.* 281.17.
13. *Comm. Ps.* 227.26; *Comm. Eccl.* 78.21 (Did.), *Comm. Ps.* 262.33–34; 300.12; *Comm. Zach.* 234.22; 259.23; 355.21 (Barn.); *Comm. Eccl.* 81.7; 86.19; *Comm. Ps.* 297.28 (Ign. *Rom.*); *Comm. Job* 184.33; 224.22; *Comm. Ps.* 262.34; *Comm. Zach.* 86.24; 234.21; 355.20 (Herm.).
14. *Comm. Eccl.* 7.34.
15. *Comm. Zach.* 341.17.
16. *Comm. Ps.* 88.12–13; *Comm. Eccl.* 167.14–15.
17. There are seventeen references to the Manicheans, twelve references to Apollinaris of Laodicea and/or his followers, eleven references to Arius or Arians, two references to Paul of Samosata, and so on. Obviously, the teachings of these figures and groups were "hot topics" in fourth century Alexandria, and Didymus did not shy away from criticizing them.

Anonymous references are also made to previous exegetes[18] and teachers who influenced Didymus.[19]

Although we may assume Didymus knew the Christian authors directly, the pagan authors were likely known through handbooks or florilegia.[20] Such were fashionable at the time of Didymus, and thus his citations of Classical authors are not as impressive as they might be if we could demonstrate direct influence. The Jewish authors are a different matter. There is no solid evidence that Philonic florilegia circulated before the time of Didymus,[21] and the variety of Jewish sources he references makes dependence on a Jewish florilegium unlikely as well. Of course, as we shall see, Didymus is resourceful, and thus he borrows at least some Josephan material from Eusebius, but he also seems to have read the Jewish sources directly as well.

Turning to the Jewish sources, which will occupy our attention in this chapter, we find references to the "Book of the Covenant,"[22] the Enoch and Elijah Apocryphon,[23] Josephus,[24] the translators Aquila, Symmachus and Theodotion,[25] and Jewish tradition.[26] Of course, Philo is the most-often cited nonbiblical source in the writings of Didymus the Blind. In this chapter we shall discuss Didymus's references to Jewish sources, excluding Philo, in an effort to demonstrate the exceptional nature of Didymus's use of Philonic material.

---

18. *Comm. Eccl.* 229.16; *Comm. Zach.* 371.27; *Comm. Ps.* 285.18; 295.27; 336.19; *Comm. Gen.* 142.7.

19. *Comm. Eccl.* 8.5–11; *Comm. Zach.* 64.28.

20. See Placid Solari, "Christ as Virtue in Didymus the Blind," in *Purity of Heart in Early Ascetic and Monastic Literature: Essays in Honor of Juana Raasch* (ed. Harriet A. Luckman and Linda Kulzer; Collegeville: Minn.: Liturgical Press, 1999), 67–88, 80.

21. No evidence has materialized to support Dominique Barthélemy's suggestion that Origen had excerpted Philonic passages on the subject of the Logos (see "Est-ce Hoshaya Rabba qui censura le 'Commentaire Allégorique?,'" in *Philon d'Alexandrie. Lyon 11–15 Septembre 1966*; *Colloques Nationaux du Centre National de la Recherche Scientifique* [Paris: Éditions du Centre National de la Recherche Scientifique], 45–78, 68).

22. *Comm. Gen.* 118.29–119.1; 121.23; 126.26; 142.27–143.1; 149.5.

23. *Comm. Zach.* 342.6 (ἐν ἀποκρύφῳ βιβλίῳ τὸν Ἐνὼχ καὶ τὸν Ἡ[λίαν]); *Comm. Eccl.* 235.27. On these references see Dieter Lührmann, "Alttestamentliche Pseudepigraphen bei Didymos von Alexandrien." *ZAW* 104 (1992): 231–49.

24. *Comm. Eccl.* 345.3; *Comm. Zach.* 364.15; 241.22; 326.16.

25. *Comm. Gen.* 174.3 (Aquila and Symmachus); *Comm. Zach.* 341.17 (Aquila and Theodotion); *Fr. Prov.* 1:6 (= PG 39:1623–24) (Theodotion and Symmachus).

26. *Comm. Zach.* 373.29.

The Jewish Sources of Didymus (Excluding Philo)

We begin our survey by examining the Jewish sources Didymus found helpful. By using the term *Jewish*, we are not necessarily claiming that Didymus knew or even cared about the religion or ethnicity of all of these sources, nor are we claiming the sources themselves received no Christian interpolation before the time of Didymus.[27] Didymus does not even introduce the Jewishness of a source unless it is apologetically relevant, but we can assume he and his audience were aware of the fact.[28] As a biblical commentator, Didymus is utilitarian, locating traditions and interpretations that are most helpful to exegesis, no matter what their origin may have been.

The Book of the Covenant

Didymus cites the "Book of the Covenant" (ἡ βίβλος τῆς διαθήκης) five times in the *Comm. Gen.* and once in the *Comm. Job*. An additional citation can be identified from the *Catena of Nicephorus* 1.175 on Gen 11:4, which has been attributed to Didymus.[29] Scholars once identified the Book of the Covenant

---

27. It is likely that the Old Testament Apocrypha known to the Alexandrian Fathers was transmitted to them through Gnostic sources (see James C. VanderKam and William Adler, eds., *The Jewish Apocalyptic Heritage in Early Christianity*, CRINT 3.4 [Assen: Van Gorcum: Minneapolis: Fortress, 1996], 162, 172, 183). In fact, this is one of the evidences cited in favor of a pre-Christian Jewish Gnosticism (162).

28. As Andrew Jacobs has emphasized, "Jewishness" in Christian works of late antiquity is not necessarily a marker of ethnicity, but of exegetical error, of extreme literalism in scriptural interpretation and application, and of hostility to Christianity (*Remains of the Jews: The Holy Land and Christian Empire in Late Antiquity* [Divinations: Rereading Late Ancient Religion; Stanford: Stanford University Press, 2004], 26–36, 60–67). Therefore, Didymus presumably would not wish to characterize an author as "Jewish" without an additional ethnic or contextual qualification.

29. Wintermute mentions the *Catena of Nicephorus* 1.175 as the only possible citation of Jubilees by the title "Book of the Covenant" in the ancient tradition (O. S. Wintermute, "Jubilees," in *Old Testament Pseudepigrapha* [ed. James H. Charlesworth; New York: Doubleday, 1985], 41), but is apparently unaware of the Tura commentaries of Didymus. In the newer introduction of Albert-Marie Denis, the Tura commentaries are included in the discussion (*Introduction à la littérature religieuse judéo-hellénistique* [Turnhout: Brepols, 2000], 1:351, 373). Denis discusses two positions on the identification of the Book of the Covenant: (1) Some have identified the work referenced in the Catena of Nicephorus with the Testament of Moses (e.g., Hermann Rönsch, *Das Buch der Jubiläen, oder die Kleine Genesis* [Leipzig: Fues, 1874], 275). But Denis notes that the *Stichometry of Nicephorus* refers 1100 lines to the *Testament of Moses* that do not correspond to the Book of Jubilees, so this option is impossible. (2) A second position is that the Testaments of the Twelve Patriarchs and Jubilees were combined and given the title Book of the Covenant (e.g., Moses Gaster, "The Hebrew Text of One of the Testaments of the Twelve Patriarchs," in *The Proceedings*

with the book of Jubilees.³⁰ However, Dieter Lührmann has attempted to demonstrate that this identification is far from certain.³¹ First of all, the title Book of the Covenant is problematic. In the ancient manuscripts, the book is known either as Jubilees or as the "Little Genesis."³² The title Book of the Covenant is known only to Didymus. Second, Albert Henrichs, the earliest translator of the Tura Papyri to encounter the title ἡ βίβλος τῆς διαθήκης translated it "the Old Testament,"³³ despite a very possible textual allusion to Jub. 17:15–18:19.³⁴

Third, and most important, the material attributed to the Book of the Covenant does not always square with our Jubilees. Pierre Nautin notes that, of the five citations of the Book of the Covenant in the *Comm. Gen.*, two of the five fail to match Jubilees at all.³⁵ Discussing the Cain and Abel sacrifices, for example, Didymus attributes to the Book of the Covenant the view that "fire, descending from heaven, received the sacrifices."³⁶ Yet this idea is found nowhere in our Jubilees.³⁷

A second passage not only fails to match Jubilees, it directly contradicts it. Didymus states that the murder of Abel could have been accomplished by a rod, by a stone, or by a stick. The last option he attributes to the Book of the Covenant.³⁸ However, Jubilees specifically states that Cain killed Abel with a rock.³⁹ These two incorrect identifications might lead us to

---

of the Society of Biblical Archaeology 16 [1893–94], 36–39). But as Denis notes, the two works belong to entirely different literary genres, and it is difficult to imagine why they would have been combined (*Introduction* 1:351–52).

30. Nautin, *Sur la Genèse* 1:28; Dieter Hagedorn and Ursula Hagedorn, "Kritisches zum Hiobkommentar Didymos des Blinden," *ZPE* 67 (1987): 59–78, 60.

31. Dieter Lührmann, "Alttestamentliche Pseudepigraphen bei Didymos von Alexandrien," *ZAW* 104 (1992): 231–49. Note also the judgment of Denis, who suggests that the Book of the Covenant is a "paraphrase de la *Gen.*, parallèle à *Jub.*, mais différent, écrit judéo-hellénistique connu à Alexandrie au 4ᵉ s." (*Introduction* 1:373).

32. Denis, *Introduction* 1:349–51.

33. In German, „das (Alte) Testament" (*Comm. Job* 6.24).

34. Albert Henrichs, *Didymos der Blinde: Kommentar zu Hiob (Tura Papyrus). Teil 1: Kommentar zu Hiob, Kap. 1–4* (Bonn: Rudolf Habelt, 1968). The most recent translator of the *Comm. Job* simply follows Henrichs, translating "the book of the testament <Old Testament>" (Edward F. Duffy, "The Tura Papyrus of Didymus the Blind's Commentary on Job: An Original Translation With Introduction and Commentary" [Ph.D. diss., Graduate Theological Foundation, 2000], 40).

35. *Sur la Genèse* 1:28–29.

36. *Comm. Gen.* 121.24.

37. In fact, it is strange that Jubilees devotes only a paragraph (six verses in modern editions) to the sacrifices of Cain and Abel (4:1–6).

38. *Comm. Gen.* 126.24–26.

39. Jub. 4:31.

believe that Didymus used a different source, lost to us, but known as the Book of the Covenant.

Although he does not list his reasons, as we have done, these are the major factors leading Lührmann to reject Nautin's identification of the Book of the Covenant with Jubilees. He concludes:

> The Book of the Covenant must therefore be considered as an entirely separate work. As far as the extant fragments allow us to draw conclusions, it is a retelling of Genesis at least from "Cain and Abel" to "Abraham." It is thus comparable with the "Book of Jubilees" or the Genesis Apocryphon of Qumran without being identical to either of these or to other similar retellings of Genesis.[40]

Nautin, although entertaining the notion that Didymus used a different source, retains his identification of the Book of the Covenant with Jubilees, explaining that Didymus's memory failed him.[41] His position is strengthened by the fact that the remaining three citations of the Book of the Covenant in the *Comm. Gen.* do match Jubilees very closely.[42] The same can be said for the singular citation in the *Comm. Job*.[43] So whether we have in the Book of the Covenant an otherwise unknown work, as Lührmann believes, or a version of Jubilees, as Nautin maintains, the work appears to have been a Jewish production, utilizing midrashic elements to fill the gaps in the biblical text. For this reason alone, Didymus's use of the work is significant, for it establishes awareness on the part of Didymus of a source that transmits Jewish tradition.

The Ascension of Isaiah

The Martyrdom of Isaiah and the Ascension of Isaiah appear to have been composed independently. The former is a Jewish work, originally written in Hebrew, and then translated into Greek.[44] Along with the translation, the work was amplified by the addition of the Ascension of Isaiah, which was

---

40. The German reads, „Das Buch des Bundes muß daher insgesamt als ein eigenes Werk angesehen werden. Soweit die erhaltenen Fragmente Rückschlüsse erlauben, handelt es sich um eine Nacherzählung der Genesis mindestens von «Kain und Abel» bis «Abraham». Es ist damit vergleichbar dem «Buch der Jubiläen» oder dem Genesis-Apokryphon aus Qumran, mit keiner dieser oder ähnlicher Nacherzählungen der Genesis aber identisch" ("Alttestamentliche Pseudepigraphen," 244).
41. Didymus "a été simplement trompé par sa mémoire" (*Sur la Genèse* 1:29).
42. *Comm. Gen.* 119.1; 143.1; 149.5.
43. *Comm. Job* 6.17–24.
44. Michael A. Knibb, "Martyrdom and Ascension of Isaiah," in *The Old Testament Pseudepigrapha* 2:143–47.

originally composed in Greek by a Christian author.[45] The date of the uniting of these two works is debated, some opting for a time in the early second century CE at Antioch.[46] Generally, the original Jewish Martyrdom of Isaiah is associated with chapters 1–5, with the exception of the obvious Christian interpolation in 3:13–4:22. The remainder of the work, chapters 6–11, is Christian in origin.

In one of the two clear citations of this work in the Tura commentaries, Didymus is obviously in possession of the Christian Ascension of Isaiah.[47] The second citation, however, cannot be precisely identified, although it appears to be from the Jewish Martyrdom of Isaiah.[48] In the former of these citations our author speaks of Jesus having ascended and descended through the "heavens," citing the ascension of Isaiah as a parallel event. The reference is clearly to chapters 6–11 of the Ascension of Isaiah, where Isaiah's ascent through the seven heavens is paralleled by Christ's descent and ascent through the same space.[49] Obviously, the section is a Christian composition. The question is whether Didymus possessed the Ascension of Isaiah separate from the Martyrdom of Isaiah. We know the two circulated independently.[50] We cannot know, however, precisely when they were joined.

In the second of Didymus's citations, we receive an extended discussion of Isaiah's martyrdom.[51] Didymus relates that Isaiah was sawn in two with a wooden saw, and that he was arrested and had charges brought against him.[52] He also closely paraphrases Isaiah's defense recorded in the Martyrdom of Isaiah 3:8–12. There is therefore no doubt that the Martyrdom of Isaiah and the Ascension of Isaiah known to Didymus is the work we now possess. What is unclear is whether Didymus believed the text is his possession was Jewish. We have already seen that the two works circulated independently. Unfortunately, as Lührmann notes, "we cannot clearly determine whether he has also taken this account from the (reworked

---

45. See Robert G. Hall, "Isaiah, Ascension of," *The Eerdmans Dictionary of Early Judaism* (ed. John J. Collins and Daniel C. Harlow; Grand Rapids: Eerdmans, 2010).

46. See Denis, *Introduction* 1:636–37.

47. *Comm. Eccl.* 329.21–25.

48. *Comm. Ps.* 218.3–14.

49. See Ascen. Isa. 10:17–11:33.

50. The second Latin translation and the Slavonic editions are proof (see Knibb, *Old Testament Pseudepigrapha* 2:147).

51. *Comm. Ps.* 218.3–14.

52. Mart. Isa. 5:11; 3:6.

Christian) Ascension of Isaiah or from an independent (Jewish?) version of the Martyrdom of Isaiah."[53]

In the citation from the *Comm. Ps.* there is nothing to preclude identification with the original Jewish Martyrdom of Isaiah, but since the text has been heavily reworked by Christian authors, it is difficult to know whether Didymus regarded the work as a Christian composition or as an ancient Jewish text. Of course, it is possible that he was uninterested in its religious origin, preferring instead to trust the work as a reliable repository of Jewish tradition.

The Apocalypse of Elijah

The work known as the Apocalypse of Elijah was apparently composed in Greek, but now exists in its entirety only in Coptic translation.[54] Modern scholars have regarded the work to have been a Christian production dating no later than the third century CE. Whether the text has Jewish antecedents is impossible to determine with certainty. The church fathers, however, claim that Paul knew and cited the work. Origen, who is apparently the source of the tradition in the fathers, refers to an Elijah work (*in secretis Eliae prophetae*), stating that Paul cites the text in 1 Cor 2:9.[55] But nothing like 1 Cor 2:9 can be found in our Apocalypse of Elijah. As Lührmann notes, it is impossible to know what Elijah text Origen had in mind.[56] Didymus, on the other hand, almost certainly possessed the same Christian Apocalypse of Elijah we have today.

In the *Comm. Eccl.* Didymus attributes to the Apocalypse of Elijah the view that in Hades there are two realms (χωρία), "a place of peace" for the righteous and "a place of condemnation" for the sinner.[57] This text, even in the Elijah Apocalypse (5:25–29), sounds as though it is influenced by the story of the Rich Man (or Dives) and Lazarus in Luke 16:19–31.[58] It is in

---

53. In German, "wir nicht eindeutig klären können, ob er diese Geschichte ebenfalls aus der (christliche überarbeiteten) AscJes übernommen hat oder aus einer noch unabhängig davon überlieferten (jüdischen?) Fassung des «Martyriums Jesajas»" ("Alttestamentliche Pseudepigraphen," 237–38).

54. O. S. Wintermute, "Apocalypse of Elijah," *Old Testament Pseudepigrapha* 1:721–753, 729. Fragments exist in many languages (see discussion of Denis, *Introduction* 1:609–31).

55. *Comm. Matt.* 27:9. See Jean Ruwet, "Origène et l'Apocalpyse d'Élie: À propos de 1 Cor 2:9," *Bib* 30 (1949): 517–19. On similar statements in the patristic period see Denis, *Introduction* 1:610–14.

56. "Alttestamentliche Pseudepigraphen," 245.

57. *Comm. Eccl.* 92.5–6.

58. Note esp. Luke 16:22–23: "The poor man died and was carried away by the angels to be with Abraham. The rich man also died and was buried. In Hades, where he was

fact in the midst of a discussion of the Lukan narrative that Didymus introduces the parallel in the Apocalypse of Elijah. In any case, while the reference Didymus provides is not an exact quotation, the material does match our Apocalypse of Elijah.

In addition, Didymus references the "Antichrist" who is mentioned for the first time in Apocalypse of Elijah chapter 3.[59] The specific κόρη to whom Didymus refers in the text is Tabitha, who "will pursue him [the Antichrist], scolding him up to Jerusalem, saying 'shameless one, O son of lawlessness.'"[60] When we compare the words of Didymus to the Apocalypse of Elijah, the material is remarkably close: "A young woman arose in this fashion to rebuke him, calling him shameless."[61] This passage is not a verbatim citation, as best we can tell, but the material closely matches the Christian Apocalypse of Elijah that we now possess.

A third passage is more difficult to pin down. Almost as though making an off-hand comment in the *Comm. Zach.* Didymus states, "I read in an apocryphal book [ἐν ἀποκρύφῳ βιβλίῳ] that Enoch and Elijah are the two sons of plenty, presumably on account of their privileges relative to other people; Enoch, remember, 'was taken elsewhere so as not to experience death,' and Elijah was taken up when a fiery horse and chariot took him up 'to heaven,' as it were."[62]

This passage is more generic than the previous two. Although Elijah and Enoch are paired in the Apocalypse of Elijah, there is no reference to the "sons of plenty" (υἱοὶ τῆς ποιότητος), which we suspect is a direct quotation.[63] Lührmann suggests that Didymus may have in mind a separate work altogether.[64] The generic reference to "an apocryphal book" leaves us with little to determine the precise source of the reference, and the quotation regarding Enoch seems to parallel Heb 11:5 better than anything in the Apocalypse of Elijah. The extemporaneous nature of the comment,

---

being tormented, he looked up and saw Abraham far away with Lazarus by his side" (NRSV).

59. *Comm. Eccl.* 235.25–28.
60. Apoc. El. (C) 4:2.
61. The Greek reads, κ[ό]ρη [τι]ς ἀναστᾶσα οὕτως αὐτὸν ἤλεγξεν λέγουσα αὐτὸν ἀναιδῆ.
62. *Comm. Zach.* 77.19–24. Trans. Robert C. Hill, *Didymus the Blind: Commentary on Zechariah*, 99. The Greek reads, Ἀνέγνων ἐν ἀποκρύφῳ βιβλίῳ τὸν Ἐνὼχ καὶ τὸν Ἡ[λίαν] τοὺς δύο υἱοὺς τῆς πιότητος εἶναι, ὡς εἰκὸς διὰ τὸ προσόνα[σθαι] παρὰ τοὺς ἄλλους ἀνθρώπους. «Ὁ μὲν γὰρ Ἐνὼχ μετετέ[θη] τοῦ μὴ ἰδεῖν θάνατον», «ὁ δὲ Ἡλίας ἀνελήμφθη» πυρίνου ἅρματος καὶ ἵππου ἀναγαγόντων αὐτὸν «ὡς εἰς τὸν οὐρανόν».
63. Apoc. El. (C) 4:7–19. This is a section Didymus probably knew since the "Tabitha" reference immediately precedes this section.
64. "Alttestamentliche Pseudepigraphen," 248.

however, probably explains our difficulty. It is possible that Didymus had no text in mind at all, but only the gist of a passage.

Josephus

Josephus was transmitted entirely by Christian scribes, and was therefore known to and used by Christians. Origen quotes Josephus rather frequently,[65] and Eusebius of Caesarea makes extensive use of Josephus as well.[66] There is nothing surprising, then, about Didymus's citation of the works of Josephus. In the works of Didymus Josephus is referred to by name only twice.[67] There are, however, three additional passages where the name of Josephus is not mentioned, but where the Jewish author is clearly quoted.

The first reference to Josephus by name is found in the *Comm. Eccl.*[68] Commenting on Eccl 12:3a ("in the day when the guards of the house shake"), Didymus introduces Josephus. He takes the "house" of the exegetical verse to be the temple and the term "guards" to refer to the priests. Didymus states,

> There was a certain Jewish historiographer, Josephus. He set forth an account in connection with the miracles that occurred after the Jews surrendered their salvation which says: "The Temple had a great door. Thirty strong men could scarcely close it, and iron bars were set to secure it once it had been closed." "Suddenly," he says, "on one night the priests who were going about heard," he says, "a voice as though of many people speaking, 'We are departing from here.'" "And suddenly," he says, "the gate opened all by itself."
>
> And this was [the fulfilment of] the fact that "the daughter of Zion will be forsaken like a tent in a vineyard" (Isa 1:8). And this is especially the case when the Savior abandoned it, saying, "I will abandon your house, leaving my inheritance" (Jer 12:7). [In the passage] "Behold your house shall be left to you" (Matt 23:38) the Savior again [speaks] to them, namely the Jews.

---

65. For a survey of the use of Josephus in early Christian literature, see Heinz Schreckenberg and Kurt Schubert, *Jewish Historiography and Iconography in Early and Medieval Christianity* (CRINT 3.2; Assen: Van Gorcum; Minneapolis: Fortress, 1992), 51–85. Schreckenberg's survey begins with the New Testament and ends with the tenth century *Epitome Antiquitatum*, but he does not mention the works of Didymus.

66. On Eusebius's use of Josephus, see Michael E. Hardwick, *Josephus as an Historical Source in Patristic Literature through Eusebius* (BJS 128; Atlanta: Scholars Press, 1989). On Eusebius's use of Jewish sources in general, including Josephus, see Sabrina Inowlocki, *Eusebius and the Jewish Authors: His Citation Technique in an Apologetic Context* (AGJU 64; Leiden: Brill, 2006).

67. *Comm. Eccl.* 345.3 and *Comm. Zach.* 364.15.

68. *Comm. Eccl.* 345.3. The Greek reads, γέγονέν τις Ἰουδαϊκὸς ἱστοριογράφος Ἰώσιππος.

Therefore this is [what the following means]: "the guards of the house were shaken" (Ecc 12:3), so as to move the guards, so as to honor the "House" no more.[69]

The preceding report is found in the *B.J.* 6.293–302. However, the exact material does not appear to be quoted directly from Josephus, but from the version found in Eusebius's *Hist. eccl.* 3.8.4–8. In all probability, Didymus borrowed the material and its apologetic application from Eusebius. Note that Didymus employs the passage to illustrate the fulfillment of scriptural prophecy, just as Eusebius does. However, Didymus utilizes different prooftexts than Eusebius so that the material now appears in an interpretation of Qoheleth's prophetic vision. Sabrina Inowlocki suggested that Eusebius might have compiled testimonia from the works of Josephus "either for chronological issues or to demonstrate the end of Judaism," and cites our passage as an example.[70] Didymus, then, could have had access to such a testimonium, although he must have adapted it for the purposes of his exegesis.

The passage in Josephus goes on to mention a certain "Jesus ben Ananias" who prophesied "a voice [φωνή] from the east, a voice from the west, a voice from the four winds, a voice against Jerusalem and the temple, a voice against the bridegroom and the bride, a voice against the people."[71] The prophetic voice associated with a certain "Jesus" probably drew the attention of alert Christian readers. While neither Didymus nor any other Father claims that this *Jesus* is Jesus, the son of Joseph, the mention of another Jesus endowed with inspiration may in fact explain why Didymus knew this section of Josephus. We can imagine that early Christian readers of Josephus paid particular attention to any Ἰησοῦς mentioned in the course of the Josephan narrative.

---

69. *Comm. Eccl.* 345.2–13. The Greek reads, γέγονέν τις Ἰουδαϊκὸς ἱστοριογράφος Ἰώσιππος· ἐκεῖνος ἐν ταῖς θεοσημίαις ταῖς γενομέναις μετὰ τὸ προδοθῆναι τὸν σ(ωτῆ)ρα ὑπὸ τῶν Ἰουδαίων καὶ τοιαύτην ἔθηκεν ἣν λέγει· θύρα μεγάλη τοῦ ναοῦ ἦν· μόλις ἔκλειον ἰσχυροὶ ἄνδρες τριάκοντα, καὶ μοχλοὶ ἐπέκειντο ἵν' ἀσφαλισθῇ κλεισθεῖσα· ἄφνω, λέγει, ἐν νυκτὶ μιᾷ οἱ ἱερεῖς περιερχόμενοι ἤκουσαν, λέγει, φωνὴν ὡς πολλῶν λεγόντων· «μεταβαίνωμεν ἐντεῦθεν»· καὶ ἄφνω, λέγει, αὐτομάτως ἠνεῴχθησαν αἱ πύλαι. καὶ τοῦτο ἦν τὸ «ἐνκαταλειφθήσεται ἡ θυγάτηρ Σιὼν ὡς σκηνὴ ἐν ἀμπελῶνι». καὶ τότε μάλιστα τοῦτο ὑπῆρκται, ὅτε ὁ σ(ωτ)ὴρ «ἐνκαταλέλοιπεν» λέγων· «ἐνκατέ|λειψα τὸν οἶκόν σου, ἀφεὶς τὴν κληρονομίαν μου»· «ἰδοὺ ἀφίεται ὑμῖν ὁ οἶκος ὑμῶν» ὁ σ(ωτ)ὴρ πάλιν αὐτοῖς τοῖς Ἰουδαίοις. τοῦτο οὖν ἐστιν τὸ «σαλευθῆναι τοὺς φύλακας [τ]ῆς οἰκ[ί]ας», τὸ μεταστῆναι τοὺς φρουρούς, τὸ μηκέτι περιέπειν τὸν «οἶκον».

70. *Eusebius and the Jewish Authors*, 153.

71. *B.J.* 6.300–301. The Greek reads, φωνὴ ἀπὸ δύσεως φωνὴ ἀπὸ τῶν τεσσάρων ἀνέμων φωνὴ ἐπὶ Ἱεροσόλυμα καὶ τὸν ναόν φωνὴ ἐπὶ νυμφίους καὶ νύμφας φωνὴ ἐπὶ τὸν λαὸν πάντα.

More importantly, Didymus does not directly quote the text of Josephus, but rather paraphrases it, jumping around in the short pericope to reconstruct the story the way he wishes to tell it. He begins by describing the large door of the temple, which took thirty men (Josephus says twenty men) to close (*B.J.* 6.293). He then jumps to the content of *B.J.* 6.299–300 where the priests hear a mysterious voice saying "we are departing from here." From there Didymus jumps back to 6.293 where he follows Josephus in describing the door opening by itself. The re-sequencing of events allows Didymus to present Josephus as claiming the opening door was indicative of the divine presence fleeing the temple. He thus makes Josephus agree with the Christian message, namely, that God manifestly declared his abandonment of the temple before its destruction. He then turns to four prooftexts from biblical prophecy to explain that all of the events reported in Josephus were foreordained in scripture.

One of the earliest and strongest Christian arguments against Judaism was the historical symbol of the temple's destruction.[72] With the assistance of Josephus, the early Christians could unite history and prophecy in an effort to solidify the claim that the destruction of the temple was a condemnation of Judaism. Although Didymus is not a polemicist by nature, we must remember that the fourth century CE is the great age of anti-Jewish Christian polemic.[73] In the wake of Julian the Apostate's failed rebuilding of the temple, the polemic only intensified.[74] Didymus's familiarity with this Josephan passage and his specific application of it has antecedents in Christian polemic against Judaism, and he is simply repeating the conventional Christian apologetic.

The second passage in which the name of Josephus occurs is in the *Comm. Zach.*[75] Didymus says, "It was noted earlier that a Jewish historio-

---

[72]. The argument seems to have been made first by Justin Martyr (see Ruth A. Clements, "Epilogue: 70 CE After 135 CE—The Making of a Watershed?," in *Was 70 CE a Watershed in Jewish History? On Jews and Judaism before and after the Destruction of the Second Temple*, ed. Daniel R. Schwartz and Zeev Weiss [AJEC 78; Leiden: Brill, 2012], 517–36). On Justin's influence on subsequent Christian apologetic, see Sarah Parvis, "Justin Martyr and the Apologetic Tradition," in *Justin Martyr and his Worlds*, ed. Sara Parvis and Paul Foster (Minneapolis: Fortress, 2007), 115–27.

[73]. See, e.g., Robert L. Wilken, *John Chrysostom and the Jews: Rhetoric and Reality in the Late 4th Century* (The Transformation of the Classical Heritage 4; Berkeley: University of California Press, 1983). For a contextualization of the polemic see Andrew Jacobs, *Remains of the Jews*, 56–100.

[74]. On this program in general see Hans Lewy, "Julian the Apostate and the Building of the Temple," *The Jerusalem Cathedra* 3 (1983): 70–96.

[75]. *Comm. Zach.* 364.15. The Greek reads, Εἴρηται καὶ πρότερον ὡς ἰουδαϊκὸς ἱστοριογράφος, Ἰώσιππος ὄνομα αὐτῷ….

grapher, Josephus by name," reported the events regarding the misfortunes that fell upon Judea. The term πρότερον means that, although Josephus is named here, he was anonymously cited earlier as "an historian, one of those who actually experienced" God's wrath.[76] That previous citation is to be found in the comments to Zech 12:1–3, specifically on 12:2 ("Behold I am setting Jerusalem as a shaken threshold"). Here Didymus writes, "In reference to the wrath that has at last befallen Judah and its inhabitants, an historian, one individual from those who actually experienced it, wrote an account in many volumes of them and their places, so that the fulfillment is indisputably visible both of what the savior said and of what Zechariah uttered in prophetic mode [προφητικῶς] ...."[77]

Didymus wishes to call to mind the content of this previous passage when he states, "It was noted above as well that a Jewish historian, Josephus by name, truthfully and precisely described the disasters befalling the nation, including starvation and other misfortunes much worse than that; the searcher after good [φιλόκαλος] can meditate on it if interested in reading directed to learning and the fear of experiencing the same fate."[78]

These passages reveal several details about Didymus's knowledge of Josephus. They reveal that Didymus knows important biographical information; namely, that Josephus is a Jewish historian, and that he devotes many books to a series of events in which he himself participates. He also refers his more interested readers to Josephus, using the term φιλόκαλος, just as he does with reference to Philo, as we shall see. However, he seems to use Josephus much as Eusebius did, to confirm the view that the destruction of Jerusalem was a form of divine punishment, and that there were even omens given directly to the Jewish people to certify divine displeasure. Didymus ties this assumption back into biblical prophecy in an attempt to establish a prophecy-fulfillment template onto which he can cast the lost fortunes of the Jewish people. Josephus's Jewishness is emphasized because his narrative is manipulated to show that even a Jew

---

76. The Greek reads, συγγραφεὺς αὐτῶν τῶν παθόντων ἴδιος (*Comm. Zach.* 326.16).

77. *Comm. Zach.* 326.15–20 (trans. Hill, *Didymus the Blind: Commentary on Zechariah*, 289). The Greek reads, Περὶ τῆς οὕτω φθασάσης ὀργῆς εἰς τέλος τῇ Ἰουδαίᾳ καὶ τοῖς οἰκοῦσιν αὐτήν, συγγραφεὺς αὐτῶν τῶν παθόντων ἴδιος πολύβιβλον σύνταξιν ἀνέγραψεν αὐτῶν τε καὶ τῶν τόπων αὐτῶν, ὡς ὁρᾶν ἀνενδοιάστως πεπληρωμένα τά τε εἶπεν ὁ Σωτὴρ καὶ ὁ Ζαχαρίας προφητικῶς ἀπεφθέγξατο....

78. *Comm. Zach.* 364.15–20 (trans. Hill, *Didymus the Blind: Commentary on Zechariah*, 321). The Greek reads, Εἴρηται καὶ πρότερον ὡς Ἰουδαϊκὸς ἱστοριογράφος, Ἰώσιππος ὄνομα αὐτῷ, ἀνέγραψεν ἀληθῶς καὶ κατὰ ἀκρίβειαν τὰς ἐπελθούσας τῷ ἔθνει συμφοράς τε καὶ λιμοὺς καὶ ἄλλας πολὺ τούτων ἀνιαρωτάτας κ[α]κοπραγίας, ἃ θεωρῆσαι ἔστιν τὸν φιλόκαλον ἀναγνώσμασιν χαίροντα συντείνουσιν πρὸς φιλομάθειαν καὶ φόβ[ο]ν τοῦ μὴ παθεῖν τὰ αὐτά.

recognized the divine judgment God poured down on his people, a judgment (in the minds of Eusebius and Didymus) in favor of the church.

Jewish Tradition

There is one reference to "Jewish tradition" in the works of Didymus.[79] The exegetical verse refers to "the earthquake in the days of Uzziah" (Zech 14:5), leading to a discussion of the "earthquake" in question. Didymus cites a Jewish tradition equating the earthquake mentioned in Amos 1:1 with the vision of Isa 6:1 which was received in the "year that Uzziah died."[80] This "Jewish tradition was in circulation" (κατὰ περιφερομένην παράδοσιν Ἰουδαϊκήν), although the source from which Didymus derives his idea is almost certainly Christian. Legends about the earthquake during the reign of Uzziah are mentioned in Josephus, and both Eusebius and Jerome follow him.[81] Eusebius believed that Josephus was reporting Jewish δευτερώσεις, and says as much.[82] It should be noted that none of these earlier interpreters connected the event explicitly with the vision of Isaiah. However, the rationale of Didymus is easily explained when we understand the treatment of Uzziah, the earthquake, and Isa 6 in rabbinic literature.

The opening line of Isa chapter 6 notes that the following vision of Isaiah was experienced on "the year in which Uzziah died."[83] The targum states, however, that the vision occurred in the year in which Uzziah was afflicted with leprosy.[84] To the rabbis "a leper is like one dead," and thus the targumic translation makes sense.[85] Now Josephus is also reporting

---

79. *Comm. Zach.* 373.29.

80. This argument presupposes that Isaiah was older than Amos, rendering invalid the view of Clement of Alexandria. that Amos (עמוס) the prophet is אמוץ, father of Isaiah. He does so because both names are transliterated Αμως in the LXX (*Strom.* 1.20). I owe these references to Louis Ginzberg, *The Legends of the Jews* (Philadelphia: The Jewish Publication Society of America, 1909–1938), 6:256–57.

81. *Ant.* 9.225. See Eusebius, *Dem. ev.* 6.18.36. Jerome does not reference Josephus explicitly, but cites the same material as "Hebrew tradition" (*Comm. Am.* 1).

82. *Dem. ev.* 6.18.34–37. For the implications of this passage regarding the attitude of the Fathers toward the historical character of the aggadah, see Adam Kamesar, "The Evaluation of the Narrative Aggadah in Greek and Latin Patristic Literature," *JTS* 45 (1994): 37–75, 63, and Kamesar, "San Basilio, Filone, e la tradizione ebraica," *Hen* 17 (1995): 129–40, 136.

83. MT 6:1: בשנת־מות המלך עזיהו, LXX: καὶ ἐγένετο τοῦ ἐνιαυτοῦ οὗ ἀπέθανεν Ὀζίας ὁ βασιλεύς.

84. בשתא דאתנגע בה מלכא עוזיה. The Aramaic root נגע means "to be stricken with leprosy" in the *ithpaal* (see Marcus Jastrow, *Dictionary of the Targumim, the Talmud Babli and Yerushalmi, and the Midrashic Literature* [New York: Title Publishing, 1943], 875).

85. See Ginzberg, *Legends* 6:357 and the references cited there.

Jewish tradition when he states that an earthquake occurred while King Uzziah attempted to offer sacrifices at the altar.[86] This is the moment in scripture at which Uzziah contracted leprosy, although scripture does not report an earthquake at that time.[87] Apparently, Jewish tradition connected the scattered dots: Uzziah attempted to officiate at the altar in the temple, at which point an earthquake occurred and he contracted leprosy (metaphorically depicted as "death" in Isa 6:1). The earthquake, also reported in Amos 1:1, was concurrent with Isaiah's vision of God.

From the information sketched here, it is clear that Didymus is relying on some Jewish source that interprets the "death" of Uzziah in Isa 6:1 as leprosy. We need not assume here any direct knowledge of rabbinic literature, nor any personal contact with contemporary Jews. Didymus lived in a monastery, and opportunities for such contact would have been scarce. The "Jewish tradition" from which Didymus learns of the earthquake is almost certainly Josephus himself, and perhaps not even directly. Eusebius cites Josephus for this exact information and refers to the comment as a "secondary tradition."[88] The "leprosy" interpretation of Isa 6 is common enough that it could have been in the Christian tradition as well. Didymus simply connects the two traditions and infers a single interpretation.

Aquila, Symmachus, and Theodotion

Like many patristic authors, Didymus refers to the Greek translators Aquila, Symmachus, and Theodotion. We are treating these authors under "Jewish sources," although we cannot be certain whether all of them were actually Jews. Irenaeus refers to Aquila and Theodotion as "Jewish proselytes,"[89] and Aquila is regarded as a Jew in rabbinic literature.[90] Eusebius describes Symmachus as an Ebionite, although we cannot be certain of this identification.[91] Because Origen's *Hexapla* included these three versions, they became widely disseminated in the Christian scholarly world, and Jerome would refer routinely to the Greek "versions" (which he terms the *recentiores*) in his exegetical and lexicographical work. Although Didymus

---

86. On the rabbinic sources, see Ginzberg, *Legends* 3:262 and 6:357.
87. See 2 Chron 26:16–21.
88. *Dem. ev.* 6.18.34–37.
89. *Haer.* 3.30.5.
90. Aquila is the only Greek translator to be claimed as Jewish by the rabbinic sources (y. Meg. 1:11; Qidd. 1:1).
91. *Hist. eccl.* 6.17.

does not mention these authors often, he does refer to them on at least three occasions by name. Each is mentioned by name twice.[92]

The first of these citations occurs at the beginning of a comment on God's promise to Noah, "I will establish my covenant with you."[93] The LXX has the traditional translation διαθήκη for the Hebrew ברית, which to Didymus implies a solemn oath to Noah alone. Although Didymus does not quote the Greek of Aquila and Symmachus,[94] he must be aware that they used the term συνθήκη, which to Didymus signifies a mere "promise."[95] The terminological distinction suggestions to Didymus that Noah had a greater reason to preach to his generation in the hope that they might be saved. Not only did God communicate his future plans with Noah alone (implying his responsibility to share it), but God also authorized the prophecy by swearing it would come true (implying the necessity of sharing it).

The second of these citations is found in a comment on Zech 12:10, specifically the words, "They shall look on me because they mistreated me" (LXX). Didymus is troubled because the Gospel of John gives a very different Greek translation: "They will look to the one whom they have pierced."[96] Didymus offers two solutions to the textual problem: (1) John made his own translation from the Hebrew, or (2) John used an alternative translation, such as "Aquila, Theodotion or another." Aquila and Theodotion were recognized to be more literal than Symmachus and the LXX, and John's quote is a more literal translation of the Hebrew than the LXX.[97] In addition, Aquila certainly had predecessors,[98] and Theodotion has been connected with the so-called καίγε recension thought to predate Aquila.[99] But none of this matters for Didymus, since he is not reporting his own opinion, but citing "those who are trained in the Hebrew language."[100] Indeed one wonders who these characters might be, and

---

92. *Comm. Gen.* 174.3 (Aquila and Symmachus); *Comm. Zach.* 341.17 (Aquila and Theodotion); *Fr. Prov.* 1:6 (= PG 39:1623–24) (Theodotion and Symmachus).

93. Gen 6:18.

94. For the Greek of Aquila and Symmachus, see Frederick Field, *Origenis Hexaplorum quae supersunt* (Oxford: Clarendon, 1875), 1:24.

95. The softer meaning of "promise" is found in *Fr. Ps.* 388.2 (on Ps 38:2).

96. LXX: ἐπιβλέψονται πρός με ἀνθ' ὧν κατωρχήσαντο; John 19:37: ὄψονται εἰς ὃν ἐξεκέντησαν.

97. והביטו אלי את אשר־דקרו (Zech 12:10).

98. See the classic work of Dominique Barthélemy, *Les Devanciers d'Aquila* (VTS 10; Leiden: Brill, 1963), and Natalio Fernandez Marcos, *The Septuagint in Context: Introduction to the Greek Versions of the Bible* (Leiden: Brill, 2000), 109–22.

99. See Barthélemy, *Les Devanciers*, 15–80.

100. *Comm. Zach.* 341.13.

particularly whether Origen might be one of them. Unfortunately, the state of Origen's works precludes certainty here. What we know is that Didymus's source(s) is reliable as to the Hebrew, but his comment adds nothing to our understanding of the text.

A third passage concerns the term "dark saying" (σκοτεινὸς λόγος) in the Greek of Prov 1:6. In a fragment from Didymus's commentary on Prov, he writes, "I am aware of Theodotion's translation, which he produced, as well as Symmachus, that they rendered it 'riddle.'"[101] There could be corruption in the scholion here since the editions of the Hexapla give the rendering of both Aquila and Theodotion as ἑρμενείαν (cf. Vulgate) and Symmachus alone as πρόβλημα.[102] Regardless, it does illustrate that Didymus was familiar with the Hexaplaric versions, although he did not make regular use of them.

Conclusion

The survey conducted in this chapter confirms that our author definitely took advantage of Jewish sources in an effort to illuminate his scriptural exegesis. In the case of Josephus, he understands that he is citing a Jewish author. In the case of the Pseudepigrapha we cannot be certain how Didymus felt about their authorship and religious background (if he cared at all). Probably, Didymus did not judge his sources by their religious background or by their reliability, but by their hermeneutical utility. In several cases he is intentionally promoting Jewish traditions, whether transmitted through the Apocrypha, Josephus, or even by Christian authors. But it is also clear that his citation of Jewish authors, sources, and traditions in no way requires contact with contemporary Jews.

---

101. The Greek reads, Ἀκούω τοῦ Θεοδοτίωνος ἑρμηνείαν, ἣν ἐξέδωκε καὶ Σύμμαχος, ὅτι πρόβλημα ἐκδεδώκασιν (trans. mine).

102. See Bernard de Montfaucon, *Hexaplorum origenis quae supersunt* 2:1; Frederick Field, *Origenis hexaplorum quae supersunt* 2:113.

5

DIRECT REFERENCES TO PHILO IN THE TURA COMMENTARIES

Introduction

We have discussed, in general, the Jewish sources of Didymus the Blind, at least partially to anticipate our case that Philo is used differently than any other source. At the heart of this case lies the direct references to Philo. Didymus mentions Philo by name nine times in the Tura commentaries and clearly refers to him anonymously an additional two times.[1] Although several publications have called attention to the importance of Philo for Didymus the Blind, no one has undertaken a comprehensive study of his influence.[2] This we shall attempt to do in the remainder of this work.

The *Comm. Gen.* is particularly rich in Philonic influence, as we would expect. Yet, despite the impressive research on Didymus's commentaries in the last three decades, comparatively little attention has been given to the *Comm. Gen.*[3] References to previous exegetes and Didymus's role in the patristic interpretation of Genesis have received less attention than other Alexandrians,[4] and no monograph-length study exists discussing the

---

1. *Comm. Gen.* 118.24; 119.2, 19; 139.12; 147.16–17; 235.27; 236.7; *Comm. Eccl.* 279.16; 300.15–16. Philo is also mentioned as τις τῶν ἀρχαίων (*Comm. Zach.* 257.12) and τις τῶν σοφῶν (*Comm. Zach.* 320.8).

2. Other than Runia's survey (*Philo in Early Christian Literature*, 197–204), we possess the contributions of Emilien Lamirande ("Le masculin et le feminin dans la tradition alexandrine: Le commentaire de Didyme l'Aveugle sur la 'Genèse,'" *Science et Esprit* 41 [1989]: 137–65), Albert C. Geljon ("Philo's Influence on Didymus the Blind," in *Philon d'Alexandrie: Un penseur à l'intersection des cultures Gréco-Romaine, Orientale, Juive et Chrétienne* [ed. Sabrina Inowlocki and Baudouin Decharneux; Monothéismes et Philosophie; Turnhout: Brepols, 2011], 357–72), and Geljon's more specific article on Cain and Abel ("Philonic Elements in Didymus the Blind's Exegesis of the Story of Cain and Abel," *VC* 61 [2007]: 282–312). The most recent monograph on Didymus's theology regularly recognizes Philonic influence (Grant D. Bayliss, *The Vision of Didymus the Blind: A Fourth-Century Virtue-Origenism* [Oxford: Oxford University Press, 2016]).

3. This is due, in part, to the tendency of scholars to focus detailed research on a single work (e.g., Prinzivalli on *Comm. Ps.*). The work of Peter D. Steiger is notable for its focus on Gen (e.g., "The Image of God in the Commentary *On Genesis* of Didymus the Blind," StPatr 42 [2006]: 243–47; Steiger's dissertation covers "Theological Anthropology in the Commentary 'On Genesis' by Didymus the Blind" (Ph.D. diss., Catholic University of America, 2006).

4. Both Geljon (*op. cit.*) and J. David Cassel, "Patristic and Rabbinic Interpretation of Genesis 3: A Case Study in Contrasts," StPatr 39 (2006): 203-11, tend to juxtapose the

Philonic material in any of the Tura commentaries. So before we turn to the *Comm. Gen.*, we shall survey the direct Philonic references in the *Comm. Zach.* and the *Comm. Eccl.*[5]

The Commentary on Zechariah

Didymus's five-volume *Comm. Zach.* was written at the request of Jerome.[6] The work survives virtually intact. Only about eight of over four hundred original pages are missing, although the occasional section is unintelligible. As far as his sources are concerned, we know that Origen had written a *Comm. Zach.* known to Jerome, but now lost.[7] We might assume that Didymus had access to this source, but his own exegesis of Zech appears not to owe a great deal specifically to his Alexandrian predecessor.[8] Of course, even if Didymus did draw on earlier exegetes, he would likely leave them unmentioned. As Robert Hill notes, Didymus refers to previous sources only five times in the entire commentary.[9]

We should not expect, therefore, a tremendous amount of Philonic influence in the *Comm. Zach.* In his extant works Philo references Zech only once, quoting from Zech 6:12, and attributing it to "one of Moses's disciples."[10] Consequently, Philo is never mentioned by name in the commentary of Didymus. However, there are at least two anonymous, but still obvious, nods to Philo as a predecessor.

In the first of these references, Didymus is in the middle of a multi-level exegesis of Zech 10:5-7, specifically the expression "the riders of horses shall be put to shame,"[11] when he introduces the following comment: "A certain sage of ancient times distinguished horseman from rider, calling the latter worthless and the former commendable: the one who rides

---

views of Philo (Geljon) or the Rabbis (Cassel) and Didymus. More limited in scope is Hanneke Reuling, *After Eden: Church Fathers and Rabbis on Genesis 3:16–21* (Jewish and Christian Perspectives 10; Leiden: Brill, 2005), 54–80.

5. The *Comm. Ps.* and the *Comm. Job* contain no obvious references to Philo as an individual exegete, although many Philonic themes can be traced as we shall see.

6. Or, so Jerome claims (*De vir. ill.* 109.2).

7. Jerome, *Comm. Zach.* praef.

8. Megan Hale Williams assumes that Origen was the primary source for Jerome's exegesis of Zech in the earlier chapters, while Didymus becomes more prominent when the Origenian material runs out. Comparison with the Origenian material cited by Jerome and Didymus illustrates the discordance (*The Monk and the Book*, 196–97).

9. R.C. Hill, trans., *Didymus the Blind: Commentary on Zechariah* (FC 111; Washington, D.C. 2006), 11.

10. *Conf.* 62–63.

11. The LXX has καὶ καταισχυνθήσονται ἀναβάτ[αι] ἵππων.

without skill, not holding the horse in check, is a mere rider [ἀναβάτης], as the aforementioned sage made clear, since it is only the one riding with equestrian skills who is rightfully referred to as a horseman [ἱππεύς]."[12]

This kind of verbal differentiation is exactly the sort of thing we expect from Philo, and there are several examples of Philo's explanation of the terms ἱππεύς and ἀναβάτης.[13] Hill interestingly states that Didymus's turn to Philo was motivated by a lack of parallel biblical material on the subject.[14] It is intriguing to consider that the mind of Didymus would turn to Philo first in the absence of scriptural parallels, as though he were at the "top of the list" of his go-to sources. Of course, Didymus's familiarity with Philo would have prompted him to think of him for such terminological antitheses. Whatever the reason, the only other author in the *Comm. Zach.* to be cited as "one of the ancients" is Aristotle, whose importance for Didymus, at least indirectly, is notable.[15]

In a second passage discussing Zech 11:17, especially the expression, "a sword shall be on his arm and on his right eye,"[16] Didymus comments on the term "sword" by introducing the following exegesis: "This sword was given to Abraham like an oracle, in order to separate him from the land and his kindred and the father's house, the 'land' meaning the body with which he was wrapped, the 'kindred' those who pursue and live the same [bodily] things, and the 'father's house,' that is the mind, the uttered word, just as one of the scholars has interpreted regarding the Mosaic instruction."[17]

---

12. Trans. Robert C. Hill, *Didymus the Blind: Commentary on Zechariah*, 240. The Greek reads, Διεστείλατό τις τῶν ἀρχαίων σοφ[ὸ]ς ἱππέα [ἀπ' ἀ]ναβάτου, καὶ τὸν μὲν ψεκτόν, τὸν δ' ἐπαινετὸν εἶπεν· ὁ γὰρ ἄνευ τέχνης ἐποχού[μ]ενος, οὐ χαλιναγωγῶν [τὸν] ἵππον, ἀναβάτης ἐστίν, ὡς ὁ προειρημένος σοφὸς π[α]ρέστησεν, τοῦ κατὰ πωλοδαμνικὴν τέχνην ὀχουμέν[ου] ἱππέως ἐν δίκῃ καλουμένου.

13. E.g., *Leg.* 2.104; *Agr.* 67–76.

14. Hill, *Didymus the Blind: Commentary on Zechariah*, 240.

15. *Comm. Zach.* 123.21, referencing Aristotle, *Eth. nic.* 5.4.7. On the importance of Aristotelian logic for Didymus, see Layton, *Didymus the Blind*, 28–29, and for the Aristotelian mean in Didymus's doctrine of virtue, see Bayliss, *The Vision of Didymus*, 148–49. We should not read too much into Didymus's knowledge of Aristotelian doctrines, however, since he is unremarkable for his times (92).

16. The LXX has μάχαιρα ἐπὶ τοὺς βραχίονας αὐτοῦ καὶ ἐπὶ τὸν ὀφθαλμὸν τὸν δεξιὸν αὐτοῦ.

17. *Comm. Zach.* 320.8 (trans. mine). The Greek reads, Αὕτη ἡ μάχαιρα χρησμοῦ δίκην τῷ Ἀβραὰμ δέδοται, ἵνα διέλῃ αὐτὸν «ἀπὸ τῆς γῆς καὶ τῆς συγγενείας αὐτοῦ καὶ τοῦ πατρῴου οἴκου», γῆς νοουμένης τοῦ σώματος οὗ περιέκειτο, συγγενείας δὲ τοὺς τὰ αὐτὰ ἐπιτηδεύοντας καὶ ἀνατραφέντας, οἶκος δὲ πατρὸς τοῦ νοῦ ὁ προφορικὸς λόγος ἐστίν, ὥς τις τῶν σοφῶν περὶ τὴν μωσαϊκὴν παίδευσιν ἡρμήνευσεν.

Louis Doutreleau is probably right to call attention to Philo's *Migr.* 2 as the ultimate inspiration here.[18] Didymus repeats the same exegesis in the *Comm. Gen.* in the comments on Gen 12:1–3, but he does not there refer to Philo in any way.[19] Here, although Philo is not mentioned by name, he is honored as one of the scholarly commentators on Moses. One wonders if the two anonymous references to Philo in the *Comm. Zach.* reflect a later practice in Didymus's exegetical life,[20] while the *Comm. Gen.* reflects his earlier habit of naming him directly.[21] We might hypothesize that Didymus had come under the influence of the times. In Gregory of Nyssa, for example, Philo can be treated as a tool in use among the Arians in support of their theology.[22] As we have seen, Didymus was no friend of the Arians, and would happily avoid naming a source that might be associated with them. Ultimately, however, we cannot be certain why he avoids the name of Philo in the *Comm. Zach.*

The Commentary on Ecclesiastes

Next we come to the *Comm. Eccl.* This work, consisting of lecture notes, covers the entire scope of Eccl, but is now badly damaged. Sources are more frequent here than in the *Comm. Zach.*, and indeed Philo is mentioned by name. The first of the Philonic passages is based on the Hagar-Sarah motif, one of the most familiar of Philonic exegeses. In the midst of a comment on Eccl 9:9 ("See life with the wife whom you have loved all the days of your life"[23]), Didymus introduces the parallel passage of Prov 5:18 ("rejoice with the wife of your youth").[24] Here Didymus suggests that the "wife of your youth" is none other than "true ethical virtue." However, before one reaches virtue, he must abide with "another man's wife," or "external wisdom." For proof of this point, he cites Philo's exegesis: "In a similar way Philo showed that Hagar produces offspring before perfect virtue. For if one does not beget children by these (women)

---

18. Note the close similarity between Philo's words and the Greek of Didymus above: τὴν μὲν γὰρ <u>γῆν σώματος</u>, τὴν δὲ <u>συγγένειαν</u> αἰσθήσεως, τὸν δὲ <u>τοῦ πατρὸς οἶκον λόγου</u> συμβέβηκεν εἶναι σύμβολον.

19. See *Comm. Gen.* 210.3.

20. Doutreleau suggests a date of 387 CE for the *Comm. Zach.* (*Sur Zecharie* 1:23).

21. Nautin does not offer a date for the work (*Sur la Genèse*), but Layton places it in the 360s (*Didymus the Blind*, 6).

22. See Runia, *Philo in Early Christian Literature*, 244–49.

23. The Greek of Didymus reads, ἰδὲ ζωὴν μετὰ γυναικός ἧς ἠγάπησας πάσας ἡμέρας ζωῆς.

24. The Greek of Didymus reads, συνευφραίνου μετὰ γυναικὸς τῆς ἐκ νεότητός σου.

of inferior status, one cannot become father of undefiled achievements and of the teachings of wisdom."[25]

Didymus then turns to Paul to clarify what Philo means, claiming, "The Apostle made the same point [as Philo] by using the terms 'letter' [γράμμα] and 'spirit' [πνεῦμα], and it is impossible to understand anagogical matters without first examining in detail the historical aspects."[26] As the passage indicates, Didymus has adopted Philo's understanding of secular or "encyclical" studies as preparatory for perfect wisdom, and has also incorporated the Philonic allegory of Sarah and Hagar to proclaim precisely this exegesis. But he prefers to locate this allegory within a Pauline frame of reference, via Origen, by analogy to the historical and allegorical senses of scripture. The "letter" of the text must be established before advancing to the "spirit" just as Hagar (secular studies) must be utilized before advancing to Sarah (wisdom/virtue).[27] This move is based on an exegesis worked out in the *Comm. Gen.* whereby Paul's allegory in Gal 4:22-31 is combined with Philo's allegorical understanding of Hagar and Sarah. We shall provide a fuller discussion below when we consider the relevant passage from the *Comm. Gen.*[28]

Next, we turn to a badly damaged text in which the name of Philo is restored by the editors.[29] In the course of his discussion of the paradoxical Eccl 10:7 ("I have seen slaves on horses and rulers walking like slaves on the ground"[30]), Didymus apparently cites Philo's *De vita Mosis* by name, specifically *Mos.* 2.2.[31] Philo states here that the only way cities can advance

---

25. The Greek reads, καὶ κατὰ τοῦτο ὁ Φίλων ἐξέλαβεν τὴ[ν] ..αν προτίκτει[ν] τῆς ἀρετῆς τῆς τελείας· εἰ μὴ γάρ τις τέχῃ ἐκ τούτων τῶ[ν μ]ικρῶν, οὐ δ[ύ]ν[ατ]αι π(ατ)ὴρ τῶν ἔργων τῶν ἀμιάντων καὶ τῶν θεωρημάτων τῆς σοφίας γενέσθαι (*Comm. Eccl.* 276.20-22; trans. Runia, *Philo in Early Christian Literature*, 199).

26. The Greek reads, τὸ δὲ αὐτὸ τοῦτο ὁ ἀπόστολος «γράμμα» καὶ «πν(εῦμ)α» λέγ[ει· κ]αὶ ἀδύνατόν ἐστιν τὰ τῆς ἀναγωγῆς νοῆσαι μὴ ἀκριβώσαντα τὰ τῆς ἱστ[ορία]ς (*Comm. Eccl.* 276.22-24; trans. mine).

27. As with Origen, the "lower levels" of exegesis are necessary and helpful to those weaker in faith (e.g., Origen, *Cels.* 4.71; 6.2; Didymus, *Comm. Gen.* 168.10-27).

28. For a more detailed presentation see Justin M. Rogers, "The Philonic and the Pauline: Hagar and Sarah in the Exegesis of Didymus the Blind," *SPhiloA* 26 [2014]: 57-77).

29. *Comm. Eccl.* 300.15 (*Didymos der Blinde: Kommentar Zum Ecclesiastes* [ed. Gerhard Binder and Michael Gronewald; vol. 5; PTA 24; Bonn: Rudolf Habelt, 1979], 100).

30. The Greek of Didymus reads, εἶδον δούλους ἐφ' ἵππους καὶ ἄρχοντας πορευομένους ὡς δούλους ἐπὶ τῆς γῆς.

31. The Greek reads [... Φίλων ἐν] τῷ Μωσέως βίῳ ... Although this Philonic work is curiously missing from the catalogue of Philonic works in Eusebius (*Hist. eccl.* 2.18), Clement cites the work by exactly the same title as we have here (*Strom.* 1.153.2-3). So we know the work was known to Christians in Alexandria prior to the time of Didymus.

toward the better is "either if kings become philosophers or philosophers kings." Didymus has nearly the same words,[32] and draws the conclusion that "They [the 'philosophers' mentioned in scripture?] were superior to the Gentiles as a 'royal priesthood' [Exod 19:6], and thus held the rule of kings, just as Abraham about whom is said, 'You are a king from God among us' [Gen 23:6]."[33]

Here Didymus references the philosopher-king motif, a doctrine Philo himself borrowed from Plato.[34] However, because Philo's entire *De vita Mosis* is intended to portray Moses as the ideal philosopher-king, one might infer that Didymus wished to reference the entirety of the treatise. Two considerations speak in favor of this suggestion. First, the Philonic line which Didymus quotes could indeed be understood as a summary statement of a utopian ideal ("what if philosophers and kings could switch places?"). Second, only here does Didymus reference a Philonic treatise by name, suggesting his appeal to the work as a whole, rather than to a specific passage within the work. Although Didymus's exegesis leading up to the Philonic reference is lacunose, he presumably discussed Moses as an example of the ideal philosopher-king, and were his comments not interrupted by a student's question (marked by the term επερ), he would have continued to expound upon the Philonic theme.[35]

David Runia adds another text from the *Comm. Eccl.* in which he thinks Philo's influence is apparent. Commenting on the expression "the almond tree should blossom" in Eccl 12:5,[36] Didymus states, "Those who have pronounced on the nature of plants say this about the almond tree: in the spring it shoots forth leaves earlier than all other plants, and it sheds them after all other trees have lost theirs. It is therefore something steadfast. For this reason the priestly rod is also called 'made of nutwood.'"[37] The Philonic passage to which Didymus likely refers is *Mos.* 2.186. Although the

---

32. Philo has, ἐὰν ἢ οἱ βασιλεῖς φιλοσοφήσωσιν ἢ οἱ φιλόσοφοι βασιλεύσωσιν ... whereas Didymus has ... ἐὰν οἱ φιλόσοφοι βασιλεῖς ἦσαν καὶ οἱ βασιλεῖς φιλόσοφοι.
33. The Greek reads, "βασίλειον γ[ο]ῦ[ν "ἱε]ρ[ά]τευμα" ὑπερέχοντες ἦσαν τῶν ἐθνῶν· καὶ οὕτως εἶχον τὸ βασιλεύε[ιν] ὡς καὶ ὁ Ἀβραάμ, πρὸς ὃν εἴρηται· "βασιλεὺς παρὰ θ(εο)ῦ σὺ εἶ ἐν ἡμῖν" (trans. mine).
34. Plato, *Resp.* 473d; Runia, *Philo in Early Christian Literature*, 200.
35. *Comm. Eccl.* 300.20.
36. The Greek reads, καὶ ἀνθήσῃ τὸ ἀμύγδαλον.
37. The Greek reads, οἱ περὶ φύσεως φυτῶν εἰρηκότες περὶ τοῦ "ἀμυγδάλου" τοῦτο λέγουσιν· πρὸ π[άντ]ων φυτῶν ἐν τῷ ἔαρι ἐκφέρει φύλ[λ]α καὶ ἀποβάλλει αὐτὰ μετὰ τὴν ἀποβολὴν πάντων τῶν ἄλλων δένδρων· παράμονον οὖν ἐστιν τοῦτο. διὰ τοῦτο καὶ ἡ "ῥάβδος" ἡ ἱερατικὴ "καρυΐνη" εἴρηται (trans. Runia, *Philo in Early Christian Literature*, 200).

name of Philo is not mentioned here, the two texts share similar language,³⁸ and the budding of Aaron's rod is probably the best-known "almond" passage in the Hebrew Bible.³⁹ Thus, if Didymus had Philo's treatise available, as *Comm. Eccl.* 300.15 suggests he did, it would make sense that he would turn to the comments regarding the budding of Aaron's rod first in his exegesis of the "almond tree." If this is correct, we are reminded of Robert Hill's comment, cited earlier, that Didymus turns to Philo when he cannot locate parallels elsewhere in the Bible. Although he does not, of course, hold the status of scripture, Philo is, among secondary exegetes, "first off the shelf."

The Commentary on Genesis

We have seen thus far that Philo is named only twice in the Tura commentaries on Zech and Eccl, although other clear references do exist. From this evidence, we might conclude that Didymus owes no great debt to Philo. When we turn to the *Comm. Gen.*, however, we find the concentration of Philonic references rising significantly. In the *Comm. Gen.* alone Didymus the Blind mentions Philo by name seven times in four passages.⁴⁰ To the modern reader, seven mentions would hardly seem to constitute dependence, but we have seen that ancient authors do not customarily name their sources.⁴¹ We have also mentioned that Origen, to whom Didymus owes a tremendous intellectual debt, is mentioned by name only once,⁴² as is Clement of Alexandria.⁴³ Considering the importance of these influences, for the name of Philo to appear at all would be significant. But his importance is highlighted when we observe that Philo's name appears more often in the Tura commentaries of Didymus than any other non-biblical exegete.

The direct Philonic references are naturally concentrated in the *Comm. Gen.*, and are to be located in the following four passages: (1) *Comm. Gen.*

---

38. The Philonic text reads, λέγεται μέντοι καὶ τῶν ἐν ἔαρι βλαστάνειν εἰωθότων δένδρων ἡ ἀμυγδαλῇ καὶ πρῶτον ἀνθεῖν εὐαγγελιζομένη φορὰν ἀκροδρύων καὶ ὕστατον φυλλορρεῖν τὴν ἐπέτειον πρὸς μήκιστον ἀποτείνουσα τῆς χλόης εὐγηρίαν.

39. Num 17.

40. In his introduction, Nautin states that Didymus names Philo only three times (*Sur la Genèse* 1:26–27), but in the index to his second volume correctly records that the Jewish author is mentioned seven times (2:276).

41. See chapter 3 above.

42. *Fr. 1 Cor.* ad 16:17–18.

43. *Comm. Eccl.* 7.34.

118.24–119.23 (on Gen 4:1-2);[44] (2) 139.10-14 (on Gen 4:18); (3) 147.15-18 (on Gen 5:3-5); and (4) 235.24-236.21 (on Gen 16:1-2). We shall now analyze each of these in succession.

(1) *Comm. Gen.* 118.24-119.2: *On Cain and Abel, the Order of Their Births*[45]

> "And she continued to bear the brother of Cain, Abel (Gen 4:2)." Now, on the one hand, Philo wants them to be twins from a single conception. It is for this reason, he [Philo] says, "the phrase 'she continued to bear his brother Abel' is added to the phrase 'she bore Cain.'" But whether he is sound in this or not, you will determine once you have pondered it, it being possible that they were born apart at different times. For also, if one is content to admit the "Book of the Covenant," he will find in it also by how much time the one preceded the other.[46]

This passage occurs at the beginning of the "literal" section of exegesis to Gen 4:1-2.[47] In the *Comm. Gen.*, Didymus offers a literal understanding of the biblical lemma first, followed by an allegorical discussion.[48] Origen himself may be credited as the inspiration behind this structure,[49] as it represents a logical application of his twofold (or threefold) theory of

---

44. Philo's name is mentioned three times in the lengthy exposition of Gen 4:1-2 (118.24; 119.2; 119.19). Runia misses the last of these in his survey (*Philo in Early Christian Literature*, 201).

45. Since the exegesis on Gen 4:1-2 is so lengthy, we shall divide it into three parts according to the number of times the author mentions Philo in the course of his exposition.

46. *Comm. Gen.* 118.24-119.2. The Greek reads, «Καὶ προσέθηκεν τεκεῖν τὸν ἀδελφὸν τοῦ Κ[άι]ν τὸν Ἄβελ». Ὁ Φίλων μὲν οὖν βούλεται διδύμους αὐτοὺς εἶν[αι] ἀπὸ μιᾶς συλλήμψεως· διό, φησίν, πρόσκειται τῷ ἔτεκεν τ[ὸν] Κάιν τὸ προσέθηκεν τεκεῖν τὸν ἀδελφὸν αὐτοῦ τὸν Ἄβελ. Π[ό]τερον ὑγιῶς ἔχει ἢ οὔ, ἐπιστήσας δοκιμάσεις, δυνατοῦ ὄντ[ο]ς καὶ χωρὶς αὐτοὺς ἐν διαφόροις χρόνοις γεγεννῆσθαι· καὶ γ[άρ], εἴ τῳ φίλον προσέσθαι τὴν βίβλον τῆς διαθήκης εὑρήσει ἐν αὐτῇ καὶ πόσον θάτερ[ο]ς θατέρου τῷ χρόνῳ προσείληφεν (trans. mine).

47. Didymus is inconsistent in the terminology he uses to describe the more basic surface meaning (e.g., ἡ ἱστορία or καθ' ἱστορίαν, πρὸς τὴν ἱστορίαν, ἁπλούστερον, σωματικόν, κατὰ τὰ γράμμα, τὸ ῥητόν, etc.). Didymus is more consistent, however, in his insistence that every scriptural passage has a legitimate literal meaning. Bayliss observes, "In the entirety of the Tura commentaries, Didymus only ever questions the historical reality of two events—the Fall account and the building of the Tower of Babel" (*The Vision of Didymus*, 69).

48. I use the term "literal" loosely since Didymus frequently does not adhere to the surface meaning in these sections. Rather, he sometimes launches into an anagogical application.

49. The structure of exegesis is more consistent in *Comm. Gen.* than in the other Tura works, but Bardy already recognized the structure of Didymus's exegesis, along with its Origenian precedents, without the aid of the Tura commentaries (see *Didyme l'Aveugle*, 201-202).

scriptural meaning.⁵⁰ The structure of a twofold reading of scripture, however, is already Philonic, and it might be that Origen was influenced by him, with Didymus simply falling in line.⁵¹

As for the comments of Didymus above, that Cain and Abel are twins is not clearly stated in the extant works of Philo, although as much is implied by *QG* 1.78.⁵² James R. Royse considers this text when he references our passage from Didymus, but ultimately follows Pierre Nautin in thinking Didymus is citing a passage no longer extant.⁵³ David Runia states that the notion of Cain and Abel being twins "is consistent with statements in Philo elsewhere."⁵⁴ Twins represent contrasting natures in Philo,⁵⁵ as the treatment of Jacob and Esau shows.⁵⁶ Since Philo consistently describes Cain and Abel in a way similar to Jacob and Esau,⁵⁷ Didymus apparently assumes the former pair were twins as well.

I believe it is likely that, in the above passage, Didymus is thinking of the early paragraphs of Philo's *Sacr*. In this treatise Philo lays out his general

---

50. The somatic level, being πρόχειρος, is the one the reader initially encounters. The psychic or pneumatic senses are not obvious, and can be accessed only by the mature. This is the theory laid out in *Princ.* 4.2.1–4. A recent discussion of Origen's three-fold theory as set forth in *Princ.* can be found in Elizabeth A. Dively Lauro, *The Soul and Spirit within Origen's Exegesis* (The Bible in Ancient Christianity 3; Leiden: Brill, 2005). She argues, in contrast to the traditional view, that Origen *is* consistent in his later homilies and commentaries with the earlier view of three-fold meaning set forth in *Princ.*

51. Philo's *QG* and *QE* are very similar in structure to the *Comm. Gen.* of Didymus, and indeed Ronald Heine has linked Origen's great Genesis commentary to the structure of Philo's *Quaestiones* ("Origen's Alexandrian Commentary on Genesis," *Origeniana Octava* 1:63–73, 64, and *Origen: Scholarship in the Service of the Church* [Christian Theology in Context; Oxford: Oxford University Press, 2010], 104–15). Henri De Lubac also observes that where Origen puts the allegorical meaning before the moral or tropological sense, it is Philo who supplies the material for the latter (*Medieval Exegesis* [trans. M. Sebanc; Grand Rapids: Eerdmans, 1988], 1:147–50).

52. *QG* 1.78: "Wherefore nature separated from him [Cain?] his twin, and made the good man [Abel] worthy of immortality ... but the wicked man [Cain] it gave over to destruction" (trans. Marcus, PLCL 10:49).

53. Nautin, *Sur la Genèse* 1:279; Royse, 'Cain's Expulsion from Paradise: The Text of Philo's *Congr.* 71," *JQR* 79 [1989)]: 219–25, 223–24). Royse repeats this judgment, although with less detail, in *The Spurious Texts of Philo of Alexandria: A Study of Textual Transmission and Corruption with Indexes to the Major Collections of Greek Fragments* (ALGHJ 22; Leiden: Brill, 1991), 23.

54. *Philo in Early Christian Literature*, 201, citing both *QG* 1.78 and *Sacr.* 4, 17.

55. Cf. especially *Praem.* 63.

56. See *Leg.* 3.2; *Sacr.* 17; *Migr.* 53.

57. This is especially true of *Sacr.* 4, 16–18.

position regarding Cain and Abel as well as Jacob and Esau.[58] Philo begins by suggesting one cannot add without first taking something away (§1). He then states that "there are two opposite and contending views of life," represented by Cain and Abel respectively (§2). Philo goes on to comment, "both these views or conceptions lie in the womb of the single soul. But when they are brought to the birth they must needs be separated, for enemies cannot live together forever" (§3).[59] These words imply that Cain and Abel are twins. How else can two ideas compete in one soul and then separate *after* birth? Later rabbinic tradition indeed also suggests that Cain and Abel were twins.[60] But it appears the rabbinic rationale was the result of overreading the Hebrew text, and Philo could well have done the same with the Greek.[61]

Furthermore, that Didymus is thinking of the beginning of *Sacr.* is suggested by the fact that Philo immediately turns to the story of Jacob and Esau to illustrate his point. He sets forth Jacob and Esau as "two contending natures" which must be separated, citing Gen 25:23 ("two nations are in thy womb" and "two peoples shall be separated from thy womb"). At this stage, Philo's opening comment on adding and taking away is resolved: "This is the remedy, that good and evil be separated and set apart from each other and no longer have the same habitation" (§4).[62]

While Philo stops short of saying Cain and Abel are twins, the entire structure of his argument depends on it.[63] The two are in the soul of one womb, must be separated *after* birth, and are compared to Jacob and Esau, who are explicitly said to have been twins (Gen 25:24). It may be that Nautin and Royse are correct, and that Philo made the idea explicit in a work now lost. However, it may not be necessary to hypothesize a lost work. Didymus does not indicate that he is quoting directly (Φίλων ... βούλεται διδύμους αὐτοὺς εἶν[αι] ἀπὸ μιᾶς συλλήμψεως), and the suggestion that Didymus is thinking of *Sacr.* 1–4 certainly is understandable in the immediate Philonic context.

---

58. Beginning in paragraph 4 of *Sacr.*, Philo draws the immediate parallel to Jacob and Esau (Royse, "Cain's Expulsion," 224, and Geljon, "Philonic Elements," 289–90, draw attention to the same text).
59. *PLCL* 2:94–97.
60. See *Gen. Rab.* 22.3; *Pirqe R. El.* 21.
61. Apparently the Hebrew expression ותסף ללדת, replicated in the Greek καὶ προσέθηκεν τεκεῖν, was taken to mean "she continued [at that moment] to bear."
62. *PLCL* 2:96–97.
63. It should be noted that Philo, in *Sacr.* 11, explicitly states that Cain is older than Abel. But he says the same thing about Jacob and Esau. Interestingly, Didymus later follows Philo's argument on the ages of Cain and Abel on the basis of the order of the biblical text (see below).

(2) *Comm. Gen.* 119.2–10: On Cain and Abel as Conditions of the Soul

Therefore, as many things as Philo states in the course of his allegorizing on this passage, the lover of learning will know, but we must, nevertheless, discuss them as best we can. Now, when the soul falls by oversight and stumbling, it bears bad offspring, but if the mind, when it sobers up, experiences some turning, at that point it certainly begins to cast off those things and to bear an introduction to virtue, which is welcome. And, little by little, as the soul increases by ethical progress, it will at some point reach the stage of perfection. But, conversely, the soul becomes detestable if, before virtue can begin, it turns back to add vice to noble reasoning.[64]

The current discussion again concerns Gen 4:1–2, and follows immediately the passage discussed above. Although the former passage belongs to Didymus's literal level of interpretation, this one is located before Didymus's own allegorical stage.[65] It would appear, then, that Didymus's appeal to Philo for the literal interpretation provokes something of an excursus on Philo's ethical portrayal of Cain and Abel as natures in the soul.[66] This point is made clearer by the immediately following comments in which Didymus discusses the professions of Cain and Abel in a way reminiscent of Philo.[67] Although there are no exact quotations or certain references to specific Philonic texts, it seems that Didymus is dependent again upon Philo's *Sacr.*, as Nautin notes.[68]

But the argument in the passage above does not relate directly to anything in the immediate context of *Sacr*. In *Sacr*. 5 Philo launches into an excursus on the progress of the soul, citing as paradigms Abraham (virtue by διδασκαλία), Isaac (virtue by φύσις) and Jacob (virtue by ἄσκησις).[69] However, Philo does not discuss the movement of each of the patriarchs through various stages of virtue, and Didymus does not bother to reference

---

64. Ὅσα μὲν οὖν Φίλων εἰς τοῦτο ἀλληγοοῶν εἶπεν, ὁ φιλόκαλος εἴσεται, λεκτέον δ' ὅμως εἰς τοῦτο τὰ κατὰ δύναμιν. Ἡ ψυχὴ τοίνυν, ὅτε μὲν παροράματι καὶ σφάλματι ὑποπίπτει, ἀπογεννᾷ φαῦλα γεννήματα, ἐὰν δὲ ἀνανήψας ὁ νοῦς ἐπιστροφήν τινα σχῇ, τότε δῆτα ἄρχεται ἐκεῖνα μὲν ἀπωθεῖσθαι, τίκτειν δὲ εἰσαγωγὴν ἀρετῆς, ὅπερ ἐστὶν ἀποδεκτόν· κατ' ὀλίγον [δὴ] προκοπῇ αὐξομένη ἐπὶ τὸ τέλειον ἥξει ποτέ, τὸ ἀνάπαλιν δὲ ἄπευκτον, ἀρετῆς προκαταρξαμένης, κακίαν προσθεῖναι τ[ο]ῦ ἀστείου λογισμοῦ παρατραπέντος (trans. mine).

65. This begins in *Comm. Gen.* 192.24 with the words πρὸς δὲ ἀ[λλ]ηγορίαν.

66. This is made explicit at the end of the discussion (*Comm. Gen.* 120.6–7: Οὗτοι δέ ... τρόποι ψυχῆς ἂν εἶεν διάφοροι κατὰ διαφόρους ἐνεργούμενοι χρόνους).

67. *Comm. Gen.* 119.11–18. The professions of Cain and Abel are given a lengthy exposition in Philo's *Sacr.* 11–49.

68. *Sur la Genèse* 1:279, 281.

69. See also *Mut.* 12, with the explanation of name changes coinciding with natures in *Mut.* 88 (cf. *Somn.* 1.168; *Abr.* 52).

the three patriarchs at all. Therefore, it would appear that Didymus is putting together several Philonic ideas.

Each of the elements of the soul's journey can be confirmed by passages in the works of Philo. Philo teaches that the soul can fall.[70] He also teaches that the soul produces offspring, both positive and negative.[71] This is because the soul is divided between good and evil parts.[72] Although Philo does not explicitly use the description φαῦλα γεννήματα, he does use its logical opposite, ἀστεῖα γεννήματα.[73] The "sobering up" of the soul can also be traced to passages in Philo,[74] as can the casting off of bad offspring, although the exact terminology is not used.[75] The idea of an εἰσαγωγὴ τῆς ἀρετῆς is not found in Philo, but one could interpret Hagar in this fashion (see below).[76] The phrase is especially characteristic of Didymus.[77] In addition, the concept of progressing toward virtue is characteristic of Philo's understanding of the soul's journey,[78] and the exact phrase ἀστεῖος λογισμός, used here, is Philonic.[79]

It should be noted that none of these concepts is unique to Philo. They are each paralleled, if not literally, at least conceptually, in Stoic literature prior to his time. Yet, Didymus does not quote the "Stoics" as his source, although he is familiar with them.[80] Nor does he refer to any pagan text, but he cites Philo explicitly. This indicates that Philo was the basis for Didymus's philosophical claims about the biblical text, even if Didymus is attributing to him something he never explicitly said.

This brings us to another key term in our passage: φιλόκαλος. The term is found a total of ten times in the Tura commentaries, always encouraging students toward additional independent research. Sometimes the research is additional scriptural investigation,[81] but it also regularly points to outside

---

70. *Agr.* 101; *Abr.* 269. Philo can also speak of the soul's fall from the passions in a positive sense (*Leg.* 2.100–101).
71. *Leg.* 2.8, 48; *Her.* 247; *Somn.* 1.202.
72. See *Praem.* 63–65; *Fug.* 24.
73. *Migr.* 142. According to a TLG search, the exact phrase φαῦλα γεννήματα is found only in Didymus the Blind.
74. *Leg.* 2.60 is especially relevant, as it associates sobering up with repenting (μετανοέω), analogous to the "turning" (ἐπιστροφή).
75. Cf. *Deus* 26; *Agr.* 25. In *Fug.* 24 Philo discusses the danger of "the worse part of the soul" overturning the better.
76. See *Congr.* 24; *Fug.* 183; *Mut.* 263.
77. *Comm. Gen.* 45.26; 119.7; 243.2; *Comm. Ps.* 248.11.
78. E.g., *Leg.* 3.140; *Agr.* 160; *Somn.* 2.235.
79. *Det.* 170; *Mos.* 1.48; cf. *Deus* 154; *Plant.* 114; *Congr.* 4.
80. Didymus cites the Stoics by name in five passages in the Tura commentaries (*Comm. Gen.* 137.12; 185.16; *Comm. Eccl.* 235.15; *Comm. Ps.* 53.23; 159.5).
81. *Comm. Job* 8.9; 143.3; *Comm. Gen.* 70.13.

sources. In the *Comm. Zach.* one reference encourages the reading of Josephus, as we have seen.[82] Didymus also can refer the φιλόκαλος to his own commentaries.[83] In the *Comm. Gen.*, the term is found an additional four times, the last two of which occur in connection with the name of Philo.[84] The related term φιλοκαλία is found once,[85] although the text is too fragmentary to determine the context and meaning. We might be inclined to associate the term with Alexandrian or even Origenist significance since Basil of Caesarea and Gregory of Nazianzus selected the term to describe their collection of Origen's biblical exegesis.[86]

Lampe provides two definitions for the term in patristic literature: (1) he who loves the ascetic life (e.g., Athanasius)[87] and (2) he who is interested in learning. Although Didymus knew Athanasius and lived in the desert himself, he never uses the term with reference to asceticism. Rather, he uses the term in the second sense. Gregory of Nazianzus had explained the term φιλόκαλος as φιλομαθής,[88] and this definition works well for Didymus. As Grant Bayliss observes, "ὁ φιλόκαλος seems to be a technical term for Didymus, naming those students who go beyond the teaching he gives them, and this very choice of language seems to me to epitomize the nature of the task in hand as he saw it."[89] In short, Didymus advises the would-be scholar, that is, anyone interested in learning, to pursue further study in Philo, Josephus, his own commentaries, or in scripture itself.

(3) *Comm. Gen.* 119.11–23: *On Cain and Abel and Their Occupations*

> It is also good that [scripture] has recorded their occupations, for "Abel" it says, "was a shepherd of sheep, but Cain was a worker of the ground." As for the historical meaning, this phrase ought not to be overlooked, when we observe the order [of their births]. For Cain's birth is set first, the chronology requiring it, but in terms of their occupations, the righteous man takes precedence. For the occupations of Abel are excellent and more

---

82. *Comm. Zach.* 364.18 (see ch. 4 above).
83. *Comm. Zach.* 377.20 (on Matt); 391.10–12 (on Isa).
84. *Comm. Gen.* 61.10; 70.13; 119.3; 139.12.
85. *Comm. Gen.* 10A.10.
86. The reason for the selection of the title φιλοκαλία is unknown. It is found already in *Epist.* 115 of Gregory of Nazianzus without explanation (for the text, see *Sur les Écritures* [ed. Marguerite Harl; SC 302; Paris: Cerf, 1983], 170–71). Harl remarks, "Le titre «Philocalie» semble n'avoir été donné à aucune ouvrage de l'Antiquité avant celuci-ci, et il ne sera repris que par la «Philocalie» russe du XVIIIe siècle" (34). However, she goes on to note that the term had been used in Eusebius to refer to a collection (*Hist. eccl.* 6.20.2).
87. Citing *Vit. Ant.* 4.
88. *Or.* 45.10.
89. Bayliss, *The Vision of Didymus*, 79.

honorable than those Cain pursued. For ensouled beings differ from unsouled beings by reason of nature. And in this way, Philo says well that those who intend to take up office over others and even over themselves should be trained beforehand in shepherding.

Now Cain is not called a "farmer," but a "worker of the ground." For he was not an excellent man in the manner of Noah, who is called a "farmer" (Gen 9:20), and not a "worker."

Now as for the allegorical interpretation, Abel is a shepherd of beasts, which means [a shepherd] of the sense perceptions, who leads these things under knowledge as an excellent herdsman; and [as] a charioteer and a commander, sets reasoning over the irascible and appetitive [parts of the soul]. But Cain, on the other hand, who is constantly focused on the ground and on earthly things, is not called a "farmer" (for he did not even seek command over these things), but is himself "a worker of the ground" alone. He is a lover of the body, having neither reason nor command. He should have said appropriately to himself, "Let us eat and drink; for tomorrow we die" (cf. Isa 22:13; 1 Cor 15:32), while doing these things with divine knowledge, according to the saying, "Whether you eat, whether you drink, whether you do anything, do all things to the glory of God" (1 Cor 10:31), being a farmer and not a worker of the ground.

But these boys, as was said before, can be different dispositions of the soul, who are at work at different times.⁹⁰

As we have already seen, the Philonic citations in this section are not exact. But there is good reason to believe that in the above comments, Didymus is thinking principally of the *QG* 1.59. We have already noted that the structure of Didymus's *Comm. Gen.* matches well with that of Philo's *Quaestiones*.

---

90. The Greek reads, Εὖ δὲ καὶ τὸ τὰ ἐπιτηδε[ύμα]τα αὐτῶν ἀναγεγράφθαι· «Ὁ μὲν» γὰρ «Ἄβελ» φησὶν «ἐγένετο πο[ι]μὴν προβάτων, Κάιν δὲ ἦν ἐργαζόμενος τὴν γῆν», ὅπερ ὡς πρὸς τὴν ἱστορίαν ἔχοι παρατήρησιν οὐκ εὐκαταφρόνητον, καὶ τ[ὴ]ν τάξιν ἡμῶν ἐπιτηρούντων. Ἐν μὲν γὰρ τῇ γενέσει τὸν Κάιν [προ]έταξεν, τοῦ χρόνου τοῦτ᾿ ἀναγκάζοντος, ἐν δὲ τοῖς ἐπιτη[δεύ]μασιν προτάττει τὸν δίκαιον. Ἀστεῖα γὰρ καὶ τιμιώτερα τ[ὰ το]ῦ Ἄβελ, ὧν ἐσπούδαζεν Κάιν· τὰ μὲν γὰρ ἔμψυχα τῶν ἀψ[ύχων] τῷ τῆς φύσεως λόγῳ διαφέρει. Καὶ ταύτῃ κ[αλῶς] ὁ Φίλω[ν] τοὺς ἀρχῆς μέλλοντας ἐπιλαμβάνεσθαι τῆς τε [ἑτ]έρων κ[αὶ] τῆς ἑαυτοῦ ἐν τῇ ποιμενικῇ προπαιδεύεσθαι ἔφη.

Κάιν δ[ὲ ο]ὐκ ἐρρέθη γεωργός, ἀλλ᾿ *ἐργαζόμενος τὴν γῆν*· οὐ γὰρ ἦν ἀ[στε]ῖος κατὰ τὸν Νῶε, ὅστις γεωργός, οὐκ ἐργάτης, εἴρηται.

Πρὸς δὲ ἀ[λλ]ηγορίαν ποιμήν ἐστιν ὁ Ἄβελ ζῴων, ὅ ἐστιν τῶν αἰσθήσ[εω]ν, ὑπὸ ἐπιστήμην ἄγων ταύτας ὡς νομεὺς ἄριστος, τῷ τ[ε θ]υμικῷ καὶ ἐπιθυμητικῷ ἡνίοχον καὶ ταξίαρχον τὸν λογισ[μὸ]ν ἐπιτιθείς. Ὁ δὲ Κάιν περὶ τὴν γῆν καὶ τὰ γήινα εἰλ[υ]σ<πώ>μενος οὐ γεωργὸς εἴρηται—ἢ γὰρ ἂν καὶ περὶ αὐτὰ τάξιν [ἐ]ζήτει—, ἀλλ᾿ *ἐργαζόμενος τὴν γῆν* αὐτὸ μόνον, φιλοσώματός [τι]ς ὤν, μηδένα λόγον ἢ τάξιν ἔχων, ὃς εἴποι ἂν προσφόρως ἑαυτῷ· «*Φάγωμεν καὶ πίωμεν· αὔριον γὰρ ἀποθ[ν]ῄσκομεν*», τοῦ σὺν ἐπιστήμῃ θείᾳ ταῦτα ποιοῦντος κατὰ τὸ λεχθὲν «*Εἴτε ἐσθίετε, εἴτε πίνετε, εἴτε τι ποιεῖτε, πάντα εἰς δόξαν Θεοῦ ποιεῖτε*» γεωργοῦ ἀλλ᾿ οὐκ ἐργάτου γῆς τυγχάνοντος.

Οὗτοι δέ, ὡς προείρηται, τρόποι ψυχῆς ἂν εἶεν διάφοροι κατὰ διαφόρους ἐνεργούμενοι χρόνους (trans. mine).

DIRECT REFERENCES TO PHILO IN THE TURA COMMENTARIES   89

Here we find evidence of Didymus's direct knowledge of that work. We shall quote the translation of Marcus:

> Why does (scripture) first describe the work of the younger man Abel, saying, "He became a shepherd of flocks, and Cain tilled the ground?"
> Even though the righteous man was younger in time than the wicked one, still he was older in activity.[91] Wherefore now, when their activities are appraised, he is placed first in order. For one of them labours and takes care of living beings,[92] even though they are irrational, gladly undertaking the pastoral work which is preparatory[93] to rulership and kingship. But the other occupies himself with earthly and inanimate things.

First Didymus notes the occupations of Cain and Abel. Since the Bible happens to mention what they did for a living, Didymus, as Philo, assumes there must be exegetical significance to their occupations. He then turns to the historical interpretation. Didymus notes the order in which the occupations of Cain and Abel are provided in the biblical text, using the exact terminology and argumentation as Philo.[94] Since the order of their occupations contrasts with the order of their birth, Didymus suggests that the more noble profession is listed first, just as Philo did. Didymus justifies his interpretation of their occupations by arguing that "ensouled beings" (ἔμψυχα) are more noble than "unsouled beings" (ἄψυχα) by nature, again just as Philo did. Finally, at the conclusion of the paragraph, Didymus cites Philo as saying those who wish to engage in politics must first train themselves by shepherding.

If we had more extensive Greek fragments of the *Quaestiones*, we could perhaps establish more direct verbal parallels between Philo and Didymus. What we have, however, is sufficient to conclude that Philo is responsible for the content of the entire paragraph, although he is cited only at the end. One may question why Didymus cites Philo at all. It is true that the shepherding profession is presented in Philo as preparatory for political office.[95] But this theme is found from the earliest times in Greek literature,

---

91. The Greek term preserved in the catenae of Procopius is ἐπιτήδευμα, the same term Didymus uses (see *PLCL* 380:36). Metzler, however, does not attribute this section to Philo, but to Didymus himself (*Prokop von Gaza*, 162).

92. The Greek of Procopius has ἔμψυχα, the same term Didymus employs (see *ibid*).

93. The Greek uses the adjective προγυμνασματικόν whereas Didymus uses the verb προπαιδεύω (see *ibid*).

94. See also *Sacr.* 11, on which Didymus depends in his exegesis of Cain and Abel, as we have already suggested.

95. *Agr.* 41, 66; *Ios.* 2-3, 54; *Mos.* 1.60.

as Philo himself recognizes.[96] Why is it that Didymus, again, cites Philo when he could have cited any number of authors for the same information?[97] It must be that Philo is valued by his audience. Whereas Homer, Plato, and others speak of shepherding in the political sense,[98] Philo applies these concepts to the Bible.[99] For that reason the φιλόκαλος should read Philo in his effort to synthesize the wisdom of the scriptures with the wisdom of the Greeks.

So much for the literal interpretation. Now we turn to the allegorical understanding of the professions of Cain and Abel. First, Didymus regards Abel as a shepherd not of animals, but of "sense perceptions" (αἰσθήσεις). Again, this theme is characteristically Philonic.[100] The leader of sense perception, Didymus tells us, is a "most excellent herdsman" (νομεὺς ἄριστος).[101] Although Philo does not use the exact terminology found here, the idea is certainly represented.[102] Didymus also describes the role of a shepherd as analogous to that of the charioteer (ἡνίοχος) and commander (ταξίαρχος).[103] In doing so, Didymus diverges from Philo's normal pair, the ship captain (κυβερνήτης) being more commonly associated with the

---

96. Cf. *Ios.* 2, where Philo cites the idea as common stock from "the race of poets" (e.g., Homer, *Il.* 1.263; 2.243; *Od.* 3.156). In *Prob.* 31 Philo explicitly names Homer for this idea ("Homer often calls kings 'shepherds of the people'").

97. Origen also references the information (*Hom. Jer.* 5.6). Origen may himself depend on Philo here (see Annewies Van den Hoek, "Philo and Origen: A Descriptive Catalogue of Their Relationship," *SPhiloA* 12 [2000]: 44–121, 89).

98. Homer is mentioned in only one passage as ὁ ποιητής (*Comm. Eccl.* 354.27-355), and Plato is mentioned only once (*Comm. Eccl.* 22.20).

99. Philo also uses the metaphor in a strictly political sense (*Legat.* 44).

100. See especially *Congr.* 96-97; cf. *Leg.* 3.111.

101. On the Platonic images of governing the soul in Didymus see Bayliss, *The Vision of Didymus*, 160–61. Geljon discusses the Philonic metaphors as a background to Didymus's own usage ("Philonic Elements," 291).

102. Philo tends to use the term ποιμήν when he wishes to extol the virtues of a shepherd. There are three reasons for this. First, and most obvious, the Bible describes Abel with the term ποιμήν (Gen 4:2). Therefore, it must be the highest description of a shepherd. Second, just as Philo distinguishes a "farmer" (γεωργός) from a "worker" (ἐργάτης), so also he distinguishes a "keeper of the flock" (κτηνοτρόφος) from a shepherd (ποιμήν) (see *Agr.* 29). Third, the term νομεύς is generic in Greek (see LSJ s.v. "νομεύς"), and Philo's vocabulary reflects the generic nature of the term (see *Agr.* 48 where it is very clearly employed as a catch-all term).

103. Philo employs the term ἡνίοχος thirty-eight times, often in the context of governing sense perception (*Leg.* 3.109; *Spec.* 2.163), the passions (*Leg.* 3.118; *Migr.* 67), and, as we find in Didymus, the irrational parts of the soul (*Leg.* 1.73; *Sacr.* 45; *Det.* 53). A short excursus on the soul as charioteer and chariot can be found in *Agr.* 72–76 (on which see Albert Geljon and David T. Runia, *Philo of Alexandria: On Cultivation* [PACS 4; Leiden: Brill, 2012], 169–71).

charioteer in Philo.[104] Although the image of the ταξίαρχος is present in Philo, he does not use the image for someone who governs the passions.[105]

Now we turn to Cain. Here too, there is clear evidence that Didymus is following Philo.[106] First, Didymus notes that Cain is always "focused on the ground and on earthly things." The term "ground" (γῆ) and its cognates are frequently negative in Philo when used in ethical contexts.[107] The "earth-born man" (ὁ γήϊνος), for example, is corruptible (*Leg.* 1.90) and is drawn to ἡδοναί (*Leg.* 3.160). Therefore, the "practicers" of virtue (ἀσκηταί) refuse to receive nourishment from earthly things (*Leg.* 3.168). They prefer rather to receive their food from heavenly things (*Leg.* 3.162). The fate of Adam, ὁ γήϊνος νοῦς,[108] is typical of "earthly" men, as he was banished from the paradise of virtues (*Plant.* 46), never to return.

Thus one can see that "earthly" elements are negative in Philo. So when the Bible states that Cain "was a worker of the ground" (ἦν ἐργαζόμενος τὴν γῆν, Gen 4:2), we are led to believe that he is a bad man (φαῦλος). But Cain's association with the ground is not the only indication of his wickedness. The Bible also describes him as an ἐργαζόμενος. Philo's typical lexical distinction between a "farmer" (γεωργός), who is superior to a "worker" (ἐργάτης), is taken over by Didymus.[109] If Cain wished to pursue the agricultural profession honorably, he ought to have been a "farmer," but as it is, the Bible assigns him the dishonor of a mere "worker."

In the *Det.* 109, in the midst of a discussion on the difference between a farmer and a worker, Philo summarizes:

---

104. The noun occurs fifty-three times in Philo, twenty-five times in concert with ἡνίοχος (e.g., *Opif.* 46; *Leg.* 3.223–24; *Ebr.* 109). Although Didymus does not use the term κυβερνήτης here, he is certainly familiar with it (found in twenty passages in the Tura commentaries, but only once in the *Comm. Gen.* [16A.3]). Didymus uses the more familiar Philonic image in *Comm. Zach.* 270.2–7. For the Platonic background to Philo's use of these and related images (borrowed primarily from the *Phaedr.*), see Anita Méasson, *Du char ailé de Zeus à l'Arche d'Alliance: Images et mythes platoniciens chez Philon d'Alexandria* (Paris: Études augustiniennes, 1986). For the background of these images in Didymus, see Bayliss, *The Vision of Didymus*, 181–82.

105. See *Migr.* 60; *Virt.* 127, in both of which ὀρθὸς λόγος is identified as the ταξίαρχος, and *Prob.* 154 where ἀρετή is cast in the same role. These three passages mark the only cases in which the term ταξίαρχος is used in an ethical sense. In its remaining seven occurrences, it is used to refer to military commanders in a literal sense.

106. Geljon presents the details well ("Philonic Elements," 294–99).

107. Γῆ occurs 849 times and γήϊνος 33 times.

108. "Adam" (אדם) in Philo in linked with אדמה in Hebrew, and thus symbolizes, as does the nation of אדום, "earth."

109. The term ἐργάτης is not always negative in Philo, however (e.g., *Leg.* 1.54 in comments to Gen 2:5).

> The worthless person [φαῦλος] never ceases spending unskilled labor [ἐργαζόμενος ἀτέχνως] on his earthly body and the sense akin to it and all external objects of sense, and he goes on doing harm to his utterly miserable soul, doing harm also to that which he imagines he is chiefly benefitting, his own body. But in the case of the worthy person [σπουδαῖος], since he is expert in the skilled work of agriculture [τέχνη γεωργική] everything that comes under his hands is managed with skill and as reason requires.[110]

One can see the direction the Philonic allegory takes. The "worker" is interested in working his body to gratify the senses, whereas the farmer is constantly attempting to cultivate his soul to yield a fruitful crop of virtue. Cain's dishonorable pursuit foreshadows his act of fratricide.[111] But lest we think that he killed a literal brother, Philo informs us that, by Abel, the Bible actually means Cain killed "the love of virtue and the God-loving position" (τὸ φιλάρετον καὶ φιλόθεον δόγμα) within himself![112] Therefore, Cain is the stereotypical bad man, eradicating in himself the possibility of seeking virtue, and resigning himself completely to the body and its passions.

Didymus clearly depends on Philo for his interpretations of Cain and Abel. He knows the Philonic etymologies of their names (see ch. 6).[113] He understands the Philonic idea of shepherding as it applies to Abel. He even accepts the notion that the term "beasts" is code for the irascible and appetitive parts of the soul. In the case of Cain also, his being called a worker instead of a farmer is significant for Didymus as it had been for Philo. Didymus introduces and concludes his discussion with the Philonic idea that Cain and Abel represent τρόποι ("dispositions") in the soul.[114] The

---

110. The Greek reads, ὁ μὲν δὴ φαῦλος τὸ γεῶδες σῶμα καὶ τὰς συγγενεῖς αἰσθήσεις αὐτῷ καὶ ὅσα ἐκτὸς αἰσθητὰ ἐργαζόμενος ἀτέχνως οὐ παύεται, καὶ βλάπτει μὲν τὴν παναθλίαν ψυχὴν ἑαυτοῦ, βλάπτει δὲ καὶ ὃ δοκεῖ μάλιστα ὠφελεῖν τὸ ἴδιον σῶμα· τῷ δὲ σπουδαίῳ—τέχνης γὰρ ἔμπειρος γεωργικῆς ἐστιν—ἡ ὕλη πᾶσα τεχνικῶς καὶ σὺν λόγῳ μεθοδεύεται (trans, *PLCL* 2:275-77, modified slightly). Philo had made the argument in §104 that a γεωργός is also a τεχνίτης because "farming is an art." Cf. *Agr.* 4: "... a husbandman [γεωργός] is guaranteed to be no unprofessional, but a skilled worker by his very name, which he has gained from the science [τέχνη] of husbandry, the science whose title he bears" (γεωργὸς δὲ τὸ μὴ ἰδιώτης ἀλλ' ἔμπειρος εἶναι καὶ τῷ ὀνόματι πεπίστωται, ὅπερ ἐκ τῆς γεωργικῆς τέχνης, ἧς φερώνυμός ἐστιν; trans. *PLCL* 3:109).
111. *Agr.* 21.
112. *Det.* 47-48.
113. Cain as κτῆσις (*Comm. Gen.* 144.16) and Abel as ἀναφέρων τῷ θεῷ (122.18).
114. The idea is quintessentially Philonic (e.g., the negative dispositions represented by the Ammonites and Moabites in *Leg.* 3.81; also *Fug.* 81; *Abr.* 52, 217ff.). Kamesar cites Plutarch, who uses the term τρόπος as equivalent to ἦθος (*Der sera numinis vindicata* 6, 515e-f), which sheds light on Philo's use of the term to refer to biblical characters as ethical dispositions ("Biblical Interpretation" 87).

opening paragraphs of the *Sacr.* are based on the notion that "Cain" and "Abel" inheres in every soul as competing natures. One nature wishes to refer all things to God (Abel) and the other wishes to retain everything for himself (Cain).[115] The universality suggested (first?) by Philo is retained and applied to Didymus's developed spirituality.[116]

(4) *Comm. Gen.* 139.10–14: *On the Posterity of Cain*

> If one wishes to assign these things an anagogical interpretation, let him do this by taking his starting point for the *anagoge* from the interpretation of names without being pedantic. Now Philo has commented on these things, the necessary benefit of which the lover of learning [φιλόκαλος] ought to accept, once he has examined them.[117]

The reference to Philo found here occurs in a short comment on the genealogy of Cain in Gen 4:18. According to his usual practice, Didymus begins by relaying the literal interpretation first. He notes that Cain's descendants lasted only seven generations, meeting their end in the Flood, whereas Seth's descendants were preserved through Noah. Didymus then turns to the allegorical interpretation, called here the ἀναγωγή, of the text. The term ἀναγωγή seems to be a favorite of Didymus,[118] and has served as the partial basis for several studies.[119] In Neoplatonism, the term carries the notion of "lifting up" the soul to God.[120] From this background, Origen applies it to the ability of scripture to "lift up" one's soul to God (i.e., the same motive as the "pneumatic" sense).[121] Bienert does not think, however, that the philosophical connotations of the term should be pressed. He argues that Origen chose the term as a synonym to ἀλληγορία simply because he wished to distinguish between secular exegesis (principally of

---

115. *Sacr.* 2–5.

116. Although Cain might be regarded as the archetypal sinner in Philo, Didymus uses Judas Iscariot for this purpose (See Layton, *Didymus the Blind*, 128–34; Bayliss, *The Vision of Didymus*, 178).

117. The Greek reads, Εἰ δέ τις καὶ ἀναγαγεῖν ταῦτα βούλεται, ἀπὸ τῆς ἑρμηνείας τῶν ὀνομάτων δεχόμενος τῆς ἀναγωγῆς τὴν ἀρχὴν μετὰ τοῦ μὴ ψυχρολογεῖν τοῦτο ποιείτω. Εἴρηται δὲ καὶ Φίλωνι εἰς ταῦτα, ἅπερ ὁ φιλόκαλος ἐπισκεψάμενος τὴν δεοῦσαν δεχέσθω ὠφέλειαν (trans. mine).

118. Didymus also uses many synonyms, as all authors of his era (e.g., the nouns διάνοια, θεωρία, νοῦς and the adjectives ἀλληγορική, ὑψηλοτέρα, μυστική, πνευματική, τροπική, etc.) (cf. the list of Bardy, *Didyme*, 202).

119. See most notably Bienert, *"Allegoria und Anagoge,"* although Tigcheler, *Didyme l'Aveugle*, 82–146 also makes valuable corrections to earlier views (e.g., those of Louis Doutreleau, see 146–47).

120. See Robert M. Grant, *The Letter and the Spirit* (London: Macmillan, 1957), 124.

121. See *Princ.* 4.3.5; Bienert comments specifically on *Hom. Jer.* 20.1–7; *Comm. Jo.* 2.21 and *Hom. Luc.* 10.30–37 (*op. cit.*, 64–67).

Homer) and Christian exegesis.[122] Later interpreters expanded the concept until it eventually becomes one of the four senses of scripture in Medieval Christian exegesis.[123]

If Bienert is correct, and if Didymus assumed the Origenian meaning of ἀναγωγή, then it is shocking to find the name of Philo, a Jew, cited as the means by which one reaches the anagogical interpretation.[124] While Didymus stops short of saying that Philo supplies the ἀναγωγή, he does state that Philo will offer sound etymology, which the reader can then employ toward the ἀναγωγή. So Philo is at least a necessary step toward the higher meaning. This places Philo in an intermediate position, above most Jewish expositors, and perhaps one level below the teacher Didymus himself, only because Philo was not a Christian.[125] For this reason Didymus refers the reader to Philo's spiritual interpretation *without commenting himself*, implying that the reader can use Philo to complete what Didymus himself fails to supply.[126]

Although no Philonic tractate is cited here, Nautin suggests that Didymus was thinking of *Post.* 66–75.[127] Here Philo quickly supplies allegorical interpretations for each of the names in the exegetical verse (Gen 4:18).[128] The etymologies of these names offer the starting point for the reader to

---

122. *Op. cit.*, 64.

123. Cf. the words of Hugh of St. Victor, *Littera gesta docet, quid credas allegoria // Moralis quid agas, quo tendas anagogia* (qtd. in Henri de Lubac, "Typology and Allegorization," in *Theological Fragments* [trans. R.H. Balinski; San Francisco: Ignatius, 1984], 138). For a full history of the question and the development of fourfold patristic exegesis, see de Lubac's magnum opus *Medieval Exegesis: The Four Senses of Scripture*.

124. While Josephus is explicitly called "Jewish" in the Tura commentaries of Didymus (see chapter four above), Philo's ethnicity is never referenced. Christians expositors before Didymus had laid the groundwork for the *Philo Christianus* legend, but the legend is not explicit until much later. Thus, there is no evidence to suggest that Didymus imagined Philo to be a Christian exegete (although see next note).

125. Eusebius divides the Jewish nation into two groups: (1) those who follow the laws according to the literal sense (κατὰ τὴν ῥητὴν διάνοιαν), and (2) those who subject themselves to the θεωρία "of the things indicated in the Laws according to the [deeper] sense" (κατὰ διάνοιαν) (*PE* 8.10.18). He then immediately mentions Philo and Josephus, and in book 11 goes on to cite Philo as an example of one of these elite Jews. Therefore, there is evidence in the patristic tradition of regarding certain Jews, especially Aristobulus, Philo and Josephus, as being on a higher level of understanding (see also *PE* 8.8.56-57; 8.9.38).

126. For more on this, see the comments on *Comm. Gen.* 147.15–18 below.

127. On Didymus's possible knowledge of *Post.*, see further Geljon, "Philonic Elements," 306–8.

128. In this passage, Γαϊδάδ means ποίμνιον (§66), Μαιήλ means ἀπὸ ζωῆς θεοῦ (§69) [the text of Didymus has Μαουιά], Μαθουσάλα means ἀποστολὴ θανάτου (§73) [the text of Didymus has Μαθουσαήλ], and Λάμεχ means ταπείνωσις (§74).

complete the allegorical interpretation which Didymus intentionally glosses over.

Manlio Simonetti observes that, in the *Comm. Gen.*, Didymus sometimes drops the name of Philo at or near the end of an allegorical discussion.[129] This move he interprets as a means of hurriedly moving on to the next passage in the commentary.[130] Although this observation can be applied to only two passages, these passages serve as a striking illustration of the role Philo occupied in Didymus's allegorical canon of go-to sources, for his favorite Jewish source was a sufficient substitute for the master himself.

(5) *Comm. Gen.* 147.15–18: *On Adam and Seth*

> The preceding shall serve as the interpretation for now. But if anyone is caught up in the number of the years and in the interpretation of the names of those who are born, Philo can offer a mystical understanding without being pedantic. So, go to him on this point, for he is beneficial.[131]

These words occur at the end of an exegesis on the chronology of Adam's life (Gen 5:3–5). Immediately before the above passage, Didymus completes his literal (historical) interpretation. Unfortunately the end of the section, where Didymus discusses the meaning of the phrases κατὰ τὴν ἰδέαν and κατὰ τὴν εἰκόνα, is lost.[132]

As we mentioned above, Didymus normally offers a literal interpretation followed by an allegorical one. Here, however, he foregoes his own allegorical interpretation, referring the reader to Philo for further information, while warning for a second time against pedantry.[133] This language is not unusual for the ancient commentators,[134] and it seems to be a concession to the audience that the commentator is not wasting their time.

---

129. Both here and in *Comm. Gen.* 147.16–17 below.

130. Manlio Simonetti, "Lettera e allegoria nell'esegesi veterotestamentaria di Didimo," *Vetera Christianorum* 20 (1983): 341–89, 354.

131. The Greek reads, Ταῦτα μὲν οὕτω νῦν ἀποδέδοται· εἰ δέ τις καὶ τῷ πλήθε[ι τῶν ἐ]τῶν καὶ τῇ ἑρμηνείᾳ τῶν ὀνομάτων <τῶν> γεννωμένων ἔ[νςχοι, Φί]λων ἀποδοίη λόγον μυστικὸν μετὰ τοῦ μὴ ψυχρολογ[εῖ]ν· πρόσεστε οὖν τούτῳ, ὠφέλιμον γάρ (trans. mine).

132. Nautin suggests that "la faute peut remonter au tachygraphe qui n'a pas eu le temps de tout prendre sous la dicteé et qui pensait compléter ensuite, soit à un copiste placé devant un modèle illisible" (*Sur la Genèse* 1:19). The "image" theory of Didymus as it relates to Origen and Philo has been discussed by Joseph Calleja, "Gn 1,26s in Filone, nelle Omilie di Origene e nel Commentario in Genesim di Didimo il Cieco," *Melita Theologica* 39 (1988): 91–102.

133. See *Comm. Gen.* 139.10–14 discussed above.

134. E.g., Simplicius, *in Phys.* 144.25–28.

The exact Philonic passage which Didymus has in mind is impossible to identify.[135] Philo discusses the names of both Adam and Seth,[136] but never their ages. Therefore, several solutions are possible. First, it is possible that Didymus had no particular Philonic passage in mind. Since both etymology and arithmology are well-known subjects in Philo, Didymus simply assumed that Philo would not pass over these subjects in consideration of Adam and Seth. David Runia, however, offers a different solution, suggesting that perhaps Didymus had access to the part of Philo's Allegorical Commentary that originally fell between the *Post.* and the *Gig.*[137] Yet a third possibility, which Runia also suggests, is that Didymus is not thinking of the "number of years" of Adam and Seth, but the 120 years before the flood, a subject he raised earlier in *Comm. Gen.* 146.20-22, and which Philo addresses.[138] Ultimately, no explanation can be proven.

The greater issue in both *Comm. Gen.* 139.10-14 above and 147.15-18 here is the fact that Didymus is comfortable referring his readers to Philo's allegorical explanations *instead of* offering his own. Didymus is not merely wrapping up a long anagogical discussion by referring to Philo. He is encouraging his readers to "fill out" their understanding of the passage (which includes allegorical exegesis) by investigating what Philo has to say. Philo is clearly more than an author within the tradition, but rather in both of these passages is "useful" (ὠφέλιμος).

In addition to the reference to Philo's utility, both of these passages associate Philo with etymological interpretation. Origen attributed to Philo the authorship of a book on Hebrew names, according to Jerome.[139] Eusebius, however, seems to doubt the authenticity of this tradition, writing, "the interpretations of the Hebrew names in the Law and the Prophets

---

135. Nautin, *op. cit.* 2:15.
136. In Philo, the former means "earth" (γῆ) (*Leg.* 1.90; *Plant.* 34), and the latter means "irrigation" (ποτισμός) (*Post.* 10, 124; cf. *QG* 1.81). See Lester L. Grabbe, *Etymology in Early Jewish Interpretation* (BJS 115; Atlanta: Scholars Press, 1988), 129 (on Adam), 205 (on Seth).
137. Runia, *Philo in Early Christian Literature*, 201.
138. *Op. cit.*, 202. Philo discusses the mystical significance of the 120 years in *QG* 1.91. But it appears that Philo devoted, or intended to devote, a much longer study to the subject. In *Gig.* 55-57 he draws the parallel between the 120 years of the flood and the 120 years of Moses's life (Deut 34:7) and proposes to dedicate a lengthy discussion of the 120 years. So far as I can tell, this discussion cannot be found in the extant works of Philo.
139. *Nom. hebr., praef.*, the relevant section of which reads as follows: "Philo, vir disertissimus Iudaeorum, Origenis quoque testimonio comprobatur edidisse librum Hebraicorum nominum, eorumque etymologias iuxta ordinem literarum e latere copulasse." Origen refers to a work by this name anonymously in *Comm. Jo.* 2.33 and in *Hom. Num.* 20.3.

are said to be his [Philo's] work."¹⁴⁰ Modern scholars have questioned whether Philo was capable of writing such a work, since he shows little knowledge of Hebrew.¹⁴¹

Didymus nowhere refers to a book of etymologies. Pierre Nautin theorizes that Didymus used one, but assumes that most of Didymus's etymologies come from Origen.¹⁴² While we do not deny Origen's influence, we shall demonstrate in the next chapter that Philo was a primary source as well. In any case, we see from the preceding references that Didymus associated Philo explicitly with etymological theory. Since Didymus borrows a number of etymologies from Philo, we may conclude that Didymus had read much of Philo himself, and assumed Philo, as a Jew, held sufficient expertise to properly etymologize Hebrew names.

(6) *Comm. Gen.* 234.31–236.21: *On Sarah and Hagar*¹⁴³

> The apostle refers these things to the two covenants by the law of allegory. But since the literal sense is present, it is itself also worthy of investigation. The saints cohabit not as though hunting after pleasure, but for the sake of procreation. For such a tradition is handed down concerning them, that they would go in to their wives only when it was time for conception. They would come together neither when she was nursing nor when she was feeding her child nor when she was pregnant. For in none of these times did they esteem intercourse appropriate. And Jacob confirms the tradition. For having proven for a long time that Rachel was not allowed to bear a child, he no longer approached her. But she, thinking that if he went in to her she would bear, said, "give me children, but if not, you have killed me"

---

140. *Hist. Eccl.* 2.18.7. The Greek reads, καὶ τῶν ἐν νόμῳ δὲ καὶ προφήταις Ἑβραϊκῶν ὀνομάτων αἱ ἑρμηνεῖαι τοῦ αὐτοῦ σπουδῇ εἶναι λέγονται.

141. The discussion has now been sufficiently lain to rest, the verdict being that Philo knew virtually no Hebrew. See David Rokeah, "A New Onomasticon Fragment from Oxyrhyncus and Philo's Etymologies," *JTS* 19 (1968): 70–82, who cites the valuable article of Jehoshua Amir ("Explanation of Hebrew Names in Philo," originally published in Hebrew [*Tarbiz* 31 (1961), 297], conveniently translated by Lester Grabbe in *Etymology in Early Jewish Interpretation*, 233–34). Of course, some have argued that Philo indeed did know Hebrew, and could author such a work. Harry Austryn Wolfson, for example, suggested that the burden of proof was on those who wish to *deny* Philo's Hebrew knowledge, concluding, "The question therefore is really not whether Philo knew Hebrew, but rather to what extent he knew it" (*Philo: Foundations of Religious Philosophy in Judaism, Christianity, and Islam* [Cambridge: Harvard University Press, 1962], 1:90).

142. Nautin, *Sur la Genèse* 1:27. Didymus knew no Hebrew (see Bärbel Kramer and Johannes Kramer, "Les éléments linguistiques hébreux chez Didyme l'Aveugle," in Ἀλεξανδρῖνα: *Hellénisme, judaïsme, et christianisme à Alexandrie* [Mélanges offerts au P. Claude Mondésert; Paris: Éditions du Cerf, 1987], 313–23).

143. Much of the material in this section has been published (Rogers, "The Philonic and the Pauline;" see also ch 8 under "Hagar and Sarah as Ethical Progress and Virtue").

(Gen 30:1). For she certainly knew that Jacob was not a creator,[144] but requested a meeting on the assumption that the saint had ceased because of the aforesaid reason in order that he might not act in vain. So he said to her, "I am not in the place of God for you, who has deprived you of the fruit of your womb, am I?" Therefore, Sarah also, being a wise and holy woman, abstained from copulation with him, since she had known for a long time that if she lay with him, she would not become pregnant. But since she knew he was able to have children, she gave her own slave girl to him to be his concubine (Gen 16:1–4). For both Sarah's temperance and absence of envy are demonstrated, as well as Abram's freedom from passion, as one drawn to this plan by his wife and not by his own desire, yielding only for the birth of children.

Therefore, the literal sense is useful, as we have discussed in detail. But the anagogical interpretation can be worked out as follows: the blessed Paul, by a typological understanding, interpeted the two women anagogically as the two covenants. Philo also, employing typology in a different way, interpreted Sarah anagogically as perfect virtue and philosophy, since she was a free and noble-born wife, cohabiting with her husband according to the laws. And virtue indeed cohabits with the sage according to the laws in order that divine offspring might be produced from it, for "Wisdom gives birth to prudence for a man" (Prov 10:23), and it is said to the pious and holy man, "Your wife flourishing like a vine ... your sons as newly-planted olive trees around your table. In this way a man who fears the Lord shall be praised" (Ps 127:3–4).

Therefore, Sarah is interpreted anagogically as perfect and spiritual virtue, but Hagar, the Egyptian slave-girl, is said by Philo to mean "the preliminary studies," but by Paul the "shadow" (Gal 4:24). For it is impossible to understand any of the spiritual or lofty conceptions without the "shadow" present in the literal sense or without the introductory aspects of the *propaideia*. For it is necessary to produce offspring from the more inferior things first. Hence they offered sacrifices according to the "shadow," they observed the Passover in a sensory fashion and circumcised in a bodily way, being led along by these things to sacrifice "a sacrifice of praise to God" (Ps 49:13), which is the same as that of the free woman. Therefore, since diligence orders the sage to go on to greater things, virtue subjects him to the divine "shadow" to make use of the introductory matters first and to produce offspring from them. For since he who is in the process of approaching virtue cannot reach perfection so as to produce offspring from it, it is advisable for him first to practice in the *propaideia* in order that he might thus advance to it completely, if he is able.[145]

---

144. The translation hearkens back to God's formation (πλάσσω) of Adam (Gen 2:7).

145. The Greek reads, Ἀνήγαγεν ταύτας ἀπόστολος εἰς τὰς δύο διαθήκας ἀλληγορίας νόμῳ· ἐπειδὴ δὲ καὶ τὸ ῥητὸν γεγένηται, καὶ αὐτὸ ἄξιον θεωρῆσαι. Οἱ ἅγιοι οὕτως συνεβίουν ὡς μὴ ἡδονὰς θηρᾶν ἀλλὰ τέκνων χάριν. Καὶ γὰρ παράδοσις τοιαύτη περὶ αὐτῶν φέρεται, ὅτι τότε μόνον συνήεσαν ταῖς γυναιξίν, ὅτε καιρὸν εἶχον συλλήψεως· οὔτε δὲ θηλαζούσῃ οὔτε τρεφούσῃ τὸ βρέφος συνήεσαν οὔτε κυοφορούσῃ· ἐν οὐδενὶ γὰρ τούτων τῶν καιρῶν οἰκείαν ἡγοῦντο τὴν σύνοδον. Βεβαιοῖ δὲ καὶ ὁ Ἰακὼβ τὴν παράδοσιν· ἐν γὰρ πολλῷ χρόνῳ δοκιμάσας ὅτι οὐκ ἐπεδέχετο ἡ Ῥαχὴλ τεκνῶσαι, οὐκέτι προσῄει αὐτῇ. ἐκείνης δ' οἰομένης ὅτι, ἐὰν προσέλθῃ αὐτῇ, τεκνοῖ, ἔλεγεν· «Ἢ δός μοι τέκνα, εἰ δὲ μή, ἀπόκτεινόν με σύ». Μὴ γὰρ οὐκ ᾔδει ὅτι οὐκ ἦν πλάστης ὁ Ἰακώβ, ἀλλὰ σύνοδον ἀπῄτει ὡς τοῦ ἁγίου

The exegetical verse for the above passage is Gen 16:1–2: "Now Sara, wife of Abram, did not bear for him. But she had an Egyptian slave girl, Hagar by name. And Sara said to Abram, 'Behold, the Lord has shut me up from bearing. Therefore, go in to my slave girl in order that you might obtain offspring by her.' And Abram obeyed the voice of Sara."[146] One might expect both Philo and Didymus to reject the literal sense of the biblical text altogether, as it contains an explicit reference to digamy.[147] Indeed, some early Christians argued on the basis of Abraham's behavior in the

---

παυσαμένου διὰ τὴν εἰρημένην αἰτίαν, ἵνα μὴ ματαιουργῇ. Ὅς δὲ πρὸς αὐτήν· «Μὴ ἀντὶ Θεοῦ σοι ἔγω εἰμι, ὃς ἐστέρησέ <σε> καρπὸν κοιλίας;»

Καὶ ἡ Σάρα οὖν, σοφὴ καὶ ἁγία οὖσα, πολλῷ χρόνῳ εἰδυῖα ὅτι συνευναζομένη οὐκ ἔλαβεν κατὰ γαστρός, ἀπέσχετο τῆς πρὸς αὐτὸν κοινωνίας καί, ἐπειδὴ ἐγίγνωσκεν ἀκόλουθον εἶναι ἔχειν ἐκεῖνον τέκνα, τὴν παιδίσκην ἑαυτῆς ἔδωκεν αὐτῷ εἰς γυναῖκα παλλακίδα. Σωφροσύνη ἅμα καὶ ἀφθονία τῆς Σάρας καὶ τοῦ Ἀβραὰμ <δείκνυται> ἀπάθεια το<ῦ> πρὸς τῆς γυναικὸς καὶ οὐκ ἀπὸ ἰδίας ὁρμῆς ἑλομένου τοῦτο ἀλλ᾽ εἴκοντος διὰ τέκνων γένεσιν.

Χρήσιμον μὲν οὖν καὶ τὸ ῥητόν, καθὰ διεξεληλύθαμεν. Ὁ δὲ τῆς ἀναγωγῆς λόγος οὕτως ἂν ἐξομαλισθείη, ὡς τύπῳ ὁ μακάριος Παῦλος εἰς τὰς δύο διαθήκας ἀνήγαγεν τὰς δύο γυναῖκας· τούτῳ καὶ Φίλων χρώμενος ἐν ἑτέροις πράγμασιν ἀνήγαγεν τὴν μὲν Σάραν εἰς τὴν τελείαν ἀρετὴν καὶ φιλοσοφίαν, αὐτὴν οὖσαν γαμετὴν ἐλευθέραν τε καὶ εὐγενίδα καὶ κατὰ νόμους σύνοικον· συνοικεῖ δὲ ἡ ἀρετὴ τῷ σοφῷ κατὰ νόμους, ἵνα θεῖα γεννήματα ἐξ αὐτῆς ἀπογεννήσῃ· «Ἡ σοφία» γὰρ «τίκτει ἀνδρὶ φρόνησιν», καὶ πρὸς τὸν εὐλαβῆ καὶ ὅσιον λέγεται· «Ἡ γυνή σου ὡς ἄμπελος εὐθηνοῦσα ***, οἱ υἱοί σου ὡς νεόφυτα ἐλαιῶν κύκλῳ τῆς τραπέζης σου. Οὕτως εὐλογηθήσεται ἄνθρωπος ὁ φοβούμενος τὸν Κύριον».

Εἰς μὲν οὖν τὴν τελείαν ἀρετὴν καὶ πνευματικὴν ἡ Σάρα ἀνάγεται, ἡ δὲ Ἀγὰρ ἡ παιδίσκη ἡ Αἰγυπτία παρὰ μὲν Φίλωνος τὰ προγυμνάσματα σημαίνειν εἴρηται, παρὰ δὲ Παύλῳ τὴν σκίαν. Ἀδύνατον γὰρ τι τῶν πνευματικῶν ἢ ὑψηλῶν νοημάτων χωρὶς τῆς κατὰ τὸ γράμμα σκιᾶς ἢ τῶν εἰσαγωγικῶν προπαιδεύσεως καταλαβεῖν· δεῖ γὰρ ἐκ τῶν ὑποδεεστέρων πρότερον τεκνοῦν. Κατὰ γοῦν τὴν σκιὰν ἐβουθύτουν, πάσχα ἐπετέλουν αἰσθητῶς καὶ περιετέμνοντο σωματικῶς, διὰ τούτων χειραγωγούμενοι ἐπὶ τὸ θύειν «τῷ Θεῷ θυσίαν αἰνέσεως», ὅπερ ἐστὶν τῆς ἐλευθέρας ἴδιον. Ἐπεὶ οὖν σπουδὴ τῷ σοφῷ τάξει χωρεῖν ἐπὶ τὰ μείζονα, ὑποβάλλει ἡ ἀρετὴ σκοπῷ θείῳ τοῖς εἰσαγωγικοῖς πρότερον χρῆσθαι καὶ ἐξ αὐτῶν τεκνοποιεῖν. Ἐπεὶ γὰρ ἄρτι προσιὼν τῇ ἀρετῇ τελειότητος ἐφάψασθαι οὐχ οἷός τε ἐστὶν ὥστε καὶ ἐξ αὐτῆς τεκνῶσαι, ὑποτίθεται αὐτῷ πρότερον ἐγγυμνάσασθαι τοῖς προπαιδεύμασιν, ἵν᾽ οὕτω καὶ αὐτὴ τελείως χωρῇ, εἰ δυνηθῇ (trans. mine).

146. Σάρα δὲ ἡ γυνὴ Ἀβράμ οὐκ ἔτικτεν αὐτῷ. ἦν δὲ αὐτῇ παιδίσκη Αἰγυπτία, ᾗ ὄνομα Ἀγάρ. εἶπεν δὲ Σάρα πρὸς Ἀβράμ Ἰδοὺ συνέκλεισέν με κύριος τοῦ μὴ τίκτειν· εἴσελθε οὖν πρὸς τὴν παιδίσκην μου, ἵνα τεκνοποιήσῃς [Didymus has τεκνοποιήσω] ἐξ αὐτῆς. ὑπήκουσεν δὲ Ἀβράμ τῆς φωνῆς Σάρας.

147. The basis would be, of course, the unseemliness of the text at face value. Aristotle, in his *Poetics* 1460b–1461b, had formulated "five categories from which critical objections are drawn:" (1) ἀδύνατα ("impossibilities"); (2) ἄλογα ("absurdities"); (3) βλαβερά ("morally harmful things"); (4) ὑπεναντία ("contradictions"); and (5) [τὰ] παρὰ τὴν ὀρθότητα τὴν κατὰ τέχνην ("things contrary to artistic correctness"). The above text could have fit into number (3) above, and therefore, could have been justified for allegorical interpretation (on the whole issue of προβλήματα in ancient texts, see A. Gudeman, "Λύσεις," *PRE* 13.2 [1927]: cols 2511–29, and especially cols. 216–17 on Aristotle).

passage that polygamy was valid.[148] Despite the potential moral implications, however, both Philo and Didymus, among others, retain the literal, "plain sense" of the text.[149]

In his treatment of Gen 16:1–2, Philo usually prefers to offer his allegorical understanding, but does not deny the text its literal meaning.[150] Likewise, Didymus insists that the literal sense (τὸ ῥητόν) in these verses is "worthy of investigation" (ἄξιον θεωρῆσαι) and "useful" (χρήσιμος), but spends the majority of his energy expounding on the allegorical sense. Philo and Didymus interpret this passage literally because they believe a moral lesson can be derived from it. Both Philo and Didymus argue that sexual activity must be motivated only by the desire to produce offspring.[151] Didymus even cites a certain "tradition" (παράδοσις) in confirmation.[152] If a woman

---

148. See Tertullian, *Mon.* 6 and Theodoret, *Quaestiones in Genesim* 68. Tertullian takes up the argument of Paul from Rom 4 and Gal 3 that Abraham was justified by faith *before* circumcision (arguing the point from Gen 15:6 prior to the institution of circumcision in Gen 17:10–14). Since the digamy of the patriarch was also posterior to his justification by faith, then anyone who wishes to follow Abraham in digamy must also admit circumcision.

149. Albert Henrichs appears to be only partially correct when he states, "To Jews and Christians alike, monogamy was the only acceptable relationship between man and woman. To accept this passage in its literal sense was beyond their capacity" ("Philosophy, the Handmaiden of Theology," *GRBS* 9 [1968]: 437–50, 439). However, at least some Jewish sources seem to permit polygamy. Polygamy, at least for men, was not banned by the rabbis. It is true that, in the Talmud, there is "not one [rabbi] who is mentioned as having lived in polygamy" (J. H. Greenstone, "Polygamy," in the *Jewish Encyclopedia* 10:120–22, 121). But avoidance of multiple wives may have been motivated by economic factors as much as anything else. Yet, it should be noted that rabbinic law was different for men than women. The latter are expressly forbidden from taking multiple partners (see B.-Z. Schereschewsky and M. Elon, "Bigamy and Polygamy," *Encyclopedia Judaica*2 3:691–94, 691).

150. See, e.g., *Abr.* 248–54; *QG* 3.20.

151. For Philo, see especially *Spec.* 3.34 (see also *Spec.* 3.313; cf. *QG* 4.86). On the issue, see Richard A. Baer, *Philo's Use of the Categories Male and Female* (Leiden: Brill, 1970), and esp. Kathy L. Gaca, "Philo's Principles of Sexual Conduct and their Influence on Christian Platonist Sexual Principles," *SPhiloA* 8 (1996): 21–39, who argues that Philo derives the idea from Pythagorean sources.

152. Didymus claims that "The saints cohabit not as though hunting after pleasure, but for the sake of procreation. For such a tradition [παράδοσις] is handed down concerning them, that they would go in to their wives only when it was time for conception" (*Comm. Gen.* 235.1–5). He goes on to argue that Jacob abstained from intercourse with Rachel once he discovered that she was barren (235.8–15), and Abraham did the same with Sarah (235.16–20). The rabbis regard the time before the flood as a time when men would take two wives, one for procreation and the other for sexual pleasure (Gen. Rab. 23.2). But the command to "be fruitful and multiply" (Gen 1:28) was taken to be all-encompassing so that one who "brings forth the seed in vain" is guilty of sin (b. Nid. 13a).

could not bear children, then her husband must not sleep with her, since he would be following πάθος and ἡδονή.[153]

As a result of their position on marital intercourse, both Philo and Didymus present Sarah as a paragon of virtue who withdraws herself from her husband since she knows she cannot bear children.[154] This position stands in contrast to the rabbinic sources, which are decisively against celibacy for any reason.[155] Nevertheless, in both Philo and Didymus Sarah's behavior leads to the conclusion that Sarah assented to the prohibition of nonprocreative intercourse, and thus her act of proposing Hagar, literally interpreted, is justifiable.[156]

Now, we turn to the allegorical interpretation. The technique Didymus employs in the above passage is highly unusual, for he weaves together the allegorical interpretations of Paul and Philo without showing even a hint of favoritism for Paul over Philo.[157] He then ignores the focal point of Paul's allegorical exegesis altogether.[158] In Gal 3:1–4:31, Paul is in the midst of

---

153. Philo may have derived the position from Pythagorean sources, as Gaca argues ("Philo's Principles"). She cites one passage as follows: "One must leave as permissible only those [sex acts] that are for the purpose of temperate and lawful reproduction of children" (*Vit. Pyth.* 210; cited in Gaca, 23). Another passage which is closer to our text above comes from a certain "Charondas," who defines semen as "the seed of a man's children," and argues that "nature made [this] seed for the sake of children, not for pleasure" (62.30–33, cited in Gaca, 24). Of the Stoic moralists, only Musonius Rufus upholds the doctrine, and "Philo and Clement are the only moralists who share it" (A. C. Van Geytenbach, *Musonius Rufus and Greek Diatribe* [Assen: Van Gorcum, 1962], 73, qtd. in David Winston, "Philo and the Rabbis on Sex and the Body," *Poetics Today* 19 [1998]: 41–62, 58 n. 26).

154. Didymus argues the same for Jacob and Rachel, suggesting that Jacob, "having proven for a long time that Rachel was not allowed to bear a child, no longer approached her" (*Comm. Gen.* 235.9). I cannot find a parallel to this interpretation in the extant works of Philo.

155. See Immanuel Jakobovits, "Celibacy," in *Encyclopedia Judaica*2 4:537. Jakobovits notes the Essene practice of celibacy and the case of Simeon ben Azzai who states, "My soul is fond of the Law; the world will be perpetuated by others" (b. Yev. 63b), as exceptions.

156. Sarah is ascribed σωφροσύνη and ἀφθονία and Abram ἀπάθεια in Didymus (*Comm. Gen.* 235.20–22). Philo composes a speech for Sarah (*Abr.* 248–52) in which she advocates a prohibition of nonprocreative intercourse.

157. Manlio Simonetti curiously argues that Didymus *rejects* the Pauline interpretation in favor of the Philonic ("Lettera e allegoria," 355). A more nuanced position is that of Runia, who states, "Didymus regards the Philonic and Pauline interpretations as of equal validity and weight, coalescing them into a single interpretation" (*Philo in Early Christian Literature*, 202). For an attempt to explain the harmonization see Rogers, "The Philonic and the Pauline."

158. The relevant portion reads, "For it is written that Abraham had two sons, one by a slave and one by a free woman. But the son of the slave was born according to the flesh, the son of the free woman through promise. Now this is an allegory: these women are two

what Hans Dieter Betz regards as his sixth and strongest argument against Christian adherence to the law of Moses.[159] Beginning in 4:21, Paul attempts to argue that Hagar allegorically represents the law of Moses. Since she was a slave, her children (observant Jews) are slaves as well. Sarah, on the other hand, was free. She apparently represents the law of Christ and the freedom Christians under the new covenant share.

The Pauline interpretation of Hagar and Sarah played, and certainly continues to play, a significant role in Jewish-Christian relations.[160] From an early period, Christians interpreted Paul's allegory with reference to God's rejection of the Jewish people.[161] However, it would appear that Didymus has little use for the Pauline allegory. He does not appear to battle Jewish opponents, and thus would not need to refute them.[162] For this reason, he turns to Philo's more useful allegorical application.

---

covenants. One is from Mount Sinai, bearing children for slavery; she is Hagar. Now Hagar is Mount Sinai in Arabia; she corresponds to the present Jerusalem, for she is in slavery with her children. But the Jerusalem above is free, and she is our mother" (Gal 4:22–26, RSV).

159. Hans Dieter Betz, *Galatians* (Hermeneia; Philadelphia: Fortress, 1979), 238–40.

160. See the history of reception in J. Louis Martyn, *Galatians* (AB 33A; New York: Doubleday, 1997), 27–41.

161. E.g., Marcion, who placed Gal first in his Pauline canon and drew the ultimate distinction between the Old and New Testaments (see Martyn, *Galatians*, 34). See also Tertullian, *Marc.* 5.4.8, who refers the allegory to the Christian church and the Jewish synagogue. Origen directs the allegory more toward the Jewish interpretation of scripture (i.e., the literal interpretation) than to the Jewish religion (*Hom. Gen.* 7.2-4). However, Origen's argument does have a anti-synagogual tone: "Is not the spiritual and mystical meaning in these words clearer than light, that that people which is 'according to the flesh' [Gal 4:23] is abandoned and lies in hunger and thirst, suffering 'not a famine of bread nor a thirst for water, but a thirst for the word of God' [cf. Amos 8:11], until the eyes of the synagogue are opened?" Then a few lines later he says, "For now the Jews lie around the well itself [i.e. the scriptures], but their eyes are closed and they cannot drink from the well of the Law and the prophets" (*Hom. Gen.* 7.6, trans. Ronald E. Heine, *Origen: Homilies on Genesis and Exodus* [FC 71; Washington, D.C.: Catholic University of America Press, 1982], 134, 137).

162. It is unclear whether the monastic environment in which Didymus taught isolated him from the political and religious pandemonium of Alexandria. Certainly during his lifetime the Church and the Synagogue were at odds. Tcherikover notes that "Towards A.D. 300 Jewish names become more frequent in the papyri and we gain the impression that all reminders of the events of A.D. 115–17 had at last vanished and Jewish life in Egypt was about to reawaken" (*CPJ* 1:96). Jewish life reawakened indeed. It was during the fourth century that the Jews began to make attempts to disrupt Christian life, such as supporting the Arians. For instance, the Jews, along with pagans, "broke into churches plundered sanctuaries, and insulted monks and nuns" (this occurred after Gregorius was appointed to succeed Athanasius as bishop in 335 CE). The Jews also participated in the expulsion of the bishop Petrus in favor of the Arian bishop Lucius (*op. cit.* 97–98). All of this seems to indicate that throughout the lifetime of Didymus Jews joined pagans as open

Philo asserts that Hagar and Sarah represent preliminary or encyclical studies (προπαιδεία/ἐγκύκλιος παιδεία) and virtue (ἀρετή), respectively. This doctrine is among the most common themes in the works of Philo, and serves as the foundation for an entire treatise, which asserts an exegesis of Gen 16:1–6 (*Congr.*). We shall attempt to highlight the peculiarities of this theme in an effort to explain why the Philonic interpretation becomes so ubiquitous in Alexandrian Christianity (particularly with Clement, Origen, and Didymus).

First of all, the groundwork for Philo's interpretation had already been laid in the Homeric scholarship of Hellenistic times. The inspiration for Philo's allegory of Hagar and Sarah can be traced to the Hellenistic interpretation of the *Odyssey*. First, we have the analogy between preliminary education and philosophy, and Penelope and her slave girls.[163] Stobaeus preserves a fragment from Ariston of Chios (ca. 250 BCE) which reads, "Ariston of Chios used to say that those who labor with the preliminary studies but neglect philosophy are like the suitors of Penelope who, when they failed to win her over, became involved with the slave girls."[164] Henrichs theorizes that Ariston intended merely to draw a comparison, and never intended to allegorize.[165] This may be true, but it is easy to see how such thinking could be turned from comparison into interpretation. Just as the suitors were distracted by the handmaidens (preliminary education), and thus lost sight of Penelope (wisdom), so Abraham became entangled with Hagar, preventing him from engaging Sarah.

Another, even more likely, consideration may have drawn Philo to the allegorical understanding of the *Odyssey*. In Homer's epic, Calypso holds Odysseus captive for seven years before he is permitted to leave Ogygia.[166] In Hellenistic interpretation, Calypso represents the sage's struggle to linger in the sciences of astronomy and astrology.[167] Odysseus is able to break away from these preliminary studies and advance to philosophy, or

---

opponents of the ever-increasing Christian influence. Toward the end of the fourth and early fifth century the Jewish-Christian conflict came to a head under Cyril of Alexandria, culminating in Jewish expulsion from Alexandria in the year 415 CE (see *op. cit.*, 98–99).

163. See Rogers, "The Philonic and the Pauline," 64–65.

164. Ἀρίστων ὁ Χῖος τοὺς περὶ τὰ ἐγκύκλια μαθήματα πονουμένους, ἀμελοῦντας δὲ φιλοσοφίας, ἔλεγεν ὁμοίους εἶναι τοῖς μνηστῆρσι τῆς Πηνελόπης, οἳ ἀποτυγχάνοντες ἐκείνης περὶ τὰς θεραπαίνας ἐγίνοντο (*SVF* 1:350). Von Arnim also lists different versions of a similar statement, which Henrichs traces to Aristotle, Aristippus, and Bion (see "Philosophy, the Handmaid," 444).

165. Ibid.

166. *Od.* 7.259–60.

167. See the discussion of Felix Buffière, *Les mythes d'Homère et la pensée grecque* (Paris: Les Belles Lettres, 1956), 388–91.

Penelope. Abraham, being from "Ur of the Chaldeans," was, according to Philo, steeped in the astral sciences. But he moved beyond these to a contemplation of God.[168] Hence Abraham could be viewed as a proto-Odysseus, representing the journey of the soul from the encyclical disciplines to philosophy.[169] The groundwork is thus set by the interpretation of Homer. Abraham must advance beyong his Chaldean learning (Hagar) to philosophy (Sarah), just as Odysseus had to advance from Calypso to reach Penelope.

Second, Philo proposes that just as Abraham must mate with Hagar before he can advance to Sarah, the student must mate with preliminary studies before he can advance to virtue (*Congr.* 9–12).[170] It was well-established at the time of Philo that encyclical studies are a necessary preparation for philosophy.[171] In fact, Willy Theiler argued that both Philo and Seneca depend on a similar source for much of their knowledge of the liberal arts.[172] The majority opinion at the turn of the Common Era seems to be that of Seneca: the encyclical studies are necessary but not sufficient for virtue.[173] Just as Seneca, Philo believes that the encyclical studies are necessary, but his view is slightly modified.

As Alan Mendelson writes, "He [Philo] endows the encyclia with inherent spiritual value; this position represents a significant shift in the history of liberal studies."[174] One may question what Mendelson means by "spiritual value." If he is referring to the idea that the encyclical studies serve the student in understanding scripture, then Philo is perhaps the first representative of this position. If, however, Mendelson is referring to the

---

168. See *Migr.* 177–87; *Congr.* 49–50; *Ebr.* 94; *Somn.* 1.53.

169. Philo quotes *Od.* 4.392 in *Migr.* 195, possibly reflecting a knowledge of the Hellenistic allegory.

170. Note especially the way Philo summarizes the paragraph: "Mind desires to have children by virtue, and, if it cannot do so at once, is instructed to espouse virtue's handmaid, the lower instruction" (*Congr.* 12).

171. On the history of this position, see the discussion in Alfred Stückelberger, *Senecas 88. Brief: Über Wert und Unwert der Freien Künste* (Heidelberg: Winter, 1965), 60–68.

172. Theiler observes, "Für den 88. Brief ist in senecaischer Bearbeitung und Stilisierung ein vorposeidonische Vorlage anzunehmen, der auch Philo *de congressu eruditionis gratia* gefolgt ist" (*Poseidonios: Die Fragmente* [TK 10; Berlin: de Gruyter, 1982], 2:383). Older scholarship tended to assume that the source for the propaideutic value of encyclical studies was Posidonius (see Stückelberger, *op. cit.*, 60).

173. See *Epist.* 88.2 and esp. §20, which reads, 'Quid ergo? nihil nobis liberalia conferunt studia?' Ad alia multum, ad virtutem nihil.... 'Quare ergo liberalibus studiis filios erudimus?' Non quia virtutem dare possunt; sed quia animum ad accipiendam virtutem praeparant."

174. Alan Mendelson, *Secular Education in Philo of Alexandria* (Cincinnati: Hebrew Union College Press, 1982), xxiv.

application of encyclical studies to "theology," then he is most certainly incorrect. Posidonius had applied the encyclia to one's search for σοφία or ἀρετή,¹⁷⁵ which was equivalent to "theology," even for the fathers.¹⁷⁶ It is likely that this position is pre-Posidonian,¹⁷⁷ and thus Philo would be dependent on the Stoic tradition.¹⁷⁸

Third, Philo cites as confirmation of his allegory the etymologies of the names of Sarah and Hagar. The former means "sovereignty of me."¹⁷⁹ According to Philo, the only "sovereignty" to which the text can refer is virtue herself, since she alone is truly sovereign over the mind.¹⁸⁰ Hagar, on the other hand, means "sojourning."¹⁸¹ This indicates to Philo that one must not linger with Hagar, the μέση παιδεία, but only sojourn therein. Another helpful element is Philo's consistent allegorization of Egypt as "the body."¹⁸² Hagar is from Egypt, and the body (through the eyes, ears, and the other senses) is involved in accessing the preliminary studies.¹⁸³ Once the student has progressed through the circuit of intermediate studies, only then is he prepared to leave the body and advance to virtue.¹⁸⁴

In two different passages in the Tura commentaries, Didymus follows the Philonic allegorical interpretation of Abraham and Sarah. In our survey of Philonic references above, we introduced a passage from the *Comm. Eccl.* in which Didymus follows Philo's allegorical theme of Hagar

---

175. Several scholars believe that Posidonius had modified the traditional Stoic definition of σοφία as ἐπιστήμη θείων καὶ ἀνθρωπίνων καὶ τῶν τούτων αἰτίων (see Max Pohlenz, *Die Stoa* 1:214, 2:106).

176. None of the Alexandrian interpreters from Philo to Didymus typically speak of "theology," but rather of the more philosophical terms σοφία, ἀρετή, etc. (Henrichs, "Philosophy, the Handmaiden," 441).

177. See Stückelberger, *Senecas 88. Brief,* 64–68.

178. Recently, Hent de Vries has argued that Philo's *Congr.* completely revolutionized the Greek concept of the ἐγκύκλιος παιδεία, and that his influence can be felt, albeit indirectly, throughout the history of education. See his "Philosophia Ancilla Theologiae," trans. Jack Ben-Levi, *The Bible and Critical Theory* 5 (2009): 41.1–41.19.

179. This is Colson's translation of ἀρχή μου. In the context of *Congr.* 2 this translation is the best one (see also *Cher.* 7; *Mut.* 77).

180. Philo apparently inherited the connection between Sarah and virtue from certain φυσικοὶ ἄνδρες (*Abr.* 99).

181. The Greek is παροίκησις (*Congr.* 20).

182. E.g., *Leg.* 2.77; *Sacr.* 48; *Post.* 62. On the issue in general see Sarah J. K. Pearce, *The Land of the Body: Studies in Philo's Representation of Egypt* (WUNT 208; Tübingen: Mohr Siebeck, 2007).

183. *Congr.* 20–21. See Pearce, 81–127.

184. Posidonius, ap. Seneca, *Epist.* 88 21–23, divided education into four "arts": (1) *artes vulgares* (= manual labor); (2) *artes ludicrae* (= entertainment); (3) *artes pueriles* (= artes liberales/ἐγκύκλιοι τέχναι); (4) *artes überae* (= for those concerned with ἀρετή). See Stückelberger, *op. cit.,* 52–55. Philo is concerned only with the third and fourth stages.

and Sarah. We shall consider this passage in greater detail here and then we will return to the analogous passage in the *Comm. Gen.* translated above.

Commenting on Eccl 9:9a,[185] Didymus introduces Prov 5:18b.[186] Although the text is fragmentary, we can get a picture of the exegesis Didymus applied. After stating that "the wife of your youth" refers to "true wisdom" or "true ethical virtue," Didymus adds, "But it is necessary [to go] 'to another wife,' [that is] to external wisdom, for a little while."[187] After several more fragmentary lines, Didymus introduces the name of Philo:

> And according to this Philo understood the ... [188] to give birth before perfect virtue. For if one does not beget from these lesser women, he cannot become father of undefiled works and of the contemplations of wisdom. The same thing the Apostle calls 'letter' and 'spirit' [2 Cor 3:6]. And it is impossible to understand the things belonging to the *anagoge* without meticulously investigating the things belonging to the *historia*.[189]

Didymus goes on to conclude his discussion by stating that Prov is not merely composed of obscurities (παροιμιῶδες), but has merit when interpreted literally as well.[190] Indeed the literal interpretation is the foundation for the spiritual.[191]

Didymus knows the interpretation he cites is Philonic, for he says as much. If more of the text had survived we could say more about how the Philonic allegory is developed here. As the text stands, we have several key components: (1) the framework of "external wisdom" as preparatory for "virtue"; (2) the identification of wives with virtue; (3) the turn to a

---

185. The text reads, "See life with the wife whom you have loved all the days of your vain life" (ἰδὲ ζωὴν μετὰ γυναικὸς ἧς ἠγάπησας πάσας ἡμέρας ζωῆς ματαιότητός σου).

186. The text reads, "rejoice with the wife of your youth" (συνευφραίνου μετὰ γυναικὸς τῆς ἐκ νεότητός σου).

187. The Greek reads, δεῖ δὲ καὶ "πρὸς ἀλλοτρίαν" ὀλίγως [ἰέναι, τουτέστιν] πρὸς τὴν ἔξωθεν σοφίαν (*Comm. Eccl.* 276.15–16; trans. mine).

188. The Greek is illegible. Gronewald hypothesizes Ἀγα<ρ> in his apparatus criticus, but has . .αν in the text. Henrichs attempts to tentatively substitute the term ταμίαν ("Philosophy, the Handmaiden," 449), but there is no space for it in the papyrus, as Gronewald states (16).

189. The Greek reads, καὶ κατὰ τοῦτο ὁ Φίλων ἐξέλαβεν τὴ[ν] . .αν προτίκτει[ν] τῆς ἀρετῆς τῆς τελείας· εἰ μὴ γάρ τις τέκῃ ἐκ τούτων τῶ[ν μ]ικρῶν, οὐ δ[ύ]ν[ατ]αι π(ατ)ὴρ τῶν ἔργων τῶν ἀμιάντων καὶ τῶν θεωρημάτων τῆς σοφίας γενέσθαι. τὸ δὲ αὐτὸ τοῦτο ὁ ἀπόστολος 'γράμμα' καὶ 'πν(εῦμ)α' λέγ[ει· κ]αὶ ἀδύνατόν ἐστιν τὰ τῆς ἀναγωγῆς νοῆσαι μὴ ἀκριβώσαντα τὰ τῆς ἱστ[ορία]ς (trans. mine).

190. The term παροιμία in patristic literature often carries the meaning "dark saying" (Origen, *Cels.* 4.87; Gregory of Nyssa, *Eun.* 3; see Lampe, s.v. παροιμία). Didymus, as Origen, regularly turns to the Solomonic trilogy as paradigmatic for ethical progress (Origen, *Comm. Cant.* praef.; Bayliss, *The Vision of Didymus*, 81).

191. See Bayliss, *The Vision of Didymus*, 81–83.

prooftext from Prov. All of these moves are characteristic of Clement's treatment of the theme.[192] But these alone are not enough to determine whether Didymus depends on Clement, or if he is making deductions similar to those of Clement on the basis of his own reading of Philo. Even if Didymus depends on Clement here, he at least recognized Clement's original source.[193] Despite the importance placed on the theme of secular education in Alexandrian patristic literature, Didymus could look through the centuries and identify the allegory with Philo.

Turning to the allegorical interpretation in the *Comm. Gen.*, we find a distinctively Philonic interpretation mixed with citations of the Solomonic works. The first feature Didymus cites as Philonic is that Sarah refers to "perfect virtue and philosophy." Philo characteristically identifies Sarah with "virtue," but less commonly with "perfect virtue."[194] Sarah can also be associated with philosophy in Philo, but the theme is not common.[195] Didymus also calls attention to Sarah as "the free and noble-born wife." The Stoics regarded the wise man alone as free and well-born.[196] Philo adopts and develops the Stoic doctrine, even writing a tractate about the subject.[197] In addition, the pair εὐγένεια and ἐλευθερία and their cognates occur together fourteen times in the extant writings of Philo.[198] Neither of these descriptions, however, is applied to Sarah. Perhaps this is because the Stoics generally regarded the wise *man* as free, and did not speak consistently of the female sage. In any case, broadly speaking, Didymus's description is sufficiently paralleled in Philo.

The idea of virtue "living in the house" (συνοικέω) with the sage is also Philonic.[199] It appears that the term "house" can occasionally be allegorized as "virtue."[200] The "soul" can also be interpreted as a "house" or

---

192. See Van den Hoek, *Clement*, 24–26, and now "Clement of Alexandria and the Book of Proverbs."

193. Clement mentions Philo's name once in this context, but only for an etymology (*Strom.* 1.31.1). Therefore, it does not seem reasonable to imagine that Didymus could have deduced the Philonic origin of the allegory by reading Clement alone.

194. See *Leg.* 3.244; *Post.* 130.

195. See *Congr.* 77-79, and esp. §79 where Philo states that the ἐγκύκλια contribute to φιλοσοφία and φιλοσοφία contributes to σοφία.

196. See *SVF* 3:365; 3:594.

197. The *Prob.*

198. E.g., *Agr.* 59; *Ebr.* 58; *Migr.* 67.

199. E.g., *Prob.* 107: "For having inured the soul from the first to hold aloof through love of knowledge from association with the passions, and to cleave to culture and wisdom, they set it wandering away from the body and brought it to make its home [συνοικέω] with wisdom and courage and the other virtues" (trans. PLCL 9:73). Cf. also *Det.* 59.

200. See *Leg.* 3.2; *Cher.* 49.

"tent."²⁰¹ Didymus suggests that the sage (Abraham) lives with virtue (Sarah) in order to produce "divine offspring" (θεῖα γεννήματα).²⁰² This doctrine accords with the literal interpretation of both Philo and Didymus, reviewed above, that a couple can come together only for the purpose of producing offspring. The same applies allegorically. According to Philo the soul can produce either the offspring of virtue or the offspring of pleasure.²⁰³ While the exact phrase θεῖα γεννήματα is not used in Philo, the equivalent phrase θεῖα σπέρματα does occur.²⁰⁴

Earlier we saw that Didymus cites Philo as describing Sarah in terms of "perfect virtue and philosophy." Here he adds a third, but related, description of Sarah as "pneumatic virtue." This terminology does not occur anywhere in the writings of Philo, and Philo normally uses the adjective πνευματικός in a materialistic sense.²⁰⁵ Next Didymus turns to his second citation of Philo in this block of interpretation. He says that Philo understands Hagar to be "preliminary studies," but Paul understands her to be a "shadow." Didymus then takes the term "shadow" (σκιά) and combines it with the Philonic interpretation: "For it is impossible to understand any of the pneumatic or lofty conceptions without the shadow which is in accord with the letter *or* without the introductory matters of the *propaideia*."

Didymus makes the argument that both "the letter" (τὸ γράμμα) and secular education are necessary to arrive at the πνευματικὰ ἢ ὑψηλὰ νοήματα. But what does Didymus mean by τὸ γράμμα? In Origenian vocabulary, τὸ γράμμα can refer to the literal, surface-level interpretation. His justification for this view is 2 Cor 3:6b: "the letter kills, but the spirit gives life" (τὸ γὰρ γράμμα ἀποκτέννει, τὸ δὲ πνεῦμα ζῳοποιεῖ), which Origen takes to mean that the spiritual interpretation is superior to the literal.²⁰⁶ On the other hand, τὸ γράμμα + adjective can refer to "scripture" as a whole.²⁰⁷ Especially when the term "shadow" occurs in connection with τὸ γράμμα, we are inclined to

---

201. E.g., *Leg.* 2.61; 3.239; *Det.* 59. The contrast between a "house" and a "tent" is common in Didymus as well (*Comm. Ps.* 58.9–15; 96.16–18; *Comm. Job* 149.25–150.4).

202. On the topic of good and bad offspring, see the discussion on *Comm. Gen.* 119.2–10 above.

203. *Leg.* 2.48; cf. *Congr.* 6.

204. *Cher.* 46.

205. See *Opif.* 67; *Abr.* 113; *Aet.* 86. Four times he speaks of τόνος as πνευματική (*Her.* 242; *Praem.* 48; *Aet.* 125; *QG* 2:3). The noun πνεῦμα, on the other hand, is frequently interpreted in terms of the πνοή of Gen 2:7. On the tension between Philo's two conceptions of "spirit," see David T. Runia, *On the Creation of the Cosmos according to Moses: Introduction, Translation and Commentary* (PACS 1; Atlanta: Society of Biblical Literature, 2001), 166–67.

206. See *Comm. Jo.* 10.26; 13.8.

207. See Lampe, s.v. "γράμμα."

think of the law. If that is what Didymus intends here then he is much closer to the thought of Clement, for whom both secular education and the Mosaic law were propaideutic (see below).

In the *Comm. Gen.* Didymus shows an awareness of both the Clementine and the Origienian understandings of τὸ γράμμα. In *Comm. Gen.* 244.8–11 Didymus seems to reflect the Clementine understanding: "For the Lord also understood that the things in the scriptures [γράμματα] that belong to the shadow would gradually cease to be by saying, 'What to me is the multitude of your sacrifices?' [Isa 1:11] and 'I will not eat the flesh of bulls nor drink the blood of goats? Sacrifice to God a sacrifice of praise and offer to the Most High your prayers [Ps 49:13–14].'"[208] Here it is clear that the Pauline meaning of σκιά is at work and the term γράμμα refers to the Mosaic law. But in *Comm. Gen.* 242.10–11 Didymus teaches, "Moreover, he who approaches divine instruction [θεία παίδευσις] ought to approach it in this way so as to understand it according to the letter, giving way to the spirit gradually."[209] This latter passage comes at the end of a description of Sarah as "virtue and the spiritual sense" (ἡ ἀρετὴ καὶ πνευματικὴ νόησις) and Hagar as "the introductory and shadowy" (ἡ εἰσαγωγικὴ καὶ σκιώδης).[210] Here it seems that Didymus intends the Origenian dichotomy between "letter" and "spirit."

So what is the sense of γράμμα in our text above? It would appear that Didymus agrees more with the interpretation of Clement than that of Origen. He speaks of offering sacrifices, observing the Passover and circumcision as preparatory for "a sacrifice of praise." These acts cannot be literal observances to be imposed on the church. Rather, it must be that (1) either Didymus is speaking historically (as is Paul) of the role the law played in leading people to Christ,[211] or (2) he is interpreting the law as a code of ethics, as Clement does.[212] So the "sacrifice of praise" is linked with

---

208. The exegetical verse is Gen 16:9. The Greek reads, Καὶ γὰρ Κύριος τὰ ἐν τοῖς γράμμασιν τῆς σκιᾶς ἠρέμα ὑπέβαλλε[ν] ἀφίστασθαι αὐτῆς διὰ τοῦ λέγειν· «Τί μοι πλῆθος τῶν θυσιῶν ὑμῶν;» καὶ «Μὴ φάγομαι κρέας ταύρων καὶ αἷμα τράγων πίομαι; Θῦσον τῷ Θεῷ θυσίαν αἰνέσεως καὶ ἀπόδος τῷ Ὑψίστῳ τὰς εὐχάς σου» (trans. mine).

209. The Greek reads, Ὁ προσερχόμενος τοίνυν τῇ θείᾳ παιδεύσει οὕτως αὐτῇ προσέχεσθαι ὀφείλει ὡς νοῆσαι αὐτὴν κατὰ γράμμα καὶ πνεῦμα ὁδῷ καὶ τάξει χωροῦντα. The term "gradually" translates ὁδῷ καὶ τάξει (cf. Nautin's "progressivement," *Sur la Genèse* 2:217).

210. The exegetical passage is Gen 16:7–8.

211. Hence the Law is a παιδαγωγός (Gal 3:24–25).

212. See *Strom.* 2.18 and Van den Hoek's discussion of Philo's *Virt.* as used by Clement in *Clement of Alexandria*, 112–114. Philo, it should be pointed out, speaks in favor of a literal observance of the Law, whereas Clement does not (*Migr.* 89–93; on the question in general see Montgomery J. Shroyer, "Alexandrian Jewish Literalists," *JBL* 55 [1936]: 261–84, and David H. Hay, "References to Other Exegetes," in *Both Literal and Allegorical:*

Sarah, the free woman, and hence with virtue. So Didymus ultimately seems to link the Pauline idea with the theory of Clement. In this immediate context, virtue is Christian wisdom and the shadow is the law. So the law is propaideutic, leading the προκόπτων toward wisdom in Christ.

Didymus does not fully work out the position he has created. To argue that, historically, the law led people to Christ is one thing. But to argue that one must *keep the law* (the shadow) in order to prepare himself for Christ would be untenable for an author such as Didymus. For this reason, Didymus must intend to suggest that the law provides an ethical basis for virtue, and thus reminds us of Clement. It is probably for this reason that Didymus argues elsewhere that the literal interpretation of the law (τὸ γράμμα), and not the keeping of the law itself, is preliminary for perfect virtue in Christ.[213]

As we have noted, this section of exegesis seems to be influenced by Clement of Alexandria, who adopts the Philonic allegory. Clement understands philosophy to hold the significance for the Greeks that the law held for the Jews.[214] Therefore, from Clement's perspective, both Greek philosophy and the Mosaic law are necessary to prepare one for Christ, who is true wisdom. Philo prefers to speak of "virtue" where Clement would speak of "wisdom," and Philo regards the law as perfect whereas Clement would regard it as imperfect, but the basic scheme is the same.[215]

So much for the interpretation of τὸ γράμμα. One final question must be addressed: from where does Didymus receive his version of the Hagar-Sarah allegory? We have already seen in the other passages surveyed above that Didymus has a *direct knowledge* of Philo. But each passage must be evaluated independently. Is Didymus dependent on Clement or Origen for the Sarah-Hagar theme? On the one hand, Didymus cites Philo directly twice in his discussion. This would lead us to believe that he is in direct contact with Philo. On the other hand, the Hagar-Sarah theme is common in Alexandrian exegesis, and Clement explicitly cites Philo in his application of it. This means that Didymus does not need to go to Philo

---

Studies in Philo of Alexandria's Questions and Answers on Genesis and Exodus [ed. David H. Hay; BJS 232; Atlanta: Scholar's Press, 1991], 81–97).

213. See *Comm. Gen.* 236.8–11; 242.7–11, lines 9–10 of which are translated above. This does not hold consistently, however. Didymus argues in *Comm. Zach.* 189.6–8 that the discussion of fasting in Zech 8:19 is meant both as a literal observance, which informs and contextualizes the allegorical understanding of fasting, namely, avoiding the teachings of heretics.

214. *Strom.* 1.5.28.1–3.

215. For this description of the different nuances in the application of the Hagar-Sarah theme in Philo and Clement, I am dependent on Eric Osborn, *Clement of Alexandria*, 90–91.

directly for this material. He could easily lift it from one of his Christian predecessors, citing Philo as the ultimate source of the allegory. So what does the evidence suggest? Let us examine the applications of the Hagar-Sarah theme in Clement and Origen, and we shall draw conclusions regarding the allegory in Didymus.

We are certain that Didymus knew Clement, as he mentions him by name.[216] Didymus mentions Origen as well.[217] Therefore, it seems possible, *a priori*, that Didymus received the Philonic interpretation of Sarah and Hagar by means of the Alexandrian Christian tradition and not from Philo directly, especially since Clement had already made the Philonic connection explicit.[218]

First, few themes are as important to Clement as his teaching that philosophy and Greek culture prepare the student for Christian scholarship. He devotes a significant portion of the first book of *Stromateis* to this theme, and Clement is heavily influenced by Philo for the explication of his doctrine.[219] Annewies Van den Hoek isolates three "components" of Clement's argument: (1) "the theme, as described in Clement's own words;" (2) "quotations from Proverbs;" and (3) "Quotations and reminiscences of Philo's *De Congressu*."[220] As we shall explain in greater detail below, elements (2) and (3) apply to Didymus as well.

In *Strom.* 1.30.1–2, Clement writes, "But as the cycle of studies contributes to philosophy, their mistress, so also philosophy itself co-operates for the acquisition of wisdom. For philosophy is the study <of wisdom> and wisdom is the knowledge of things divine and human and their causes. Wisdom is therefore mistress of philosophy, as philosophy is of preparatory education."[221] The entire paragraph is lifted from Philo's *Congr.* 79. Here Clement is stating Philo's general premise, which he reinforces in *Strom.* 1.30.3–4: "And scripture will afford a testimony to what has been said by

---

216. *Comm. Eccl.* 7.34.
217. *In 1 Cor* 16:17–18.
218. Henrichs demonstrates that the Philonic interpretation of Hagar and Sarah is present in each of the great Alexandrian fathers ("Philosophy, the Handmaiden of Theology," 437–50).
219. Van den Hoek devotes an entire chapter of her study to this theme, regarding it as one of the "four blocks" of Clement's use of Philo (see *Clement of Alexandria*, 23–47).
220. Van den Hoek, *Clement of Alexandria*, 24.
221. I cite here the translation of Van den Hoek because she usefully italicizes the phrases that are direct quotations from Philo (*Clement of Alexandria*, 31). The Greek reads, Ἀλλ' ὡς τὰ ἐγκύκλια μαθήματα συμβάλλεται πρὸς φιλοσοφίαν τὴν δέσποιναν αὐτῶν, οὕτω καὶ φιλοσοφία αὐτὴ πρὸς σοφίας κτῆσιν συνεργεῖ. ἔστι γὰρ ἡ μὲν φιλοσοφία ἐπιτήδευσις <σοφίας>, ἡ σοφία δὲ ἐπιστήμη θείων καὶ ἀνθρωπίνων καὶ τῶν τούτων αἰτίων. Κυρία τοίνυν ἡ σοφία τῆς φιλοσοφίας ὡς ἐκείνη τῆς προπαιδείας.

this; Sarah was at one time barren.... Having no child, Sarai assigned her maid, by name Hagar the Egyptian, to Abraham in order to get children. Wisdom, therefore, that dwells with the man of faith ... was still barren ...."[222]

Here we can see that Clement has incorporated the Philonic interpretation of Sarah and Hagar, identifying Sarah with σοφία. He will go on to allegorize Egypt as κόσμος, which diverges from Philo, who identifies Egypt with σῶμα, as we saw above (*Strom.* 1.30.4).[223] But the two definitions accomplish the same interpretive goal. Clement goes on to cite Philo by name for the first of four times in the *Stromateis*: "And Philo interprets *Hagar* to mean '*sojourning*'. For it is said in connection with this: Be not much with a strange woman' (Prov. 5:20). *Sarai* he interprets to mean '*sovereignty over me*' ...."[224]

After discussing "self-taught" Isaac and the "practicer" Jacob, Clement turns to an exegesis of Gen 16:6: "Wherefore also, when Sarah was jealous of Hagar who surpassed her in favor, Abraham, as choosing only what was profitable in secular philosophy, said '*Behold, the maid is in your hands: deal with her as it pleases you*' (Gen. 16:6a), manifestly meaning: *I embrace* secular *culture* as *younger and* your *handmaid; but* your *knowledge I honour and* revere *as fullgrown mistress.*"[225] This marks Abraham's rejection of elementary studies as he is now prepared to advance on to virtue. His submission to virtue requires leaving behind "secular culture."

It is obvious from the passages cited above that Clement borrows his application of Gen 16:1–6 from Philo. But the two authors are not without their differences. Van den Hoek notes two fundamental changes in Clement's version. First, Clement's intention is to *prove* to his opponents

---

222. The Greek reads, Τῶν εἰρημένων μαρτυρίαν παρέξει ἡ γραφὴ διὰ τῶνδε· Σάρρα στεῖρα ἦν πάλαι ... μὴ τίκτουσα ἡ Σάρρα τὴν ἑαυτῆς παιδίσκην ὀνόματι Ἄγαρ τὴν Αἰγυπτίαν εἰς παιδοποιίαν ἐπιτρέπει τῷ Ἀβραάμ. ἡ σοφία τοίνυν ἡ τῷ πιστῷ σύνοικος ... στεῖρα ἦν ἔτι....

223. Van den Hoek notes that Philo associates the μέση παιδεία with the κόσμος αἰσθητός in *Congr.* 19ff, and perhaps this explains Clement's etymology (*Clement of Alexandria*, 35). Still, the fact that Clement drops the αἰσθητός is an indication that he, at the least, is reinterpreting Philo in light of the early Christian concept that the κόσμος is evil (cf. John 8:23; Rom 12:2; 2 Cor 4:4), as Van den Hoek points out (*loc. cit.*).

224. *Strom.* 1.31.1 (cf. Philo, *Congr.* 2, 20). The Greek reads, ἑρμηνεύει δὲ ὁ Φίλων τὴν μὲν Ἄγαρ παροίκησιν (ἐνταῦθα γὰρ εἴρηται· «μὴ πολὺς ἴσθι πρὸς ἀλλοτρίαν»), τὴν Σάραν δὲ ἀρχήν μου.

225. *Strom.* 1.32.1 (cf. Philo, *Congr.* 153–54). The Greek reads, διὰ τοῦτο καὶ ὁ Ἀβραάμ, παραζηλούσης τῆς Σάρρας τὴν Ἄγαρ παρευδοκιμοῦσαν αὐτήν, ὡς ἂν τὸ χρήσιμον ἐκλεξάμενον μόνον τῆς κοσμικῆς φιλοσοφίας, «ἰδοὺ ἡ παιδίσκη ἐν ταῖς χερσί σου, χρῶ αὐτῇ ὡς ἄν σοι ἀρεστὸν ᾖ» φησί. δηλῶν ὅτι ἀσπάζομαι μὲν τὴν κοσμικὴν παιδείαν καὶ ὡς νεωτέραν καὶ ὡς σὴν θεραπαινίδα, τὴν δὲ ἐπιστήμην τὴν σὴν ὡς τελείαν δέσποιναν τιμῶ καὶ σέβω.

that secular education indeed is necessary for the Christian sage.[226] Philo does not appear to be polemicizing at all. Second, the two authors fundamentally disagree on the relationship between virtue and wisdom and their definition of wisdom. For Clement, "virtue as an autonomous concept had to make way for wisdom," but "in Philo virtue and wisdom remain separate."[227] For Philo, wisdom must be identified with the Mosaic law. For Clement, wisdom is Christ. Despite their differences, Clement is able to take what he found beneficial in Philo and apply it to his own unique understanding of education.

Now we turn to Origen. We know that Origen published a commentary on the early chapters of Gen in twelve or thirteen books,[228] but continued the rest of his exegesis with *scholia*.[229] The life of Abraham was probably never covered in commentary fashion. Nevertheless, in a fragment of Origen's exegesis of Gen 16:4 we can clearly see that the basic parameters of the Philonic allegory of Hagar and Sarah are present: "'And her mistress was dishonored before her' (Gen 16:4). The 'by whom' is deliberately unexplained in order that we might find, once we have sought it out, that virtue is naturally dishonored when preliminary studies give birth, by no means by Abraham, but either by the slave girl or by those who rejoice in its offspring before the birth of better things."[230] The apparent interpretation of Hagar as προπαιδεύματα and Sarah as ἀρετή reveals that Origen was certainly aware of the Philonic interpretation.

The same interpretative tradition appears in the *Hom. Gen.* 11:1-2. Here Origen is discussing the marriage of Abraham and Keturah when he asks,

> What then? Are we to suppose that inducements of the flesh have flourished in so great a patriarch at that time? And shall he who is said to have been dead long ago in his natural impulses now be supposed to have been revived for passion? Or, as we have already often said, do the marriages of

---

226. It is also possible that Clement is arguing against the Epicurean-Cynic view, which denied any validity to the liberal arts (see Stückelberger, *Senecas Ep. 88. Brief*, 31-39).

227. Van den Hoek, *Clement of Alexandria*, 46.

228. Eusebius claimed that twelve books on Gen were known (*Hist. Eccl.* 6.24.2), but Jerome claims there were thirteen (*Epist.* 33.4).

229. The extent of the original commentary is unknown. Ronald Heine argues that the commentary stopped with the story of Seth in Gen 4 ("Origen's Alexandrian *Commentary on Genesis*," *Origeniana Octava* 1:65).

230. *Sel. in Gen. 16:4*, PG 12:116A (trans. mine). The Greek reads, 'Καὶ ἠτιμάσθη ἡ κυρία αὐτῆς ἐναντίον αὐτῆς.' Ἐπίτηδες οὐκ ἐσαφηνίσθη τὸ ὑπὸ τίνος, ἵνα ἡμεῖς ζητήσαντες εὕρωμεν, ὅτι πέφυκεν ἀτιμάζεσθαι ἀρετή, ἡνίκα προπαιδεύματα γεννήσῃ· οὐ πάντως ὑπὸ τοῦ Ἀβραάμ, ἀλλ' ἤτοι ὑπὸ τῆς παιδίσκης, ἢ τῶν χαιρόντων πρὸ τῆς γενέσεως τῶν κρειττόνων τοῖς γεννήμασιν αὐτῆς (I owe the reference to Henrichs, "Philosophy, the Handmaiden," 445).

the patriarchs indicate something mystical and sacred, as also he suggests who said of wisdom, "I decided to take her as my wife?" [cf. *Wis* 8:9].[231]

Origen's interpretation here seems to be based on the absurdity of Abraham's ability to have intercourse at such an old age. This justifies his turn to the allegorical understanding of the patriarchs and their marriages. He also mentions that such a figurative reading is familiar to his audience. Yet Origen does not cite Philo as his authority but Wis.[232] This may be due to the fact that he is preaching to a popular audience. In any case, his premise that wives represent virtues is in conformity with Philonic theory.[233]

As he attempts to prove his thesis, Origen declares that "although he was wise" (*sapiens*), Abraham "knew that there is no end of wisdom nor does old age impose a limit on learning."[234] And although Abraham had lived with virtue, that is Sarah, "the death of Sarah is to be understood as the consummation of virtue."[235] So Abraham continues to "perfect virtue" by further training himself. Then, based on Rom 4:19,[236] Origen declares that Abraham was "dead" to his members,[237] which further frees him for wisdom. Abraham then advances to Keturah, whose name means "incense" or "good odor" (θυμίαμα),[238] for "we are the good odor of Christ" (2 Cor 2:15).[239]

After extolling the benefits of age in the acquisition of wives (meaning the acquisition of wisdom), Origen goes on to note that "scripture designates the progress of the saints figuratively by marriages."[240] Since

---

231. Trans. Ronald E. Heine, *Origen: Homilies on Genesis* (FC 71; Washington, D.C.: Catholic University of America Press), 168. The Latin text reads, *"Quid ergo? Putamus quod in tanto patriarcha per idem tempus incitamenta carnis viguerint? Et qui olim naturalibus motibus emortuus dicitur, nunc ad libidinem redivivus putabitur? An, ut saepe iam diximus, patriarcharum coniugia mysticum aliquod indicant sacrimentum, sicut et ille, qui dicebat de sapientia: "Hanc ego cogitavi uxorem adducere mihi?"*

232. The Greek of *Wis* 8:9 is as follows: ἔκρινα τοίνυν ταύτην ἀγαγέσθαι πρὸς συμβίωσιν.

233. E.g., *Cher.* 41; *Congr.* 25ff.

234. The Latin reads, ... *sciebat quod sapientiae nullus est finis nec discendi terminum senectus imponit.*

235. The Latin reads, *Sarae namque dormitio, virtutis est intelligenda consummatio.*

236. "He did not weaken in faith when he considered his own body, which was as good as dead because he was about a hundred years old, or when he considered the barrenness of Sarah's womb" (RSV).

237. Cf. Col 3:5.

238. Franz Wutz considers the etymology Philonic (*Onomastica Sacra: Untersuchungen zum Liber interpretationis nominum hebraicorum des hl. Hieronymus* [TU 41; Leipzig: J.C. Hinrichs, 1914], 1:87, 457), although it is not precise (Philo has θυμιῶσα, *Sacr.* 43).

239. Trans. Heine, *Origen: Homilies on Genesis*, 168–69.

240. Trans. Heine, *Origen: Homilies on Genesis*, 170–71. The Latin reads, *Profectus etenim sanctorum Scriptura figuraliter per coniugia designat.*

"wife" means "virtue," Origen reasons that the patriarchs who take on multiple wives possess more virtues than those who retain just one. It seems clear that the germs of Origen's exposition come from Philo. The idea that one can progress in virtue itself is Philonic.[241] The Stoics taught that one was in vice until he attained perfection.[242] The scheme that Seneca provides in *Epist.* 75, for example, is based on how much vice the προκόπτων may still possess.[243] But in Philo the patriarchs are called "virtuous" while they are progressing. For Philo, virtue was merely the beginning of perfection, and it was possible for one to fall away after becoming virtuous.[244] Thus, theoretically, Abraham could advance beyond Sarah (virtue) to further learning, as Origen explicitly states. Whether Philo taught that Keturah represents a further advance in sagacity for Abraham we cannot say for certain. We are inclined to answer in the negative since Philo, in the singular reference to Keturah in his extant works, interprets her, along with Hagar, as preparatory for virtue.[245] This means, of course, that Philo is basing his understanding on Keturah as a "concubine" (cf. Gen 25:6), and not on her being a "wife" (Gen 25:1). Naturally, a concubine would enjoy inferior status. Still, if Keturah is married *after* Abraham acquires virtue (Sarah), Origen's position seems more logical than Philo's.

The death of Sarah would theoretically represent the death of virtue in Philo (since Keturah apparently does not represent ethical advancement),

---

241. E.g., *Agr.* 160; *Abr.* 34; *Virt.* 67. John Dillon writes, "Philo's innovation here [scil. *Leg.* 3.125ff.] (if it *is* his) is thoroughly un-Stoic, as the Stoics would not recognize the *prokopton* as possessing virtue at all (at best he would possess 'sparks' or adumbrations of virtues)...." ("Plotinus, Philo and Origen on the Grades of Virtue," in *Platonismus und Christentum* [ed. Horst-Dieter Blume and Friedhelm Mann; JAC 10; Münster: Aschendorffshe Verlagsbuchhandlung, 1983, 92–105, 103). We shall return to this topic in chapter 8, as Didymus affirms the same.

242. Plutarch is representative: "'Yes,' they [the Stoics] say, 'but just as in the sea the man an arm's length from the surface is drowning no less than the one who has sunk five hundred fathoms, so even those who are getting close [οἱ πελάζοντες] to virtue are no less in a state of vice than those who are far from it. And just as the blind are blind even if they are going to recover their sight a little later, so those progressing [οἱ προκόπτοντες] remain foolish and vicious right up to their attainment of virtue'" (trans. A. A. Long and D.N. Sedley, *The Hellenistic Philosophers*, 61.T). The Greek reads, "ναί," φασίν, "ἀλλὰ ὥσπερ ὁ πῆχυν ἀπέχων ἐν θαλάττῃ τῆς ἐπιφανείας οὐδὲν ἧττοι πνίγεται τοῦ καταδεδυκότος ὀργυιὰς πεντακοσίας, οὕτως οὐδὲ οἱ πελάζοντες ἀρετῇ τῶν μακρὰν ὄντων ἧττόν εἰσιν ἐν κακίᾳ· καὶ καθάπερ οἱ τυφλοὶ τυφλοί εἰσιν κἂν ὀλίγον ὕστερον ἀναβλέπειν μέλλωσιν, οὕτως οἱ προκόπτοντες ἄχρι οὗ τὴν ἀρετὴν ἀναλάβωσιν, ἀνόητοι καὶ μοχθηροὶ διαμένουσιν."

243. *Epist.* 75.12–14.

244 E.g., *Spec.* 1.252: "... the perfect man [ὁ τέλειος], in so far as he is a created being, never escapes from sinning...."

245. *Sacr.* 43.

but Philo does not allegorize her death.²⁴⁶ Perhaps he knows the implications of doing so. Therefore, while Origen does not depend on Philo for his understanding of Keturah, it seems that his hypothesis seems to work out what Philo did not.

One other text from the hand of Origen indicates that he borrows part of the allegorical theme of education and virtue from Philo.²⁴⁷ In his *Hom. Gen.* 6.2 Origen speaks of Abimelech's marriage to Sarah in ethical terms (Gen 20). He states that Abimelech wishes to associate with Sarah because she represents virtue.²⁴⁸ To support his hypothesis Origen supplies a Philo-based etymology of Sarah as *princeps vel principatum agens*.²⁴⁹ While no role is assigned to Hagar in this homily, Origen assumes that Abimelech had prepared himself to accept virtue ἐν καθαρᾷ καρδίᾳ (Gen 20:5). How did he prepare himself? Origen explains, "*Abimelech* means 'my father is king.' It seems to me, therefore, that this Abimelech represents the studious and wise men of the world, who by giving attention to philosophy, although they do not reach the complete and perfect rule of piety,²⁵⁰ nevertheless, perceive that God is the father and king of all things."²⁵¹ Origen goes on to explain that Abimelech was not permitted to touch Sarah (Gen 20:6)

---

246. The death of Sarah (Gen 23) is interpreted in a literal way in Philo, and therefore is not "the death of virtue" (see *Abr.* 245ff.; *QG* 4.73).

247. The *Ep. Greg.* is often cited as reflecting a similar ideology, but since there are no parallels to the Hagar-Sarah allegory, we relegate the text to a footnote. At the beginning of the letter Origen writes, "I should like you to select even from Greek philosophy those encyclopedic disciplines or preliminary studies that can be applied to the Christian teaching, and also those parts of geometry and astronomy that are useful for the exegesis of the Holy Scriptures. The reason for this advice is that we have to regard pagan philosophy as an assistant of Christian doctrine, just as the adherents of pagan philosophy themselves regard geometry, music, grammar, rhetoric and astronomy as assistants of their philosophy" (trans. Henrichs, "Philosophy, the Handmaiden," 446). The Greek reads, ...ηὐξάμην παραλαβεῖν σε καὶ φιλοσοφίας Ἑλλήνων τὰ οἱονεὶ εἰς χριστιανισμὸν δυνάμενα γενέσθαι ἐγκύκλια μαθήματα ἢ προπαιδεύματα, καὶ τὰ ἀπὸ γεωμετρίας καὶ ἀστρονομίας χρήσιμα ἐσόμενα εἰς τὴν τῶν ἱερῶν γραφῶν διήγησιν· ἵν', ὅπερ φασὶ φιλοσόφων παῖδες περὶ γεωμετρίας καὶ μουσικῆς γραμματικῆς τε καὶ ῥητορικῆς καὶ ἀστρονομίας, ὡς συνερίθων φιλοσοφίᾳ, τοῦθ' ἡμεῖς εἴπωμεν καὶ περὶ αὐτῆς φιλοσοφίας πρὸς χριστιανισμόν (*Ep. Greg.* 1).

248. *Hom. Gen.* 6.1.

249. Philo describes Σάρα (= שרי) as "my rule" (αρχή μου) and Σάρρα (= שרה) as "ruling" (ἄρχουσα) (*Cher.* 5, 7; *Congr.* 2; *Mut.* 77). Origen clearly understands the latter meaning here.

250. Philo terms εὐσέβεια "queen of the virtues" (e.g., *Spec.* 4.147). See Gregory Sterling, "'The Queen of the Virtues:' Piety in Philo of Alexandria," *SPhiloA* 18 (2006): 103–23.

251. Trans. Heine, *Origen: Homilies on Genesis*, 123–24. The Latin reads, *Abimelech interpretatur 'pater meus rex.' Et videtur ergo mihi quod hic Abimelech formam teneat studiosorum et sapientum saeculi, qui philosophiae operam dantes, licet non integram et perfectam regulam pietatis attigerint, tamen senserunt Deum patrem et regem esse omnium.*

because he was not fully prepared for the acceptance of virtue. So Origen has taken the idea of Philo and expanded it.[252]

As we can see, Didymus received a rich tradition of exegesis that had its roots in Philo. Based on the evidence available to us, it seems that, in the case of the Hagar-Sarah story, he is influenced more by Clement than by Origen. Of Van den Hoek's three "components" of Clement's argument cited above, the quotations from Prov and the quotations and reminiscences of Philo's *Congr.* apply also to Didymus. In the *Comm. Eccl.* Didymus introduces Prov and mentions Philo, just as Clement does. In the *Comm. Gen.*, Didymus seems to develop his own exegesis, intertwining the Pauline and Philonic interpretations of Hagar and Sarah, but his description of the law as propaideutic sounds very much like Clement. With the preceding considerations in mind, it seems that Didymus read Clement, who pointed him to Philo. Being familiar with Philo's writings already, Didymus investigated the Philonic references for himself, and developed his own exegesis from them. In this process, he becomes the model φιλόκαλος he encourages his students to be.

Conclusion

From the clear references to Philo in the Tura commentaries, we can draw the following conclusions: (1) Didymus has read Philo directly, and thus is not always dependent on others for his Philonic knowledge; (2) he sometimes follows a specific Philonic treatise successively in his own argumentation (as we saw with *Sacr.* above); (3) he recommends Philo as an author from whom his audience can benefit, twice foregoing his own allegorical interpretation and encouraging the reader to consult Philo to complete the exegesis of the passage; (4) Like Clement and Origen, Didymus develops Philonic ideas, and alters them from the author's original application (such as the intertwining of the Pauline and Philonic interpretations of Hagar and Sarah).

From our analysis of the *Comm. Gen.*, there is no doubt that Didymus knew and used Philo. He cites Philo by name seven times in the commentary and reveals a thorough knowledge of the Philonic corpus. From the explicit references in this chapter, he appears to have been in contact most closely with the *Sacr.*, the *Congr.*, *Mos.* and the *QG*. However, we have seen that Didymus presents ideas that can be located in every part of the

---

252. Philo refers to Abimelech, like Keturah, only once (*Plant.* 169), and this text treats Isaac and Rebekah in Gen 26:8.

Philonic corpus.[253] Therefore, Didymus was most certainly well-acquainted with the works of Philo of Alexandria, and the remaining sections of the monograph shall deal with methodological and conceptual parallels.

---

253. The only Philonic works in which we do not cite parallels above are *Sobr.*, *Jos.*, *Virt.*, *Cont.*, *Prov.*, *Hypoth.*, *Flacc.* and *Legat.*

6

BORROWINGS FROM PHILO: ETYMOLOGY

Introduction

In the previous chapter we focused on the seven mentions of Philo's name. In the remaining chapters we shall cast a broader net, attempting to show that Philonic influence on Didymus extends even to his methods of exegesis. First, we shall consider the use of etymology as a means to allegory. Second, we shall examine Didymus' use of arithmology as a springboard to allegory (ch. 7). Finally, we shall examine several general Philonic themes that Didymus incorporates into his own exegesis without necessarily citing the Jewish author (ch. 8).

Didymus and the Semantics of Biblical Language

As virtually all early Christian authors, Didymus assumes the Bible contains the verbal manifestation of divine thought.[1] Therefore, everything in the Bible is beneficial (ὠφέλιμος) and nothing is superfluous.[2] Early Christianity inherited this view from Judaism, and we find typical expression of it in Philo.[3] For Philo, the Pentateuch was "a divinely inspired, didactic, and even 'super-didactic' work, that is, every part of it is inspired and contains divine wisdom."[4] The task of the interpreter is to tap into this divine wisdom by means of exegesis.

Exegesis was not always so easy, however. Ancient interpreters found a number of biblical texts, taken at face-value, to be contradictory and

---

1. E.g., *Comm. Ps.* 39.23; *Comm. Eccl.* 7.9. One can see this attitude clearly in his response to Porphyry, where the Bible's divinely inspired character elevates it above the poetry of the Greeks (see Bienert, *Allegoria und Anagoge*, 141–45, and Stefaniw, *Mind, Text and Commentary*, 80–86). On the polemic more generally see Antonio Carlini, "La polemica di Porfirio contro l'esegesi 'tipologica' dei Cristiani," SCO 46 (1998): 385–94.

2. The New Testament itself affirms this (2 Tim 3:16–17), and the fathers merely expand the concept. For Origen, see Neuschäfer, *Origenes als Philologe*, 259–60. For an example see Didymus, *Comm. Gen.* 174.13–18 (for discussion see Bayliss, *The Vision of Didymus*, 76–78).

3. E.g., *Leg.* 3.147; *Fug.* 54.

4. Adam Kamesar, "Biblical Interpretation in Philo," in *The Cambridge Companion to Philo*, ed. Adam Kamesar (Cambridge: Cambridge University Press, 2009), 65–91, 80.

absurd. While most modern scholars are content to admit these contradictions as the result of human frailty, most ancient Jewish and Christian exegetes invested the apparent contradictions with divinely inspired truth.[5] Philo, for example, believed the biblical description of the two trees in Eden cannot be taken literally, "for no trees of life or understanding have ever appeared on earth in the past or are ever likely to appear in the future."[6] Rather, Moses must be "hinting at [αἰνίττομαι] the ruling part of the soul." Similiarly, it is absurd to believe God removed a rib from man and built a woman.[7] God is actually describing here the faculty of sense-perception (ἡ αἰσθητική).[8] In Philo, the allegorical interpretation dispenses with the offensive literal meaning.[9] Wherever the surface meaning is absurd, a philosophical truth is intended.[10] Allegorical interpretation unlocks the philosophical truth.[11]

One might ask why God couched important truths in "myth-like" (μυθώδης) stories at all.[12] The answer which Origen provides is telling.

---

5. E.g., Aristobulus, *fr.* 2.1, 2.5. For Origen, see the well-known passage in *Princ.* 4.2–3 (and for general discussion, see Dively Lauro, *The Soul and Spirit*, 47–50). This is also the view of many Homeric interpreters of antiquity. Heraclitus the Allegorist, for example, believes Homer to have produced, in the words of David Dawson, "a surface level of seemingly mythical poetry (the literal sense) and a deeper level of truth or philosophical insight (the allegorical sense)" (*Allegorical Readers and Cultural Revision in Ancient Alexandria* [Berkeley: University of California Press, 1992], 41).

6. *Opif.* 154 (trans. Runia, *On the Creation*, 88). The Greek reads, δένδρα γὰρ ἐπὶ γῆς οὔτε πέφηνέ πω πρότερον οὔτ' αὖθις εἰκὸς φανεῖσθαι ζωῆς ἢ συνέσεως.

7. The precise language Philo uses is τὸ ῥητὸν ἐπὶ τούτου μυθῶδές ἐστι.

8. *Leg.* 2.19–24.

9. His words in *Agr.* 97 are representative: "But in the explanations that uncover the deeper meaning the mythical element disappears and the truth is discovered in full clarity" (trans. Geljon and Runia, *On Agriculture*, 62). Philo is, of course, inconsistent, often positing the literal sense as valid (more attention to the literal meaning is characteristic of the *Quaestiones*; for an introduction, see Giovanni M. Vian, "Le Quaestiones di Filone," *Annali di Storia dell'Esegesi* 9 [1992]: 365–88).

10. For a summary of textual "absurdity" and the move to allegory, see Jean Pépin, "À propos de l'histoire de l'exégèse allégorique: l'absurdité, signe de l'allégorie," StPatr 1 (1955): 395–413.

11. Compare the view of Strabo on Homer: "and when Homer indulges in myths he is at least more accurate than the later writers, since he does not deal wholly in marvels, but for our instruction [πρὸς ἐπιστήμην] he also uses allegory, or revises myths, or curries popular favour, and particularly in his story of the wanderings of Odysseus" (1.2.7; trans. LCL).

12. Philo's view of biblical "myth" is more nuanced than we can discuss here. For further information see Adam Kamesar, "Philo, the Presence of 'Paideuctic' Myth in the Pentateuch, and the 'Principles' or *Kephalaia* of Mosaic Discourse," *StPhA* 10 (1998): 34–65. More generally on the Hellenistic-Jewish critique of Greek myth compared with Mosaic truth, see René Bloch, *Moses und der Mythos: Die Auseinandersetzung mit der griechischen Mythologie bei jüdisch-hellenistischen Autoren* (JSJSup 145; Leiden: Brill, 2011).

Speaking of Plato's authorial brilliance in mythological composition (*Symp.* 203 B–E), Origen writes:

> If readers of this were to imitate the malice of Celsus (which no Christian would do) they would ridicule the myth and would make a mock of so great a man as Plato. But if they could find Plato's meaning by examining philosophically what he expresses in the form of a myth, they would admire the way in which he was able to hide the great doctrines as he saw them in the form of a myth on account of the multitude, and yet to say what was necessary for those who know how to discover from the myths the true significance intended by their author.[13]

According to Origen, Plato had two reasons for composing mythologically: (1) he could communicate great truths to the "multitude" (οἱ πολλοί) by means of the story, and (2) he could embed the residue of deeper truths within the mythological fabric of the story for those advanced enough to pursue them. Origen goes on to declare later, "For our scriptures have been written to suit exactly the multitude of the simple-minded, a consideration to which no attention was paid by those who made up the fictitious stories of the Greeks."[14]

While Origen is prepared to assign credit to Plato for thinking of the benefit of his audience in composition, no such honor will be attributed to the myth-makers of the Greeks. They composed purely for entertainment, and not for education.[15] The point Origen is trying to make is that *everything* in the Bible is "beneficial" (ὠφέλιμος) and "educational" (διδασκαλικός).[16] Kamesar characterizes this attitude as "pan-Scriptural didacticism," basing himself on the wording of 2 Tim 3:16.[17] If everything in scripture is intended for instruction, then to overcome the apparent absurdities and contradictions in the Bible, one must resort to allegorical interpretation. In fact, the Bible is deliberately set in language difficult to understand.[18]

---

13. Origen, *Cels.* 4.39 (trans. Chadwick, 215). The Greek reads, Ἆρα γὰρ οἱ ἐντυγχάνοντες τούτοις ἐὰν μὲν τὴν κακοήθειαν τοῦ Κέλσου μιμῶνται, ὅπερ Χριστιανῶν ἀπείη, καταγελάσονται τοῦ μύθου καὶ ἐν χλεύῃ θήσονται τὸν τηλικοῦτον Πλάτωνα· ἐὰν δὲ τὰ ἐν μύθου σχήματι λεγόμενα φιλοσόφως ἐξετάζοντες δυνηθῶσιν εὑρεῖν τὸ βούλημα τοῦ Πλάτωνος, <θαυμάσονται> τίνα τρόπον δεδύνηται τὰ μεγάλα ἑαυτῷ φαινόμενα δόγματα κρύψαι μὲν διὰ τοὺς πολλοὺς ἐν τῷ τοῦ μύθου σχήματι, εἰπεῖν δ' ὡς ἐχρῆν τοῖς εἰδόσιν ἀπὸ μύθων εὑρίσκειν τὸ περὶ ἀληθείας τοῦ ταῦτα συντάξαντος βούλημα.

14. Origen, *Cels.* 4.50 (trans. Chadwick, 225). The Greek reads, Τὰ γὰρ ἡμέτερα ἐστόχασται καὶ τοῦ πλήθους τῶν ἁπλουστέρων, ὅπερ οἱ τὰ ἑλληνικὰ πλάσματα ποιήσαντες οὐκ ἐφυλάξαντο.

15. On the debate on the purpose of literature in ancient literary criticism, see D. S. Russell, *Criticism in Antiquity* (Berkeley: University of California Press, 1981), 84–98.

16. E.g., *Hom. Num.* 14.2; *Hom. Jes. Nav.* 20.4; *Comm. Matt.* 16.2; *Comm. Rom.* 2.6.

17. πᾶσα γραφὴ θεόπνευστος; see Kamesar, "Biblical Interpretation in Philo," 84.

18. For Origen, see Marguerite Harl, *Sur les Écritures*, 75–79 (and *Philoc.* 2.2; 10.2).

Only by means of figurative exegesis can one peel away the layers of mythic material and arrive at the spiritual intention of the inspired text.[19]

Etymology and Biblical Interpretation

Etymology can be found in the earliest of Greek authors. Homer etymologizes the name of Odysseus as though it derives from ὀδύρομαι, meaning "to grieve" (*Od.* 1.55) and ὀδύσσομαι, meaning "to hate" (*Od.* 1.62). Aeschylus associates Zeus with ζῆν, meaning "to live" (*Supp.* 584), and Helen of Troy with ἑλεῖν, meaning "to destroy" (*Ag.* 681–90).[20] As Robert Maltby writes, "The popular assumption that the study of a name could reveal τὸ ἔτυμον, 'the truth,' about the thing accounts for the importance attached to etymology in ancient thought and literature."[21]

Personal names were a primary target of the etymologist from the beginning. It was believed that proper names changed spelling and meaning less often than generic names, and they were also bestowed with greater care. One can see in both Homer and in the Bible the ancient assumption that a name bore a striking truth about the character of the person named.[22] In Greek thought, this lesson applies particularly to the names of the gods. While Plato is skeptical about the reliability of human names and the names of heroes, he is willing to acknowledge greater reliability in the case of divine names. He suggests two reasons for this: (1) divine names are given with greater care than human names, and (2) perhaps divine names were given by the gods themselves.[23]

Although cautious, Plato still believes that generic nouns can reveal deep truths. The noun θεός, Plato argues, received its name because the ancient Greeks believed the gods to be cosmic entities (sun, moon, earth, stars, and so on) who were thought to be "running" (θεῖν) since they were in constant motion.[24] Δαίμονες, likewise, were so named "because they were wise and knowing" (δαήμονες).[25] But other names, such as ἄνθρωπος, are more difficult to interpret.[26] Still some words leave us with the impression

---

19. See *Comm. Jo.* 10.5.
20. Examples provided in R. Maltby, "Etymology," *OCD*4 542–43, 542.
21. Ibid.
22. For biblical examples see, e.g., Gen 17:5; 32:28.
23. *Crat.* 397B–C.
24. *Crat.* 397D.
25. *Crat.* 398B.
26. See *Crat.* 398E–399C.

that they mean the opposite of what they appear.[27] Plato provides a number of etymologies in the *Cratylus* which he himself either accepts, rejects, or about which he remains neutral. This indicates that, whatever he might argue in terms of the validity of etymology, he himself valued the practice to an extent.[28]

In the *Cratylus* three points of view are proposed with regard to etymological analysis: (1) The position of Cratylus that "names" and "things" are identical (ὄνομα = πρᾶγμα);[29] (2) The position of Hermogenes that "correctness of a name is by convention and agreement" among human beings (ὀρθότης ὀνόματος = συνθήκη καὶ ὁμολογία);[30] (3) The position of Socrates that "things that exist must be learned from themselves and not from their names" (τὰ ὄντα ἐξ αὑτῶν μαθητέον and not ἐξ ὀνομάτων).[31] Socrates acknowledges certain aspects of the positions of both Cratylus and Hermogenes, but ultimately argues that etymology is not *always* a reliable guide toward "knowledge." In the words of Mark Amsler, "*etymologia* is a suspect science for Plato since it produces subjective knowledge and tells us more about the knower than the known."[32]

Aristotle sought to advance beyond Plato's uncertainty, but is aware of the problems he raises. Fundamentally, Aristotle agrees with the position of Hermogenes that names are conventional. He states, "No sound is by nature a noun: it becomes one, becoming a symbol."[33] In this sense, Aristotle can define "spoken words" as "symbols or signs of affections or impressions of the soul," while "written words are the signs of words spoken."[34] By describing words as "symbols of affections in the soul," Aristotle is able to accommodate the various changes in the written as well as the spoken form, while regarding the symbol itself as static. Thus, the πρᾶγμα does not

---

27. Plato concludes his discussion with the remark, "And so names which we believe have the very worst meanings appear to be very like those which have the best" (437C).
28. On the entire question see the discussion of David Sedley, "The Etymologies in Plato's *Cratylus*," *JHS* 118 (1998): 140–54.
29. The clearest passage is 435D: "this is the simple truth, that he who knows the names [τὰ ὀνόματα] knows also the things named [τὰ πράγματα]."
30. The clearest passage is 384C: "I ... cannot come to the conclusion that there is any correctness of names other than convention and agreement."
31. The clearest passage is 439B: "How realities [τὰ ὄντα] are to be learned or discovered is perhaps too great a question for you or me to determine; but it is worth while to have reached even this conclusion, that they are to be learned and sought for, not from names but much better through themselves than through names" (trans. LCL).
32. Mark Amsler, *Etymology and Grammatical Discourse in Late Antiquity and the Early Middle Ages* (Amsterdam Studies in the Theory and History of Linguistic Science 3.44; Amsterdam: Benjamins, 1989), 35.
33. *Int.* 16a26.
34. *Int.* 16a3–5 (trans. LCL).

change, but only the ὄνομα, a mere symbol of the πρᾶγμα by common agreement. The science of etymology, then, "can explain [only] what is the consensus view of truth and how names are imposed on things, but it cannot guarantee the absolute truth about these things."[35] With the advent of the Stoics, however, language became a supreme guide toward truth.

The Stoics believed that language could be divided into "signifiers" (σημαίνοντα) and "things signified" (σημαινόμενα).[36] Signifiers are equivalent to sounds (φωναί), but things signified are the πράγματα to which the sounds refer (the position of Cratylus). In fact, primordial words, according to the Stoics, conveyed meanings which represented exactly the essence of the thing named.[37] Thus, whereas Aristotle had referred to words as mere symbols and Plato had argued that one can never reach certain knowledge of the πράγματα through the ὀνόματα, the Stoics developed a precise grammatical science to break down words in an attempt to reach the "things" subsisting under their surface. This was the science of etymology.[38]

But why were the Stoics concerned with word analysis at all? The Stoics adopted the pan-Hellenic idea that the distant past was part of a pristine golden age. Since, as the Stoics argued, the philosopher-kings who belonged to this golden age first applied words to things, one could enter the minds of these ancient sages by examining words and thus arrive at the original ἔτυμον.[39] Since the Stoics believed etymology allowed one to uncover the wisdom of the ancients, one might think the Stoics accepted the conventional theory of language (words were assigned to things "by imposition," θέσει). But the Stoics also acknowledge that words are natural (φύσει).[40] Since the θέσις/φύσις debate is already present in Plato's *Cratylus*, we might accuse the Stoics of vacillating here between two contradictory positions.[41] But their view was more nuanced.

---

35. Amsler, *op. cit.*, 34.
36. See, e.g., *SVF* 2:166.
37. Dawson, *Allegorical Readers*, 31.
38. Note the remark of Dirk M. Schenkeveld, "The term ... ἐτυμολογία is to all appearances a Stoic coining, by which they indicate that the search for the reason why a particular name has been given to a particular thing is related to the search for truth" ("Language," in the *Cambridge History of Hellenistic Philosophy* [ed. Keimpe Algra, Jonathan Barnes, Jaap Mansfeld, and Malcom Schofield; Cambridge: Cambridge University Press, 1999], 177–225, 183).
39. This is the assumption of Cornutus' *Epidrome* (see Glenn W. Most, "Cornutus and Stoic Allegoresis," in *ANRW* 2.36.3: 2014–65).
40. This was indeed the impression of Origen, who associated the position that names were "the product of imposition" with Aristotle (*Cels.* 1.24).
41. See the discussion of Schenkeveld, 179–80.

Michael Frede argues that the Stoics realized words could not be completely natural since all human beings would necessarily speak the same language.[42] So they intermingled aspects of both θέσις and φύσις. The result is that ancient sages imposed names, but "they have been imposed in such a way that they naturally reflect the nature of things by somehow imitating them."[43] According to the Stoics, there were a limited number of natural words. Varro cites Cosconius who placed the original number at 1000, meaning that there could be a possible 500,000 permutations of those 1000 original words.[44] Varro goes on to speculate that the number could reach 5,000,000 if prefixes are added.[45]

In addition to a base number of original words the Stoics proposed that these words phonetically or actually represent the "things" they imitate.[46] Perhaps the most famous example of actual representation comes from Chrysippus. When pronouncing the word ἐγώ, he stated, the chin points to the chest, the center of human consciousness.[47] Phonetic representation, however, accounts for the bulk of etymological discussion. The very sounds of letters were thought to be fundamental in this regard. *Rho*, for example, represents "speed, motion and hardness," while *lamda* is associated with "smoothness" and "softness."[48] At other times, combinations of letters could unlock the essence of the πρᾶγμα, such as the sound -ηρ to indicate that Hera ("Ηρα) represents the ἀήρ.[49] In the language of the *Principia dialecticae*, similarity of sounds is classified as *similitudo*. But sounds can also be employed to refer to the opposite of what we would normally think. The term *bellum* ("war") is the oppposite of *bellus* ("beautiful"), and *lucus* ("grove") is the opposite of *lux* ("light"). This is the principle of *contrarium*.[50]

---

42. Synonyms and homonyms also posed a problem for a purely natural view of language (see Dawson, *Allegorical Readers*, 33–34).

43. Michael Frede, "Principles of Stoic Grammar," in *The Stoics* [ed. John M. Rist; Berkeley: University of California Press, 1978), 27–75, 69.

44. *De ling. lat.* 6.36 (cited in Frede, *loc. cit.*).

45. *De ling. lat.* 6.38 (cited in Frede, *loc. cit.*).

46. *SVF* 2:146: "primary sounds imitate things." It could be that the Stoics regarded letters and syllables as primary, and words as derivative from them, as is implied by *SVF* 2:148 (see A. A. Long, *Hellenistic Philosophy* [2nd ed.; Berkeley: University of California Press, 1986], 133–34).

47. *SVF* 2:884.

48. See Plato, *Cratylus* 434C.

49. See Cornutus, *Epidrome* 17.1 and Dawson, *op. cit.*, 31.

50. See Long, *op. cit.*, 134. For other examples from the *Principia dialecticae* see A. C. Lloyd, "Grammar and Metaphysics in the Stoa," in *Problems in Stoicism* (ed. A. A. Long; London: Athlone, 1971), 58–71, 64–65.

When one considers how the Stoics conceived of original words and sounds, it might seem that the ἔτυμον is completely out of reach. Indeed, Chrysippus remarked, "Every word is ambiguous by nature since two or more meanings can be understood from it."[51] But rather than abandoning the study of language and ceding to the impossibility of recovering the original forms, the Stoics redoubled their efforts through the science of etymology. By peeling away the layers of human imposition, the Stoics maintained the fundamental possibility of understanding πράγματα by means of ὀνόματα. In order to do this, they needed to identify the kinds of mutations words could suffer over time.

The Stoics developed a four-stage scheme applied to changes in words.[52] The parts are (1) ἀφαίρεσις (*detractio*), "subtraction," equivalent to "syncope," or the reduction of a syllable or syllables within a word (e.g., in English, "prolly" instead of "probably"); (2) πρόθεσις (*adiectio*), "addition," usually indicating a prefix or preposition (e.g., the scores of compound words in Greek); (3) μετάθεσις (*transmutatio*), "methathesis," or the transposition of sounds (e.g., in English "ax" instead of "ask"); and (4) ἐναλλαγή (*immutatio*), "interchange," or the change of letters or sounds, tense or case (e.g., "we was tired" instead of "we were tired").

By classifying the development of words into these four categories, the Stoics were in a much better position to trace the words back through time to their original form. They would simply take the current form as the starting point, and ask if one or more of the four changes had occurred. At the end of the analysis, one would be left with a form which was, presumably, original. The original term, now excavated, would be equivalent to the word first applied to the thing and depict perfectly the essence of that thing. Or so went the theory.

Etymology as a Means of Biblical Interpretation

The Alexandrian interpreters of scripture adopted the Stoic system of etymological interpretation. Words are mere symbols, adequate only insofar as they represent the incorporeal objects to which they refer.[53] The

---

51. *SVF* 2:151.
52. See Wolfram Ax, "Quadripertita ratio: Bemerkungen zur Geschichte eines aktuellen Kategoriensystems (Adiectio–Detractio–Transmutatio–Immutatio)," in *The History of Linguistics in the Classical Period* (ed. Daniel J. Taylor; Amsterdam Studies in the History of Linguistic Science 3.46; Amsterdam: Benjamins, 1987), 17–40.
53. I.e., the Stoic theory of language dominates the verbal discussions (see Diogenes Laertius, *Vit. phil.* 7.57; Origen, *Cels.* 1.24).

exegete must decode these symbols not by hermeneutical skill alone, but by divine aid as well.[54] Largely, the procedures of etymology yielded the same results for the biblical interpreters as it did for the interpreters of Greek poetry. The "true meaning" (ἔτυμον) of the word revealed an ancient truth which was not obvious to the casual reader. But one major distinction is the fact that the Greeks worked entirely on their own language. In fact, etymology was one of the criteria of "Hellenicity" in rhetoric.[55] This was due to the assumption that the original namers spoke flawless Greek.[56]

But the biblical text was not originally written in Greek, but in Hebrew. Therefore, etymologies must be performed on the basis of the Hebrew, and not on the Greek language. Although many early interpreters viewed the Septuagint to be an inspired translation, this view does not seem to alter their etymologizing.[57] Hebrew was the language the biblical authors spoke, and Hebrew would be the foundation of etymological analysis. This important difference distinguishes etymological work on the Bible from that done on Homer and the poets.

Etymology in Philo

The first interpreter to etymologize the Bible on a grand scale is Philo of Alexandria.[58] Philo was certainly familiar with the Greek tradition of etymologizing, as the following passage makes clear: "Elsewhere the universal practice of people as a body is to give to things names which differ from the things, so that the objects are not the same as what we call them. But with Moses the names assigned are manifest images [ἐμφαντικώταται] of the

---

54. The theme of divine aid can be traced throughout the Alexandrian tradition (e.g., Philo, *Mut.* 18; Origen, *Hom. Num.* 13.1; Didymus, *Comm. Zach.* 314.16–19; prayer, e.g., Origen, *Hom. Gen.* 11.3; Didymus, *Comm. Zach.* 182.23–26). This is a general theme of Late Antique Commentators (e.g., Proclus, *In Parm.* 617).

55. See Sextus Empiricus, *Adv. math.* 1.241ff. Hellenicity is defined as φράσις ἀδιάπτωτος ἐν τῇ τεχνικῇ καὶ μὴ εἰκαίᾳ συνηθείᾳ (Diogenes Laertius, *Vit. phil.* 7.59).

56. See Frede, "Principles," 68–70.

57. Philo believes that the Greek text is inspired and even asserts that it represents exactly the Hebrew words in their etymological senses (see *Mos.* 2.37–40 with the comments of Kamesar, "Biblical Interpretation in Philo," 66–71). However, this high view of the LXX does not seem to affect his etymologizing. If it had, Philo should have performed his etymologies on the basis of the Greek. In point of fact, he rarely does so (for a list of Philo's Greek etymologies, see Grabbe, *Etymology in Early Jewish Interpretation*, 237–38). David Winston explains the Greek etymologies of Philo as examples of *paranomasia*, and therefore are not to be regarded as serious attempts at etymological analysis ("Aspects of Philo's Linguistic Theory," *SPhiloA* 3 [1991]: 109–25, 120).

58. "Aristobulus is really the only certainly pre-Philonic Jewish exegete who gives us any material on the use of etymology" (Grabbe, *Etymology*, 53).

things, so that the name and the thing are inevitably the same from the first and the name and that to which the name is given differ not a whit."⁵⁹ Philo uses the key terms ὄνομα and πρᾶγμα, and reflects the traditional notion that words are (or should be) mere symbols of true realities.⁶⁰ Moses was not the first to assign names, but his imposition of names is fully consonant with the original essence of the "thing." Therefore, the Mosaic legislation has preserved the perfect form of the original name. One needs only to understand the Hebrew of Moses to access the essence of the thing named.⁶¹

Although Moses properly applied names to things, he was not the first to do so. Adam stands in this role as the first human (Gen 2:19–20). Philo remarks:

> What we admire in the Lawgiver's literal statement is his ascription to the first man of the fixing of names. Indeed, Greek philosophers said that those who first assigned names to things were wise men. Moses did better than they, first of all in ascribing it not to some of the men of old but to the first man created.... Again, had many persons bestowed names on things, they would inevitably have been incongrous and ill-matched, different persons imposing them on different principles, whereas the naming by one man was bound to bring about harmony between name and thing, and the name given was sure to be a symbol, the same for all men, of any object to which the name was attached or of the meaning attaching to the name.⁶²

As we saw above, human corruption was one of Plato's key objections to the validity of etymology. Philo has a response. The biblical record is

---

59. *Cher.* 56 (trans. *PLCL* 2:43, modified slightly). The Greek reads, ὁ μὲν ἄλλος ἅπας ἀνθρώπων ὅμιλος ὀνόματα τίθεται πράγμασι διαφέροντα τῶν πραγμάτων, ὥσθ' ἕτερα μὲν εἶναι τὰ τυγχάνοντα, ἑτέρας δὲ κλήσεις τὰς ἐπ' αὐτοῖς· παρὰ Μωυσεῖ δὲ αἱ τῶν ὀνομάτων θέσεις ἐνάργειαι πραγμάτων εἰσὶν ἐμφαντικώταται ὡς αὐτὸ τὸ πρᾶγμα ἐξ ἀνάγκης εὐθὺς εἶναι τοὔνομα καὶ τοὔνομα καὶ καθ' οὗ τίθεται διαφέρειν μηδέν. For a similar statement, see *Agr.* 1–2.

60. That etymological interpretation aims at the πρᾶγμα holds true throughout the Greek tradition. Compare the definition of Orion, a fifth century grammarian: Ἐτυμολογία ἐστὶ τὸ ἐξ αὐτῆς τῆς τοῦ πράγματος ὀνομασίας εὑρίσκειν τὴν αὐτοῦ ἑρμενείαν. καὶ τὸ διὰ τί οὕτως ὀνομάζεται (qtd. in Peraki-Kyriakidou, "Aspects of Ancient Etymologizing," *CQ* NS 52 [2002]: 473–98, 481).

61. See *Congr.* 44.

62. *Leg.* 2.14–15 (trans. *PLCL* 1:233–35). The Greek reads, ἡ μὲν ῥητή, παρόσον τὴν θέσιν τῶν ὀνομάτων προσῆψε τῷ πρώτῳ γενομένῳ ὁ νομοθέτης. καὶ γὰρ οἱ παρ' Ἕλλησι φιλοσοφοῦντες εἶπον εἶναι σοφοὺς τοὺς πρώτους τοῖς πράγμασι τὰ ὀνόματα θέντας· Μωυσῆς δὲ ἄμεινον, ὅτι πρῶτον μὲν οὔ τισι τῶν πρότερον, ἀλλὰ τῷ πρώτῳ γενομένῳ, ... ἔπειτα ὅτι πολλῶν μὲν τιθέντων ὀνόματα διάφωνα καὶ ἄμικτα ἔμελλεν ἔσεσθαι, ἄλλων ἄλλως τιθέντων, ἑνὸς δὲ ὤφειλεν ἡ θέσις ἐφαρμόττειν τῷ πράγματι, καὶ τοῦτ' εἶναι σύμβολον ἅπασι τὸ αὐτὸ τοῦ τυγχάνοντος ἢ τοῦ σημαινομένου.

superior to the Greek tradition because Moses ascribes to the first man the imposition of names, thereby leaving no room for corruption over time.

If Moses properly applied the Adamic names to things and if the very words of scripture are perfect and contain no superfluity, as we saw above, then changes in names are highly significant.[63] Names are normally static, as is proven by Issac's naming of the wells (Gen 26:18).[64] But if a name is changed, the basic essence of the thing is changed as well. For this reason, personal name changes are didactic, marking for the reader a shift in the soul of the protagonist. Philo states, "... Abraham and Sarah had not yet received their change of names, that is they had not yet been changed in character to the betterment of soul...."[65] And again, "Cease then to suppose that the Deity's gift was a change of name instead of a betterment of character symbolized thereby."[66] So name changes have exegetical significance because they reflect a fundamental change in "thing."[67]

It is typical for Philo to provide a name, its etymology, and an allegorical interpretation based on the etymology.[68] In the case of Cain and Abel, for example, Philo notes that "Cain" means "possession" (κτῆσις) whereas "Abel" means "referring to God" (ἀναφέρων ἐπὶ θεόν). He immediately shifts to the allegorical equivalents based on the respective etymologies of the names, labeling Abel "the God-loving position" (τὸ φιλόθεον δόγμα) and Cain "the self-infatuated" (τὸ φίλαυτος).[69] These titles reflect, in accordance with the etymology, the essence of character. Cain is "self-loving," but Abel is "God-loving." The same procedure applies to Sarah. Her name means "ruling" (ἄρχουσα), but the allegorical equivalent is "virtue." Why? Because

---

63. The Bible represents most name changes as being directed by God (Gen 17:5; 32:28). But even where Moses (not God) changes Hosea's name to Joshua (Num 13:16), the incident is treated no differently in Philo (see *Mut.* 121–22).

64. *QG* 4.194 reports that Isaac was content with the names imposed by Abraham, "for he knew that if he should change the names, he would change the things at the same time" (trans. *PLCL* Suppl. 1:482).

65. *Cher.* 4 (trans. *PLCL* 2:11).

66. *Mut.* 70 (trans. *PLCL* 5:179). Cf. Gen. Rab. 44:10: "Abram and Sarai cannot have children, but Abraham and Sarah can have children."

67. Dawson compares Philo's theory to a geometrical diagram: "changing the diagram (e.g., from O to Δ) automatically changes the meaning (from 'circle' to 'triangle')" (*Allegorical Readers*, 86).

68. Runia identifies four steps in Philo's etymological interpretation: (1) the Hebrew name; (2) its translation into Greek; (3) symbolism of the translation; (4) justification of the translation by means of interpretation ("Etymology as an Allegorical Technique in Philo of Alexandria," *StPhA* 16 [2004]: 101–21, 104).

69. *Sacr.* 2–3.

virtue is to rule one's life.[70] These etymologies often govern Philo's entire presentation of biblical characters, such as Rebekkah.[71]

Etymologizing stands at the forefront of Philo's biblical exegesis. He often uses etymology at the beginning of an allegorical discussion to ground a particular interpretation.[72] Rarely does Philo pass up an opportunity to explain the symbolism of a name, although sometimes the allegorical interpretation of the name is so familiar that he skips the etymology altogether.[73] This procedure indicates that his audience was well-acquainted with the allegorical equivalents of biblical names, either through Philo's own preaching or through the pre-Philonic tradition.[74]

Etymology in Origen

When we turn to Origen, we find that he too adopts the Stoic theory of language.[75] Words are mere symbols of higher realities. For this reason the intuitive interpreter "should pay more attention to what is meant than to how it is expressed in words."[76] Indeed, words are incapable of precisely expressing realities: "Our aim has been to show that there are certain things, the meaning of which it is impossible adequately to explain by any human language, but which are made clear rather through simple apprehension than through any power of words."[77] In this respect, in the scriptures "gold is applied to the intellect and mind, whereas silver is referred only to language and the power of speech."[78]

---

70. *Congr.* 2–4; cf. *Cher.* 3.

71. Rebekkah would seem to be portrayed negatively in the biblical text, at least in her deception of Isaac (Gen 27). But Philo's interpretation of Rebekkah as "constancy" colors every passage in which she is discussed, and she is never painted negatively in Philo (see Valentin Nikiprowetzky, "Rébecca, vertu de constance et constance de vertu chez Philon d'Alexandrie," *Sem* 26 [1976]: 109–36).

72. See Runia, "Etymology," 111.

73. E.g., *Leg.* 2.24 (Eve as sense perception); *Det.* 59 (Sarah as virtue); *Fug.* 24 (Rebekkah as constancy).

74. On the question of Philo's predecessors in biblical etymologizing, see Grabbe, *Etymology in Early Jewish Interpretation*, 89–109.

75. See *Philoc.* 4 with the comments of Harl (*Sur les Écritures*, 274–81). See also R. P. C. Hanson, "Interpretations of Hebrew Names in Origen," *VC* 10 (1956): 103–23; Catherine M. Chin, "Origen and Christian Naming: Textual Exhaustion and the Boundaries of Gentility in *Commentary on John* 1," *JECS* 14 (2006): 407–36.

76. *Princ.* 4.3.15 (trans. Butterworth, *On First Principles* [New York: Harper, 1966], 312).

77. *Loc. cit.* (trans. Butterworth). Unfortunately, this section of Princ. survives only in Latin translation, which reads, ... *quod sunt quaedam, quorum significatio proprie nullis omnino potest humanae linguae sermonibus explicari.*

78. *Comm. Cant.* 2.8 (trans. R. P. Lawson, *Origen, The Song of Songs: Commentary and Homilies* [Ancient Christian Writers 26; London: Longmans, Green and Co., 1957], 152).

Language is necessary, however, "for the sake of those who cannot understand [ideas] unless they are thus couched in terms to which they are accustomed. The words in which we hear them, therefore, will be well known and familiar; but our perception of them, if we give them the perception they deserve, will be of things divine and incorporeal."[79] The aim of the exegete is to advance beyond the mere shell of words, the "earthen vessels," and to arrive at the "treasure" contained therein.[80] Etymology is of great assistance in reaching this exegetical goal, for it enables the interpreter to locate the πράγμα subsisting under the ὄνομα.[81]

While names are symbols, meanings (σημαινόμενα) signify higher realities (πράγματα).[82] For Origen, as for Philo, the words of the biblical text represent the divine mind. In fact, Origen declares that Jesus as the Logos inspired the biblical authors.[83] In a fragment of his exegesis of Col,[84] Origen writes,

> Furthermore, the law of Moses was (given) through angels by the hand and by the power of a mediator who is Christ, who when he was in the beginning was the Word of God and was with God and the Word was God and served the Father in all things. Everything was made by him, that is, not only creatures, but also the law and the prophets. And he is himself the mediator between God and men.[85]

But Christ was no simple mediator. Origen declares, "The words of Christ, however, according to our understanding, are not only those which he taught in the flesh when he was made man, for also before this time Christ was the Word of God in Moses and in the Prophets."[86] The same Logos

---

The Latin reads ... *aurum ad sensum mentemque revocetur, argentum vero ad verbum atque eloquia referatur.*

79. *Hom. Cant.* 3.9 (trans. Lawson, *Origen*, 201). The Latin reads, ... *qui aliter audire non possunt, nisi his verbis, quae in usu habentur, a scriptura divina humani more referuntur eloquii, ut verbis quidem notis ea et solitis audiamus, sensu tamen illo, quo dignum est, de divinis rebus et incorporeis sentiamus.*

80. This is Origen's interpretation of 2 Cor 4:7. See Harl, "Origène et la sémantique du langage biblique," *VC* 26 (1972): 161–87.

81. On the importance of etymology for Origen see, e.g., *Hom. Num.* 27.5; *Comm. Jo.* 2.196.

82. See *Philoc.* 4.1.

83. E.g., *Comm. Matt.* 12.43; *Comm. Jo.* 1.15.

84. The exact exegetical verse in Col is unclear from the fragment.

85. Quoted in Torjesen, *Hermeneutical Procedure*, 108 (PG 14, col. 1297C). The Latin reads, Data est autem lex Moysi per angelos in manu et virtute mediatoris Christi, qui cum esset in principio Verbum Dei, et apud Deum esset, et Deus esset Verbum, Patri in omnibus ministravit. *Omnia* enim *per ipsum facta sunt* [John 1:3], id est non solum creaturae, sed et lex, et prophetae; et ipse est *mediator Dei et hominum* [1 Tim 2:5]."

86. *Princ.* 1.1 (trans. Butterworth, 1).

who communes with Moses and the Prophets is present in us since we too possess Logos.[87] Interpretation then is engaging one's own Logos with that of scripture.

If the names of scripture are inspired by Christ, then they must, as Philo assumes, be perfect. Therefore, names represent things. Like Philo, Origen recognizes that changes in name represent changes in character. Commenting on the phrase "hallowed be your name" (ἁγιασθήτω τὸ ὄνομά σου) in the Sermon on the Mount, Origen declares, "The word 'name' is a proper noun indicative of the individual quality [ἰδία ποιότης] of the thing named."[88] When a change in name occurs, a change in character is represented: "In the case of men, when individual qualities change, names are also appropriately [ὑγιῶς] changed according to scripture."[89] Origen cites the cases of Abram (changed to Abraham), Simon (changed to Peter), and Saul (changed to Paul) to prove his point. These name "changes" signify changes in quality. But human names are to be contrasted with God's name (τὸ ὤν), which never changes because the Divine "quality" never changes.

So Origen accepts the importance of etymologies. In his exegetical work we find a number of etymologies given, of names in both the Old Testament and the New Testament. Approximately one fourth of Wutz's first volume on etymology is devoted to Origen, and he identifies an "Origenesgruppe" of etymologies in early Christianity.[90] A number of Origen's etymologies are borrowed from Philo.[91] Some, however, are borrowed from other sources.[92] It is questionable that Origen made any of his own etymologies from the Hebrew.[93] In any case, we find in Origen the

---

87. *Hom. Jer.* 17.1–2.
88. *Orat.* 24.2. The Greek reads, "ὄνομα" τοίνυν ἐστὶ κεφαλαιώδης προσηγορία τῆς ἰδίας ποιότητος τοῦ ὀνομαζομένου παραστατική (trans. mine).
89. *Loc. cit.* In classical thought ὑγιής indicates a "word" appropriate to render an "idea" (Harl, *Sur les Écritures*, 275).
90. *Onomastica Sacra: Untersuchungen zum* liber interpretationis nominum hebraicorum *des hl. Hieronymus.* (TU 41; Leipzig: Henrichs, 1914), 1:50–56.
91. In Van den Hoek's catalogue, she lists around 100 etymologies that Origen borrows from Philo ("Philo and Origen," 48–113).
92. Wutz hypothesized a pre-Origenian list of wilderness toponyms in the book of Num (see *op. cit.*, 136–43).
93. Whether Origen knew Hebrew at all can be debated, and those who acknowledge at least some acquaintance with the language find it difficult to determine how much Hebrew he knew. A summary of the evidence may be found in Nicholas De Lange, who himself gives a fairly negative assessment of the scholar's knowlege of Hebrew: "We shall not be far from the truth if we conclude that Origen could not speak or read Hebrew, but that he was fortunate in having acquaintances who did, and who gave him such help as he demanded" (*Origen and the Jews*, 22). The ancient view was that Origen knew Hebrew well,

normal Philonic procedure of name, etymology, and allegorical interpretation. This is the case, for example, with the name "Eden," meaning "delight." Origen cites Ps 36:4 ("delight in the Lord") and proceeds to explain that we must delight in the Logos of God.[94] Origen also interprets "manna" as "what is this?" following Philo.[95] His allegorical interpretation that manna is the divine Logos is similar to Philo's as well.[96] The familiar etymology of "Israel" as "mind seeing God" is inspired by Philo.[97] Thus, it is certain that Origen and Philo shared the same rationale for their etymological exegesis, and it can be conclusively demonstrated that Origen borrowed etymologies and their allegorical interpretations from Philo.

Etymology in Didymus the Blind

Like Philo and Origen, Didymus the Blind found great value in etymological interpretation.[98] For Didymus, etymology was necessary because the literal sense of the biblical text was insufficient to carry the divine νοῦς. He follows Origen in his low view of language as an adequate means of divine revelation. In discussing Zech 4:8–9, Didymus writes:

> In keeping with God's communication by revelations to people who discern interiorily, the psalmist says in the Psalms, 'Then you spoke in a vision to your sons' [Ps 89:19], since God the Word does not speak by ears and voice to those in possession of the spirit of adoption. As the true light, you see, he enlightens the mind of those he wishes to receive his divine communications, speaking by visions rather than by hearing; for example, when God spoke this way to Isaiah in the verse, 'A vision which Isaiah saw' [Isa 1:1], it was not visible things that followed but words.[99]

---

as evidenced by his compilation of the Hexapla (e.g., Jerome, *Vir. ill.* 89.6). Vesey argues that Jerome's Origen is carefully crafted after his own scholarly struggles with the language ("Jerome's Origen: The Making of a Christian Literary Persona," StPatr 28 [1993]: 135–45). Nevertheless, it is not necessary for Origen to have known Hebrew to etymologize. A number of sources would have been available to him, namely Philo, etymological lists, or contemporary Jewish friends.

94. *Comm. Cant.* 1.
95. *Hom. Ex.* 7.5.
96. Cf. *Her.* 79. On manna as "the most generic τί" in Philo see *Leg.* 2.86; *Det.* 118.
97. See *Hom. Gen.* 15.3–4; *Hom. Num.* 11.4; *Hom. Is.* 9.4.
98. Doutreleau calls etymological interpretation "a Didymean characteristic" (*Sur Zacharie* 1:111).
99. *Comm. Zach.* 71.28–72.7 (trans. Hill, *Didymus the Blind: Commentary on Zechariah*, 94). The Greek reads, Συμφώνως τῷ ἐν ἀποκαλύψεσιν ὁμιλεῖν τὸν Θεὸν τοῖς διορατικοῖς οὖσιν κατὰ τὸν ἔσω ἄνθρωπον, ὁ ὑμνωδὸς ἐν Ψαλμοῖς· «Τότε ἐλάλησας ἐν ὁράσει τοῖς υἱοῖς σου», οὐκ ἐν ὠσὶ οὐδὲ φωνῇ τοῖς τὸ πνεῦμα τῆς υἱοθεσίας ἔχουσιν λαλοῦντος τοῦ Θεοῦ Λόγου. Ὢν γὰρ φῶς ἀληθινόν,

One can see Didymus follows Origen's idea that the Logos communicates with the authors of scripture, and human language is an unsuitable medium. He communicated with them "mind to mind," an idea present in Philo and the Fathers in the form of the Stoic λόγος προφορικός and λόγος ἐνδιάθετος.[100] Despite the fact that the biblical text now exists in verbal form, the inspiration of it took place entirely through visions of the mind.[101]

The idea that the Logos never communicated in material language for Didymus is likely related to the Plotinian view of the material and noetic worlds.[102] For Plotinus, the material cosmos is "merely the insubstantial expression of higher realities."[103] The natural world can be compared to a mirror which reflects the higher realities of the noetic cosmos.[104] So language, as a part of the material world, is merely a reflection of a higher, noetic language. Plotinus explains:

> For as language (λόγος) spoken by voice is an imitation (μίμημα) of that in the soul, in the same way that one in the soul is an imitation of the one in the other (hypostasis, mind); likewise, just as the language pronounced by the lips is fragmented (into words and sentences) in contrast to that in the soul, so is the one in the soul (which is the interpreter of that previous language) fragmented by comparison with the one that precedes it.[105]

φωτίζει τὴν διάνοιαν ὧν θέλει δέξασθαι αὐτοῦ τὰς θείας ὁμιλίας· ἐν ὁράσει μᾶλλον ἢ ἐν ὠσὶ λαλεῖ. Αὐτίκα γοῦν καὶ τῷ Ἡσαΐᾳ οὕτω λαλοῦντος Θεοῦ, τῷ· «Ὅρασις ἣν εἶδεν Ἡσαΐας», οὐχ ὁρατά, ἀλλὰ λόγοι ἐπιφέρονται.

100. On Didymus' description of "mind to mind" speech and its relation with the Stoic doctrine see *Comm. Zach.* 320.8 (on Zech 11:17). On the Philonic imposition of the idea see Kamesar, "The Logos Endiathetos." On the Stoic idea in general, see M. Mühl, "Der λόγος ἐνδιάθετος und προφορικός von der älteren Stoa bis zur Synode von Sirmium 351," *Archiv für Begriffsgeschichte* 7 (1962): 7–56.

101. Didymus' view is similar to Philo's. Winston observes, "In the majority of passages Philo seems to emphasize the inferiority of the spoken word to that which is within the mind alone" ("Aspects of Philo's Linguistic Theory," 125). Since divine speech is, of necessity, immaterial (*Deus* 83), the term λόγος προφορικός is never used of divine speech in Philo (an important observation made in Max Pohlenz, *Philo von Alexandria* (*NAWG*; Philologisch-historische Klasse 5; Göttingen: Vandenhoeck & Ruprecht, 1942), 410–87, 447). Apparently *all* divine speech takes places within the minds or souls of the biblical authors in Philo's imagination.

102. Giovanni Reale believes that Plotinus drew inspiration from Philo: "not only is it probable but it is nearly certain that Philo of Alexandria influenced Plotinus" (*A History of Ancient Philosophy: The Schools of the Imperial Age*, ed. and trans. John R. Catan [Albany: SUNY Press, 1990], 4:310).

103. Robert Lamberton, *Homer the Theologian: Neoplatonist Allegorical Reading and the Growth of the Epic Tradition* (Berkeley: University of California Press, 1986), 95.

104. *Enn.* 1.1.8.

105. *Enn.* 1.2.3, 27–30 (qtd. in Lamberton, *Homer the Theologian*, 87–88). The Greek reads, Ὡς γὰρ ὁ ἐν φωνῇ λόγος μίμημα τοῦ ἐν ψυχῇ, οὕτω καὶ ὁ ἐν ψυχῇ μίμημα τοῦ ἐν ἑτέρῳ. Ὡς

As we see in this passage, Plotinus divides language into three categories: (1) the fragmented, material language of voice; (2) the immaterial but fragmented language of the soul; (3) the immaterial and wholly unified language of the mind.[106]

For Plotinus, human language can never capture both image and object (*Enn.* 5.8.5), although the Egyptians come closest with their hieroglyphics (*Enn.* 5.8.6). "Fragmentations" take place the further one moves from the Mind. Given these fragmentations, "direct expression on the part of a god in human language is finally an impossibility."[107] So the bare letters of the biblical text cannot communicate divine thought, although they retain some relative value. The goal is to advance beyond the letter and locate the divine "idea."[108]

In order for an exegete to understand the "idea" behind a text, it is necessary to operate on the level of the λόγος, one step removed from the highest language of the mind, but still accessible to the reader since it subsists under the letter. Philo had already identified the λόγος as the "place" of the thoughts of God (*Opif.* 20), and Origen had identified the λόγος with Christ who impressed these thoughts into the minds of the biblical authors (*Princ.* 1.1). Didymus likewise locates the Logos in the minds of both scriptural author and modern interpreter.[109] The interpreter is thus a pen with which the Logos writes, pointing the reader to itself.[110] Therefore, the level of the λόγος was, from their point of view, equivalent to the level of the divine νοῦς.[111]

Connected with this Judeo-Christian idea is the doctrine of Plotinus that "knower" and "known" are identical.[112] If the biblical exegete can properly tap into the λόγος of scripture, that is, into the mind of God, then he too

---

οὖν μεμερισμένος ὁ ἐν προφορᾷ πρὸς τὸν ἐν ψυχῇ, οὕτω καὶ ὁ ἐν ψυχῇ ἑρμηνεὺς ὢν ἐκείνου πρὸς τὸ πρὸ αὐτοῦ.

106. It is important to keep in mind that virtually all texts were considered as *spoken language* since they were read aloud, even in the context of private study (see the introduction to the recent study of William A. Johnson, *Readers and Reading Culture in the High Roman Empire* [Oxford: Oxford University Press, 2010], 3–16). Thus, the distinction between written and spoken language as such is not important for the authors discussed in this study.

107. Lamberton, *Homer the Theologian*, 169.

108. Didymus uses a number of illustrations (e.g., human speech, which has both reason and voice [*Comm. Gen.* 142.24–27]; the body of Christ, which has both flesh and spirit [*Comm. Ps.* 39.21–25]).

109. E.g., *Comm. Zach.* 4.5–10 and 94.10–16.

110. *Comm. Ps.* 332.2–3; 336.4–5.

111. See David G. Robertson, "Mind and Language in Philo," *JHI* 67 (2006): 423–41, 424–26.

112. See Giovanni Reale, *A History of Ancient Philosophy*, 4:345–46 for a discussion.

becomes, in a way, divine. Didymus says, "It [the Logos] comes to Spirit-filled men without remaining, since it is there at the time it comes to them; then, in fact, then is the time they will also be gods whom he enlightens by coming."[113] Didymus then cites the proof-text Ps 82:6 in the form of John 10:35–36 ("you are gods"). So those who contemplate divine reason are gods, united with the mind of God.[114] This process is described most characteristically in Didymus by the term ἀναγωγή.[115]

So exegesis performed on the letter of the biblical text is of only relative value, although it contains some benefit.[116] Commenting on Ps 1:3 ("like trees planted by streams of water, which yield their fruit in its season"), Didymus likens "fruit" to the "mystical and spiritual understanding of the scriptures" and the leaves to the "common readings which guard the fruit and nourish more naïve men."[117] Discussing Job 5:26 Didymus writes, "And because humans could not understand (the wisdom of God), it was mixed with words, so that they became able to comprehend the 'mixture,' since they cannot understand the (teachings) of wisdom in unveiled form."[118] In his explanation of Eccl 11:7 Didymus compares the spiritual sense of scripture to "honey" and the "letter" to the "comb," an analogy reminiscent of Origen's more biblical "treasure in earthen vessels."[119] These passages make clear that Didymus was perfectly in line with Philo, Origen, and the Neo-Platonists in maintaining the insufficiency of material language to convey divine thought. One must work behind the veil of language to

---

113. *Comm. Zach.* 94.23–25. The Greek reads, Γίνεται δέ, καὶ οὐκ ἔστιν, πρὸς τοὺς πνευματοφόρους ἄνδρας, ὧν καὶ τότε πρὸς αὐτοὺς ὅταν γένηται. Τότε γὰρ τότε καὶ θεοὶ ἔσονται πρὸς οὓς ἐπεφοίτησεν καὶ γέγονεν.

114. Plotinus also maintained that Ideas exist not only in the Mind, but Ideas are actually identical to the Mind. He states, "No Idea is distinguishable from the Mind, each actually being that Mind" (*Enn.* 5.6.6). On this doctrine and its importance, see Reale, *A History of Ancient Philosophy*, 4:343–50.

115. The term in Neo-Platonism carried mystical significance (see Bienert, "*Allegoria*" *und* "*Anagoge*," 62–63).

116. Every word of scripture is useful (e.g., *Comm. Gen.* 174.13–18).

117. Fr. 3 (Mühlenberg) *ad* Ps. 1:3 (trans. Layton, *Didymus the Blind*, 27). The Greek reads, Ἀλλὰ καὶ τοῦ ξύλου τοῦ πεφυτευμένου παρὰ τὰς διεξόδους τῶν ὑδάτων (τοῦτο δέ ἐστιν ἡ τοῦ θεοῦ σοφία) καρπὸς μέν ἐστιν ἡ μυστικὴ καὶ πνευματικὴ τῶν γραφῶν διάνοια, φύλλα δὲ σκέποντα τὸν εἰρημένον καρπὸν αἱ πρόχειροι λέξεις εἰσὶν αἳ πρὸς τῷ ποιεῖν τὸ ἴδιον ἔργον ἐν τῷ φυλάττειν τοὺς καρποὺς καὶ τροφὴ γίνονται τῶν ἀκεραιοτέρων ἀνθρώπων τῶν δι' ἁπλότητα κτηνῶν λεγομένων κατὰ τὸ Ἀνθρώπους καὶ κτήνη σώσεις, κύριε.

118. *Comm. Job* 121.2 (trans. Stefaniw, *Mind and Text*, 214). The Greek reads, [x]αὶ ἐπε[ὶ οὐχ οἷ]ά τε ἦν ταῦτα διανοηθῆ[ναι ἀ]ν(θρώπ)οις, ἀνθρωπίναις λέξε[σιν συνε]κεράσθησαν, ἵν' οὕτως ἐ[φί]κωνται τοῦ «κράματος» λαβέ[σθαι γυ]μνῶν ἀκούειν τῶν τῆς [σοφίας μ]ὴ δυνάμενοι.

119. *Comm. Eccl.* 330.11–15.

access the divine message. Such is possible, in at least one way, by etymological interpretation.

Etymological interpretation is as much a part of the exegetical repertoire of Didymus as it is for Philo and Origen. Although Didymus knew no Hebrew, he understands the polysemic nature of Hebrew terms and the potential of misunderstanding them.[120] In the *Comm. Gen.*, Didymus discusses the fact that both Adam and Enosh mean ἄνθρωπος, and states, "For among the Hebrews, there are many words for 'man,' just as the Greeks also use the words ἄνθρωπος, μέροψ, βροτός, and φῶτα; but these words correspond to their etymologies by nature and are not imposed."[121] It is unclear why Didymus believes the Greek words for man are natural, but the language of the passage suggests that Didymus was acquainted with the ancient debate regarding the development of names.[122]

A second text from the *Comm. Gen.* demonstrates that a name-change reflects a change in nature. Commenting on the name "cherubim" in Gen 3:24, Didymus states:

> Thus, they were called "cherubim" from what inheres in them; for "cherubim" means "multitude of knowledge." Therefore, the name comes from the very thing present in them. In this way also the name of Abram was changed to Abraham and Sara to Sarra and Jacob to Israel. And Peter too, the chosen head of the apostles, received this name on account of progress in virtue, just as those mentioned before. For passing from a more inferior virtue, which was signified by the first names, to a greater one, they appropriately received the names characteristic of virtue, as it is possible to see when reading the translations of these names.[123]

---

120. See *Comm. Gen.* 139.9–14; 147.15–18. On Didymus' lack of Hebrew knowledge see Kramer and Kramer, "Les elements linguistiques."

121. *Comm. Gen.* 146.5–9 (trans. mine). The Greek reads, παρ' Ἑβραίοις γὰρ πολυώνυμος ὁ ἄνθρωπος, ὥσπερ καὶ παρὰ τοῖς ἑλληνιστὶ λαλοῦσιν ἄνθρωπον, μέροπα, βροτόν, φῶτα· ἐτυμολογίαις δὲ ταῦτα ὑποπίπτοντα φύσει καὶ οὐ θέσει εἰσίν.

122. At least some authors attempted to harmonize the two conflicting views. For example, Varro writes, *Duo igitur omnino verborum principia, impositio et declinatio, alterum ut fons, alterum ut rivus* ("therefore the origins of words are two in number: imposition and declension, the one as the source, the other as the stream") (*De lingua latina* 8.5). Of course, Varro regards etymology to be useful for uncovering only imposed names, since derivative words ultimately go back to an original corpus of imposed words. But he acknowledges that some words are unrecoverable in their original form (7.5).

123. 113.15–25 (trans. mine). The Greek reads, Οὕτω χερου<βεὶ>μ ἐκ τοῦ ἐνυπάρχοντ[ος] αὐτοῖς ἐκλήθησαν· 'πλῆθος' γὰρ 'γνώσεως' ἑρμηνε[ύε]ται χε[ρο]υβείμ. Ἀπ' αὐτοῦ οὖν τούτου τοῦ προσόντος αὐτοῖς ἡ προσηγο[ρία] εἴρηται. Ταύτῃ τοι καὶ ἀπὸ τοῦ Ἀβρὰμ Ἀβραὰμ μετωνο[μά]σθη καὶ ἀπὸ Σάρας Σάρρα καὶ ἀπὸ Ἰακὼβ Ἰσραήλ, καὶ Πέ[τρο]ς δ' ὁ πρόκριτος τῶν ἀποστόλων τῆς προσηγορίας ταύτη[ς τ]ετύχηκεν διὰ προκοπὴν ἀρετῆς ὡς καὶ οἱ προεκτεθ[έν]τες. Ἀπὸ γὰρ ὑποδεεστέρας ἀρετῆς, ἥτις διὰ τῶν πρώτω[ν ὀ]νομάτων ἐσημαίνετο, διαβάντες ἐπὶ μείζονα, οἰκείως [ἀρετ]ῆς τὰς προσηγορίας ἐδέξαντο, ὡς ἔνεστιν ἐντυχοντα τα[ῖς τ]ούτων ἑρμηνείαις θεωρῆσαι.

As we have seen above, both Philo and Origen express the idea that changes in name indicate changes in character. In fact, the examples Didymus' examples here are paralleled in Origen's *Or.* 24.2 cited above.[124] So it would seem that Didymus is perfectly in line with his Alexandrian predecessors, if not directly dependent.

When we turn to the mechanics of how an etymological interpretation is conducted, we find that Didymus again falls in line with the tradition. The sequence of name-translation-interpretation present in both Philo and in Origen holds for Didymus as well. In the *Comm. Gen.* Didymus rarely introduces an etymology without some interpretive signal, such as ἑρμηνεύω or μεταλαμβάνω. This structure does not hold true with the same consistency in the other Tura commentaries.[125] Commenting on Gen 12:4–5, Didymus states, "The anagogical interpretation also contains much benefit for the one who is capable of working through everything. Now 'Harran' means 'holes' [τρῶγλαι], which is a symbol of the senses. For the locations of the senses are, as it were, holes. Therefore, God wishes to elevate him [Abraham] from the sense-perceptible objects."[126]

It is noteworthy that the etymology of Haran launches the allegorical portion of Didymus' interpretation.[127] The *Comm. Gen.* maintains a rigid structure of (1) biblical lemma, (2) literal interpretation, designated variously by ῥητόν, ἱστορία, and the like, and finally (3) the allegorical/ anagogical interpretation.[128] Here, citing a word from the biblical lemma at the beginning of the ἀναγωγή helps to focus the audience back onto the verse under consideration.[129] It also functions to ground the anagogical

---

124. The name changes of Abraham, Sarah, and Jacob are also paralleled in Origen, *Hom. Jes. Nav* 23.4.

125. See Nelson, "The Classroom," 152.

126. *Comm. Gen.* 213.4–7 (trans. mine). The Greek reads, Ἔχει δὲ καὶ ὁ τῆς ἀναγωγῆς λόγος πολλὴν τὴν ὠφελίαν τῷ ἅπαντα ἐξομαλῖσαι δυναμένῳ. Χαρρὰν μὲν οὖν ἑρμηνεύεται 'τρῶγλαι', ὅπερ σύμβολόν ἐστιν τῶν αἰσθήσεων· οἱ τόποι γὰρ τῶν αἰσθήσεων ὡσανεὶ τρῶγλαί εἰσιν. Βούλεται οὖν ὁ Θεὸς ἀπαναστῆναι αὐτὸν ἀπὸ τῶν αἰσθητῶν.

127. Didymus explicitly states that the "interpretation of names" is a good starting point for allegorical interpretation in *Comm. Gen.* 139.10–14 (discussed in chapter five above).

128. This structure is not carried out consistently in the other Tura commentaries to the extent to which we find it in the *Comm. Gen.*

129. In the course of Didymus' literal interpretation, he frequently quotes and discusses passages from all over the Bible. This practice, characteristic of Philo (at least with the Pentateuch) and Origen as well, is a long-standing Alexandrian tradition going back at least as far as Aristarchus, who is attributed the statement, Ὅμηρον ἐξ Ὁμήρου σαφηνίζειν, or, in some versions, "each author is his own best interpreter" (see Pfeiffer, *History of Classical Scholarship*, 1:225–26). Porphyry echoes the same idea: ὡς αὐτὸς μὲν ἑαυτὸν

interpretation in scripture. This is important since Didymus is primarily a biblical exegete, as Philo and Origen before him. Etymology is not only an important tool for allegorical interpretation, it is an important structural tool as well.

A second example of etymological interpretation is performed on the term "Nod" (Ναΐδ in Philo; Ναΐν in Didymus). Didymus writes, "For the word 'Nod' means 'tossing;' for where must the one who has withdrawn from peaceful virtue live if not in 'tossing,' an unstable and unreliable thing, which is vice?"[130] Didymus explains that Cain, whose name means "possession," has withdrawn from virtue and is thus condemned to be "tossed" by vice. This moralizing interpretation assists Didymus in painting Cain in Philonic fashion as the stereotypical φαῦλος.[131]

It is important to note that the etymology of "Harran" and its attendant interpretation are borrowed almost verbatim from Philo.[132] The same can be said about his interpretation of "Nod."[133] Didymus is entirely dependent upon others for his etymologies. Some of these were probably so well known that it is futile to seek their "source" (e.g., Adam meaning ἄνθρωπος). But I believe it is possible to locate the origin of most of the etymologies. This is because Didymus usually cites an etymology and proceeds to provide an allegorical interpretation based on the etymology. If both etymology and allegorical interpretation match a predecessor, then we can determine with greater probability that Didymus is dependent on that predecessor.[134] Below is a chart of etymologies provided in the *Comm. Gen.* Although other commentaries feature etymologies, we are seeking to highlight the greatest concentration of potential Philonic influence.

τὰ πολλὰ Ὅμηρος ἐξηγεῖται (*Quaest. hom.* 1.12–14). Unfortunately, the practice often draws the interpreter far away from the lemma under discussion (for Origen see Neuschäfer, *Origenes als Philologe*, 276–85).

130. *Comm. Gen.* 135.26–136.2 (trans. mine). The Greek reads, 'Σάλος' γὰρ ἡ Ναῒν ἑρμηνεύεται· ποῦ γὰρ ἔδει τὸν ἀποστάντα τῆς εἰρηνικῆς ἀρετῆς οἰκεῖν ἢ ἐν τῇ 'σάλῳ', ἀστάτῳ πράγματι καὶ ἀβεβαίῳ, ὅπερ ἐστὶν ἡ κακία;

131. *Comm. Gen.* 131.14. For Cain as "bad man" in Philo see, e.g., *Det.* 119, 140.

132. "For the translation of Haran is 'hole,' and holes are figures of openings used by sense-perception" (*Migr.* 188; see also *Fug.* 45 and *Abr.* 72).

133. See especially *Cher.* 12.

134. The same methodology was applied by Van den Hoek in her analysis of Philonic etymologies in Origen (see "Philo and Origen," 46).

Name	Meaning	Passage	Provenance
Ἄβελ	ἀναφέροντα	144.10–11	Philo[135]
Ἀβράμ	πατὴρ υἱοῦ[136]	113.25	Origen[137]
Ἀβαάμ	πατὴρ υἱῶν	113.25	ibid.
Ἀδάμ	ἄνθρωπος	146.5	Origen[138]
Ἀραριάδ [sic][139]	μαρτυρία καταβάσεως	195.18	—[140]
Βαιθήλ	οἶκος θεοῦ	220.1–2	Origen[141]
Βάραδ	ἀστραπή	249.7	—[142]
Ἐνώς	ἄνθρωπος	145.3, 146.5	Philo[143]
Εὕα	πάντων τῶν ζώντων μήτηρ[144]	105.31	Gen 3:20
Ἰακώβ	πτερνιστής	114.6	Philo[145]
Ἰάφετ	πλατυσμός/καλλονή	165.25	Origen[146]
Ἰσραήλ	νοῦς ὁρῶν Θεόν	114.12	Philo[147]
Καδής	ἅγιος	249.7	Philo[148]
Κάιν	κτῆμα	144.16	Philo[149]
Λώτ	ἀπόκλισις λελυτρωμένος	213.23	Philo[150]
Ναΐν	σάλος	135.26	Philo[151]

---

135. *Sacr.* 51; *Det.* 32.

136. Didymus acknowledges a multiplicity of meanings without listing any others (Ἀβράμ...ἑρμενεύε[ται] πρὸς ἑτέραις καὶ πατὴρ υἱοῦ).

137. *Hom. Num.* 11.4.

138. *Comm. Jo.* 1.1.

139. For Ἀραράτ.

140. Found elsewhere only in Cyril of Alexandria (see Wutz, *Onomastica Sacra*, 2:1059). This term is not etymologized at all, as far I can determine, in the extant works of Philo or Origen.

141. *Comm. Jo.* 20.10.

142. A different etymology is given in Philo (ἐν κοινοῖς or ἐν κακοῖς [there is a textual issue], *Fug.* 213).

143. *Abr.* 8, attributing the definition to the Χαλδαῖοι; *Abr.* 12, *Praem.* 14 and *Det.* 138 interprets Ἐνώς as ἐλπίς.

144. Eve is named Ζωή in the LXX of Gen 3:20, and thus once Eve is called Zoe (*Comm. Gen.* 105.23).

145. *Leg.* 1.61; 2.89; 3.15, 93, 180; *Sacr.* 42, 135; *Migr.* 200, also found in Origen (*Cels.* 5.45).

146. Not represented in Greek among Origen's writings, but in Latin translation (*latitudo* in *Hom. Jes. Nav.* 3.4; both of the etymologies given in Didymus are found also in the Armenian onomastica (Wutz, *Onomastica Sacra*, 2:919).

147. This famous Philonic etymology is technically "the one seeing God" (e.g., *Leg.* 2.34; 3.15; *Sacr.* 134), apparently standing for איש ראה אל, but even Philo himself gives ὁρατικὴ διανοία (*Mig.* 14) and ὁρατικὸς νοῦς (*Mut.* 209). The "mind seeing God" was the etymology taken up in Origen (e.g., *Hom. Num.* 11.4).

148 *Fug.* 196, 213, also in Origen (*Hom. Num.* 19; *Hom. Jes. Nav.* 20).

149. The synonym κτῆσις is used in Philo (*Cher.* 52; *Sacr.* 2; *Det.* 32) and Origen (*Comm. Jo.* 13.62).

150. Philo has simply ἀπόκλισις (*Mig.* 148).

151. The more Hebraic term Ναΐδ is found in Philo, but the etymology is the same (*Cher.* 12).

Σάρα	μικρότης	114.3	—[152]
Σάρρα	ἀρχοῦσα	114.5	Philo[153]
Σήθ	ποτισμός	144.10	Philo[154]
Σήμ	τέλειος	165.25	—[155]
Σούρ	συνοχή	243.4	Origen[156]
Συχέμ	ὠμίασις	215.2	Philo[157]
Χάμ	τολμηρός/προπετής/θέρμη/ἔκτασις	165.26	Philo[158]
Χαναάν	ἡτοιμασμένη	214.6	Origen[159]
Χαρράν	τρῶγλαι	213.4	Philo[160]
Χερυβείμ	πλῆθος γνώσεως	113.17	Origen[161]

In the *Comm. Gen.*, Didymus provides etymologies for twenty-six proper names. Of these, twenty-one are found in the extant works of Philo and/or Origen (over 80 percent). Exactly half can be found in Philo (thirteen of twenty-six), and eight in Origen. The remaining five etymologies can be found in some later source, and thus Didymus gives no etymology that is unrepresented in the patristic tradition, whether before or after his time. It is probable that onomastic lists were in circulation well before the time of Didymus,[162] but the influence of the works of Philo and Origen in the transmission of such etymologies is notable. Wutz recognizes this fact as he speaks of Philo and Origen as the primary influences on Jerome's etymological knowledge.[163] The same can be said for Didymus.

We can gather from the statistical information cited above that Didymus often repeats etymologies found in Philo and Origen, even if he rarely cites his source. In the previous chapter we discussed two different passages in which Didymus explicitly associates Philo with etymological interpretation,

---

152. The etymology ὀλιγοστή is found in de Lagarde (1:204, 1 41) in a list of Origenian etymologies from codex Colbertinus 4124.

153. *Cher.* 7, 41; *Mut.* 77; *Abr.* 99 (cf. *Leg.* 2.82; *Congr.* 6).

154. *Post.* 124.

155. No etymology given in Philo. Wutz lists ὄνομα, but this is an apparent misreading of *Sobr.* 52 (ἔφαμεν πάλαι, ὅτι Σήμ ἐπώνυμός ἐστιν ἀγαθοῦ ...). The etymology τέλειος is found in Lagarde 1:177, 71

156. *Comm. Matt.* 11.

157. *Leg.* 3.25; *Migr.* 221. The alternate form ὦμος is also in Philo (*Det.* 9; *Mut.* 193).

158. θερμή is represented in Philo (*Sobr.* 44).

159. This is Origen's interpretation of Χαναναία (ἡτοιμασμένη ταπεινώσει, *Comm. Matt.* 11), which Didymus apparently mistook for Χαναάν.

160. *Fug.* 188; *Mig.* 88; *Abr.* 72. Philo also gives another option along with τρῶγλαι (ὀρυκτή) in *Somn.* 1.41.

161. *Hom. Num.* 5.3; *Comm. Rom.* 1:3. Cf. Philo, *Mos.* 2.98: Χερουβὶμ ἐπίγνωσις καὶ ἐπιστήμη πολλή.

162. We have a number of manuscripts containing onomastic lists (see Wutz, *Onomastica Sacra*, 1:1–11).

163. *Onomastica Sacra*, 1:13–51.

although he does not assign to Philo a "book of Hebrew names."[164] Pierre Nautin believes the etymologies in the *Comm. Gen.* derive primarily from Origen, with the additional assistance of onomastic lists.[165] Our survey shows that Philo was just as important a source of Didymus' etymologizing interpretations, although we do not deny other potential influences.

Conclusion

Etymological interpretation is one of Philo's greatest gifts to Alexandrian Christianity, although Philo himself must be dependent on predecessors. The Philonic influence is most apparent in the case of Didymus the Blind. First, Didymus explicitly assigns Philo pride of place in etymologizing. Based on our current state of knowledge, it seems unlikely that he derived this opinion from Origen, who never in his extant writings connects Philo with etymologizing.[166] And, although Jerome reports that Origen assigned to Philo the authorship of a "book of Hebrew names," we have no confirmation of it.[167] Second, where Didymus cites Philo, he is often very close to Philo's own language, and often borrows large chunks of allegorical interpretation based on the Philonic etymologies. Van den Hoek takes such cases as evidence of Origen's dependence on Philo, and we should do the same for Didymus. Doubtless, as Nautin acknowledges, Didymus knew Philo directly.[168] Therefore, there seems to be no cogent reason to deny Philo as a primary source, along with Origen, for the etymological exegesis of Didymus the Blind.

---

164. We discuss these passages in ch 5. *Comm. Gen.* 139.10–14 states, "If one wishes to assign these things an anagogical interpretation, let him do this by taking his starting point for the anagoge from the interpretation of names without being pedantic. Now Philo has commented on these things, the necessary benefit of which the lover of learning ought to accept once he has examined them." And *Comm. Gen.* 147.15–18 says, "But if anyone is caught up in the number of the years and in the interpretation of the names of those who are born, Philo can offer a mystical interpretation without being pedantic. So go to him on this point, for he is beneficial."

165. *Sur la Genèse* 1:27.

166. Origen does not cite Philo by name in conjunction with any particular etymology, although he does refer to "one of our predecessors" in etymologizing "Jordan" as κατάβασις (*Comm. Jo.* 6.25; see Philo, *Leg.* 2.89). In addition, Van den Hoek has documented around 100 etymologies that Origen shares with Philo ("Philo and Origen," 48–113).

167. *Nom. hebr., praef.* Eusebius also assigns Philo a work of this sort, but his order (last in the list of Philonic works) and his language (λέγονται) may indicate the tradition was in doubt: τῶν ἐν νόμῳ δὲ καὶ προφήταις Ἑβραϊκῶν ὀνομάτων αἱ ἑρμηνεῖαι τοῦ αὐτοῦ σπουδὴ εἶναι λέγονται (*Hist. eccl.* 2.18.7).

168. Van den Hoek, *Sur la Genèse*, 1:26–27.

7

BORROWINGS FROM PHILO: ARITHMOLOGY

Introduction

To the modern rationalist, numbers in scripture are of little significance. Modern interpreters do not read the Bible's report that Abraham had 318 fighting men in his house (Gen 14:14) as an invitation to numerological symbolism.[1] But the author of *Barn.*, probably an Alexandrian, explains that 318 is actually a veiled reference to Jesus and the cross.[2] And we find similar interpretations in Clement of Alexandria and in Ambrose.[3] For most of the patristic interpreters, all biblical numbers are significant. Just as every word in the Bible is important, so also every number requires deeper explanation. François Bovon explains, "God is the master of names and numbers, thus conferring an ontological quality to any creation."[4] R. Alan Culpepper has documented the various patristic interpretations of the 153 fish that the disciples of Jesus catch in John 21:11, noting the mystical interpretations offered.[5] Many scholars have proposed explanations of numbers in Rev, most commonly 666, or the variant 616.[6] While numbers are symbols in virtually every culture, the Greeks honed the method of linking number with interpretation. And the Hellenistic-Jewish and early Christian interpreters of the Bible put the arithmological science to great use.

---

1. Claus Westermann states emphatically, "it is not necessary to attribute a special significance to this number" (*Genesis 12–36* [trans. John J. Scullion Jr.; A Continental Commentary; Minneapolis: Fortress, 1995], 201).
2. In the LXX the word "eighteen" precedes "three hundred." From this "Barnabas" deduces that "ten" (I in Greek) and "eight" (H in Greek) represent Jesus (ΙΗΣΟΥΣ), whereas "three hundred" (T in Greek) represents the cross (*Barn.* 9:8). See François Bovon, "Names and Numbers in Early Christianity," *NTS* 45 (2001): 267–88, 281–82. For the role of numbers in early Christian theology, see Joel Kalvesmaki, *The Theology of Arithmetic: Number Symbolism in Platonism and Early Christianity* (Hellenic Studies 59; Washington, D.C.: Center for Hellenic Studies, 2013).
3. Clement, *Strom.* 6.85 and Ambrose, *Abr.* 1.3.15.
4. Bovon, "Names and Numbers," 268, citing Irenaeus, *Haer.* 2.25.1.
5. "Designs for the Church in the Imagery of John 21:1–14," in *Imagery in the Gospel of John* (ed. Jörg Frey, Jan G. van der Watt, and Ruben Zimmermann; WUNT 200; Tübingen: Mohr Siebeck, 2006), 369–402.
6. On the use of numbers in Rev in general, see Adela Yarbro Collins, "Numerical Symbolism in Apocalyptic Literature," *ANRW* 2.21.2: 1221–87, 1268–84.

Arithmology in Hellenistic-Jewish Interpretation

Philo was not the first Jewish exegete to recogize the importance of numbers in explaining the Bible. Wis praises God in Pythagorean terms: "You have arranged all things by measure and number and weight."[7] Aristobulus had earlier boasted that Plato and Pythagoras had plagarized the Mosaic doctrines and passed them off as their own.[8] The vestige of such a notion might well be preserved in the Pythagorean tradition, for Ps-Iamblichus records that Pythagoras spend time in Palestine "consorting with the descendants of Mochos, the prophet and philosopher."[9] Other sources place Pythagoras in Egypt, a claim that, if taken seriously, could contextualize the appeal of mathematics in Alexandria.[10] But we need not place geographical restrictions on Pythagoras to understand his influence.[11] Isocrates had called him "the first to bring to the Greeks all philosophy."[12] Such a reputation is sufficient to explain his popularity, but the most famous contribution of the Pythagoreans would be in the realm of mathematics.

Aristotle informs us that the Pythagoreans had invested in numbers ontological significance applicable to every concept in the physical universe.[13] The theoretical doctrines of the Pythagoreans were, by the time of Philo, associated with Platonism, so that many of them could identify the

---

7. Wis 11:20.
8. Fragment 3 (= *Praep. ev.* 13.12.1).
9. *Vit. Pyth.* 14 (trans. John Dillon, *The Middle Platonists: 80 CE to AD 220* [Ithaca, N.Y.: Cornell University Press, 1977], 143).
10. Isocrates, *Bos.* 11.28. Gerald Bostock argues that Pythagorean mathematical theory originated in Egypt and continued to thrive, especially in Alexandria ("Origen and the Pythagoreanism of Alexandria," in *Origeniana octava: Origen and the Alexandrian tradition = Origene e la tradizione alessandrina: papers of the Eighth International Origen Congress, Pisa, 27–31 August 2001* (ed. Lorenzo Perrone, Leuven: Leuven University Press, 2003), 465–78, 465–66).
11. The quest of the "historical Pythagoras" is one of the most elusive problems in ancient philosophy (see Christoph Riedweg, *Pythagoras: His Life, Teaching and Influence*, trans. Steven Rendall [Ithaca, NY: Cornell University Press, 2005], 42–97, and now the summary in Geoffrey Lloyd, "Pythagoras," in *A History of Pythagoreanism* [ed. Carl A. Huffman; Cambridge: Cambridge University Press, 2016], 24–45).
12. Isocrates, *Bos.* 11.28. Diogenes Laertius also knows this tradition (1.13; 8.1). Isocrates implies that Pythagoras learned his "philosophy" from a study of Egyptian religion. The Egyptian visit of Pythagoras is greatly expanded in Ps-Iamblichus's *Vit. Pyth.* 3–4, who adds later that Pythagoras first called himself a "philosopher" (12).
13. *Met.* 985b22–986a3. It is remarkable, however, how few discussions of numbers occur in Pythagorean texts of the Hellenistic age (see further Holger Thesleff, ed. *The Pythagorean Texts of the Hellenistic Period* [Acta Academiae Aboensis A: 30; Åbo: Akademi, 1965]).

ideal forms with numbers. Walter Burkert has theorized that such syncretism between Pythagoreanism and Platonism can be explained by a desire on the part of the more dogmatic Platonists to redefine their system against the dominant Skeptical trends then current in the Academy. In so doing, they actually claimed, on the one hand, to be restoring Plato's original intention, and on the other hand, to be reaching beyond Plato to his teacher, Pythagoras.[14]

Philo, for his part, makes explicit mention of Pythagoras twice and the Pythagoreans on eight different occasions.[15] In fact, he quotes the earliest Pythagorean writer we know, Philolaus (ca. 470–390 BCE)[16] and also refers to the Pseudo-Pythagorean treatise, *On the Nature of the Universe* by Ocellus of Lucania.[17] John Dillon goes so far as to suggest that Philo's *Mos.* was patterned after "the existing life-myth of Pythagoras."[18] There is much Pythagoreanism in Philo to be sure. In his physics he adopts the notions that the Platonic Ideas are reducible to numerical quantities.[19] In his ethics, he seems to fall under the influence of Pythagorean mores.[20] Even his famous scheme of Abraham, Isaac, and Jacob as φύσις, μάθησις, and ἄσκησις is paralleled in the Pythagorean tradition.[21] Many of Philo's comments on specific numbers are probably borrowed from arithmological handbooks, which are probably of Pythagorean origin.[22] It thus seems clear

---

14. Walter Burkert, *Lore and Science in Ancient Pythagoreanism* (trans. Edwin L. Minar Jr.; Cambridge, Mass.: Harvard University Press), 94.
15. Pythagoras: *QG* 1.17; 3.16; Pythagoreans: *Opif.* 100; *Leg.* 1.15; *Prob.* 2, 19; *Aet.* 12; *QG* 1.99; 3.16, 49.
16. *Opif.* 100. On Philolaus, see Carl A. Huffman, *Philolaus of Croton: Pythagorean and Presocratic* [Cambridge: Cambridge University Press, 1993]).
17. *Aet.* 12. This treatise is probably to be dated around 150 BCE (John Dillon, "Ocellus," in *OCD*[4], 1030).
18. John Dillon, *The Middle Platonists*, 142.
19. *Her.* 156. Dillon refers also to *Opif.* 102, but Runia follows Radice in suggesting that the term "ideas" in this passage is not the Platonic *terminus technicus* (*On the Creation*, 277, citing Roberto Radice, "Commentario a La creazione del mondo," in *Filone di Alessandria: La filosofia mosaica* [ed. Clara Kraus Reggiani et al.; Milan: Rusconi, 1987], 286).
20. See Kathy Gaca, "Philo's Principles of Sexual Conduct and their Influence on Christian Platonist Sexual Principles," *SPhiA* 8 (1996): 21–39.
21. Archytas, *De educ.* 3, who has the scheme, φύσις, ἄσκησις, and εἴδησις. I owe the reference to Dillon, *The Middle Platonists*, 152.
22. To my knowledge, no one has devoted a separate study to Philo's use of arithmological handbooks. We can, however, assume that he utilized such sources based on a few examples. Philo's claim that 64 and 729 form both squares and cubes is paralleled in the handbooks (*Opif.* 91–93; see Anatolius 25.14–21; Ps-Iamblichus, *Theol. Arith.* 54.13–55.1 [cited in Karl Staehle, *Die Zahlenmystik bei Philon von Alexandreia* (Leipzig: Teubner, 1931),

that the Pythagorean tradition certainly exerted an influence on Philo's biblical exegesis.

When searching for a proximate influence on Philo's number theory we are met with frustration. Nikolaus Walter once theorized that a floriligium on the number seven was created from Pythagorean sources, and placed in circulation among Hellenistic Jews.[23] The strongest evidence in favor of such a source would be the works of Philo.[24] But it seems just as likely to me that Philo was influenced by the syncretism of Platonism and Pythagoreanism immediately before his time, exemplified most prominently in Eudorus of Alexandria.

Eudorus is indeed the foremost witnesses to the blending of Pythagoreanism and dogmatic Platonism in the first century BCE.[25] Since Eudorus was also from Alexandria, then it stands to reason that the wave of interest in Pythagoreanism in general, and mathematics in particular, would have carried Philo away. Indeed, John Dillon uses Philo to assert that Eudorus regarded the Platonic Ideas as the thoughts of God,[26] and that the Ideas were numbers.[27] Whether or not we accept any specific area of Eudorus's influence on Philo, it is reasonable to assume that the commingling of Pythagoreanism and Platonism, so characteristic of Philo, was initiated by a previous Alexandrian philosopher such as Eudorus, and that number theory was part of this synthesis. Alexandrian Judaism had already inherited the desire to utilize Pythagorean number theory, as is clear from the discussion of the number seven in Aristobulus's fragment 5. The "Pythagorean" arithmological handbooks were also responsible for passing

---

35]). The phrase "walk not on the highways" (*Prob.* 2) is paralleled in Diogenes Laertius 8.17 in a list of Pythagorean quips.

23. *Der Toraausleger Aristobulos* (TU 86; Berlin: Akademie-Verlag, 1964), 200.

24. Kalvesmaki introduces "Pythagorean and Platonist number symbolism in the First Century" with Philo and Plutarch before moving to Eudorus and Moderatus (*The Theology of Arithmetic*, 7–25).

25. John Dillon remarks, "For with Eudorus there enters into Platonism a new influence, an influence which completes the amalgam of doctrine to which we give the name of Middle Platonism, that of NeoPythagoreanism" (*The Middle Platonists*, 115). For an evaluation of whether Eudorus really represents a new version of Pythagoreanism or a continuation of earlier philosophical traditions, see Charles H. Kahn, *Pythagoras and the Pythagoreans: A Brief History* (Indianapolis: Hackett, 2001), 94–104, and John Dillon, "Pythagoreanism in the Academic Tradition," in *A History of Pythagoreanism*, 250–73, 261–66 on Eudorus and Philo.

26. *The Middle Platonists*, 128. Philo is the first author on record to assert this exact doctrine, and Roberto Radice theorized that Philo indeed is its originator ("Observations on the Theory of the Ideas as the Thoughts of God in Philo of Alexandria," *SPhilA* 3 [1991]: 126–34).

27. *The Middle Platonists*, 129.

along this wisdom, and Philo's own discussions of arithmology sound very much like "book wisdom." What is clear is that Philo belonged to a world filled with arithmological interest.

Arithmology in Philo

As we have seen, the science of arithmology was well-established before the time of Philo, and Philo is especially fond of arithmology. He informs us on at least two occasions that he wrote a separate treatise on numbers.[28] While there is no reason to doubt Philo's claim, the treatise was apparently unknown to Eusebius of Caesarea, who produces our earliest catalogue of Philo's works.[29] Still, so many discussions of numbers occur in Philo's writings that we cannot imagine the lost treatise would add much substance to what we already know of his number theory. *Opif.*, for example, features forty-nine paragraphs devoted to the study of numbers, most prominently the number seven.[30] This is why it is surprising that only one short monograph has been devoted to arithmology in Philo, and no study focused exclusively on arithmology in Philo has been published, to my knowledge, in over thirty-five years![31]

A comprehensive study of Philonic arithmology would be a welcome addition, especially in light of recent decades of work in the field of ancient Pythagoreanism. The importance of Philonic arithmology would

---

28. *Mos.* 2.115; *QG* 4.110. The treatise is alluded to in *Opif.* 15, 52 and *Spec.* 2.200.

29. See Eusebius, *Hist. eccl.* 2.18. No certain quotations from the Greek fathers have been identified, but a possible Armenian fragment has been published by Abraham Terian, "A Philonic Fragment on the Decad," in *Nourished with Peace: Studies in Hellenistic Judaism in Memory of Samuel Sandmel* (ed. Frederick E. Greenspahn et al.; Chico, Calif.: Scholars, 1984), 173–82, and several Latin fragments have been tentatively identified by Françoise Petit, *L'ancienne version latine des Questions sur la Genèse de Philon d'Alexandrie* (TU 113–14; Berlin: Akademie Verlag, 1973), 1:71–72 with commentary, 2:89–91.

30. Over 25 percent of Philo's *Opif.* is taken up with comments on numbers (Runia, *On the Creation*, 25).

31. The monograph was released over eighty years ago (Staehle, *Die Zahlenmystik*). Other helpful studies include the contributions of Frank Egleston Robbins, "Posidonius and the Sources of Pythagorean Arithmology," *CP* 15 (1920): 309–22; "The Tradition of Greek Arithmology," *CP* 16 (1921): 97–123, and especially "Arithmetic in Philo Judaeus," *CP* 26 (1931): 345–61. More recently, Horst Moehring has explored the subject with special emphasis on the number seven ("Arithmology as an Exegetical Tool in the Writings of Philo of Alexandria," in SBLSP 1 [1978]: 191–227, republished in *The School of Moses: Studies in Philo and Hellenistic Religion in Memory of Horst R. Moehring* [ed. J.P. Kenney; BJS 304 = SPhiloM 1; Atlanta: Scholar's Press, 1995], 141–76). Most recently on the number five, see Beatrice Wyss, "Philo und die Pentas: Arithmologie als exegetische Methode," in *Alexandria* (ed. Reinhard Feldmeier, Tobias Georges, and Felix Albrecht; COMES 1; Tübingen: Mohr Siebeck, 2013), 361–79.

also assist in the field of patristics, since the Philonic heritage of arithmological interpretation is indeed rich in the Alexandrian patristic tradition. Although this is not the place to offer such a study, an updated comprehensive discussion of Philo's arithmology is a real *desideratum*.

The Philonic View of Arithmology

When we turn to Philo's comments on numbers, we learn that he is a man of his time. We have already seen the potential influence of Eudorus, and whether or not we can attribute Philo's "Pythagoreanism" to such a specific influence, it is true that Philo accepts the superiority of the first ten numbers, as virtually all Pythagorean thinkers do. He writes in *QG* 4.110, "for one is the beginning of the numbers, and ten is the end."[32] Philo also distinguishes in the same paragraph between "one" and the Monad: "And the monad differs from one as the archetype surpasses and differs from the copy, for the monad is the archetype while one is a likeness of the monad."[33] In this passage, "one" refers to the number, and "Monad" to the principle underlying number. Such a statement accords with Pythagorean and Middle Platonic thought in general, but did not characterize the earlier Pythagoreans.[34] Thus we see, by way of example, that Philo is aware of the contemporary developments in arithmological theory.[35]

While it can be established that Philo is a man of his time, it can also be said that Philo does little more than repeat accepted wisdom in the field of arithmological science. Frank Egleston Robbins wrote over eighty years ago, "Philo was no mathematician, in the professional sense, and made no contributions ... to the mathematical sciences."[36] There is no reason to revise this statement today. Still, Philo left his impression on later Christian authors who drew from him methodologically, if not directly. Clement of Alexandria, for example, refers to Philo on two occasions as "the Pythagorean," which, among other potential references, must include his interest in explaining biblical numbers.[37] Origen likewise borrows a few

---

32. Trans. *PLCL* Supp. 10:395.

33. This passage agrees with a parallel in John Lydus (Staehle, *Die Zahlenmystik*, 20).

34. Robbins theorizes that distinguishing the unity from the one is Middle Platonic, being found also in Moderatus and later in Theon ("The Tradition," 120–21). Theon explicitly says that Philolaus and Archytas did not distinguish the terms (see Robbins, "Arithmetic," 348).

35. Philo is not always consistent in distinguishing the "One" from the "Monad" (e.g., *Deus* 11).

36. "Arithmetic," 346.

37. See David T. Runia, "Why Does Clement of Alexandria Call Philo the 'Pythagorean?,'" *VC* 49 (1995): 1–22. On Clement's Pythagoreanism, see Eugene Afonasin, "The

arithmological interpretations from Philo.[38] These authors did not learn mathematics from Philo, but how to apply their mathematics to biblical exegesis. Indeed, they shared with Philo the fundamental Pythagorean assumption that number was inherent in everything that truly exists.[39]

Moses, of course, understood the principles of number better than anyone. In *Spec.* 4.105 Philo writes:

> For as he [Moses] always adhered to the principles of numerical science, which he knew by close observation to be a paramount factor in all that exists, he never enacted any law great or small without calling to his aid and as it were accommodating to his enactment its appropriate number. But of all the numbers from the unit upwards ten is the most perfect and, as Moses says, most holy and sacred.[40]

The preceding comment has as its base the idea that the Jews are permitted to consume the flesh of only ten animals.[41] Thus Moses is obedient to the most perfect number. The more important idea here is that Moses not only knew the mathematical sciences, but always embedded the principles of mathematics in the biblical legislation. This is why all numbers must be interpreted. Aristoblus had already asserted that Moses was the teacher of Pythagoras,[42] a view Philo probably knew and accepted.[43] Thus, by utilizing arithmological interpretation, Philo is merely extracting by means of allegory what Moses intended long ago.

Pythagorean Way of Life in Clement of Alexandria and Iamblichus," in *Iamblichus and the Foundations of Late Platonism* (ed. Eugene Afonasin et al.; Leiden: Brill, 2013), 13–36.

38. E.g., *Hom. Gen.* 16.6 (borrowing from *Migr.* 204) and *Comm. John* 28.1–5 (borrowing from *Opif.* 13; *Leg.* 1.3). On Origen's Pythagoreanism, see Gerald Bostock, "Origen and the Pythagoreanism of Alexandria," in *Origeniana Octava: Papers of the Eight International Origen Congress* (ed. Lorenzo Perrone; Leuven: Peeters), 1:465–78.

39. This was true of Pythagorean number theory already at the time of Aristotle (*Met.* 985b22–986a3).

40. Trans. *PLCL* 8:71–73. The Greek reads, ἀεὶ γὰρ τῆς ἀριθμητικῆς θεωρίας περιεχόμενος, ἣν ἀκριβῶς κατανενόηκεν ὅτι πλεῖστον ἐν τοῖς οὖσι δύναται, οὐδὲν οὐ μικρὸν οὐ μέγα νομοθετεῖ μὴ προσπαραλαβὼν καὶ ὥσπερ ἐφαρμόσας τὸν οἰκεῖον τοῖς νομοθετουμένοις ἀριθμόν. ἀριθμῶν δὲ τῶν ἀπὸ μονάδος τελειότατος ἡ δεκὰς καί, ὥς φησι Μωυσῆς, ἱερώτατός τε καὶ ἅγιος.

41. Deut 14:4–5.

42. Fragment 3.3 (= Clement, *Strom.* 1.22.150; Eusebius, *Praep. ev.* 13.12.3).

43. Ps-Iamblichus records in his *Vit. Pyth.* 14 that Pythagoras spend time in Palestine "consorting with the descendants of Mochos, the prophet and philosopher."

Arithmology in Origen

When we turn to the writings of Origen, we find that arithmology plays a lesser role than in Philo. Origen often bypasses prime opportunities to launch into discussions of number mysticism.[44] Therefore, his influence on Didymus in the field of arithmology does not appear to be as great as Philo's. However, it is certain that Origen had studied mathematics, and his writings reveal at least a basic knowledge of Neo-Pythagoreanism.[45] Porphyry, commenting on the education of Origen, represents him as having a thorough education in Pythagorean literature, stating, "For he was always consorting with Plato, and was conversant with the writings of Numenius and Cronius, Apollophanes and Longinus and Moderatus, Nicomachus and the distinguished men among the Pythagoreans."[46] Porphyry (in Eusebius) also informs us that Origen and the famous Plotinus had the same teacher, Ammonius Saccas.[47]

If Origen and Plotinus shared a similar educational background under Ammonius Saccas, then perhaps the greatest Neo-Platonist and the greatest Christian scholar were born out of the same intellectual environment.[48] But some modern scholars doubt the veracity of Eusebius's citation, claiming that Porphyry did not intend to describe the Christian Origen.[49] If this is correct, then Eusebius's quotations of Porphyry have no historical value for our purposes. If Porphyry is describing the Christian Origen, however, as some scholars argue, then Origen would have been well-educated in Neo-Pythagorean literature.[50]

The evidence from Origen's own writings indicates that he had some knowledge of the Pythagoreans. The terms "Pythagoras" or "Pythagoreans"

---

44. For an example, see the contrast between Philo and Origen on the number fifty (as explained in Bostock, "Origen and the Pythagoreanism of Alexandria," 475 n. 91).

45. The *Panegyric* of Gregory Thaumaturgus lists Origen's geometrical and astronomical studies (*Pan.* 8).

46. Reported in Eusebius, *Hist. eccl.* 6.19.8 (trans. LCL). The Greek reads, συνῆν τε γὰρ ἀεὶ τῷ Πλάτωνι, τοῖς τε Νουμηνίου καὶ Κρονίου Ἀπολλοφάνους τε καὶ Λογγίνου καὶ Μοδεράτου Νικομάχου τε καὶ τῶν ἐν τοῖς Πυθαγορείοις ἐλλογίμων ἀνδρῶν ὡμίλει συγγράμμασιν.

47. For Origen, see Eusebius, *Hist. eccl.* 6.19.6–7; for Plotinus, see Porphry, *Vit. Plot.* 7.

48. See Heinrich Dörrie, "Ammonios, der Lehre Plotins," *Hermes* 83 (1955): 439–78, where Ammonius is interpreted as being heavily Pythagorean in orientation and an ecstatic philosopher.

49. Mark Edwards has argued for two Origens and two Amonii, making it impossible to link Plotinus with the Christian Origen ("Ammonius, Teacher of Origen," *JEH* 44 [1993]: 168–81, and *Origen against Plato*, 53–55).

50 On the view that Porphyry was describing the Christian Origen, see Ilaria Ramelli, "Origen, Patristic Philosophy, and Christian Platonism: Re-thinking the Christianization of Hellenism," *VC* 63 (2009): 217–63.

occur thirty-nine times in the Greek works of Origen. Most of these occurrences, however, simply list Pythagoras among the φιλόσοφοι of ancient times, and the overwhelming majority occur in an apologetic context.[51] In his exegetical works, Origen seems uninterested in typical Pythagorean concepts. He often by-passes prime opportunities to launch into arithmological interpretation, and even when he does engage the arithmological meaning, he usually limits his discussion to no more than a few lines.[52] Even where we find Pythagorean mathematics driving his interpretation, Origen's proof-texts do not come from the philosophical tradition, but rather from the Bible without further comment.

When discussing the dimensions of the ark, Origen launches into a lengthy discussion of the 300 cubits, which he interprets as three sets of one hundred: "Now the number one hundred is shown to be full and perfect in everything and to contain the mystery of the whole rational creation."[53] This sounds very Pythagorean indeed, but Origen's proof is not from mathematics, but from scripture. The number one hundred symbolizes "the whole rational creation" because the shepherd left the ninety-nine to retrieve the sheep that went astray (Luke 15:4–5). The shepherd's descent from the mountains to locate the one lost sheep represents the condescension of the Trinity, which is represented by the tripling of the number one hundred.[54]

When discussing "the fifth part" the Egyptians were to pay to the Pharaoh (Gen 47:24), Origen offers a Philonic explanation that the "five senses in the body are designated, which carnal people serve; for the Egyptians always submit to things visible and corporal. But on the other hand, the Israelite people honor ten, the number of perfection."[55] Origen

---

51. According to a TLG search, almost all occur in *Cels.* (34).

52. A good example is *Comm. Jo.* 10.261–262. Here Origen cites Heracleon's arithmological interpretation of the forty-six years that the Temple was being built (John 2:20). Heracleon interprets "six" as "matter" and "forty" as a reference to the "tetrad." Origen responds by saying, "But see if it is possible to understand forty with reference to the four elements ... and the six with reference to the fact that man came to be on the sixth day" (Ὅρα δὲ εἰ δυνατὸν τὸν μὲν τεσσεράκοντα διὰ τὰ τέσσαρα τοῦ κόσμου στοιχεῖα ἐν τοῖς ἀφωρισμένοις εἰς τὸν ναὸν ἐγκατατασσόμενα λαμβάνειν, τὸν δὲ ἓξ διὰ τὸ τῇ ἕκτῃ ἡμέρᾳ γεγονέναι τὸν ἄνθρωπον; trans. Ronald E. Heine, *Origen, Commentary on the Gospel according to John Books 1–10* [FC 80; Washington, D.C.: Catholic University of America Press, 1989], 313).

53. *Hom. Gen.* 2.5 (trans. Heine, *Origen, Homilies on Genesis*, 82). The Latin reads, *centarius autem numerus plenus in omnibus et perfectus ostenditur et totius rationabilis creaturae continens sacramentum.*

54. Another example can be found in the *Sel. Ps.*, where Origen discusses the Hebdomad, the One and the Dyad, each time appealing to biblical passages for proof of their λόγοι ἀριθμητικοί (PG 12, cols. 1075–1076).

55. *Hom. Gen.* 16.5 (trans. Heine, *Origen, Homilies on Genesis*, 223).

borrows this from Philo's *Migr.* 203–204, in which the Jewish author associates the five senses with the number five. However, whereas Philo goes on for several paragraphs about the significance of the number five, Origen enumerates in short order scriptural prooftexts from both Testaments in an effort to "prove" his hypothesis.

Whereas Philo launches into arithmological interpretations seemingly every time the opportunity presents itself, Origen rarely does so. Contrasting the two authors, Donald Nielsen writes, "Although arithmology was also a tool for Philo, its spirit had a deeper inner connection with the older Jewish images undergoing interpretation. While these tools remain a convenient part of Origen's intellectual equipment, they have a less integral connection with the understanding of creation, or even retribution, than they had in Philo's cosmology."[56] What Nielsen argues is that Origen was aware of the arithmological explanations of the cosmos, but is much less concerned with exploiting the symbolic significance of numbers.

In *Princ.* 1.1.6, Origen describes God as μόνας and ἑνάς, indicating that he regarded God as the transcendent first principle, as did the Pythagoreans and Philo.[57] God cannot be divided, but the Logos (Christ) participates both in the unity of the Monad and in the diversity of matter.[58] Elsewhere Origen writes, "God, therefore, is altogether one and simple. Our Savior, however, because of the many things ... becomes many things, or perhaps even all these things, as the whole creation which can be made free needs him."[59]

That Christ can be both unity and diversity at once is explained by an allegorical interpretation of the dimensions of the Mercy Seat in the *Comm. Rom.*[60] Origen states that Christ is "one and a half" because the number participates equally in the Monad, the absolute transcendent principle, and in the Dyad, associated with matter.[61] The length of "two and a half," likewise, refers to the Holy Spirit since reducing its number to "two" would reduce its own independent powers. Since "two" is "consigned to bodies"

---

56. Donald A. Nielsen, "Civilizational Encounters in the Development of Early Christianity," in *Handbook of Early Christianity: Social Science Approaches*, ed. Anthony J. Blasi, Paul Andre Turcotte and Jean Duhaime (Walnut Creek, CA: AltaMira, 2002), 267–90, 286.

57. See Kalvesmaki, *The Theology of Arithmetic*, 175–82.

58. On the influence of Neo-Pythagorean metaphysics on Origen see Bostock, "Origen and the Pythagoreanism of Alexandria," 468–71.

59. *Comm. Jo.* 1.119 (trans. Heine, 1:58). The Greek reads, Ὁ θεὸς μὲν οὖν πάντη ἕν ἐστι καὶ ἁπλοῦν· ὁ δὲ σωτὴρ ἡμῶν διὰ τὰ πολλά...πολλὰ γίνεται ἢ καὶ τάχα πάντα ταῦτα, καθὰ χρῄζει αὐτοῦ ἡ ἐλευθεροῦσθαι δυναμένη πᾶσα κτίσις.

60. In Exod 25:17 the mercy seat is to be two and a half cubits long and one and a half cubit wide.

61. On Origen's identification of the Dyad with matter see *Fr. in Luc.* 212.

and "sometimes appointed even for unclean things," Origen assumes that scripture would never link divine principles with the Dyad (matter) directly.

The background to this discussion is the usual Neo-Pythagorean linkage of the Dyad both to the Monad and to the material world. But Origen's explanation of this familiar concept is anything but Pythagorean. He has altered the very foundation of Pythagorean mathematics by allowing half-numbers to be explained as having arithmological significance. Only whole numbers exist as principles in Pythagorean thought. Origen seems to assume that his audience would balk at such an unorthodox arithmology since he cites the principle that Christ is "meditator,"[62] and acknowledges that he is being "bold" in offering this interpretation.[63] Still, this passage reveals that accepted arithmological principles could be altered in order to accommodate his biblical exegesis.

In addition to the comments on the first three principles, Origen occasionally refers to Pythagorean concepts of the other numbers. For example, he can refer to six as a "perfect number," citing the six days of creation as proof.[64] Six also "seems to indicate someone industrious and hardworking, but seven indicates rest."[65] Origen also comments on the number ten: "And since the tenth number has been observed to be holy, no few mysteries being recorded to have occurred in the number ten [lit. the decad], we must think that it is not without reason that in the gospel too the tenth hour is recorded as the time when John's disciples went down with Jesus."[66] Unfortunately, no further details are provided to explain why ten is holy.[67]

In one passage in particular Origen refers to the δύναμις ἀριθμῶν, listing several numbers. For example, "seven" is "much honored in divine Scripture," Origen says, citing the Sabbath, Pentecost, and the Jubilee.[68] He then speaks of the Dyad as ἀκάθαρτος ἀριθμός, not because of its divisiveness

---

62. 1 Tim 2:5.
63. See *Comm. Rom.* 3.8.4 (trans. Thomas P. Scheck, *Origen, Commentary on the Epistle to the Romans, Books 1–5* [FC 103; Washington, D.C.: Catholic University of America Press, 2001], 218–19).
64. *Princ.* 4.12. The passage concerns the "six stone water pots" in John 2:6.
65. *Comm. Matt.* 14.5. The Greek reads, ἔοικεν οὖν ὁ μὲν ἓξ ἀριθμὸς ἐργαστικός τις εἶναι καὶ ἐπίπονος, ὁ δὲ ἑπτὰ περιέχειν ἀνάπαυσιν.
66. *Comm. in Ioh.* 2.220 (trans. Heine, 1:154). The Greek reads, Ἐπεὶ δὲ ὁ δέκατος ἀριθμὸς τετήρηται ὡς ἅγιος, οὐκ ὀλίγων μυστηρίων ἐν τῇ δεκάδι ἀναγραφομένων γεγονέναι, νοητέον οὐ μάτην καὶ ἐν τῷ εὐαγγελίῳ τὴν δεκάτην ἀναγράφεσθαι ὥραν τῆς τῶν Ἰωάννου μαθητῶν παρὰ τῷ Ἰησοῦ καταγωγῆς.
67. Origen also suggests that the number "ten" holds a "privileged position in many passages of Scripture" at the beginning of book 10 of the *Comm. Joh* (10.1).
68. "Seven" is often linked with "rest" (e.g., *Comm. Jo.* 13.408).

or identification with evil (as in Pythagorean literature), but because Noah was commanded to take only one pair of the "unclean" (ἀκάθαρτος) animals into the ark. He then says that the Monad is "much before" and "itself first" among all the other numbers, which we might take as a statement of simple mathematics if not for the term "Monad." But Origen then reaches his main point: every Psalm is numbered according to the δύναμις ἀριθῶν. He then says that Ps 50 (MT = 51) is perfectly numbered because the "fiftieth year marks a release of all debt."[69] Again, a passage on the discussion of numbers is not driven by Pythagorean theory, but by references to the Bible.

By comparison, Philo's interpretation of fifty, which Origen may have known, also recognizes the biblical associations with "release," but Philo then proceeds to make an arithmological point about fifty being a perfect number.[70] Philo is rarely content to note the biblical data and move on, but feels compelled to consider the mystical significance of the numbers as well. Although Origen shows himself aware of Pythagorean number theory, he is much more interested in how scripture uses numbers. Whereas Philo is happy to carry his readers along on vast arithmological excurses, Origen rarely spends more than a few lines discussing numbers, even when he notes their importance in context.

Arithmology in Didymus the Blind

With respect to arithmology, Didymus the Blind stands firmly in the Philonic and Origenian tradition. In the *Comm. Gen.* alone there are over twenty separate discussions of numbers, almost all of which lead to an allegorical interpretation. Didymus is far more interested in arithmology than Origen. Ann Browning Nelson observes that the Tura commentaries of Didymus "offer one of the densest uses of numerological interpretation in any patristic author."[71] We can see the mathematical training of Didymus in references to psephic illustrations, indicating that Didymus had studied mathematics in a scholastic setting of some kind.[72] He also understands the

---

69. This is David's confession of guilt (according to the superscription, following Nathan's coming to him after his adultery with Bathsheba). PG 10, cols. 1075–76. Didymus offers a similar explanation of Psalm 50, although he diverges from Origen's understanding (*Comm. Ps.* 106.23–26; cf. Clement, *Strom.* 7.87.2).

70. *Det.* 63–64.

71. "The Classroom of Didymus the Blind" (Ph.D. diss., University of Michigan, 1995), 155.

72. Didymus even states ψῆφος signifies ἀριθμός in the Bible (*Comm. Eccl.* 226.2–3), a point doubtless based on illustrating mathematical principles with small stones (cited in Nelson, "The Classroom," 155).

language of geometry, referring to squares, cubes, tetragons, and even discussing three-dimensional figures.[73] It is interesting to think of a blind student handling pebbles and imagining their arrangement into geometric shapes. It would stand to reason that such concrete illustrations would have held particular interest for a young Didymus. However, Didymus, like Philo, does not discuss mathematics for its own sake, but always utilizes the science in service to anagogical exegesis.

We know Didymus had received a broad education, including studies in rhetoric, astronomy, geometry, arithmetic, and philosophy.[74] In his book on Didymus, Gustave Bardy discusses each of these subjects in relation to the writings of Didymus known to him at the time. When he comes to the subject of arithmology, Bardy remarks, "There is nothing here particularly original, and which implies a robust arithmetical culture."[75] After the discovery of the Tura commentaries, Bardy's assessment needs partial revision. While it is still true that no mathematical originality can be seen in Didymus, it is not true that he was uninfluenced by the "arithmetical culture" of late antiquity.

Even though Didymus probably learned mathematics in school, his arithmological interpretations point to the almost certain conclusion that he, like Philo before him, utilized textbooks. In his brief survey of arithmology in his edition of the *Comm. Zach.*, Louis Doutreleau states, "There were collections of arithmology and it appears that Didymus had his own, or at least that he knew in detail the contents of them."[76] A little later in his survey, Doutreleau opens up another possible influence on Didymus's arithmological theory: "We can see that these speculations [on the mystical significance of numbers], if they do not derive directly from the treatises of Iamblichus, seem to come, without much modification, from the manuals from which Didymus borrowed."[77] Unfortunately, Doutreleau does not cite any parallels from Iamblichus, nor does he develop this idea any further. However, since Iamblichus wrote several textbooks on arithmology and

---

73. See *Comm. Zach.* 4.19–5.7; *Comm. Job* 10.16; *Comm. Gen.* 184.20–21; *Comm. Ps.* 156.20–27; see Nelson, "The Classroom," 158–59.

74. Sozomen, *H.E.* 3.15.1; Theodoret, *H.E.* 3.30.3.

75. *Didyme l'Aveugle* (Études de Théologie Historique 1; Paris: Beauchesne, 1910), 220. The French reads, "il n'y a rien là de particulièrement original, et qui suppose une forte culture arithmétique."

76. *Sur Zacharie* 1 (SC 83; Paris: Editions du Cerf, 1962), 112. The French reads, "Il y avait des recueils d'arithmologie et il apparaît bien que Didyme avait le sien, ou que, du moins, il en connaissait en détail le contenu."

77. *Sur Zacharie* 1: 113–114. The French reads, "On voit que ces spéculations, si elles ne dérivent pas directement des traités de Jamblique, semblent sortir sans grande modification des manuels auxquels Didyme les emprunte."

these were heavily influential in the fourth and fifth centuries CE, it is not too much of a stretch to imagine Didymus had access to Iamblichus's writings on the subject.[78]

The influence of Iamblichus is yet to be traced out, but a more important influence for our purposes is Philo of Alexandria. While both Clement and Origen practice arithmology, neither of them is as enthusiastic about the science as Philo and Didymus.[79] Even without the aid of the Tura commentaries, which were discovered over three decades after his study was published, Bardy could suspect the influence of Philo and Origen on Didymus's arithmological exegesis. Having surveyed some of Didymus's numerological intepretations, he writes, "One recognizes in these speculations the influence of Philo and Origen."[80] Doutreleau likewise mentions that Christian authors in general followed Philo in arithmological interpretation, and the same holds true for Didymus.[81]

What these scholars suspect Didymus himself acknowledges, on one occasion connecting Philo with both arithmology and etymology. Commenting on the chronology of Adam's life (Gen 5:3–5), he writes, "If anyone is caught up in the number of the years and in the interpretation of the names of those who are born, Philo can offer a mystical understanding without being pedantic. So, go to him on this point, for he is beneficial."[82] This passage informs us that Didymus is aware of Philo's comments on numbers, and feels they would assist his students' understanding of the biblical text.

---

78. Additional study is needed to investigate the extent to which Iamblichus may have influenced Didymus in general. But the interest in unifying the classical philosophers (esp. Plato and Aristotle) is present in Didymus, as it was in Iamblichus (on Iamblichus's aims, see Dominic J. O'Meara, *Pythagoras Revived: Mathematics and Philosophy in Late Antiquity* [Oxford: Clarendon, 1989], 87). Also, Didymus was certainly aware of Porphyry (see Philip Sellew, "Achilles or Christ? Porphyry and Didymus in Debate Over Allegorical Interpretation," *HTR* 82 [1989]: 79–100).

79. Clement's extant writings utilize arithmology more for theological proofs than exegetical ones (see Kalvesmaki, *The Theology of Arithmetic*, 125–51). Therefore, we have chosen to omit him from our survey in this work, which is focused on biblical exegesis.

80. *Didyme*, 220. The French reads, "On reconnaît dans ces spéculations, l'influence de Philon et d'Origène." Curiously, this is one of only two references to Philo in Bardy's entire book on Didymus (see index). This point is noted by Runia, *Philo in Early Christian Literature*, 198 n. 74.

81. *Sur Zacharie* 1:112.

82. *Comm. Gen.* 147.15–18. See our discussion of this passage in ch 5 above.

The Methodology of Didymus's Arithmology

The methodology of Didymus's arithmological exegesis indicates that he had read both Philo and Origen. First, as Anne Browning Nelson observes, almost all of Didymus's arithmological discussions occur in the context of allegorical interpretation.[83] This detail reflects Philo's tendency to locate in numbers universal truths embedded in the allegorical sense of scripture. Didymus also tends to cite the biblical occurrences of a particular number before launching into arithmology, and sometimes cites only biblical testimony. This tendency reminds us of Origen, who almost always cites biblical prooftexts instead of arithmological theories. For example, the number ten is holy, according to Didymus, because there are ten commandments.[84] The number forty is "distressing" (κακωτικός) because the Israelites wandered in the desert for forty years and Jesus was tempted for forty days in the desert.[85]

Didymus also appears to temper his enthusiasm for number symbolism on occasion. First, he acknowledges that not every number carries symbolic significance.[86] He will often by-pass prime opportunities to interpret numbers allegorically.[87] While God is the creator of numbers, and every number in scripture is put there by God, not every number demands a spiritual interpretation.[88] This attitude seems to approximate the position of Origen. However, his technical discussions of the mathematical sciences and the mystical properties of numbers remind us much more of Philo. Therefore, Didymus occupies a position halfway between Origen, whose primary source on numbers is the Bible itself, and Philo, who frequently offers more "Pythagorean" explanations familiar from the arithmological handbooks.

A good example of a typical arithmological interpretation in Didymus can be found in his discussion of Gen 6:3: "Their days shall be 120 years." He writes:

> Everything which God does or says, he both does and says for a good reason [κρίσει τινὶ ἀληθινῇ]. So since he says, as though a necessary point, "their days shall be 120 years," and this does not seem right, it is necessary to search out another meaning [διάνοια] for the passage at hand. For the numbers which

---

83. "The Classroom," 154.
84. *Comm. Gen.* 35.3 (cited in Nelson, "The Classroom," 157).
85. *Comm. Gen.* 190.10 (cited in Nelson, "The Classroom," 158).
86. *Comm. Ps.* 259.32.
87. The example Nelson cites comes at the beginning of the *Commentary on Zechariah*, where Didymus allegorizes neither the age of the prophet nor the date of his prophecy (1.1–3), "The Classroom," 156.
88. *Comm. Ps.* 108.26–27 (cited in Nelson, "The Classroom," 156).

158   CHAPTER 7

> are used in the scriptures are not used by chance [ὡς ἔτυχεν], but for some reason. And often they are introduced in a way unsuitable to the literal meaning (ἱστορία), and are thus used for some [other] reason. For when scripture says, "I have left for myself 7000 men who have not bowed the knee to Baal,"[89] there is no literal meaning—so many men could not have escaped the notice of Elijah [lit. "the saint"]![90] Rather, for the sake of clarifying the meaning, it is stated clearly that everyone who surpasses the sense-perceptible objects and the world created in six days, having come into the hebdomad, that is, into the higher sense [ἀναγωγή], is left behind by God as a watcher and helper of others. So the number six is used for the creation of the world, as a perfect number, just as was mentioned earlier. "He will deliver you six times from necessities,"[91] is not mentioned because of a number or because he will deliver from necessities only so many times, but the text states this since, as long as one is in the affairs of the [world] which was created in six [days], he is subject to necessities. They do not have the purification of rest, which is indicated by the hebdomad, as the Savior says to his disciples, "You are not of this world," having surpassed the necessities in it.[92] The preceding discussion was provided in order to explain that the number 120 was not used in vain, but it is necessary to notice that scripture, in utilizing numbers, fits their natural senses [οἰκεῖα] to them, as in the case of the world being created in six days.[93]

The foregoing quotation is a thesis statement on the purpose of biblical numbers in Didymus. The scriptures contain no superfluity, and thus every number must carry significance. However, one must beware of taking biblical numbers literally. Oftentimes, numbers are intended for allegorical interpretation. Such is the case with "120 years." The number cannot be literally applied to length of years in one's physical lifespan any more than 7000 can be the number literally intended in God's conversation with Elijah.

After a few more lines of discussing the greatness of the number six, Didymus returns to his discussion of 120, which reminds us of Philo's own comments on the same number:

> Let us, moreover, investigate the properties of the number. It is said that this number, when its own factors are added together, is doubled. For if one adds half of 120, which is sixty, a third, which is forty, a fourth which is thirty, a fifth which is twenty-four, a sixth which is twenty, an eighth which is fifteen, a tenth which is twelve, a twelfth which is ten, a fifteenth which is

---

89. Rom 11:14; cf. 1 Kgs 19:18.
90. Origen is not so blatant in his rejection of the literal meaning, but he too allegorizes the 7000 men as those who have received "rest" (because of the number seven; *Comm. Rom.* 8.7.3–4).
91. Job 5:19.
92. Cf. John 8:23; 15:19.
93. *Comm. Gen.* 154.3–155.3.

eight, a twentieth which is six, a twenty-fourth which is five, a thirtieth which is four, a fortieth which is three a sixtieth which is two and a one hundred and twentieth which is one, this makes 240, double of 120, which consists of fifteen numbers.[94] Now the number fifteen, when increasing by a progression makes 120.[95] But the fifteen has been used to the most perfect degree, for there are six degrees of the number itself [...].[96] But the phrase "Give a part to the seven" refers to the Old Testament, and "to the eight," which is a symbol for resurrection and the New Testament, making a total of fifteen.[97] Hence the Jews, accepting only the Old Testament, give "a part to the seven," but fail to listen when it says "give to the eight." But also the heretics who reject the Old Testament, while giving a part to the eight, fail to offer to the seven. But the orthodox man [ἐκκλησιαστικός] accepts both covenants, giving both parts. Therefore, since the number 120 doubles itself, it is a symbol of the teaching which produces the true life honored according to both action and contemplation, in order that, by doubling the lifespan [βίος] one might have this life [ζωή] which is indicated by the number ....[98]

It is interesting to note that Philo interprets the number 120 in a generic way as indicating human life.[99] Didymus, however, refers the number not to physical life, but to spiritual life. In order to do this he moves from 120 to fifteen (the number of the factors of 120), and this makes him think of

---

94. 1, 2, 3, 4, 5, 6, 8, 10, 12, 15, 20, 24, 30, 40, 60.
95. I.e., 120 is the sum of the first fifteen numbers added together. The same point is made by Philo in an exegesis of Gen 6:3 (see QG 1.91).
96. The manuscript goes blank (see Nautin, *Sur la Genèse*, 2: 34).
97. Eccl 11:2. This passage is central to Didymus's doctrine of the coherence of scripture (see Bayliss, *The Vision of Didymus*, 72).
98. *Comm. Gen.* 155.15–156.16 (trans. mine). The Greek reads, Ἴ[δωμε]ν τοίνυν τὸ ἰδίωμα τοῦ ἀριθμοῦ. Λέγεται τοίνυν ὅ[τι οὗτος] ὁ ἀριθμὸς ἐκ τῶν ἑαυτοῦ μερῶν συντεθέντων δι[πλασιά]ζεται· ἐὰν γὰρ συντεθῇ τὸ ἥμισυ, ὅ ἐστιν ἑξήκον[τα, τρ]ίτον μ, τέταρτον λ, πέμπτον εἴκοσι τέσσερα, ἕκτο[ν] εἴκοσι, ὄγδοον δέκα πέντε, δέκατον ιβ, δωδέκατ[ον] ι, πεντεκαιδέκατον ὀκτώ, εἰκοστὸν ϛ εἰκοστοτέ[ταρ]τον πέντε, τριακοστὸν τέσσερα, τεσσερακοστὸν τρεῖς[, ἑξ]εκοστὸν δύο, ἑκατοστοεικοστὸν ἕν, ἀποτελεῖ τὸν δ[ιακό]σια τεσσεράκοντα, διπλασίονα ὄντα τοῦ ἑκατὸν εἴκο[σι, οὗ] τὰ μέρη δέκα πέντε τυγχάνει, ὥσπερ δέκα πέντε αὐ[ξόμ]ενος κατὰ παραύξησιν ποιεῖ τὸν ἑκατὸν εἴκοσι. Ὁ δὲ δέκ[α π]έντε ὅτι εἰς τὸν τελειότατον βαθμὸν παρελήμφθη, δῆλόν ἐστιν· τοῦ γὰρ [αὐ]τοῦ ἀριθμοῦ ἓξ βαθμοί *** Ἀλλὰ καὶ τὸ «δὸς μερίδα τοῖς ἑπτά», [ὅπε]ρ δηλοῖ τὰ τῆς παλαιᾶς διαθήκης, «καί γε τοῖς ὀκτώ», ὅ[περ] ἀναστασίμου [καὶ] καινῆς διαθήκης ἐστὶν σύμβολ[ον, τ]ὸν δέκα πέντε [συ]νάπτει. Ἰουδαῖοι γοῦν τὴν πα[λαιὰ]ν μόνον δεχόμενοι τοῖς ἑπτά διδόασιν μερίδα, [μὴ] ἀκούοντες τοῦ καὶ τοῖς ὀκτὼ αὐτὴν διδόναι· ἀλλὰ [καὶ] οἱ ἑ]τερόδοξοι ἀθετοῦντες τὴν παλαιάν, τοῖς ὀκτὼ μ[ερίδα] διδόντες, παραιτοῦνται τοῖς ἑπτά παρέχειν· τοῦ ἐκ[κλησια]στικοῦ ἀμφοτέρας δεχομένου τὰς διαθήκας, ἀ[μφοτέ]ροις μερίδα δίδωσιν. Ἐπεὶ οὖν καὶ ὁ ἑκατὸν εἴκοσι [ἀριθμὸς] διπλασιάζεται, σύμβολον ὑπάρχει διδασκαλ[ίας διε]γειρούσης ἐπὶ τὴν ἀληθῆ ζωὴν κατά τε πρᾶξιν [καὶ θε]ωρίαν τιμωμέν[η]ν, ἵνα διπλασιάσαντες τὸν βίο[ν τὴν] ζωὴν ταύτην ἔχωσιν διὰ τοῦ ἀριθμοῦ δηλουμ[ένην]....
99. QG 1.91.

Eccl 11:2, where the numbers seven and eight are found together.[100] With the assistance of allegorizing those numbers, he arrives at the idea that the number 120 is actually positive rather than negative. Since the fifteen factors of 120 equal 120 doubled (240), Didymus thinks of a double measure of life, both physical and spiritual. One is characterized by physical action and the other by spiritual contemplation. Thus, by accepting both the seven (Old Testament) and the eight (the New Testament) one is offered a double portion of "life." The Philonic insight is combined with an allegorical interpetation in the Origenian fashion.

It is interesting to note that, in *QG* 1.91, commenting on the same number, Philo makes the most of the mathematical observations also found in Didymus. He notes that 120 is a double number, and also comments on the fifteen factors of 120. But Philo's explanation is much more mathematically complex. Therefore, if Didymus is borrowing from Philo here, he simplifies the mathematics—a move his students likely appreciated.[101] He also tacks on his interpretation of Eccl 11:2 which is, of course, absent in Philo. This passage provides an example of Philo's potential generic influence, but it is apparent that Didymus has added plenty of information on his own.

Another example can be located in Didymus's discussion of Gen 1:14–19, which drifts into an excursus on numbers. He notes that the six days in Gen 1 are not to be taken literally (since days are measured by the sun, which was not created until the fourth day).[102] Rather, the days of Gen 1 must be intended to reflect the symbolic power of numbers.[103] This principle is born out by the fact that six is a perfect number. Didymus writes, "For the first of the perfect numbers is six. And they say that perfect numbers are equal to the sum of their own parts, and there are only four

---

100. Eight is associated with the resurrection in early Christianity, probably because the resurrection occurred on Sunday (if the Sabbath is the seventh, then Sunday would be the eighth day [cf. John 20:26]). This is the explanation in article no. 349 of the Catechism of the Catholic Church. Also, by gematria, the numerical equivalent to both Ἰησοῦς and ἡ ἡμέρα ἡ τρίτη, the day of the resurrection, is 888.

101. In *QG* 1.91, as often in the *Quaestiones*, Philo simply extols the arithmological characteristics of the biblical number. Here, in connection with the number 120, Philo lists seven explanations of the number. Strangely, though, he concludes with a literal interpretation: "But perhaps a hundred and twenty years are not the universal limit of human life, but only of the men living at that time, who were later to perish in the flood after so great a number of years, which a benevolent benefactor prolonged, allowing repentance for sins" (trans. *PLCL* Supp. 10:60).

102. Philo makes a similar argument (*Leg.* 1.2–3).

103. The argument that God is beyond time and thus the days of Gen 1 cannot be literal is Philonic (*Opif.* 13, 28; *Leg.* 1.20).

such numbers from four to 10,000.[104] Six is the first, of which half is three, a third is two, a sixth is one, and adding these together produces six."[105]

Discussions of perfect numbers are standard in the mathematical handbooks of late antiquity, and both Philo and Didymus were aware of them.[106] The number six is the most often discussed perfect number, probably because the proofs of its perfection are much simpler.[107] Philo uses the argument in order to establish the sacred nature of the number in Gen 1. On its mathematical properties Philo writes, "Of the numbers (proceeding) from the unit, six is the first perfect number. It is equal to (the product of) its parts [1 × 2 × 3], and is also formed by their sum [1 + 2 + 3], namely the three as its half and the two as its third and the unit as its sixth."[108] Now this line of reasoning is common, and thus Didymus need not depend on Philo for it. However, Didymus's comment on the number six comes right after a comment that the days of creation cannot be literal, just as in Philo's *Opif.*[109] So the order in which the arguments are made likely indicates Philonic influence, as Pierre Nautin has noted.[110]

A way in which Philonic influence is perhaps more apparent can be found in Didymus's discussion of the hebdomad. Didymus, like Philo, devotes more space to seven than to any other number.[111] Didymus associates the hebdomad with the "epoptic power" of God on one occasion.[112] He also frequently associates it with perfection, rest and purity.[113] These connections are found in many patristic authors, and need not come from

---

104. Didymus continues in this context to discuss the next perfect number, 28.

105. *Comm. Gen.* 34.10–13. The Greek reads, Πρῶτος γὰρ ὁ ἓξ τελείων ἐ[στί]ν· τελείους δὲ ἀριθμοὺς φασιν τοὺς ἐκ τῶν ἑαυτῶν με[ρ]ῶν ἀ[π]αρτιζομένους, τέσσαρες δὲ μόνοι εἰσὶν ἀπὸ μονάδος ἕως μυρίων. Πρῶτος οὖν ἐστιν ὁ ἕξ, οὗ ἥμισυ τρία, τρίτον δ[ύ]ο, ἕκτον ἕν, ὧν συντεθέντων ὁ ἓξ ἀποτελεῖται.

106. See Theon of Smyrna 45.9ff; Nicomachus, *Ar.* 1.16; Iamblichus, *In Nic.* 32.20ff (cited in Burkert, *Lore and Science*, 431 n. 27).

107. Four perfect numbers were known in antiquity: six, 28, 496 and 8128 (Nelson, "The Classroom" 163 n. 106).

108. *Opif.* 13 (trans. Runia, *On the Creation*, 49). The Greek reads, τῶν τε γὰρ ἀπὸ μονάδος [ἀριθμῶν] πρῶτος τέλειός ἐστιν ἰσούμενος τοῖς ἑαυτοῦ μέρεσι καὶ συμπληρούμενος ἐξ αὐτῶν, ἡμίσους μὲν τριάδος, τρίτου δὲ δυάδος, ἕκτου δὲ μονάδος.

109. περὶ τῶν ἓξ ἡμερῶν δεῖ νοεῖν ὡς οὐ χρονικῆς ἕνεκα παρ[εκτάσεως] παρειλημμένων, ἀλλὰ λόγου οἰκείου τῇ δημιουργίᾳ τ[οῦ θεοῦ] καὶ τῆς τοῦ ἀριθμοῦ δυνάμεως (*Comm. Gen.* 34.7–10).

110. *Sur la Genèse* 1:93.

111. In *Comm. Gen.* see 35.25–27; 56.23–25; 154–55; 177.8–10; 183. 25-184.21; see also *Comm. Eccl.* 317.15–26; 319.9–10; *Comm. Job* 135.28–29; *Comm. Ps.* 88.19–24; 107.18; 120.28; 125.7; 257.17; 291.27; *Comm. Zach.* 11.23–24; 117–118; 198.20-200.20; 154.20–25; 210.20-211.10; 406.6–8 (this list is taken from Nelson, "The Classroom," 196).

112. *Comm. Gen.* 56.23–24.

113. See, e.g., *Comm. Gen.* 133.15; 154.23; *Comm. Zach.* 11.24; *Comm. Eccl.* 317.15–17.

162   CHAPTER 7

Philo at all.[114] But one passage from the *Comm. Gen.* suggests a much closer relationship between the two thinkers.

Didymus states:

> All the numbers inside the decad are produced by doubling or tripling except for seven. For example, one produces two, and two produces four after it has been produced by one, and four produces eight after it has been produced by two, and five produces ten. Now six, once it has been produced, does not itself produce. But seven is neither produced by what comes before nor produces anything that comes after itself in the decad. But two produces six and three produces nine when these are multiplied by three. But it has another property as well. For if you multiply by two the numbers starting from the monad seven times, they will produce an equilateral square: 1, 2, 4, 8, 16, 32, 64.[115] Now 64 is a square (8 × 8 = 64) and a cube (4 × 4 × 4 = 64). But if you multiply the numbers by three seven times, again starting from the monad, you get 729 which is itself also both a square and a cube: 1, 3, 9, 27, 81, 243, 729. 729 is a square (27 × 27 = 729) and a cube (9 × 9 × 9 = 729). Now a square signifies solidity, but the cube ....[116] Therefore it is not without reason that the comments made about numbers are embedded in [ἔγκειμαι] the divine scriptures in a believable way.[117]

The preceding explanation of the number seven is inspired by Philo's discussion in *Opif.* 91–101, although not in precise sequential order.[118] First, Didymus notes that all the numbers from one to ten are produced by

---

114. See G.W.H. Lampe, *A Patristic Greek Lexicon* (Oxford: Oxford University Press, 1969), s.v. "ἑπτά."

115. Note that there are seven numbers in the series.

116. The manuscript breaks off.

117. *Comm. Gen.* 183.27–184.23. Πάντες οἱ ἐντὸς δεκάδος ἀριθμοὶ διπλασιαζόμε[νοι ἢ τ]ριπλασ[ιαζόμενοι π]λὴν τοῦ ἑπτὰ καὶ γεννῶσιν καὶ γεν[νῶνται, ο]ἷον ὁ εἷς γεννᾷ τὸν δύο, καὶ ὁ δύο τὸν τέσσε[ρα] οὕτ[ως γεννη]θεὶς ὑπὸ τοῦ ἑνός, ὁ δὲ τέσσερα τὸν ὀκτὼ γεν[νη]θεὶς [καὶ αὐτὸς] ὑπὸ τῶν δύο, ὁ δὲ πέντε τὸν δέκα, καὶ ὁ ἓξ δέ ποτ[ε γεννώμεν]ος οὐ γεννῶν, ὁ δὲ ἑπτὰ οὔτε ὑπὸ τῶν φθασάντων γ[εννᾶται οὔ]τε τινὰ μεθ' ἑαυτὸν ἕως δεκάδος γεννᾷ· ἀλλὰ καὶ ὁ δύο τὸν ἓξ καὶ ὁ τρία τὸν ἐννέα τριπλασιαζόμενοι γεννῶσιν. Ἔχει δὲ κα[ὶ] ἕτερόν] τι προνόμιον· ἐὰν γὰρ ἐν διπλασίονι λόγῳ πολυπλασιά[ζῃς το]ὺς ἀπὸ μονάδος ἀριθμοὺς ἕως ἑπτά, ἴσος ἅμα καὶ τετράγ[ωνος] γίνεται· εἷς γάρ, δύο, τέσσερα, ὀκτώ, δέκα ἕξ, τριάκοντα δύο, [διπ]λασιασθέντα τὸν ἑξήκοντα τέσσερα, ὅστις τετράγωνος [μέν ἐ]στιν, ὀκτὼ γὰρ ὀκτὼ ἑξήκοντα τέσσερα, κύβος δέ, τέτρα γ[ὰρ τέ]σσερα τέτρα ἑξήκοντα τέσσερα. Ἀλλὰ καὶ τριπλασιαζόμ[ενοι] ἕως ἑπτὰ πάλιν ἀπὸ μονάδος ἀποτελεῖ τ[ὸν] ἑπτακόσια ε[ἴκοσι ἐνν]έα καὶ αὐτὸν ὄντα τετράγωνον ἅμα κ[αὶ] κύβον· εἷς [γάρ, τρία], ἐννέα, εἴκοσι ἑπτά, ὀγδοήκοντα εἷς, δ[ιακόσια τ[εσσε[ράκοντα τρ]ία, ἑπτακόσια εἴκοσι ἐννέα, ὡς εἴρηται, κ[ύβον] ἅμα κ[αὶ τετράγων]ον συμπληροῖ, τετράγωνον μὲν οὕτως· [ἑπτὰ εἰ]κοσάκ[ις εἴκοσι ἑπ]τὰ ἑπτακόσια εἴκοσι ἐννέα, κύβον οὕτως· ἐ[ννεά]κις ἐν[νέα ἐννεά]κις ἑπτακόσια εἴκοσι ἐννέα. σημαίνει μ[ὲν] τὸ τετρ[άγωνον] βεβαιότητα, ὁ δὲ κύβος *** Οὐκ ἀπεικ[ότως] οὖν ἂν εἴη τὰ περὶ τῶν ἀριθμῶν εἰρημέ[να] τῷ μηδὲ[ν ἀρ]γὸν ἐγκεῖσθαι τοῖς θείοις γράμμασιν πεπιστω[μέ][ν]ως.

118. Nautin is quite clear: "Ce qui suit sur l'hebdomad vient de Philon, *De Opif.* 93–94" (2:97).

doubling or tripling other numbers except for seven. Philo too affirms that the number seven alone is neither generated nor generates, as the handbooks claim.[119]

Second, the examples cited by Didymus conform to Philo's three categories of numbers within the decad: (1) those which generate but are not generated; (2) those which are generated but do not generate; (3) those which are both generated and who themselves generate.[120] Didymus does not list these categories, as Philo does, but his examples confirm the Philonic system, beginning with the number which generates, but is not generated (number one), then moving to examples of the numbers that both are generated and generate. Then he notes that the number six is generated, but does not itself generate. Finally, he mentions the number seven, which corresponds to none of these three categories.

Didymus then switches to another property of the number seven. Multiplying by two or three the numbers in the decad until one reaches seven will produce sixty-four or 729, respectively.[121] Both of these numbers form both squares and cubes.[122] Philo has the exact information in similar language. He writes that seven is "a number whose starting-point in each case is the unit in accordance with the double or the triple or with numbers generally corresponding to these, such as sixty-four and 729, the former attained by doubling (seven times) from the unit, the latter by tripling."[123]

Didymus then notes that the numbers formed in this fashion, sixty-four and 729 being examples, form both cubes and squares. Philo notes that "the seventh term of any regular progression, starting from unity and with a ratio of two, three, or any other number, is both a cube and a square...." He then cites the two numbers sixty-four and 729 again. Philo's text is even important for determining where the manuscript of Didymus is lacunose. Didymus writes, "Now a square signifies solidity, but the cube...." Philo explains that "this number [seven] contains the kinds of both incorporeal and corporeal being, the former [incorporeal] through the surface produced by squares, and the latter [corporeal] through the solidity produced

---

119. Anatolius, cited in Ps-Iamblichus, *Theol. Arith.* 54.18ff. states that this distinction belongs to both one and seven.
120. *Opif.* 33, 99, and see Robbins, "Arithmetic" 351–52.
121. On Philo's use of ratios, see Robbins, "Arithmetic," 352–53.
122. These discussions occur also in the handbooks (Anatolius 25.14–21; Ps-Iamblichus, *Theol. Arith.* 54.13–55.1 [cited in Staehle, *Die Arithmetik*, 35]).
123. *Opif.* 91 (trans. Runia, *On the Creation*, 71). These numbers are cited as examples in Anatolius 35.14–21.

by cubes."[124] We may surmise that the lacuna in Didymus's text originally had a similar discussion about the properties of cubes, and he may have even discussed corporeality in connection with them.[125] Both Philo and Didymus depend on handbooks here, but the discussion of Didymus is too similar to Philo's not to see a more direct influence.

The two lengthy passages we have discussed from the *Comm. Gen.* offer the clearest parallels between the arithmology of Philo and that of Didymus. Other parallels exist, but they are too generic to argue definitively in favor of influence.[126] I have been unable to locate any indisputable parallels between Origen and Didymus in the mathematical sciences. It would appear that Didymus frequently uses his own knowledge of mathematics to interpret biblical numbers. In contrast to etymology, where he is often directly dependent upon predecessors, in the realm of arithmology Didymus has less need for the mathematical explanations of Philo and Origen. Even when his arithmology is the same, his interpretation often differs from his predecessors.

Nevertheless, a more generic influence can be noted. The Alexandrian model of "scripture interpreting scripture" must be applied also to biblical numbers. Didymus usually allows biblical passages to direct his explanations of numbers. Even where he discusses Greek arithmology, parallel scriptures are still cited. Likewise, Philo has taught Didymus to use the mathematical sciences, and not just the Bible, to interpret biblical numbers. While Philo applies mathematics to elucidate the biblical text, he does not normally seek parallels in scripture beyond the textual lemma.[127] This is especially the case in his *Quaestiones*. Didymus does associate Philo with arithmological exegesis, and certainly used him as a source, but it is difficult to determine in most cases where he is following Philo and where he is applying his own knowledge, whether repeated from his first-hand education, or borrowed from the mathematical handbooks that circulated widely in late antiquity. Philo is most certainly a source of arithmological interpretation for Didymus, but Didymus is more than capable of continuing the Philonic legacy of arithmological exegesis.

---

124. *Opif.* 92 (trans. Runia, *On the Creation*, 71).

125. That the number seven comprises both the corporeal (solid) and the incorporeal (surface) is found in Macrobius, although the parallel is inexact (1.6.35; see Runia, *On the Creation*, 272).

126. E.g., that the number two refers to divisible matter, or that five refers to the five senses (*Comm. Gen.* 44.8–9; 48.1–7; 165.8–13).

127. Of course, Philo is focused, on the whole, on a much smaller segment of scripture (the Pentateuch).

8

PHILONIC BORROWINGS:
GENERAL EXEGETICAL AND PHILOSOPHICAL THEMES

Introduction

Our study thus far leaves no doubt that Didymus was influenced by the works of Philo. This influence extends beyond direct references to include specific borrowings from the exegetical tools of etymology and arithmology, complete with allegorical interpretations. Now we turn to major exegetical and philosophical themes illustrative of Didymus's dependence on Philo. We shall discuss these parallels under four major headings: (1) Didymus's psychology; (2) his doctrine of divine Powers; (3) his concept of virtue; and (4) his exegesis of the creation account.

The Philonic Impact on Didymus's Doctrine of the Preexistence of Souls

Central to Didymus's presentation of the soul is the doctrine of the soul's preexistence, ostensibly extracted from Gen. This is one of the primary reasons cited for his condemnation, along with Origen and Evagrius, in 553.[1] Because of the ancient associations between Origen and Didymus on this doctrine, it is often assumed that Didymus merely copied Origen's sentiments.[2] Didymus's own writings, however, reveal that he does not uncritically incorporate Origenian doctrines. In fact, Grant Bayliss has discovered that Didymus's articulation of the doctrine of preexistence is much more similar to Philo's than has previously been acknowledged.[3] We do not wish to deny Origen's influence altogether, for it is indeed strong as we shall see. But we wish to demonstrate that Didymus has used the Philonic stone to sharpen his Origenian sword.

---

1. For the ancient testimonies, see PG 39:239ff. For analysis see Brian E. Daley, "What Did 'Origenism' Mean in the Sixth Century?," in *Origeniana Sexta* (ed. Gilles Dorival and Allain Le Boulluec; Leuven: Leuven University Press, 1995), 627–38.

2. E.g., Manlio Simonetti, "Didymiana," *Vetera Christianorum* 21 (1984): 129–55, 134–42.

3. Bayliss, *The Vision of Didymus*, 98–119.

Origen on the Preexistence of Souls

Origen's doctrine of preexistence is well-covered in modern academic literature.[4] The attention is warranted since Origen's ancient critics also fixated on his doctrine of the soul.[5] Although it is tempting to locate inspiration for the doctrine within Platonism specifically, or the Greek philosophical tradition generally,[6] a more natural and immediate influence is Philo of Alexandria.[7] Gerald Bostock writes, "The doctrine of preexistence in Origen is not simply derived from a Platonism artificially grafted on to the Christian faith. It is derived rather from Philo, who has absorbed both Platonic and Jewish elements into his thinking."[8] Although this is true, it should be noted that Origen never mentions Philo in connection with the doctrine. And we may add that Origen has not uncritically adopted Philo without running him through his pan-scriptural filter.[9] Nevertheless, while Origen's additional scripture references add

---

4. See, e.g., Marguerite Harl, "La preexistence des ames dans l'œuvre d'Origène," in *Origeniana Quarta*, 238–58; Peter Heimann, *Erwähltes Schicksal: Präexistenz der Seele und christlicher Glaube im Denkmodell des Origenes* (Theologische Beiträge und Forschungen 5; Tübingen: Katzmann, 1998).

5. Already, Pamphilus and Eusebius are responding to Origen's teachings on the soul (*Apol.* 159–88). Epiphanius and Theophilus would take up the issue again several decades later (see Clark, *The Origenist Controversy*, 86–104 [on Epiphanius], 105–21 [on Theophilus]).

6. Origen himself is aware of the Platonic origins of the doctrine (*Cels.* 4.40) and believes the philosophical origins are preempted by the teaching of Moses (*Cels.* 6.43).

7. Earlier generations of scholars saw Origen's doctrine of preexistence to be a corruption of biblical doctrine derived primarily from Greek philosophy (e.g., Eugène de Faye, *Origen and His Work*, trans. Fred Rothwell [London: Allen & Unwin, 1926], 92–94; René Cadiou, *Origen: His Life at Alexandria*, trans. John A. Southwell [London: Herder, 1944], 224; Jean Daniélou, *Origen*, trans. Walter Mitchell [New York: Sheed & Ward, 1955], 75). Regardless of the influences, Origen refers to the doctrine of preexistence as "the generally-held theory about the soul" (ὁ καθόλου περὶ ψυχῆς λόγος; *Comm. Jo.* 2.182).

8. "The Sources of Origen's Doctrine of Pre-existence," in *Origeniana Quarta* (ed. Lothar Lies (Innsbruck: Tyrolia, 1987), 259–64, 259. Peter Martens also recognizes Philo's importance ("A Fitting Portrait of God: Origen's Interpretations of the 'Garments of Skins' [Gen 3:21]," in *Hidden Truths from Eden: Esoteric Readings of Genesis 1–3* [ed. Caroline Vander Stichele and Susanne Scholz; Atlanta: SBL Press, 2014], 55–84).

9. There are multiple scriptural texts that presuppose the preexistence of souls in Origen's mind. For example, Jacob and Esau serve as paradigms of all souls achieving praise or blame before incarnation (*Princ.* 2.9.7; 3.1.22, both discussing Rom 9:8–23; see A. Castagno Monaci, "L'idea della preesistenza delle anime e l'esegesi di Rm 9,9–21," in *Origeniana Secunda*, 69–78). Origen's ignorance of the parallelism in Jer 1:5 also leads him to insist Jeremiah's soul preexisted his body (*Hom. Jer.* 1.10). The term καταβολή in Eph 1:4 sparks the idea that souls were "cast down" (*Princ.* 3.5.4; *Comm. Jo.* 19.149–50).

depth and consistency to the doctrine, the basis would appear to be his Philo-inspired exposition of Gen 1–3.[10]

Few passages could be clearer than Origen's *Princ.* 1.8.4:[11]

> Whole nations of souls are stored away somewhere in a realm of their own, with an existence comparable to our bodily life .... But by some inclination towards evil these souls lose their wings and come into bodies, first of men; then through their association with the irrational passions, after the allotted span of human life they are changed into beasts; from which they sink to the level of insensate nature.[12]

Human life can be characterized in Platonist terms as the soul's search for release from the body. As Origen states in the same passage, "On earth by means of virtue souls grow wings and soar aloft, but when in heaven their wings fall off through evil and they sink down and become earth-bound and are mingled with the gross nature of matter."[13] This is the standard Platonist narrative, which Philo also accepts.[14] But Origen is no mere philosopher. He also locates the preexistence of souls in a number of scriptural passages.

To cite just one exegetical example, Origen is concerned with the statement that John the Baptist "was sent from God" (John 1:6). When combined with the prophecy that John would "be filled with the Holy Spirit, even from his mother's womb" (Luke 1:15), Origen sees only one interpretive option: John's soul preexisted his body in the heavenly abode. He was, Origen says, "sent from some other region when he was placed in

---

10. Scholars have sometimes ignored or downplayed Origen's attempt to defend the pre-existence of souls from Gen, but Peter Martens has shown that the first three chapters of Gen are central to his theory ("Origen's Doctrine of Pre-Existence and the Opening Chapters of Genesis," *ZAC* 16 [2013]: 516–49).

11. See also *Princ.* 1.6.2; 2.1.1; 2.6.3–6 (on the soul of Christ); 2.8.3–4; 2.9.1–2; 2.9.5–6.

12. If Koetschau is correct about the validity of the fragments, the Greek reads, ἔθνη τινὰ τῶν ψυχῶν ἀποτίθεται ἐν ἰδιαζούσῃ τινὶ πολιτείᾳ πρὸς τὴν ἐν σώματι ζωήν...ῥοπῇ δέ τινι τῇ πρὸς κακίαν πτερορρυούσας τὰς ψυχὰς ἐν σώμασι γίνεσθαι, πρῶτον μὲν ἀνθρωπ[ίν]οις, εἶθ' οὕτως διὰ τῆς πρὸς τὰ ἄλογα τῶν παθῶν ὁμιλίας μετὰ [τὴν] τοῦ ἀνθρωπίνου βίου ἐγχώρησιν ἀποκτηνοῦσθαι, κἀκεῖθεν μέχρι τῆς φυσικῆς ταύτης καὶ ἀναισθήτου καταπίπτειν ζωῆς (*Origenes Werke 5, De Principiis* [Περὶ Ἀρχῶν], ed. Paul Koetschau [GCS 22; Leipzig: Hinrichs, 1913], 102–3; trans. G.W. Butterworth, *Origen On First Principles* [New York: Harper, 1966], 72–73).

13. The Greek reads, ἐντεῦθεν δι' ἀρετῆς πτεροφυῆσαι μετεωροπορούσιν, ἐκεῖθεν δὲ διὰ κακίας τῶν πτερῶν ἐκπιπτόντων χαμαιπετεῖς πρόσγειοι γίνονται, τῇ παχύτητι τῆς ὑλικῆς καταμιγνύμεναι φύσεως.

14. The classic presentation is *Phaedr.* 245–49. Edwards's statement that "Origen never embraced this doctrine, either as a hypothesis or as an edifying myth" stands against the entire ancient tradition (*Origen Against Plato*, 89).

the body."¹⁵ Therefore, one is forced to "admit that John's soul, being older than his body and subsisting prior to it, was sent."¹⁶ Indeed, Origen says, this is a general truth, applicable in a different way to all humanity.¹⁷

This exegetical agenda was extended to the early chapters of Gen. Doubtless, the "tunics of skins" was Origen's most controversial interpretation predicated on psychic preexistence (Gen 3:21).¹⁸ For this interpretation not only validated the preexistence of souls, but located the entire Edenic existence in a heavenly, preincarnate world. Origen was aware of the potential objections, and responded to them.¹⁹ Although only three extant passages in Origen's writings directly address the "tunics of skins," and none clearly require him to have interpreted the phrase in reference to psychic preexistence,²⁰ his ancient critics are unanimous in attributing the interpretation to him.²¹ He seems to have held Adam to be paradigmatic for all humanity when he is clothed with "tunics of skins," writing,

> And the statement that the man who was cast out of the garden with the woman was clothed with "coats of skins" (Gen 3:21), which God made for those who had sinned on account of the transgression of mankind, has a certain secret and mysterious meaning, superior to the Platonic doctrine of the descent of the soul which loses its wings and is carried hither "until it finds some firm resting-place."²²

---

15. *Comm. Jo.* 2.180 (trans. Heine, *Origen: Commentary on John*, 1:143).

16. *Comm. Jo.* 2.181 (trans. *ibid*).

17. *Comm. Jo.* 2.182–84. For a similar interpretation, note Origen's explanation of Jer 1:5 (*Hom. Jer.* 1.10).

18. The academic bibliography on the subject is massive (see, e.g., Pier Franco Beatrice, "Le tuniche di pelle: Antiche letture di *Gen.* 3,21," in *La tradizione dell'Enkrateia: Motivazioni ontologiche e protologiche* [ed. Ugo Bianchi; Rome: Edizioni dell'Ateneo, 1985], 433–82; Hanneke Reuling, *After Eden: Church Fathers and Rabbis on Genesis 3,16–21* [Leiden: Brill, 2006], 74–76; Anna Tzvetkova-Glaser, *Pentateuchauslegung bei Origenes und den frühen Rabbinen* [Early Christianity in the Context of Antiquity 7; Frankfurt: Lang, 2010], 98–108).

19. The strongest objection is the plain sense of Gen 2:23, where Adam says of Eve, "She is bone of my bones and flesh of my flesh" (see Martens, "A Fitting Portrait," 65–70).

20. *Cels.* 4.40; *Hom. Lev.* 6.2; *Sel. Gen.* ad Gen 3:21 (PG 12.101; this last reference is equivalent to Metzler's frg. D 22 [Karin Metzler, *Origenes: Werke mit deutscher Übersetzung 1/1. Die Kommentierung des Buches Genesis* [Berlin: de Gruyter, 2010], 190–97]).

21. Methodius is already attacking Origen's doctrine (*Res.* 1.4; 2.1; 23.3; see also Epiphanius, *Pan.* 64.4.9; 63.5–64.66.6; Jerome, *Epist.* 51.5). It is unlikely that all the critics could be wrong.

22. *Cels.* 4.40 (trans. Chadwick, 216–17). The Platonic reference is to the *Phaedr.* 246b–c. The Greek reads, Καὶ ὁ ἐκβαλλόμενος δὲ ἐκ τοῦ παραδείσου ἄνθρωπος μετὰ τῆς γυναικός, τοὺς «δερματίνους» ἠμφιεσμένος «χιτῶνας», οὓς διὰ τὴν παράβασιν τῶν ἀνθρώπων ἐποίησε τοῖς ἁμαρτήσασιν ὁ θεός, ἀπόρρητόν τινα καὶ μυστικὸν ἔχει λόγον, ὑπὲρ τὴν κατὰ Πλάτωνα κάθοδον τῆς ψυχῆς, πτερορρυούσης καὶ δεῦρο φερομένης, «ἕως ἂν στερεοῦ τινος λάβηται».

One can clearly see that Origen here rejects the literal interpretation of the biblical text, which he entertains elsewhere.[23] For how else could the text contain "a secret and mysterious meaning?"[24] And why would this meaning lead him to think of Plato's doctrine of psychic preexistence? Although no single extant Origenian text captures the essence of the interpretation ascribed to him, the presence of the notion in Philo before him and Didymus after him serve to bolster the claim that Origen indeed interpreted Gen 3:21 in this fashion.[25]

Philo on the Preexistence of Souls

Philo almost certainly accepts the preexistence of souls.[26] He writes in *Somn.* 1.180–81,

> For excellent would it have been for the reasoning faculty to have remained in its own keeping and not have left its home for that of sense-perception;

---

23. See *Sel. Gen.* ad Gen 3:21. Martens actually suggests that four different interpretations of the tunics of skin can be found in Origen: (1) a literal interpretation of God fashioning animal skins into clothing; (2) an allegorical interpretation of the skins as symbols of human mortality; (3) a literal interpretation of the skins as symbols of human mortality [*sic*]; (4) an allegorical interpretation that the skins were symbols of bodies assigned to human souls that preexisted them. The first two of these Origen rejects, and the last two he accepts ("A Fitting Portrait").

24. See Martens, "Origen's Doctrine of Pre-existence," 540–41.

25. This interpretation is also found among the gnostics (e.g., Hippolytus, *Haer.* 10.13.4; Irenaeus, *Haer.* 1.5.5; Tertullian, *Res.* 7). Origen may well have been aware of this fact, as Clement of Alexandria was before him (*Strom.* 3.95.2).

26. See Sami Yli-Karjanmaa, *Reincarnation in Philo of Alexandria* [SPhiloM 7; Atlanta: SBL Press, 2015], 31–36. John Dillon disagrees, "There is no need, however, to postulate a pre-incarnate existence for individual souls" ("Philo of Alexandria and Platonist Psychology," in *The Afterlife of the Platonic Soul: Reflections of Platonic Psychology in the Monotheistic Religions* [ed. Maha Elkaisy-Friemuth and John M. Dillon; Leiden: Brill, 2009], 17–24, 23). Instead, Dillon envisions "individual *logoi* emanating from the Form of Man to join with the appropriate matter" (ibid). He taps into Philo's idea that Gen 1 is the creation of the ideal Forms, and thus Gen 1:26 is the Ideal man (e.g., *Opif.* 134). While this is true, Gen 1:26 cannot be regarded exclusively as the Form of man, for Gen 2:7 is interpreted in a materialist sense, a body being provided for the mind (or soul) created earlier (e.g., *Opif.* 69; *Leg.* 1.31–32). If only the Form of man is created in Gen 1:26, then Philo has no exegetical rationale in Gen for the creation of mind or soul. I think Dillon assumes, reasonably enough, that Philo will be consistent in his interpretation of Gen 1 with reference to the Forms. Indeed, he is not (see Richard A. Baer Jr., *Philo's Use of the Categories Male and Female* [ALGHJ 3; Leiden: Brill, 1970], 22–26). On the complications of locating the interpretive traditions on these passages, see Tobin, *The Creation of Man*, 56–101 (on the single creation of man), 102–34 (on the double creation of man). The competing nature of these traditions in Philo was not appreciated by the church fathers, who tend to mix the two.

but, failing that, it is well that it should return to itself again. Perhaps, too, in these words [Gen 28:15] he hints at the doctrine of the immortality of the soul: for ... it forsook its heavenly abode and came into the body as into a foreign land.[27]

This passage is one of many in which Philo stresses the soul's desire to release itself from the body.[28] Although Philo mostly speaks of the soul's ascent in conjunction with his allegorical interpretation of the Pentateuch,[29] it has a certain literal application as well, for the soul is released from the body at death.[30] The intended result of death is the soul's ascent to its place of origin.[31] Philo appears to locate souls in the air, and to equate them with demons, which are the same to Philo as the biblical angels.[32] These descend to enter bodies for a variety of reasons,[33] but their ultimate return to the air seems to be Philo's basic eschatology.[34] In other words, Philo simply adapts the Platonic scheme to his own biblical theology.

Philo's interpretation of the tunics of skins seems to have influenced both Origen and Didymus.[35] He writes,

> But according to the deeper meaning, the tunic of skin is symbolically the natural skin of the body. For when God formed the first mind, He called it Adam; then he formed the sense, which He called Life; in the third place, of necessity He made his body also, calling it symbolically a tunic of skin, for it was proper that the mind and sense should be clothed in the body as in a

---

27. Trans. *PLCL* 5:393. The Greek reads, καλὸν μὲν γὰρ ἦν, τὸν λογισμὸν ἐφ' ἑαυτοῦ μείναντα μὴ ἀποδημῆσαι πρὸς αἴσθησιν· δεύτερος δὲ πλοῦς, ἐφ' ἑαυτὸν ὑποστρέψαι πάλιν. ἴσως δὲ καὶ τὸ περὶ ἀφθαρσίας ψυχῆς ὑπαινίττεται δόγμα διὰ τούτου· ἀπολιποῦσα μὲν γὰρ τὸν οὐράνιον τόπον, ὡς καὶ μικρῷ πρότερον ἐλέχθη, καθάπερ εἰς ξένην χώραν ἦλθε τὸ σῶμα.

28. E.g., *Ebr.* 101; *QG* 3.10; cf. *Congr.* 59.

29. David Winston writes, "The central thrust and fundamental aim of Philo's biblical commentary is to trace the return of the human soul to its native homeland by means of the allegorical method of interpretation" (*Logos and Mystical Theology*, 36). On the correspondence between levels of reading and the constitution of the human being, see David Dawson, "Plato's Soul and the Body of the Text in Philo and Origen," in *Interpretation and Allegory: Antiquity to the Modern Period* (ed. Jon Whitman; Brill's Studies in Intellectual History 101; Leiden: Brill, 2000), 89–107.

30. E.g., *Leg.*1.105; *Conf.* 36; *Abr.* 258. John T. Conroy Jr. regards "the death of the soul" as both metaphorical and ontological in Philo ("Philo's 'Death of the Soul:' Is This Only a Metaphor?," *SPhiloA* 23 [2011]: 23–40).

31. E.g., *Conf.* 77–78; *QG* 3.11.

32. *Somn.* 1.141 (see the comments of Winston, *Logos and Mystical Theology*, 27–42).

33. Winston isolates five reasons why the soul incarnates (ibid), but these have been expanded recently to nine (Yli-Karjanmaa, *Reincarnation*, 44–81).

34. See Lester L. Grabbe, "Eschatology in Philo and Josephus," in *Judaism in Late Antiquity: Death, Life-After-Death, Resurrection, and the World-to Come in the Judaisms of Antiquity* (ed. Alan J. Avery-Peck and Jacob Neusner; HO 1.49; Leiden: Brill, 2000), 163–86, 164–73.

35. On Philo's interpretation of this passage, see Beatrice, "Le tuniche," 463–67.

tunic of skin, in order that His handiwork might first appear worthy of the divine power.³⁶

Immediately before this allegorical understanding, Philo had offered a "literal" interpretation of the tunics. Made from simple leather, the garments teach the aspiring sage to wear plain clothing and to dispense with fancy garments dyed a variety of colors, especially purple. But the allegorical interpretation is even more fascinating.

Like Origen after him, Philo distinguished the "man" of Gen 1:26 from that of Gen 2:7. The former was made "in the image" of God, and is thus heavenly, whereas the latter was "molded" (πλάσσω), and is thus earthly.³⁷ One wonders whether both thinkers did not interpret Gen 2:7 and Gen 3:21 in exactly the same fashion, both reflecting the embodiment of the preexistent soul. If we do not assume that Philo and Origen read Gen sequentially, that is, Gen 3 follows chronologically *after* Gen 2, then it is likely that they regarded the two passages as mutually enlightening and not inherently contradictory.³⁸ We would thus have two passages that for Philo and Origen pointed to the embodiment of preexistent souls. This is how Didymus the Blind read his predecessors.

Didymus on the Preexistence of Souls

It is typical to associate Didymus's doctrine of psychic preexistence with that of Origen, for the two were condemned together. But Origen was not Didymus's only influence for the doctrine.³⁹ I believe Didymus recognized Origen's primary source, and so studied Philo carefully for himself. As any good student, he did not take his teacher's word as truth, but conducted a thorough investigation and reached most of the same conclusions.

---

36. *QG* 1.53 (trans *PLCL* Supp 1:31). The passage is paralleled in *QG* 4.1. Unfortunately, these texts are preserved only in Armenian, making precise verbal comparisons impossible.

37. See Philo, *Leg.* 1.32–33; Origen, *Hom. Gen.* 1.13; *Comm. Matt.* 14.16.

38. This is Martens's argument with regard to Origen's explanation of Gen 2:7 and 3:21: "Rather than read the references to corporeality before Gen 3:21 literally, so that the first couple was already embodied in paradise before their fall and subsequent reception of 'garments of skins,' he [Origen] read passages such as Gen 2:7 allegorically to signify bodies received after the fall" ("Hidden Truths," 69–70), that is, being cast from Eden.

39. Bayliss has offered the most recent study of Didymus's doctrine of the preexistence of the soul, and rightly recognizes Philo's influence, along with Origen's (*The Vision of Didymus*, 98–119). I largely follow his presentation here.

Didymus's doctrine is presented exegetically in several places.[40] We shall cite just one example here. Commenting on the curse of Job 3:3–5,[41] Didymus drifts into an excursus on the soul: "The human soul is immortal, and is not only different in substance from the body but also more divine, since it is knit together with it for [two] different reasons: it is united either because its own sense of self-worth provokes an inclination and yearning for communion with bodies, or because it is led by its own goodness to those who need its benefits."[42]

Didymus then proceeds to attack the materialists who think an immortal and incorporeal entity can arise from the body. Indeed, says Didymus, their position requires ongoing creations subsequent to God's "resting" on the seventh day (Gen 2:2). Didymus then turns to Eccl 1:9–10 to support his general hypothesis: "What is that which has happened? It is that which will happen! And what is that which has been done? It is that which will be done. And there is nothing novel under the sun. As for the person who will speak and say, 'See this is new!'—it has already happened in the ages that have been before us."[43]

Then Didymus reels off the same scriptural references to intrauterine souls as we saw with Origen above. Jeremiah (Jer 1:5), Jacob and Esau (via Rom 9:13), and John the Baptist (Luke 1:44) are all indications of souls sent to earth for the good of humankind (his second reason for the soul's descent). Didymus concludes, "Now these passages demonstrate that souls are not co-temporal with bodies."[44] Obviously, then, Didymus was well-

---

40. E.g., *Comm. Gen.* 153.23–27; *Comm. Job* 62.18–22; 74.27–75; *Comm. Eccl.* 193.25–194.1.
41. "May the day on which I was born perish, and the night on which they said, 'See, a male.' May that day be darkness, and may the Lord above not seek it, nor brightness come to it. But may darkness and the shadow of death seize it, may gloom come upon it" (trans. mine). The Greek reads, ἀπόλοιτο ἡ ἡμέρα ἐν ᾗ ἐγεννήθην καὶ ἡ νὺξ ἐν ᾗ εἶπαν ἰδοὺ ἄρσεν. ἡ ἡμέρα ἐκείνη εἴη σκότος καὶ μὴ ἀναζητήσαι. αὐτὴν ὁ κύριος ἄνωθεν μηδὲ ἔλθοι εἰς αὐτὴν φέγγος. ἐκλάβοι δὲ αὐτὴν σκότος καὶ σκιὰ θανάτου ἐπέλθοι ἐπ' αὐτὴν γνόφος.
42. *Comm. Job* 56.20–29 (trans. mine). The Greek reads, ἡ τοῦ ἀνθρώπ[ου] ψυχὴ ἀθάνατος ὑπάρχουσα κα[ὶ] οὐ μόνον ἑτέρας οὐσίας παρὰ τὸ [σ]ῶμα, ἀλλὰ καὶ θειοτέρας, τούτωι συνεπλάκη κατὰ διαφόρους λόγους, ἢ τῆς ἀξίας αὐτῆς τῆς κατὰ ῥοπὴν ἰδίαν καὶ πόθον πρὸς τὰ σώματα κοινωνίαν πρὸς αὐτὰ ἐργασαμένης, ἢ διὰ τὸ χρήσιμον τῶν ὠφελίας δεομένων τούτῳ συναφθείσης.
43. Eccl 1:9–10 corroborates his apparently literal interpretation of Gen 2:2. The Greek of Didymus reads, τί τὸ γεγονός αὐτὸ τὸ γενησόμενον καὶ τί τὸ πεποιημένον αὐτὸ τὸ ποιηθησόμενον καὶ οὐκ ἔστιν πᾶν πρόσφατον ὑπὸ τὸν ἥλιον. ὃς λαλήσει καὶ ἐρεῖ· ἰδὲ τοῦτο καινόν ἐστιν ἤδη γέγονεν [ἐν] τοῖς αἰῶσιν τοῖς ἐπερχομέν[οις] [LXX: γενομένοις] ἀπὸ ἔμπροσθεν ἡμῶν.
44. *Comm. Job* 57.27–29. The Greek reads, ταῦτα γὰρ οὐ συγχρόνους τοῖς σώμασιν ἀπ[ο]δείκνυσιν τὰς ψυχάς (trans. Bayliss, *The Vision of Didymus*, 99 [modified slightly]).

versed with the presentation of Origen, and felt compelled to defend it.[45] In this respect he goes beyond Origen in his insistence that souls *must* pre-exist bodies, and that those who disagree are heretical.[46]

Didymus's defense of the doctrine extended to the passages we have already discussed with reference to Philo and Origen: the "man" of Gen 1:26 as opposed to the "man" of Gen 2:7, and the "tunics of skins" (Gen 3:21). With regard to the former, Didymus, like his Alexandrian predecessors, thought it absurd that God would create a material being κατ' εἰκόνα: "It was not in accord with the [body-soul] compound that God made man in his image, for God is not in human form."[47] Like Philo and Origen, Didymus did not interpret the man of Gen 1:26 corporeally.[48]

Unfortunately, the *Comm. Gen.*'s section of exegesis on Gen 2:7 is missing from the Tura papyrus. But Didymus links his interpretation of Gen 3:21 with his earlier comments on the man made "according to the image:"

> While we said earlier that man was made "according to the image," which refers to an immaterial substance [τὸ ἄϋλον], it is also true that he needed an instrumental body [ὀργανικόν σῶμα], since he was made in a different condition that required something he could use. But here "skins" are made. Now of these skins the statement is fitting, "for a corruptible body weighs down the soul" [Wis 9:15a], the "corruptible body" meaning this dense, earthly substance [τὸ παχύ], and then, "the earthly tent overloads the mind full of thoughts" [Wis 9:15b], the "earthly tent" referring to the means by which the soul moves to different places once it is released from this body. Now the tent is an intermediate substance uniting the noetic with the dense, earthly substance. The dense, earthly substance "weighs down" the soul, but the tent "overloads" the mind rather than the soul.[49]

---

45. His argument matches nearly perfectly *Princ.* 1.7.4. We will remind the reader that Didymus authored a commentary on *Princ.*, according to Jerome (*Ruf.* 1.6; 2.16).

46. Bayliss writes, "In fact the suggestion that the soul is co-sown with the body is portrayed not only as a mistaken interpretation of Scripture but a major heresy and one particularly associated with the Egyptian Hieracas" (*The Vision of Didymus*, 100).

47. *Comm. Gen.* 56.14–16. The Greek reads, Οὐ κατὰ τὸν σύνθετον τοίνυν κατ' εἰκόνα Θεοῦ ὁ ἄνθρωπος γέγονεν· οὐ γὰρ ἀνθρωπόμορφος ὁ Θεός (trans. mine). David Runia regards this comment as a direct quotation from Philo's *Opif.* 69. The verbal match between the two passages is with the words ἀνθρωπόμορφος ὲ θεός (*On the Creation*, 234; see also Runia's essay, "L'exégèse philosophique et l'influence de la penseé philonienne dans la tradition patristique," in *Philon d'Alexandria et le langage de la philosophie*, 327–48, 336–42).

48. We shall further discuss the Philonic references in Didymus's interpretation of Gen 1:26–28 below under the "Image of God."

49. *Comm. Gen.* 107.4–15. The Greek reads, Πρότερον μὲν οὖν κατ' εἰκόνα ὁ ἄνθρωπος γεγενῆσθαι εἴρηται, ὅπερ δηλοῖ τὸ ἄϋλον· ἐπειδὴ δὲ καὶ ἐν ἑτέρᾳ καταστάσει γεγένηται ὡς δεῖσθαί τινος ᾧ χρήσεται, ἐδέησεν αὐτῷ ὀργανικοῦ σώματος, νῦν δὲ καὶ δερμάτινοι γίνονται. Τούτων παραστατικόν ἐστιν τὸ λεγόμενον·«Φθαρτὸν γὰρ σῶμα βαρύνει ψυχήν», τοῦ φθαρτοῦ σώματος δηλοῦντος τὸ παχὺ τοῦτο, εἶθ' ἑξῆς «[κ]αὶ βρίθει τὸ γεῶδες σκῆνος νοῦν πολυφροντίδα», γεῶδες σκῆνος λέγων ᾧ κέχρηται

This dense passage unfortunately is not fleshed out as the modern interpreter might wish. Consequently, it is tempting to read the Neo-Platonist conception of psychic satiety into Didymus (and Origen before him).[50] The three-step descent would seem to work well exegetically: Pure mind (Gen 1:26) descends into soul (the intermediate body, Gen 2:7), and then further descends into flesh (Gen 3:21).[51] But, as we have seen, it seems that neither Philo nor Origen wishes to read Gen 2:7 as an event separate from Gen 3:21. In fact, such an error is the result of an assumption that ancient expositors read the text chronologically. Didymus does not wish to posit a fall from mind to soul to body any more than Origen and Philo, but rather to understand two stages of creation: incorporeal man (Gen 1:26), and corporeal man (Gen 2:7; 3:21). Martens's reading of Origen, referenced above, is anticipated already by Didymus's reading of the great Alexandrian. And both Origen and Didymus appear to have received the idea from Philo.

Didymus juxtaposes, just as Philo and Origen, the soul's being made (ποιέω) with the body being molded (πλάσσω).[52] In other words, his typical approach is to distinguish immaterial mind or soul (Gen 1:26) from material flesh (Gen 2:7). To cite one example, interpreting Ps 103:4, Didymus says,

> Scripture does not say "he who molded [ὁ πλάσας] angels," but "he who made [ὁ ποιῶν] his angels spirits" (Ps 103:4 [MT = 104:4]; Heb 1:7) For about the earth it is said as of a dense body [παχέος σώματος], "And his hands molded the dry land" (Ps 94:5 [MT = 95:5]). These things are not said because God molds things with his hands like a human being, but because divine instruction bestows on each thing the exact meaning suitable to it, "molding" being appropriate to the body, and "making" appropriate to the soul.[53]

ἡ ψυχὴ ἀπαλλαττομένη τοῦδε τοῦ σώματος πρὸς τὰς μεταβατικὰς ἑαυτῆς κ[ι]νήσεις, ὅπερ μέσον ἐστὶ συνάπτον τὴν νοερὰν οὐσίαν πρὸς τὸ [π]αχύ· τοῦτο τὴν ψυχὴν βαρεῖ, τοῦ σκήνους οὐ τὴν ψυχὴν ἀλλ[ὰ] τὸν νοῦν βρίθοντος (trans. mine).

50. Bayliss is certainly right to reject this tendency, as satiety has no role in Didymus's psychology (*The Vision of Didymus*, 103–5, 222–24).

51. This is Hermann Schibli's reading of Didymus ("Origen, Didymus, and the Vehicle of the Soul," in *Origeniana Quinta*, 381–91, 383), and Caroline Bammel's reading of Origen ("Adam in Origen," in *The Making of Orthodoxy: Essays in Honour of Henry Chadwick* [ed. Rowan Williams; Cambridge: Cambridge University Press, 1989], 62–93).

52. *Comm. Job* 273.15–33; 75.31–276.11.

53. *Comm. Job* 275.34–276.11. The Greek reads, γὰρ περὶ τῶν ἀγγέλων οὐκ εἴρηται· ὁ πλάσας ἀγγέλους, ἀλλ' "[ὁ π]οιῶν [ἀγ]γέλους αὐτοῦ πν(εύμ)ατα." καὶ περὶ τῆς γῆς εἴρηται ὡς παχέος σώματος· "καὶ τὴν ξηρὰν αἱ χε[ῖρ]ες αὐτοῦ ἔπλασαν." ταῦτα δὲ οὐ[χ, ὅ]τι κατὰ τοὺς ἀνθρώπους θ(εὸ)ς χερ[σὶ] διαπλάττει, εἴρηται, ἀλλ' ὅτι ἑκ[άσ]τῳ τὸ οἰκεῖον ἡ θεία παίδευσις ἐπιφέρει ὄνομα, τὴν μὲν πλάσιν ὡς εἴπομεν τῷ σώματ[ι, τ]ὴν δὲ ποίησι(ν) [τῇ ψυχῇ] (trans. mine).

Didymus goes on to insist the soul is immortal, and thus cannot have been "molded," but only "made." For when scripture declares that Adam is earth and would return to the earth (Gen 3:19), it must be referring to the "molded" body and not to the "made" soul. This passage is sufficient for us to conclude that Didymus would never have interpreted Gen 2:7 in reference to the soul's being "molded," which is terminologically ruled out (thanks to Philo). Thus for Didymus both Gen 2:7 and 3:21 refer to the body in its postlapsarian state.

Didymus's comments about the tunics of skins can now be appreciated. After citing the biblical lemma, Didymus writes:

> It is appropriate that the "tunics of skins" are made for the soon-to-be mother of all things (Gen 3:20) along with her husband who helped her in the effort. For one might say the tunics are nothing other than bodies.[54] For if the lovers of the literal sense [οἱ φιλίστορες] want to believe God made tunics out of skins, why is the phrase added "he clothed them," since they could clothe themselves? For it so happens that those who stitched together aprons for themselves out of leaves were not ignorant of how to make coverings (Gen 3:7). But it is possible to find that the body is referred to as skin often in the divine instructions, for the blessed Job says, "For I know the one about to release me is eternal, to resurrect on earth my skin which has born these things" (Job 19:25–26). It is obvious to everyone that Job said these things about the body itself. And again, the same man says something similar about himself, "You have clothed me with skin and flesh, and with bones and tendons you have strung me together" (Job 10:11). For this is a clear and most obvious proof of the tunics of skins being the body, that Job also mentions "you clothed," which is said also in the case of the protoplasts.[55]

Didymus then turns to the specific language of the text, noting that God made different "tunics for Adam and his wife," rather than the same tunic for "both of them." He takes this to mean that each was clothed with skin

---

54. Didymus appears to be quoting from Origen: οὓς οὐκ ἂν ἑτέρους τις τῶν σωμάτων εἴποι, whereas Origen's fragment has οὐκ ἄλλους εἶναι τοῦ σώματος (*Sel. Gen.* ad Gen 3:21).

55. *Comm. Gen.* 106.10–26 (trans. mine). The Greek reads, Καταλλήλως τῇ μελλούσῃ πάντων ἔσεσθαι μητρὶ μετὰ τοῦ ἀνδρὸς εἰς τοῦτο συμβαλλομένου οἱ δερμάτινοι κιτῶνες γίνονται, οὓς οὐκ ἂν ἑτέρους τις τῶν σωμάτων εἴποι. Εἰ γὰρ καὶ οἱ φιλίστορες ἐκ δερμάτων κιτῶνας τὸν Θεὸν πεποιηκέναι οἰήσονται, τί πρόσκειται καὶ τὸ «ἐνέδυσεν αὐτούς», δι' ἑαυτῶν τοῦτο ποιῆσαι δυναμένων; Οὐ γὰρ ἀνεννόητοι ἐτύγχανον σκεπασμάτων, οἵ γε ῥάψαντε[ς] ἑαυτοῖς ἐκ φύλλων περιζώματα. Ὅτι δὲ πολλαχοῦ τῶν θ[εί]ων παιδευμάτων τὸ σῶμα δέρμα καλεῖται, ἔστιν εὑρεῖν. Ἰὼ[β] γὰρ ὁ μακάριός φησιν· «Οἶδα γὰρ ὅτι ἀέναός ἐστιν ὁ ἐκλύειν με μέλλων· ἐπὶ γῆς ἀναστῆσαι τὸ δέρμα μου τὸ ἀναντλοῦν ταῦτα», παντὶ δέ τῳ σαφὲς ὡς ταῦτα περὶ τοῦ σώματος ἑαυτοῦ ὁ Ἰὼβ ἔφασκεν· Καὶ πάλιν ὁ αὐτὸς περὶ ἑαυτοῦ τοιαῦτά φησιν· «Δέρμα καὶ κρέας με ἐνέδυσας, ὀστέοις δὲ καὶ νεύροις με ἐνείρας.» Σαφὲς γὰρ καὶ ἀριδηλότατον δεῖγμα τοῦ τοὺς δερματίνους κιτῶνας εἶναι τὸ σῶμα, ὅτι καὶ τοῦ ἐνέδυσας μνημονεύει ὁ Ἰώβ, ὅπερ καὶ ἐπὶ τῶν πρωτοπλάστων εἴρηται.

appropriate to his or her gender. Then he returns to his earlier interpretation of Gen 1:26, which we quoted above, and concludes that Paradise cannot have been a real place on earth.[56]

The similarities between Didymus and his predecessors are obvious. First, he offers an interpretation "appropriate" to the nature of God. Philo had noted, "And could the apparel of the human body be better or more fittingly made by any other power than God?"[57] Origen, perhaps more dramatically, scoffs at the notion that God could be considered a mere leatherworker (σκυτοτόμος), since such a profession is "unworthy" (ἀνάξιος) of him. So these expositors rejected the possibility of a literal reading on the grounds that it is ἀπρεπής.[58] Didymus, however, adds an exegetical reason to reject God's making of literal tunics: Adam and Eve already knew how to make their own clothes (Gen 3:7). They did not need God's help to make clothing, and thus the apparent meaning is ruled out textually as well.

Second, Didymus locates meaning not only in God's making, but also in his clothing the protoplasts. He seems to borrow the point from Philo, who asserts, "For in the case of human clothing, there are some who make it and others who put it on. But this natural tunic, that is, the body, was the work of Him who had also made it, and having made it, also clothed them in it."[59] Just as Adam and Eve were capable of making their own clothes, so also they were capable of putting on clothes. God's action here must refer to something that the protoplasts could not do themselves.

Third, all three thinkers assume the paradise of Eden to be a heavenly, spiritual, or incorporeal place. Both Philo and Origen reject the possibility that God could plant a garden (Gen 2:8),[60] and Didymus agrees that paradise was "a supercelestial place."[61] Once this decision had been made, the exegetes had to locate a scriptural passage when the current human

---

56. Origen makes the same points in the fragment from *Sel. Gen.* ad Gen 3:21 (cf. *Comm. Jo.* 2.175–76).

57. *QG* 1.53 (*PLCL* Supp. 1:31). Richard Layton has fleshed out the topic of divine "appropriateness," and recognizes both Philo and Origen as influences on Didymus ("Didymus the Blind and the *Philistores*: A Contest over *Historia* in Early Christian Exegetical Argument," in *Studies on the Texts of the Desert of Judah: New Approaches to the Study of Biblical Interpretation in Judaism of the Second Temple Period and in Early Christianity* [ed. Gary Anderson, Ruth Clements, and David Satran; Leiden: Brill, 2013], 243–67, 257–66).

58. This category of objection is standard in literary criticism from the earliest time (see Plato, *Phaedr.* 274b; Aristotle, *Rhet.* 1404b; 1408a; 1414a).

59. *QG* 1.53 (*PLCL* Supp. 1:31).

60. Philo: E.g., *Leg.* 1.43–47; *QG* 1.6; Origen: *Princ.* 4.3.1; *Sel. Gen.* ad Gen 3:21.

61. Didymus's χωρίον ὑπεραναβεβηκός (*Comm. Gen.* 107.21) reminds us of Origen's θεῖόν τι χωρίον (*Sel. Gen.* ad Gen 3:21). Cf. also Didymus, *Comm. Gen.* 91.7–9.

body came into existence. Gen 3:21 became one of those passages, along with Gen 2:7. Both were interpreted similarly to refer to the construction of the physical body of humankind. Didymus offers the clearest expression of this interpretation, but he is clearly dependent upon his predecessors.

The Philonic Impact on Didymus's Doctrine of Virtue

No issue is more central to Didymus's thought than his doctrine of virtue.[62] In Didymus's mind, every scriptural verse, every biblical character (e.g., Hagar and Sarah), and even the structure of biblical books as a whole (e.g., Job, Ps) aim at the moral advancement of the reader. Like Philo and Origen, Didymus views the soul's journey to be an attempt to ascend beyond the body to the contemplation of higher realities (a process termed ἀναγωγή). The ultimate goal for these thinkers was to progress toward virtue, which was equivalent to becoming like God.[63] One can thus understand the appeal of Philo's interpretations for Didymus, who is, according to Bayliss, generally more personal than Origen. It is the Philonic focus on the individual soul that draws Didymus to his articulation of the doctrine of virtue.

The Philonic Impact on Didymus's Doctrine of Prepassions and Passions

The Stoic doctrine of prepassions (προπάθεια) has received much attention in modern scholarship.[64] The Stoics wished to assert that all passions (πάθη) were due to an "excessive impulse" in the soul, being both "irrational and unnatural."[65] Passions fundamentally represent a lack of control,

---

62. Bayliss, *The Vision of Didymus*, offers the most comprehensive treatment of Didymus's doctrine of virtue.

63. E.g., Philo, *Fug.* 63. The combination of the Stoic concept of προκοπή with the Platonic ideal of ὁμοίωσις θεῷ (*Theaet.* 176b) is curious, although Philo generally falls on the Platonic (and Peripatetic) side of viewing the "progressor" (προκόπτων) in a positive sense (see Geert Roskam, *On the Path to Virtue: The Stoic Doctrine of Moral Progress and Its Reception in [Middle-]Platonism* [Ancient and Medieval Philosophy 1; Leuven: Leuven University Press, 2005], 146–219 on Philo).

64. See e.g., Karlhans Abel, "Die Propatheia-Theorem: ein Beitrag zur stoischen Affektenlehre," *Hermes* 111 (1983): 78–97; Richard Sorabji, "Chrysippus-Posidonius-Seneca: A High-Level Debate on Emotion," in *The Emotions in Hellenistic Philosophy* (ed. Juha Sihvola and Troels Engberg-Pedersen; The New Synthese Historical Library 46; Dordrecht: Kluwer, 1998), 149–70; Margaret Graver, *Stoicism and Emotion* (Chicago: University of Chicago Press, 2007), 85–108.

65. E.g., Diogenes Laertius 7.110: ἔστι δὲ αὐτὸ τὸ πάθος κατὰ Ζήνωνα [the reputed founder of the Stoic school] ἡ ἄλογος καὶ παρὰ φύσιν ψυχῆς κίνησις ἢ ὁρμὴ πλεονάζουσα.

and thus must be completely eradicated.[66] This hard line created a problem, at least for the later Stoics.[67] Their solution was to distinguish an impression (φαντασία) or impulse (ὁρμή) involuntarily made on the soul from mental assent (κατάληψις) to that impression. The former they called a prepassion or προπάθεια, which allowed the movement (κίνησις, ὁρμή) of the soul without requiring this movement to become excessive, and thus result in a passion in the purest sense.[68]

Philo on Prepassion

Philo is one of the earliest Greek authors to attest the doctrine of προπάθεια.[69] The Greek term occurs only once in a fragment discussing Gen 4:26. "Why," Philo asks, "did Seth's son Enosh hope to call the name of the Lord God?" He answers: "'Enosh' is interpreted as 'man.' And this is now taken, not as a mixture, but as the logical part of the soul, the mind, to which hope is peculiarly fitting, for irrational animals are bereft of hope. And hope is a certain anticipation of joy (προπάθεια τις τῆς χαρᾶς); before joy there is an expectation (προσδοκία) of good."[70] Margaret Graver reasonably asks why hope should be regarded as a προπάθεια rather than an εὐπάθεια.[71] The answer seems to be that hope "requires a certain element of uncertainty; i.e., that it necessarily stops short of assent."[72] But Philo seems to suggest more.

This passage illustrates that προπάθειαι are inherently neutral, and thus can precede either πάθη (negative) or εὐπάθειαι (positive). Philo's application is contrary to the Stoic sources, which tend to posit προπάθεια as a potential negative to excuse the sage from total imperturbability. The concept functions as a loophole, technically anomalous, but practically

---

66. Contrast the Stoic ideal of ἀπάθεια from the Platonic/Aristotelian μετριοπάθεια (see John M. Dillon, "Metriopatheia and Apatheia: Some Reflections on a Controversy in Later Greek Ethics," in *Essays in Ancient Greek Philosophy* 2 [ed. John P. Anton and Anthony Preus; Albany: SUNY, 1983], 508–17).

67. Abel argues that the doctrine of prepassions goes back to Zeno himself ("Die Propatheia-Theorem"), but others have questioned if it dates back that far in the history of Stoicism (Brad Inwood, *Ethics and Human Action in Early Stoicism* [Oxford: Oxford University Press, 1985], 165–73; Inwood, *Reading Seneca: Stoic Philosophy at Rome* [Oxford: Oxford University Press, 2005], 23–64).

68. Regularly cited is the tale in Aulus Gellius 19.1 (= Epictetus frag. 9).

69. On Philo's position, see Margaret Graver, "Philo of Alexandria and the Origins of the Stoic ΠΡΟΠΑΘΕΙΑΙ," in *Philo of Alexandria and Post-Aristotelian Philosophy* (ed. Francesca Alesse; Studies in Philo of Alexandria 5; Leiden: Brill, 2008), 197–221.

70. *QG* 1.79 (trans. *PLCL* Sup 1:49).

71. Graver, "Philo and the Stoic ΠΡΟΠΑΘΕΙΑΙ," 212.

72. Graver, "Philo and the Stoic ΠΡΟΠΑΘΕΙΑΙ," 213.

necessary. Philo, however, has placed the concept positively as the potential first stop on the road to assent.

Another relevant passage is preserved in Procopius of Gaza. The text is now listed as *QG* 4.73 in the Philonic corpus (translated into Armenian), but it has been recognized since the time of Max Pohlenz that the Greek is a paraphrase of Procopius himself rather than Philo's original.[73] Even if this is the case, however, it shows that Philo was understood, at least by one ancient reader, to attest the doctrine of προπάθεια, and thus the passage remains relevant for the reception history of Philo.

The Greek as we have it may be translated: "'And Abraham went to mourn Sarah' (Gen 23:2). These words make clear that Abraham was guilty of a prepassion rather than a passion. For scripture does not say he mourned, but that 'he went to mourn.' This is made clear by the statement, 'Abraham arose from the dead' (Gen 23:3), which comes before 'he mourned.'"[74] This passage clearly shows a more traditional apologetic use of prepassion. Abraham perhaps *intended* to mourn Sarah, but indeed did not. Thus Abraham can be presented as the rare Stoic sage, never having succombed to passion.

Origen on Prepassion

Origen too adopts the Stoic concept of prepassion. Usually, the term occurs in apologetic contexts, as we would expect from the Stoic sources, as a tool to explain that the sage is not actually guilty of passion. For example, the wording of Ps 4:5a (LXX) ("be angry and sin not") is troubling, for anger (ὀργή) is regarded as a passion in Stoicism.[75] Origen's answer is to suggest that the scriptural lexicon applies the term much more broadly than we might otherwise think. Whereas some (the Stoics?) might define anger as "something decisive" (τι προαιρετικόν), and therefore, as an excessive movement of will, Origen maintains that scripture is using the

---

73. *Die Stoa* 2:254; see Graver, "Philo of Alexandria," 202–3, n. 13.

74. The Greek reads, «Ἦλθε δὲ Ἀβραὰμ κόψασθαι Σάρραν.» Προπάθεια καὶ οὐ πάθος τοῦ Ἀβραὰμ διὰ τούτων δεδήλωται· οὐ γὰρ εἴρηται, ὅτι ἐκόψατο, ἀλλ' ὅτι »ἦλθε κόψασθαι«· τοῦτο δηλοῖ καὶ τὸ »ἀνέστη Ἀβραὰμ ἀπὸ τοῦ νεκροῦ« μὴ προλεχθέντος τοῦ 'ἐκόψατο' (trans. mine). I have reproduced Metzler's text (*Prokop von Gaza: Eclogarum in libros historicos Veteris Testamenti epitome* [GCS n.s 22; Berlin: de Gruyter, 2015], 1:300). Metzler labels the fragment as unidentified, but says regarding Philonic influence "die Exegese scheint inspiriert von Ph., quaest. Gen. V [*sic*, read: IV] 73" (1:300, n. ad Gen 23.2.2–5).

75. Although ὀργή is not regarded as one of the four cardinal passions of Stoicism, it is associated with "an excessive desire [ἐπιθυμία] to take vengeance against one who allegedly committed an injustice" (see *SVF* 3:395–97).

term as something "indecisive" (ἀπροαίρετον), or "what some call a προπά-θεια."[76]

Such a solution is exegetically necessary for Origen, who equates sin with passion. This creates an obvious problem with Christ himself being ascribed a passion in Matt 26:37: "he [Jesus] began to be grieved and anxious."[77] Could Christ actually be guilty of grief (λυπή), one of the four cardinal passions in Stoicism? "No," says Origen, despite the clear wording of scripture. Origen first fixates on the verb "begin" (ἄρχομαι), insisting that Christ did not enter into the state of grief, but only approached it. Origen establishes his point by an appeal to Heb 4:15, noting that Christ was "without sin," and therefore without passion. Christ was not literally grieved (λυπεῖσθαι), as the scriptures seem to say, but experienced only the prepassion preceding grief. Just as Philo rescues Abraham from the charge of passion, so also Origen saves Jesus from the same.

Didymus on Prepassion

In comparison with the authors discussed thus far, the material attesting to Didymus's doctrine of prepassion is far more extensive. Didymus uses the noun προπάθεια forty-one times, or a little less than half the total number of attested Greek usages in the TLG. It should come as no surprise that Didymus's doctrine of προπάθεια has attracted a fair amount of attention in recent years, especially in the publications of Richard Layton.[78] Layton believes Origen is the most important influence on Didymus's articulation of this originally Stoic theme. He writes, "Didymus does not seem to have direct contact with the function of *propatheia* in Stoic writings and depends completely on Origen's use of the concept. In this way, he obtains the psychological concept already attached to scriptural narratives, along with this resonant ambiguity."[79]

There is much to commend Layton's assessment. In one instance, Didymus makes exactly the kind of argument we saw with Origen on Matt 26:37. After a student asks why his instructor insists that Christ suffered only προπάθειαι, Didymus answers that it is an apologetic necessity. First,

---

76. *Sel. Ps.* ad Ps 4:5. For a discussion of this passage see Layton, *Didymus the Blind*, 114–19.

77. The Greek reads ἤρξατο [Christ] λυπεῖσθαι καὶ ἀδημονεῖν (*Comm. Matt.* Ser. 92, quoted in Layton, *Didymus the Blind*, 121–22).

78. Richard Layton, "Judas Yields a Place to the Devil: The Appropriation of Origen's Commentary on Ephesians by Didymus of Alexandria," in *Origeniana Septima*, 531–41; esp. "Propatheia: The Origins of the Passions in the Exegesis of Origen and Didymus" *VC* 54 (2000): 242–62; *Didymus the Blind*, 114–34.

79. Layton, *Didymus the Blind*, 123.

Heb 4:15 claims that Christ committed no sin (and hence no passion). Second, if we admit that Christ did suffer passion, then his soul would not be perfect.[80] Third, Matt 26:37 states Christ only *began* to suffer grief, and thus distances him from actually experiencing the passion.[81] A passion is a state of mind, and thus one cannot properly "begin to be" in that state.[82] As Didymus says later, "Sometimes, it [the λογικὴ οὐσία] immediately stops the disturbance so that nothing comes after it. This they call a προπάθεια."[83] This is just one example, but it seems to confirm Layton's thesis, namely that Didymus is at least partially dependent upon Origen for the doctrine of προπάθεια..

But Bayliss feels that Philo is a much more important influence. He writes, "I would suggest that it is not Origen's stretching of the terminology of prepassion to fit biblical archetypes which results in an inherent ambiguity unconsciously exaggerated by Didymus [as Layton argues] but Didymus's wish to express a psychological continuum which moves him to a more Philonic usage." Now Bayliss does not wish to dismiss the influence of Origen, but feels that Didymus's application of προπάθεια owes more to Philo.

For Didymus, as for Philo apparently, prepassion is a preliminary stage that can be understood as positive, negative, or even indifferent.[84] On the negative side, Didymus states, "Pre-passion alone acquits from any charge, it does not subject someone to a charge; but passion [πάθος] subjects one to a moderate charge; while disposition [διάθεσις] is evil-doing [κακία]; and much worse the action which is added to it."[85] Here, although prepassion can lead to sin, it is morally neutral by itself. But there is a much more

---

80. The soul of Christ was an essential element in the Apollinarian controversy (see Michael Ghattas, "Didymus der Blinde von Alexandrien in der Auseinandersetzung mit Apollinaris von Laodicea und seinen Lehren," in *Patristica et Oecumenica: Festschrift für Wolfgang A. Bienert zum 65. Geburtstag* [ed. Peter Gemeinhardt and Uwe Kühneweg; Marburg: Elwert, 2004], 45–49).
81. *Comm. Ps.* 222.8–12.
82. See Didymus, *Comm. Ps.* 293.6–12.
83. *Comm. Ps.* 222.13–14 (trans. mine). The Greek reads, ἐνίοτε δὲ ἵστησιν εὐθέως τὴν ταραχὴν ὡς μηδὲν μετ' αὐτὴν γενέσθαι. ταύτην προπάθειαν λέγουσιν.
84. Didymus explicitly says, "leave aside for now pre-passion, which involves an inclination toward indifferents" (ἐάσθω γὰρ νῦν ἡ προπάθεια ὡς ῥοπὴν εἰς τὰ ἀδιάφορα ἔχουσα; *Comm. Gen.* 165.18–20). This comment comes right after Didymus claims that a πάθος is not necessarily "something objectionable" (τὸ ψεγόμενον). Unfortunately, the thought is not fleshed out more fully.
85. *Comm. Ps.* 43.23–25 (trans. Bayliss, *The Vision of Didymus*, 208). The Greek reads ἡ προπάθεια μόνη ἀπολύει ἐνκλήματος, οὐχ ὑποβάλλει ἐνκλήματι· τὸ πάθος δὲ μετρίῳ ἐνκλήματι· ἡ δὲ διάθεσις κακία ἐστὶν λοι[π]όν· πολλῷ πλέον καὶ ἡ πρᾶξις προσλημφθεῖσα.

positive application of the doctrine, which Didymus utilizes to great Christological benefit.

After declaring that Christ can be said to enter into prepassion, but not into passion, Didymus writes:

> We are not saying that pre-passion occurs in what is immutable; for we do not call anything else immutable besides the Trinity. Therefore since the soul, which Jesus assumed, is different from the Trinity, it naturally admits pre-passion and a beginning of being astonished and sorely troubled (Mark 14:33). And I quote an apostolic verse: "Instead of the joy set before him he endured the cross, having despised its shame" (Heb 12:2). Unless he was in a state of pre-passion and shunned it, there was no brave deed, nor prize.[86]

Προπάθεια for Didymus is not only a preparatory state, but also a rational and positive one. In fact, Didymus rejects outright the competing notions that Christ actually did sin as well as that he had no rational faculty and thus could not sin.[87] Assigning a positive role to prepassion allows him to walk the line between these two extremes. For Origen, prepassion was merely an apologetic tool, truer to the pure Stoic usage. Christ approached, but did not enter sin. Didymus, however, extends Christ's experience of prepassion in a positive way. Bayliss summarizes,

> To his mind, if there was no potential for moral decline and sin within Christ, then there is nothing praiseworthy in his sinlessness and no soteriologically essential conquest over sin and death. Thus, there must have been a state of crisis within the incarnation which could have led to sin but in fact did not, because of the Saviour's active pursuit of virtue. It is this role that Didymus attributes to pre-passion.[88]

Whereas Layton feels that Didymus, by placing prepassion on a scale, makes a false deduction based on Origen, Bayliss sees Didymus as continuing a tradition from Philo that ultimately is picked up by later authors, such as Jerome.[89] It is tempting to see Philonic influence in Didymus's application of προπάθεια, for Origen is much more Stoic than Philo and Didymus, and while Didymus's usage does not perfectly match Origen's, it certainly does match Philo's. Nevertheless, Bayliss is forced to make his

---

86. *Comm. Ps.* 282.2–7 (trans. Ibid., 210). The Greek reads, προπάθεια[ν] οὐ λέγομεν ἐν ἀτρέπτῳ γίνεσθαι· οὐ λέγομεν γάρ τινα ἄλλον ἄτρεπτον παρὰ τὴν τριάδα. ἐπεὶ τοίνυν ἡ ψυχή, ἣν ἀν[έλα]βεν Ἰησοῦς, ἄλλη ἐστὶν παρὰ τὴν τριάδα, πέφυκεν δέχεσθαι προπάθειαν καὶ ἀρχὴν τοῦ θαμβεῖσθαι καὶ ἀδημονεῖν. καὶ λ[έγ]ω ἀποστολικόν· "ἀντὶ τῆς προκειμένης χαρᾶς ὑπέμεινεν σταυρὸν αἰσχύνης καταφρονήσας." εἰ μὴ γέγονεν ἀλ[ύ]σκων ἐν προπαθείᾳ, οὐκ ἦν ἀνδραγάθημα οὐδὲ ἆθλον.

87. See *Comm. Ps.* 43.12–20; 293.7–9.

88. Bayliss, *The Vision of Didymus*, 209.

89. Bayliss, *The Vision of Didymus*, 206.

case from only one Philonic passage.[90] While significant, one wonders if Philo is consistent in his application of the doctrine.[91] However, despite any other parallels in previous authors, we can surmise that Didymus must have known Philo's usage and developed it in a Christological direction following Origen.

The Philonic Impact on Didymus's Doctrine of Ethical Progress and the Stages of Virtue

Few Philonic themes are more prominent in the Alexandrian patristic tradition than the interpretation of Hagar as encyclical studies and Sarah as virtue.[92] The theme was most useful for arguing that secular education is a necessary preparation for virtue. Van den Hoek regards the theme as one of four major borrowings from Philo in Clement of Alexandria.[93] We have also seen the theme in the works of Origen.[94] In chapter 5 we established that Didymus knew the versions of Clement and Origen but had certainly read the Philonic allegory of Hagar and Sarah for himself. So there is no need to rehash what we have already discussed. Here, we wish to set the broader context of the allegory in the thought of Philo, and to discuss how the allegory influenced Didymus's concept of secular education in general.

In Philo, Hagar represents the encyclical studies and Sarah perfect virtue.[95] The connection between secular studies and philosophy was already established by the time of Philo. In fact, Seneca shows knowledge of the same background information in his *Epist.* 88.[96] For his information on the προκόπτων Philo again is dependent on the traditional literature, with an important modification.[97] But Philo's primary purpose was exegetical. He

---

90. Bayliss is apparently unaware that the Greek fragment from Procopius is likely unoriginal (see above).
91. As an example in a similar category, Abraham is attributed only μετριοπάθεια in one passage (*Abr.* 257), while in another he is attributed ἀπάθεια (*QG* 4.73). See Sharon Weisser, "Why Does Philo Criticize the Stoic Ideal of *Apatheia* in *On Abraham* 257? Philo and Consolatory Literature," *CQ* 62 (2012): 242–59.
92. See, e.g., Henrichs, "Philosophy, the Handmaiden of Theology"; Johan Leemans, "After Philo and Paul"; Miyako Demura, "Origen and the Exegetical Tradition of the Sarah-Hagar Motif in Alexandria," SPatr 56 (2013): 73–81; Rogers, "The Philonic and the Pauline."
93. See *Clement* 23–47.
94. See ch. 5 above, on *Comm. Gen.* 234.31–236.21.
95. See, e.g., *Congr.* 9–12, 23.
96. See our discussion in ch. 5 above.
97. The modification is that one can progress *in* virtue, a point Didymus maintains as well (see ch. 5 above).

wished to show that the biblical patriarchs, each through different means, reached the ethical ideal of "becoming like God" (ὁμοίωσις θεῷ).

This ethical ideal is borrowed from Plato's *Theaet.* 176b. For Philo as for any moralist, God was free from all vice and all passion. Thus, the normal Middle Platonic doctrine of μετριοπάθεια had to be revised to the Stoic ethical summit of ἀπάθεια.[98] David Winston writes, "Inasmuch as, according to Philo, God is completely ἀπαθής, his ὁμοίωσις θεῷ formula clearly implies that man's highest ethical ideal is constituted by a state of ἀπάθεια."[99] Each of the patriarchs reaches ethical perfection, Isaac by φύσις,[100] Jacob by ἄσκησις,[101] and Abraham by διδασκαλία.[102] Not every biblical character is able to completely eradicate the passions, however. Aaron lives his entire life as a προκόπτων, content to "moderate" the passions (μετριοπάθεια), but never able to extirpate them.[103]

Another dimension exists in the thought of Philo that makes the assimilation to God possible. For Philo, the cosmic Logos is akin to the highest part of our nature, the mind (νοῦς). Hence, the idea that humanity is made in the image of God (Gen 1:26) has ethical significance. The connection enables Philo to define the Stoic οἰκείωσις in terms very similar to the Platonic ὁμοίωσις θεῷ.[104] This leads, as Carlos Lévy explains, to "two levels of kinship between man and God: (1) the level intended by providence through the process of the creation, and (2) the level reached by the human being who, in his search for rationality, consciously takes the resemblance upon himself."[105] Thus, every man has an opportunity to pursue this innate "ember of wisdom" (*Spec.* 2.47) to reach ethical perfection by becoming like God.[106]

The ethical ideal is plainly set forth in Philo, but the road to it is long and arduous. In *Agr.* 159–161 Philo identifies three different stages moral

---

98. See Lilla, *Clement of Alexandria*, 99–117, who demonstrates that Neo-Platonism typically links ἀπάθεια with the doctrine of ὁμοίωσις θεῷ.

99. "Philo's Ethical Theory," *ANRW* 2.21.1:372–416, 400.

100. *Fug.* 166–67.

101. *Leg.* 2.89.

102. *Abr.* 52–53.

103. *Leg.* 3.129, 132.

104. See Carlos Lévy, "Philo's Ethics," in *The Cambridge Companion to Philo*, 146–71, 147–49.

105. Carlos Lévy, "Philo's Ethics," 149.

106. Wendy Helleman points out an important distinction made by Philo: "Assimilation does not ... involve the individual in a participation or sharing of the divine nature as such; more characteristically, it aims at an imitation or clear reflection in the individual of the qualities, or 'virtues' which are properly attributed to the divine nature" ("Philo of Alexandria on Deification and Assimilation to God," *SPhiloA* 2 [1990]: 51–71, 63).

development: (1) beginners (ἀρχόμενοι), (2) progressors (προκόπτουσι), and (3) the [just] perfected (τετελειωμένοι).[107] The last category does not refer to those who have conquered vice once and for all. In fact, they may not even be aware that they have reached "perfection" (*Agr.* 161).[108] This likely would be Philo's explanation of Abraham who, although mating with Sarah (perfect virtue), also grieves over her death, exhibiting a passion (λύπη).[109] Lévy suggests that Philo is influenced by the Peripatetic notion that the passions can be beneficial,[110] and he may indeed be correct.[111] If so, we have further reason to imagine Philo invoked the Stoic doctrine of prepassion.[112] Therefore, there is a tension in the thought of Philo between complete freedom from emotion, which is the result of divine grace,[113] and moderation of the passions, which is possible through human effort alone.[114]

In this scheme the stage of perfection contains two levels: those who can fall back into the passions and those who cannot.[115] Philo would apparently link the final stage with the ideal of *visio dei*, which is complete ὁμοίωσις θεῷ.[116] The "perfected" souls who have just entered virtue, and who can still fall away, such as Abraham, reach the level only of contemplating God's δυνάμεις.[117] The occasional sage, such as Moses, however, reaches the stage of contemplating God in his essence.[118] Of these two characters, Philo remarks, "The highest point of wisdom reached by Abraham is the initial course in Moses' training."[119] So Abraham is the more common sage, and

---

107. The larger discussion in *Agr.* 146–68 covers progress and ethical perfection.
108. This distinction is Stoic (see *SVF* 3:539–42).
109. *Abr.* 256–57 (see Weisser, "Why Does Philo Criticize").
110. E.g., *Leg.* 2.8.
111. "Philo's Ethics," 161.
112. See the discussion of prepassion above.
113. See Walther Völker, *Fortschritt und Vollendung bei Philo von Alexandrien* (TUGAL 4.49.1; Leipzig: Henrichs, 1938), 266 (cited in Lévy, "Philo's Ethics," 160). See Philo's words in *Leg.* 1.89.
114. Lévy expresses this distinction as "bad apathy" and "good apathy" ("Philo's Ethics," 160).
115. Seneca, *Epist.* 75.9 has the exact same scheme.
116. See *Migr.* 168–175.
117. See *Mut.* 15–24.
118. See Scott D. Mackie, who cites *Ebr.* 152 as an indication that it is possible in Philo's thought for one to reach a vision of τὸ ὄν ("Seeing God in Philo of Alexandria: the Logos, the Powers or the Existent One?," *SPhiloA* 21 [2009]: 25–47, 34–36).
119. *Post.* 174. The Greek reads, τὴν δὲ τούτου [Noah] τελείωσιν Ἀβραὰμ ἄρχεται παιδεύεσθαι, ἡ δὲ ἀκροτάτη τοῦδε σοφία Μωυσέως ἐστὶν ἄσκησις ἡ πρώτη (trans. PLCL 2:433). This statement follows a chain of progressively better patriarchal exemplars: The heights reached by Seth set the stage for Noah; those reached by Noah set the stage for Abraham, and so on.

Moses the rare wise man who is able to extirpate the passions and ascend to a contemplation of τὸ ὄν. The appearance of the true sage, however, is extremely rare. Seneca quips, "The wise man, like the phoenix, appears once every five hundred years."[120]

Now the purpose of Philo's Allegorical Commentary is to lead his readers along the path of ethical progress. David Hay writes that Philo's primary purpose is "the means of turning to God, the barriers people encounter when they try to grow closer to God, and the stages of spiritual progress."[121] Secular education and biblical interpretation provide essential steps in one's spiritual progress in both Philo and in the Alexandrian Fathers. The Fathers also continue the ethical ideal of ὁμοίωσις θεῷ.[122] The exegesis of Didymus the Blind is traditional, and reflects a similar thought world.

Didymus on Virtue

Didymus encourages his students to "live according to philosophy and virtue" (*Comm. Eccl.* 165.17). In order to reach this stage they must progress throughout their lives. In connection with this theme, Richard Layton has shown that Didymus understands the Book of Psalms as an allegory of the individual's "pilgrimage" to ethical perfection.[123] This goal is exemplified in Job, who displays a number of sagacious qualities, including εὐδαιμονία and καρτερία.[124] When we turn to the *Comm. Gen.* we find the foundation for the ethics of Didymus in general: humanity must return to the state of perfection prior to the Fall.

In *Comm. Gen.* 104.13–17 Didymus remarks, "Virtue is a toilsome object, since the heart of men is attentively engaged in the evil; for this reason, scripture says 'you shall eat your bread by sweat all the days of your life' (Gen 3:19), which could not have been said with regard to angels. For they are more content to practice in the things of virtue."[125] Didymus under-

---

120. *Epist.* 42.1.
121. David Hay, "Philo of Alexandria," in *Justification and Variegated Nomism*, ed. Donald A. Carson, Peter T. O'Brien, and Mark A. Siefrid [WUNT 2/140; Tübingen: Mohr Siebeck; Grand Rapids: Baker, 2001], 1:357–80, 365.
122. E.g., Clement, *Strom.* 2.19.97; Origen, *Princ.* 3.6.1 (on the whole question and its relation to Platonism, see Lilla, *Clement of Alexandria*, 60–117).
123. See Layton, *Didymus the Blind*, 54–55.
124. See Layton, *op. cit.*, 70 (on εὐδαιμονία, on which he believes Didymus to reflect Plotinian influence) and 80–81 (on καρτερία, on which Didymus is following Stoic sources).
125. The Greek reads, Ἐπίμοχθον οὖν ἡ ἀρετή, ὅπου καὶ ἡ καρδία τῶν ἀνθρώπων ἐπιμελῶς ἐπὶ τὸ κακὸν ἔγκειται· διὰ τοῦτο «πάσας» φησὶν «τὰς ἡμέρας τῆς ζωῆς σου ἐν ἱδρῶτι φαγῇ τὸν ἄρτον σου», ὅπερ οὐκ ἂν λεχθείη ἀγγέλοις· εὐκολώτερον γὰρ παρ' ἐκείνοις τὰ τῆς ἀρετῆς ἐνεργεῖται (trans.

stands the Fall of man in terms of a loss of the angelic condition in which virtue was dominant.[126] As we have seen, the Fall was not merely psychological; it was also physiological, the "skins" being fashioned as earthly bodies (Gen 3:21).

The way in which humanity recovers their originally perfect condition is through progress. Basing himself on the omission of καθ' ὁμοίωσιν in Gen 1:27, Didymus writes,

> For when the mind enters into piety [θεοσέβεια], it is formed at first in accord with the image of God, but later, through moral progress which turns into perfection, it comes to exist in accord with the likeness of God, which the blessed John posits when he says, "Beloved, now we are children of God and it has not yet been revealed what we will be; we know that if he is revealed, we will be like him [ὅμοιοι αὐτῷ] (1 John 3:2). For since they already exist in accord with the image, they hope to become in accord with the likeness.[127]

Education plays a prominent role in this process, as well as repentance.[128] But it is possible for humanity to reach the level of ὁμοίωσις θεῷ, at least theoretically.

Humanity is thus involved in an eternal struggle to return to the original state of virtue. In this struggle, three categories of ethical advancement can be identified: (1) "initiation" (εἰσαγωγή); (2) "progress" (προκοπή); and (3) "perfection" (τελείωσις).[129] Didymus interprets the command to "grow and multiply" (Gen 1:28) along these lines: "Since divine instruction [θεία παίδευσις] involves an initiation [εἰσαγωγή], a progression [προκοπή], and a perfection [τέλος], we must understand the command to 'grow' in this sense."[130] The scheme is traditional, with one exception. Didymus regards

---

mine). For the motif of virtue as a toilsome pursuit, cf. Philo, *Leg.* 3.135; *Sacr.* 35–36 (for elsewhere in Didymus, cf. *Comm. Ps.* 274.24–25; *Comm. Eccl.* 44.28–45.2).

126. Chrysostom makes the same argument (*Hom. Gen.* 16:1, 6; 17:1; cited in Layton, *Didymus the Blind*, 188, n. 82).

127. *Comm. Gen.* 58.27–59.1 (trans. mine). The Greek reads Ὁ γὰρ ν[οῦς] προσελθὼν τῇ θεοσεβείᾳ τυποῦται μὲν κατὰ τὴν εἰκόνα τ[οῦ Θ]εοῦ, ὕστερον δὲ διὰ προκοπῆς τῆς ἐπὶ τελειότητα καθ' ὁμοίωσιν Θεοῦ γίνεται ὅπερ <παρ>ιστὰς ὁ μακάριος Ἰωάννης φησίν· «Ἀγαπητοί, νῦν τέκνα Θεοῦ ἐσμεν καὶ οὔπω ἐφανερώθη τί ἐσόμεθα· οἴδαμεν ὅτι ἐὰν φανερωθῇ ὅμοιοι αὐτῷ ἐσόμεθα.» Ἤδη γὰρ κατ' εἰκόνα ὄντες ἐλπίζουσιν καθ' ὁμοίωσιν γενέσθαι.

128. *Comm. Gen.* 59.18–23. Μετάνοια for Philo and Christian thinkers is positive, whereas for Stoicism it had been negative (see Monique Alexandre, "Le lexique des vertus: Vertus philosophiques et religieuses chez Philon: μετάνοια et εὐγένεια," in *Philon d'Alexandrie et le langage de la philosophie*, 17–46, 22).

129. *Comm. Gen.* 26.25; 165.17–23 (see Bayliss, *The Vision of Didymus*, 208).

130. *Comm. Gen.* 69.8–9 (trans. mine). The Greek reads, Καὶ ἐπεὶ ἡ θεία [παίδε]υσις καὶ εἰσαγωγὴν ἔχει καὶ προκοπὴν καὶ τέλος, κατὰ τ[αύτην τὸ] «αὐξάνεσθε» νοητέον.

the distinctively "divine" instruction to be the key to ethical advancement. This move represents a break from Philo, who describes ethical advancement largely in (pagan) philosophical terms, although his proofs are biblical.[131] This may be a hint that Didymus regards *Christian* education as a key element in ethical advancement, as Layton attempts to show.[132]

When discussing Hagar and Sarah, there is evidence that Didymus has altered the Philonic model, although he is certainly dependent on it. In his discussion, Didymus mentions Philo by name twice.[133] He accepts Philo's identification of Hagar with the *propaideia*, and regards Sarah as "perfect virtue and philosophy,"[134] and once as "the perfection of virtue."[135] But Didymus differs from Philo in that his concept of the *propaideia* seems not to be entirely secular. We saw in the previous paragraph that the ethical stages of humanity comprise what Didymus terms θεία παίδευσις. He also interprets the "seed" of woman in Gen 3:15 as "the inherent virtues" that come from the woman (i.e., the church), which are the "teachings of the θεία παίδευσις."[136]

It seems that Didymus links Philo's Hagar-Sarah allegory not only with ethical advancement, but also with the distinctively "spiritual" interpretation of the Bible. Commenting on Hagar's flight from Sarah in Gen 16:7–8, he writes, "The one who approaches the θεία παίδευσις ought to enter her in such a way that he understands her by letter and by spirit."[137] Now these are exegetical terms. Those who follow only a literal sense are, like Hagar, attempting to "flee from virtue," and remain only in the introductory stage. "But when the beauty of the spiritual law becomes present, [the sage] flees the shadowy parts [literal sense/sacrifices]."[138] Now this whole discussion is directed against "the Israelites" who are identified with Hagar. But Didymus is not involved in a battle of religion. Rather, his problem with the "Israelites" is that they adhere to a literal interpretation of the Old

---

131. For Didymus, Greek philosophy is typically negative (e.g., *Comm. Eccl.* 158.6–8; *Comm. Zach.* 233.15–20).

132. Layton, *Didymus the Blind*, 135–58.

133. *Comm. Gen.* 235.24–236.21.

134. *Comm. Gen.* 235.29.

135. *Comm. Gen.* 114.5.

136. *Comm. Gen.* 99.6.

137. *Comm.* Gen. 242.9–11 (trans. mine). The Greek reads, Ὁ προσερχόμενος τοίνυν τῇ θείᾳ παιδεύσει οὕτως αὐτῇ προσέχεσθαι ὀφείλει ὡς νοῆσαι αὐτὴν κατὰ γράμμα καὶ πνεῦμα ὁδῷ.

138. *Comm.* Gen. 243.16–17 (trans. mine). The Greek reads, Ἀλλὰ καὶ τοῦ κάλλους τοῦ πνευματικοῦ νόμου ἐνστάντος φεύγει τὰ σκιώδη....

Testament, both theoretically (in hermeneutics) and practically (in application).[139]

At this juncture we should untie the knots of Didymus's exegesis. Ethical progress for Didymus permeates every aspect of one's life. When one arrives at perfection, virtue, or philosophy through training, he is the ultimate sage, reaching what Philo also calls ὁμοίωσις θεῷ. The mind of God unites with the mind of man so that the sage can perceive divine realities as God sees them. Didymus explains, "For sometimes the human melts and the material falls away from thought and from the hearts, so that the mind no longer has any attachments, but is completely immaterial, as it was at the beginning."[140] Later in the same work, Didymus states, "There are visible and invisible things created by God. And their creator is seen from their greatness and beauty. The eye, however, which sees invisible things is our mind, the pure heart, which also sees God."[141] This *visio dei* is also described in Philo, as we saw above. But the twist that Didymus provides is that only the appropriate understanding of the spiritual sense of scripture leads one to contemplate divine realities.

It would seem that the Neo-Platonic interpretation of Homer has exercised its influence heavily.[142] The "spiritual" reading of sacred texts found a unique place, especially in the Plotinian philosophy of late antiquity. Robert Lamberton says that "the *Odyssey* was for Plotinus and his circle already a poem that, in subtly manipulated allegories, recounted a spiritual journey through a Platonized universe."[143] This reading strategy is clearest in Porphyry's *On the Cave of the Nymphs*, in which he presents the cave as a symbol:

> Homer says that all outward possessions must be deposited in this cave and that one must be stripped naked and take on the persona of a beggar and, having withered the body away and cast aside all that is superficial and turned away from the senses, take counsel with Athena, sitting with her

---

139. This attitude is already present in Clement and Origen, for whom Ἰουδαϊκός means "slavishly literal" (Clement, *Paed.* 1.6; Origen, *Princ.* 2.11.2).

140. *Comm. Ps.* 352–4 (trans. Stefaniw, *Mind, Text and Commentary*, 241). The Greek reads, τήκεται οὖν ποτε ὁ ἄνθρωπος, τὸ ὑλικόι ποτε ἀποπίπτει τῆς νοήσεως καὶ τῆς καρδίας, ὥστε τὸν νοῦν μηκέτι ἔχειν τι προσπεπλεγμένον, ἀλλὰ πάντῃ ἄϋλον εἶναι ὡς καὶ τὴν ἀρχὴν ὑπῆρκται.

141. *Comm. Ps.* 84.24–25 (trans. Stefaniw, *Mind, Text and Commentary*, 243). The Greek reads, εἰσὶν ὁρατὰ καὶ ἀόρατα θεοῦ ποιήματα· καὶ ἐκ μεγέθους τούτων καὶ τῆς καλλονῆς ὁ κατασκευάσας αὐτὰ θεωρεῖται. ὀφθαλμὸς δέ ἐστιν ὁ τὰ ἀόρατα ὁρῶν ὁ νοῦς ἡμῶν, ἡ καθαρὰ καρδία, ἥτις καὶ τὸν θεὸν βλέπει.

142. On this point see Lamberton, *Homer the Theologian*, 83–143.

143. Lamberton, *Homer the Theologian*, 132.

beneath the roots of the olive, how he might cut away all the destructive passions of his soul.[144]

Clearly, Porphyry sees the cave as much more than a mere geological formation. It is a spiritual symbol teaching us to leave behind our vices and enter the world of virtue. Didymus believed the spiritual meaning of the Bible served the same purpose.

Secular education provides no more value in reaching ἀρετή than the surface meaning of scripture provides in reaching the ἀναγωγή. Both the literal meaning and the *propaideia* are of relative value to be sure, but he who stops there will never advance beyond the stage of προκοπή. Just as in Philo, the ethical ideal in Didymus is to attune one's νοῦς to the divine νοῦς, and to strip away all vice to arrive at perfection—a mental *visio dei*.[145] This can only occur through a concentrated practice in moral discipline and a focused study on the spiritual sense of the scriptures.

The Philonic Impact on Didymus's Doctrine of the Divine Powers

The doctrine of the divine powers (δυνάμεις) is one of Philo's most characteristic teachings about God. The doctrine is rooted in a philosophical tension: Philo's Platonist belief in divine transcendence must be balanced with his Stoic belief in divine immanence.[146] Scripture confronts Philo with the fact that God governs his creation, but the biblical description of how such governance occurs aggravates Philo's theological sensibilities.[147] The ultimate answer, worked out Platonically, is that God acts in the world not directly, but through his δυνάμεις.

A number of passages set forth Philo's doctrine of the powers. One can be located in his exegesis of the troubling narrative of Gen 18. Here three "men" visit Abraham, one of whom appears to be none other than God himself (v. 10). Philo feels compelled to explain how this can be:

---

144. *Antr. nymph.* 79.12–19 (translation Lamberton, *Homer the Theologian*, 130, modified slightly). The Greek reads, Εἰς τοῦτο τοίνυν φησὶν Ὅμηρος δεῖν τὸ ἄντρον ἀποθέσθαι πᾶν τὸ ἔξωθεν κτῆμα, γυμνωθέντα δὲ καὶ προσαίτου σχῆμα περιθέμενον καὶ κάρψαντα τὸ σῶμα καὶ πᾶν περίττωμα ἀποβαλόντα καὶ τὰς αἰσθήσεις ἀποστραφέντα βουλεύεσθαι μετὰ τῆς Ἀθηνᾶς, καθεζόμενον σὺν αὐτῇ ὑπὸ πυθμένα ἐλαίας, ὅπως τὰ ἐπίβουλα τῆς ψυχῆς αὐτοῦ πάθη πάντα περικόψῃ.

145. *Comm. Gen.* 210.21; 217.15ff.

146. In general, see Luis Angel Montes-Peral, *Akataleptos Theos: der unfassbare Gott* (ALGHJ 16; Leiden: Brill, 1987); Cristina Termini, *Le potenze di Dio: Studio su δύναμις in Filone di Alessandria* (SEAug 71; Rome: Institutum Patristicum Augustinianum, 2000).

147. The tension renders the subject of providence particularly problematic for Philo (see Peter Frick, *Divine Providence in Philo of Alexandria* [TSAJ 77; Tübingen: Mohr: Siebeck, 1999], 26–32).

the central place is held by the Father of the Universe, Who in the sacred scriptures is called He that is [ὁ ὤν] as His proper name, while on either side of Him are the senior potencies the nearest to Him, the creative and the kingly. The title of the former is God [θεός], since it made [τίθημι] and ordered the All; the title of the latter is Lord [κύριος], since it is the fundamental right of the maker to rule and control what he has brought into being.[148]

Although here the transcendent ὁ ὤν appears more immanent, the next paragraph explains that the One can only be contemplated through mental vision (ὁρατικὴ διάνοια), a gift Abraham has. At the more generic level, Philo's exegesis is based on the two primary names for God in the Pentateuch, יהוה and אלהים. Modern source-critical method highlights these names as being indicative of the J and E sources,[149] but both Philo and the rabbis take the names to express different powers (δυνάμεις) or attributes (מידות) of God.[150]

As the language of the text above implies, God possesses more than two powers. This passage also fails to express God's absolute transcendence, and hence the role of the Logos in the world. Another passage more fully explains Philo's doctrine of divine transcendence and the role of the powers. In a series of discussions of the Cherubim, Philo asks what God means when he says "I will speak to you ... from between the cherubim."[151] *QE* 2.68 states:

> First there is He who is more venerable than the unit and the monad and the first principle (ἀρχή). Then there is the Logos of Him who is, the spermatic substance of those things which exist. From the divine Logos, as from a spring, two powers split off. The one is the creative power, in accordance with which the craftsman placed all things and ordered them, and this power is named "God" (θεός). The other is the kingly power, in accordance with which the creator rules what has come into being, and this power is called "Lord" (κύριος). From these two powers others have grown forth. Beside the creative power the gracious power sprouts forth, and its name is "beneficent." Beside the kingly power the legislative power sprouts

---

148. *Abr.* 121 (trans. *PLCL* 6:63). The Greek reads, πατὴρ μὲν τῶν ὅλων ὁ μέσος, ὃς ἐν ταῖς ἱεραῖς γραφαῖς κυρίῳ ὀνόματι καλεῖται ὁ ὤν, αἱ δὲ παρ' ἑκάτερα αἱ πρεσβύταται καὶ ἐγγυτάτω τοῦ ὄντος δυνάμεις, ἡ μὲν ποιητική, ἡ δ' αὖ βασιλική· προσαγορεύεται δὲ ἡ μὲν ποιητικὴ θεός, ταύτῃ γὰρ ἔθηκέ τε καὶ διεκόσμησε τὸ πᾶν, ἡ δὲ βασιλικὴ κύριος, θέμις γὰρ ἄρχειν καὶ κρατεῖν τὸ πεποιηκὸς τοῦ γενομένου.

149. See the classic presentation in Julius Wellhausen, *Prolegomena to the History of Israel* (trans. John Sutherland Black and Allan Menzies; Edinburgh: Black, 1885).

150. See b. Ber. 60b; Gen. Rabb. 33.3. The Divine "attributes," מדת הרחמים and מדת הדין often are hypostatized in rabbinic literature (b. Shabb. 55a; Meg. 15a; San. 111b). In general, see David Winston, "Philo and Rabbinic Literature," in *The Cambridge Companion to Philo*, ed. Adam Kamesar (Cambridge: Cambridge University Press, 2010), 231–53, 238–41.

151. Exod 25:21.

forth, and its correct name is the "punitive" (power). Below these and beside these is the ark. The ark is the symbol of the intelligible cosmos.[152]

Philo goes on to allegorize the ark of the covenant, and then adds, "The divine Logos who is in the middle has a superior position, but above the Logos is He who speaks."[153] This yields the following seven powers, each given in order of rank:

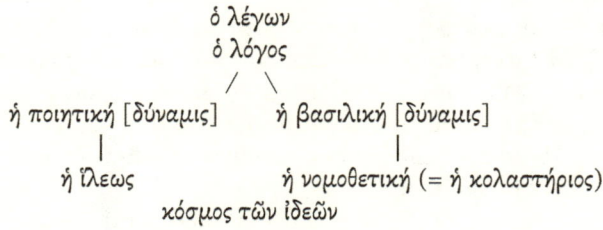

Although the text is lacunose, a similar scheme can be located in *Fug.* 94–95. This important passage discusses the six cities of refuge (Num 35), which Philo identifies as the Logos and the five powers. The final two powers in his scheme have not been preserved, but Philo does mention ἡ ποιητική, ἡ βασιλική, and ἡ ἴλεως. Wendland also proposes a textual emendation, which would place ἡ νομοθετική as the fourth. Hence, it would appear that the basic scheme of *QE* 2.68 can be confirmed in an least one other Philonic text.

The background to the doctrine of divine powers has long occupied the minds of scholars. Rabbinic literature furnishes exact parallels to the idea, although the meanings of the names יהוה and אלהים are usually reversed.[154] Whereas Philo links mercy with the creative power, or θεός, the rabbinic

---

152. Trans. David Runia, "A Neglected Text of Philo of Alexandria: First Translation into a Modern Language," in *Things Revealed: Studies in Early Jewish and Christian Literature in Honor of Michael E. Stone* (ed. Esther G. Chazon, David Satran and Ruth A. Clements; JSJSup 89; Leiden: Brill, 2004), 199–207, 205–6.

153. There is no parallel to the "speaker" anywhere in Greek thought (Dillon, *Middle Platonists*, 166). It seems to me that Philo adds it here so that he can emphasize that there are seven powers. First, he mentions ὁ λέγων only *after* he has enumerated the other six powers, almost as an afterthought. Second, if we compare *Fug.* 94–95, where only six powers are mentioned (ὁ λέγων being absent), then it seems rational to conclude that the addition of the "speaker" to the scheme in *QE* 2.68 is artificial.

154. An exception is found in Mekhilta baḥodesh 5, translated in Winston, *Logos and Mystical Theology*, 21–22. But, as Winston explains, this passage is better understood as an exegesis of the biblical passages under consideration than as an all-embracing theory of God's attributes.

literature links this attribute with the name יהוה (κύριος). Also, the rabbinic literature identifies the punitive power with the name אלהים, but Philo identifies it with the name κύριος (יהוה).

Scholars of ancient Judaism have long searched for an explanation for this difference. Arthur Marmorstein argues that the rabbis deliberately altered the tradition they received in response to Christian and/or gnostic attacks. In fact, as Marmorstein attempts to show, older traditions agreeing with Philo can be found throughout the midrashic literature.[155] More recently, the theory of Marmorstein has been revived by Alan Segal.[156] Segal argues that the rabbis are not polemicizing against Christians or gnostics specifically, but against any group who posited a divine mediator.[157] Therefore, just as Marmorstein, Segal would argue that Philo preserves an older tradition which the rabbis inherited and altered for polemical purposes.

Both Marmorstein and Segal argue that the doctrine of the divine powers developed within Judaism. Harry Austryn Wolfson provides a possible exegetical explanation of the doctrine. First, in Exod 33:18 Moses asks to be shown the δόξα of God. Second, in Ps 23:9-10 (LXX), the "king of glory" (βασιλεὺς τῆς δόξης) is identified precisely with "the lord of the powers" (κύριος τῶν δυνάμεων). Hence the term κύριος is linked scripturally with the βασιλικὴ δύναμις of God. When Moses requests a vision of God's glory, he is asking to see his ruling power and not the transcendent ὁ ὤν.[158] Wolfson's explanation is unlikely, however, since there is not a single reference to the Psalms passage anywhere in the works of Philo.[159]

More recently, Cristina Termini has also taken an exegetical approach to the problem of Philo's doctrine of the powers. She argues that the Hellenistic Jewish assumption that God makes use of divine intermediaries was parlayed into a comprehensive doctrine of the δυνάμεις (usually in the plural in Philo).[160] This doctrine explains the mysterious role of the

---

155. See "Philo and the Names of God," *JQR* 22 (1931): 295–306.
156. See the article he composed with Niels A. Dahl, "Philo and the Rabbis on the Names of God," *JSJ* 9 (1978): 1–28. Segal later expanded the ideas present there in his book, *Two Powers in Heaven: Early Rabbinic Reports about Christianity and Gnosticism* (Leiden: Brill, 2002).
157. Segal, *Two Powers*, 121–34 (on the rabbinic evidence), 159–81 (on Philo).
158. Wolfson, *Philo* 1:218–19.
159. Runia states, "It is remarkable but true, I believe, that Philo never cites a biblical text which speaks literally of God's *dunamis*" ("Clement of Alexandria and the Philonic Doctrine of the Divine Powers," *VC* 58 [2004]: 256–76, 260).
160. See Termini, *Le potenze di Dio*, 59–75. See also Termini's summary of her findings in "Philo's Thought within the Context of Middle Judaism," in *The Cambridge Companion to Philo*, 95–123, 100–101.

Cherubim (*Cher.* 27–28), the theophanies in Gen 18 (*Abr.* 107–32), and the divine "let us" passages in Gen 1:26 and 11:7 (*Opif.* 72–75; *Conf.* 168–82). Therefore, Philo's doctrine was conceived as a comprehensive *solutio* to these otherwise problematic texts.

Another background which has been discussed in the context of Philo's doctrine of the powers is more philosophical. It is argued that parallels from Pythagoreanism, Platonism, Aristotelianism, and Stoicism shed light on Philo's discussions.[161] Certainly, all of these backgrounds cannot be of equal relevance. A passage in the Ps-Aristotelian tractate *De mundo* seems to distinguish between God's οὐσία and his δύναμις (6.397b19–28), felt by Abraham Bos to be an important influence on Philo.[162] But Philo's system is more elaborate than that of the *De mundo*.[163]

John Dillon tries to emphasize the Pythagorean background of the absolute transcendence of God, but also acknowledges the Stoic discussions of the powers. A passage from Diogenes Laertius furnishes an important parallel: "He [God] is, however, the artificer of the universe and, as it were, the father of all, both in general and in that particular part of him which is all-pervading, and which is called many names according to its various powers."[164] As the passage goes on to show, the Olympian deities represent manifestations of the Logos in the created world. The analogy to Philo is striking. Not only is the Logos the representative of the transcendent God, but himself gives rise to functionaries to accomplish his work in the material universe. Confirmation of this doctrine may be found in a near-contemporary of Philo, Cornutus, who identifies δίκη and the Graces with the powers of God, a scheme Philo himself knows.[165]

While these philosophical conceptions serve as background to Philo's doctrine, they do not fully elucidate it. For Philo the doctrine of God's powers is much more important than it appears to be in any of the Hellenistic philosophical systems. Dillon acknowledges as much, concluding, "All this explains a certain amount, but it does not, I think, account entirely for the very prominent role which the two chief Powers play in Philo's metaphysics. That may, after all, be his own contribution."[166]

---

161. See Dillon, *Middle Platonists* 161–63; Winston, *Logos and Mystical Theology* 19–20.

162. Abraham P. Bos, "Philo of Alexandria: A Platonist in the Image and Likeness of Aristotle," *SPhA* 10 (1998): 66-86, 75-79.

163. See Dillon, *op. cit.*, 161.

164. 7.147. The Greek reads, εἶναι δὲ τὸν μὲν δημιουργὸν τῶν ὅλων καὶ ὥσπερ πατέρα πάντων κοινῶς τε καὶ τὸ μέρος αὐτοῦ τὸ διῆκον διὰ πάντων, ὃ πολλαῖς προσηγορίαις προσονομάζεσθαι κατὰ τὰς δυνάμεις (trans. LCL).

165. See *Post.* 32; *QE* 2.61 and Dillon, *op. cit.*, 163.

166. *Loc. cit.*

The biblical view of God's immanent involvement in the world seems to contradict the divine transcendence of Platonic metaphysics. The Bible does not seem to assign as comprehensive a role to angels and other divine intermediaries as Philo and many other Jews and Christians in Antiquity would like.[167] Thus Philo, or perhaps his predecessors, had to magnify the doctrine of divine powers, mentioned only sporadically in Greek philosophy, to distance the One from the world while maintaining the traditional position of heavenly intermediaries.

Didymus on the Divine Powers

When we turn to the writings of Didymus the Blind we have enough information to determine that he adopted the Philonic doctrine of the divine powers. Unfortunately, much of the information he originally provided is now lost. For example, Didymus writes in *Comm. Gen.* 102.8–11, "Since, we previously interpreted paradise allegorically as a divine place for the dwelling of the blessed powers, it is only appropriate that we understand the things about the man and the woman in the same way."[168] Unfortunately, the pages where this exegesis was carried out are now missing from the manuscript.

Again in *Comm. Gen.* 134.4–6 Didymus writes,

> It ought to be noted that the phrase "anyone who kills Cain" is used either in place of the vocative, that is, "O Cain, anyone who kills," or is directed at others about him [Cain], in order that it might read "*anyone* who kills Cain." Now he who claims that these others are certain powers [δυνάμεις] would make no mistake. And it is to these others that he [God] has given a "sign not to destroy him," which is a command from God himself; for no such punishments should occur without his consent.

Although one could interpret the above passage to refer to angels or to the "evil powers, the devil and his angels,"[169] it is also possible to understand Didymus to be referring to God's punitive power (ἡ κολαστική δύναμις).[170]

---

167. For a general presentation, see Michael Mach, *Entwicklungsstadien des jüdischen Engelglaubens in vorrabinischer Zeit* (TSAJ 34; Tübingen: Mohr Siebeck, 1992).

168. The Greek reads, Ἐπειδὴ δὲ ἐν τοῖς ἔμπροσθεν ὁ παράδεισος ἡμῖν ἐν ἀλληγορίᾳ ἐλαμβάνετο χωρίον εἶναι θεῖον ἐνδιαίτημα μακαρίων δυνάμεων, καταλλήλως καὶ τὰ περὶ τοῦ ἀνδρὸς καὶ τῆς γυναικὸς ἐκλημπτέον (trans. mine). This passage corresponds to our earlier discussion that Didymus adopted the incorporeal habitation of man and woman in the garden of Eden (see the discussion in this chapter above on the doctrine of preexistence).

169. Didymus understands "the great sea monsters" (κήτη μεγάλα; Gen 1:21) to be the devil and his angels, or αἱ πονηραὶ δυνάμεις (*Comm. Gen.* 45.4–15).

170. This is how Didymus interprets the angel guarding the Garden of Eden (*Comm. Gen.* 115.9).

Unfortunately, the manuscript goes blank at this point, and what additional information Didymus may have provided is now lost.

Also confusing is the fact that Didymus does not utilize the doctrine of the powers for his exegesis of Gen 1:26 or 11:7, as we see in Philo.[171] We do not know how Didymus interpreted the theophany of Gen 18 since his commentary covers only the first seventeen chapters of Gen, and he does not refer to the passage elsewhere.[172] We are left, then, with only a few passages.

The clearest text that reveals Philo's influence is located at *Comm. Gen.* 31.15–22. In discussing the divine epithets κύριος and θεός, Didymus writes,

> For by the name "God" [θεός] the text means the creative aspect [τὸ δημιουργικόν], but by the name Lord [κύριος] indicates a ruler and king. This is why scripture says "in the beginning *God* [θεός] created," not "the king" or "the Lord." Now it says this not because "God" is different from the "Lord," but because the name "God" more clearly expresses the creative aspect. Thus, when he gives a commandment to Adam, it says, "The Lord God commanded Adam," and this is appropriate, for it is characteristic of a lord and king to give laws and commandments.[173]

We can see that the explanation of the divine titles clearly goes back to Philo, although Didymus does not specifically mention the names as "powers" in this passage.[174]

Further confirmation on a larger scale that Didymus adopts the Philonic doctrine of the powers can be found in the comments of Didymus on the Cherubim. From these passages we can see that Didymus was dependent upon Philo for his doctrine of the divine powers, although he changes the doctrine in a significant way.

In his exegesis of Gen 3:24, Didymus writes,

---

171. Strangely, Didymus does not comment on the hortatory subjunctive ποιήσωμεν at all. Origen, by contrast, seems to reflect an awareness of the Philonic discussion (e.g., *Princ.* 1.5.2).

172. Clement interpreted the three visitors along Philonic lines, however (see Runia, "Philo and Clement," 261–62).

173. The Greek reads, μάλιστα γὰρ διὰ ταύτης τῆς προσ[ηγορ]ία[ς τὸ] δημιουργικὸν δηλοῦται, ἡ δὲ *Κύριος* ὀνομασία ἄρχοντος κ[αὶ β]ασί[λε]ως ἐμφαίνει σημασίαν. Καὶ «*ἐν ἀρχῇ*» οὖν «*ἐποίησεν ὁ Θεός*» εἴρηται, οὐχ ὁ Βασιλεὺς ἢ Κύριος, οὐχ ὅτι ἕτερός ἐστιν, ἀλλ᾽ ὅτι ἐμφατικώτερον τὸ δημιουργὸν παρίστησιν τὸ *Θεός* ὄνομα. Ὅτε οὖν ἐντολὴ δίδοται τῷ Ἀδάμ, λέγεται· «*Ἐνετείλατο Κύριος ὁ Θεὸς τῷ Ἀδάμ*», καὶ εἰκότως· κυρίου γὰρ καὶ βασιλέως ἐστὶν τὸ νόμους καὶ ἐντολὰς διδόναι (trans. mine).

174. Didymus preferred to follow Origen in speaking of the "powers" in accord with Col 1:16 (e.g., *Comm. Jo.* 2.34.204; 10.39.269).

> The names of the superior powers, as one might say, are not simply called "proper" nouns [κύρια] among us, but signify ruling functions [πολιτεῖαι]. They are called "rulers, authorities, thrones, and dominions" (Col 1:16) on account of their ruling, having authority, and reigning. For this is what the word "throne" means, according to what is said in Proverbs, "For the throne of rule is established with righteousness" (Prov 16:12). And they are called "dominions" because of their having dominion. Hence they were called "cherubim" from what inheres in them, for "cherubim" means "multitude of knowledge."[175]

Didymus informs us here that the Cherubim are "superior powers" (ὑπερβεβηκυῖαι δυνάμεις). Later he will claim that they are "transcendent rational creatures" (τὰ ὑπερανεβεβηκότα λογικά).[176] The initial focus of the passage above is not what the Cherubim are, but what they do. They rule, hold authority, have dominion, and the like. All of this accords with Philo's idea that the Cherubim indicate divine rule, even if Didymus appeals to the Origenian proof-text Col 1:16.[177] The Philonic background is driving his exegesis, although he probably depends on Origen as well.

The etymology of the name Cherubim does not take up significant space in Philo. Two passages, however, are relevant. In *Mos.* 2.97 Philo notes that "Cherubim" means "full knowledge and science" (ἐπίγνωσις καὶ ἐπιστήμη πολλή), and in *QE* 2.62 he shortens it to "full knowledge" (ἐπίγνωσις πολλή). Origen picks up this etymology, and Didymus may have borrowed it from him.[178] However, the etymology of the name "Cherubim" does not mean as much for Philo or Origen as it does for Didymus.

After calling attention to the fact that the term "sword" is in the singular while "Cherubim" is in the plural, Didymus writes, "The fact that there is one sword guarding, which is indicative of the punitive power [κολαστικὴ δύναμις], but a 'multitude of knowledge' leading to divine virtue signifies the philanthropy of the God of the universe."[179] Here the sword and the

---

175. *Comm. Gen.* 113.9–17 (trans. mine). The Greek reads, Αἱ προσηγορίαι τῶν ὑπ[ε]ρβεβηκυιῶν δυνάμεων, ὡς ἂν εἴποι τις, οὐχ ἁπλῶς κα[τὰ] τὰ παρ' ἡμῖν κύρια καλούμενα ὀνόματά εἰσιν, ἀλλὰ πολ[ιτ]ειῶν σημαντικαί· ἀρχαὶ καὶ ἐξουσία<ι>, θρόνοι, κυριότητε[ς δ]ιὰ τὸ ἄρχειν καὶ ἐξουσιάζειν καὶ βασιλεύειν, —τοῦτο γὰρ ὁ θ[ρό]νος δηλοῖ κατὰ τὸ ἐν Παροιμίαις λεγόμενον· «Μετὰ γὰρ [δικ]αιοσύνης ἑτοιμάζεται θρόνος ἀρχῆς», —καὶ κυριότητες δ[ὲ δ]ιὰ τὸ κυριεύειν λέγονται. Οὕτω χερου<βεὶ>μ ἐκ τοῦ ἐνυπάρχοντ[ος] αὐτοῖς ἐκλήθησαν· "πλῆθος" γὰρ "γνώσεως" ἑρμηνε[ύε]ται χε[ρο]υβείμ.
176. *Comm. Gen.* 115.1.
177. On Philo's doctrine of the Cherubim as powers see Termini, *Le potenze di Dio*, 99–136.
178. *Hom. Num.* 5.3.
179. *Comm. Gen.* 115.8–11 (trans. mine). The Greek reads, Φιλανθρωπίαν μὲν οὖν τοῦ Θεοῦ τῶν ὅλων σημαίνει τὸ μίαν εἶναι ῥομφαίαν, ὅπερ σημεῖόν ἐστι κολαστικῆς δυνάμεως, τὴν φυλάσσουσαν, "πλῆθος" δὲ "[τ]ῆς γνώσεως" τῆς ἐπὶ τὴν θείαν ἀρετὴν ἀγούσης.

Cherubim signify the two highest powers of God, the former signifying the punitive power and the latter the creative or beneficent power. Didymus immediately takes his cue from the text that God provides much knowledge to man, but mitigates his punishment. Philo normally identifies the two powers with the Cherubim and interprets the sword as heaven, the sun, or the Logos.[180] Only in *Cher.* 20 can one perhaps find an indication that the sword signifies a "power" of God as well. So Didymus is in slight disagreement with the normal Philonic scheme.

Philo also does not make much of the etymology of Cherubim as "full knowledge." In *QG* 1.57 he refers to the Cherubim (i.e., the powers) as "overseers of wisdom," noting that the "wisdom of the world" (i.e., philosophy) reflects the wisdom of the powers as a mirror. Didymus avoids such praises of Greek philosophy, preferring rather to emphasize that while God corrects little (with one sword), he offers wisdom in abundance. Paradise is equivalent to virtue, and God assists the progressor, utilizing his beneficent and punitive powers, in his search for perfection.[181]

Didymus concludes his discussion,

> Therefore the guardianship for which the "sword" and the "cherubim" have been appointed, as I mentioned before, should be beneficial, so that, if one should desire entrance [into Paradise/virtue], he could come by means of these things [i.e. the powers], the cherubim hinting at the knowledge of the truth, of which it is necessary for him who enters to have a share, and the sword hinting at the painful leading, as it is written, "through many tribulations" (Acts 14:22) it is possible to obtain entrance into the kingdom.[182]

As we can observe, Didymus adopts the Philonic doctrine that the term Cherubim refers to the divine powers. But he develops the doctrine in a more practical way than Philo normally does, arguing that the Cherubim as "full knowledge" assist the man who seeks to return to Paradise.

---

180. *Cher.* 28; *Mos.* 2.99; *QG* 1.57; *QE* 2.62. On the image of the sword in general, see Aristide M. Serra, "La 'spada:' simbolo della 'parola di Dio,' nell'Antico Testamento biblica-guidaico e nel Nuono Testamento," *Marianum* 63 (2001): 17–89, 32–46. The Logos as "cutter" is most clearly articulated in *Her.*, on which see David M. Hay, "Philo's Treatise on the Logos-Cutter," *SPhiloA* 2 (1973): 9–22.

181. This theme is not unfamiliar to Philo, who also assigns a moral quality to the powers (e.g., *Fug.* 95ff.; *Abr.* 119ff.). This is very close to Didymus's doctrine of conscience (Bayliss, *The Vision of Didymus*, 129–30).

182. *Comm. Gen.* 116.15–20 (trans. mine). The Greek reads, Ἡ φυλακὴ ο[ὖν, εἰ]ς ἣν τέθεινται ἡ ῥομφαία καὶ τὰ χερουβείμ, ὡς πρ[οείρ]ηται, εἴη πρὸς ὠφέλειαν, ἵνα, εἰ γένοιτο πόθος τινὶ τῆς εἰσόδου, [δι]ὰ τούτων ἡ χειραγωγία γένηται, τῶν μὲν χερουβείμ αἰνιττο[μέν]ων τὴν γνῶσιν τῆς ἀληθείας, ἧς μετέχειν δεῖ τὸν εἰσεῖνα[ι β]ουλόμε[νο]ν, τῆς δὲ ῥομφαίας τὴν ἐπίπονον ἀγωγήν· καὶ γὰρ δι[ὰ π]ολλῶν [θλ]ίψεων τῆς εἰσόδου ἔστιν τῆς βασιλείας τυχεῖν, ὡ[ς γ]έγραπται.

The image of virtue as the goal of humanity represents a greater emphasis than what we can observe in Clement and Origen. In this respect Bayliss believes Didymus restores a more Philonic emphasis.[183] It is also true that the positive cosmic forces, such as the powers, even assist humanity in the goal of becoming like God. Although Didymus utilizes Origenian vocabulary and proof-texts in his articulation of the theory, the contours of his discussion appear more Philonic. He has once again, it seems, utilized both Philo and Origen to articulate his own conclusions.

Further Areas of Philonic Influence on Didymus's Interpretation of the Genesis Creation Account

The creation account in Gen was central to the theology, anthropology, psychology, and soteriology of the Alexandrian interpreters of the Bible. It is thus not surprising that Philo devotes special attention to Gen 1–2.[184] Didymus likewise devotes a great deal of attention to the creation account (covering Gen 1:1–2:3). Although the beginning sections are lacunose and some pages are missing altogether, we can see that originally 80 of the 251 pages of the Tura manuscript covered Didymus's discussion of the creation.[185] Didymus never cites Philo by name in these sections, but it is clear that he is dependent upon him.[186] We have already seen Didymus's interpretations of the names for God.[187] We have also seen that he interprets the concept of *imago dei* in Gen 1:26 in the ethical sense of ὁμοίωσις θεῷ.[188] The remainder of the chapter will be taken to discuss further the issue of human hegemony over animals and the implications of God's image.

---

183. Bayliss, *The Vision of Didymus*, 121

184. There are 585 quotations or allusions to Gen 1–2 in the works of Philo (based on the list in *Biblia Patristica. Supplément. Philon d'Alexandrie* [ed. J. Allenbach et al.; Paris: Éditions du centre national de la recherche scientifique]), 27–31.

185. The papyrus is missing pages 77–80, which would have continued the discussion of Gen. 2:3.

186. Nautin lists parallels to Philo in no less than nineteen of the eighty sections on the creation (*Sur la Genèse* 1:32–188).

187. *Comm. Gen.* 31.15–22 (see above).

188. *Comm. Gen.* 58.27–59.1 (see above).

Human Hegemony over Animal Creation

Like Philo, Didymus emphasizes human superiority over animals, utilizing examples from nature. On the literal level, animals and humans are "ensouled creatures" (ἔμψυχα). For Philo and Didymus this means that animals possess the sense-perceptible elements of the soul (the five senses). We may also surmise that Philo granted to animals the generative part, although he does not say so explicitly. Of course, this interpretation requires an adoption of the Stoic concept of the unitary soul, as opposed to the Platonic and Aristotelian conceptions.[189]

Commenting on the expression, "And there was evening and there was morning, a fifth day" in Gen 1:23, Didymus writes,

> For it is fitting that irrational creatures which participate much in sense-perception should be created on the fifth which is indicative of sense-perception. For even if people have a share in sense-perception, they also have something greater than sense-perception, that is mind and reason, but the irrational creatures have sense-perception alone.[190]

The ideas here presented are largely based on a mixture of traditional Pythagorean and Stoic concepts. The connection between the number five and sense-perception can be found throughout the arithmological tradition.[191] In addition, the Stoics taught that the animal's soul was composed only of the five senses and the generative element. The ἡγεμονικόν, or the "command center," alone is characteristic of humans. At birth, it is "like a sheet of paper ready for writing upon."[192] After the first seven years of life, the Stoics believed, rationality was complete.[193]

Later in the *Comm. Gen.* Didymus explains the difference between the souls of animals and the human soul: "the souls of irrational animals offer impressionistic and impulsive movement to their bodies, for they are themselves also corporeal, or rather, being in the body itself, the souls [of

---

189. On Philo's adoption of the Stoic concept of the soul see Gretchen Reydams-Schils, "Stoicized Readings of Plato's *Timaeus* in Philo of Alexandria," *SPhilA* 7 (1995): 85–102.

190. *Comm. Gen.* 44.8–11. The Greek reads, «Καὶ ἐγένετο ἑσπέρα καὶ ἐγένετο πρωΐ, ἡμέρα πέμπτη» καὶ εἰκότως· ἔπρεπεν γὰρ τὰ πολὺ τῆς αἰσθήσεως μετέχοντα ἄλογα ζῷα ἐν τῇ πεντάδι δηλούσῃ τὰς αἰσθήσεις γενέσθαι. Κἂν γὰρ ἄνθρωποι αἰσθήσεως κοινωνῶσιν, ἀλλ' ἔχουσιν τὸ μεῖ<ζ>ον τῆς αἰσθήσεως, τὸν νοῦν καὶ λογισμόν, τῶν ἀλόγων περὶ μόνην αἴσθησιν ἐχόντων (trans. mine).

191. E.g., Anatolius 33.19; Ps-Iamblichus, *Theol. arith.* 34.3–5. On the number five in Philo see Wyss, "Philo und die Pentas."

192. Aetius 4.11.1 (*SVF* 2:83), trans. Long and Sedley, *Hellenistic Philosophers* 1:238.

193. Ibid.

irrational animals share] in the body's composition."[194] The idea that the soul sends φαντασίαι and όρμαί in both human and animal can be paralleled in both Philo and Origen, and is apparently derived from Stoicism.[195] What distinguishes humanity is that they also possess νοῦς and λογισμός.[196] This is why man (νοῦς) is created before woman (αἴσθησις), so that the mind can rule over the senses.[197]

The content of the above citation could have been derived from external sources, and is not necessarily borrowed from Philo. But the combination of the Stoic and Pythagorean elements seems to indicate that Didymus did borrow from Philo here. Certainly Nautin believes he did.[198] He cites *Opif.* 62, where Philo writes that God "proceeded to undertake the formation of the kinds of mortal living beings. He started with the acquatic creatures on the fifth day, considering that nothing bears such a family-resemblance to anything else as the five does to living beings. The chief difference between living beings with [ἔμψυχα] and without soul [ἄψυχα] is the possession of sense-perception."[199] Here Philo distinguishes animals from plants, providing a hierarchy of inanimate, animate, and rational creatures. Nautin also cites *Plant.* 133, where Philo, commenting on Lev 19:25 ("on the fifth year you may eat of its fruit"), remarks that since fruit is connected with the number five, this can only mean that αἴσθησις supplies nourishment to man's νοῦς. The senses supply the impressions, but the mind, or rationality, must rule. The combination of the interpretation of the number five and the Stoic conception of the movements of the soul (for which Philo is the principle witness) seems to indicate that Nautin is right in detecting Philonic influence on Didymus here.

A final text should be discussed regarding man's literal hegemony over animal creation. Commenting on Gen 1:26, Didymus writes,

---

194. *Comm. Gen.* 48.26–49.1 (trans. mine). The Greek reads, ...τὴν φανταστικὴν καὶ ὁρμητικὴν κίνησιν αἱ τῶν ἀλόγων ψυχαὶ τοῖς σώμασιν παρέχουσιν, σωματικαὶ ὑπάρχουσαι καὶ αὐταί, μᾶλλον δὲ ἐν αὐτῷ οὖσαι τῷ σώματι καὶ ἐν τῇ τούτου συστάσει.
195. Philo, *Leg.* 2.23; Origen, *Princ.* 2.8.1. *SVF* cites Philo for this doctrine.
196. See Philo, *loc. cit.*
197. Philo, *Leg.* 2.23–24; 3.49; *Cher.* 41; *Fug.* 188. See also Didymus, *Comm. Gen.* 83.1. On the connection between the interpretations of Philo and Didymus on woman in general, see Émilien Lamirande, "Le masculin et le feminin dans la tradition alexandrine: Le commentaire de Didyme l'Aveugle sur la 'Genèse,'" *Science et Esprit* 41 (1989): 137–65, and Reuling, *After Eden*, 54–79.
198. He writes, "L'idée vient de Philon" (*Sur la Genèse* 1:117).
199. The Greek reads, τὰ θνητὰ γένη ζωοπλαστεῖν ἐνεχείρει, τὴν ἀρχὴν ἀπὸ τῶν ἐνύδρων ποιούμενος ἡμέρᾳ πέμπτῃ, νομίσας οὐδὲν οὕτως ἕτερον ἑτέρῳ συγγενὲς ὡς ζῴοις πεντάδα. διαφέρει γὰρ ἔμψυχα ἀψύχων οὐδενὶ μᾶλλον ἢ αἰσθήσει (trans. Runia, *On the Creation*, 61). See also *Plant.* 133; *QG* 4.110.

The passage "And let him rule over the fish of the sea and over the birds of the air and over the beasts and over all the earth, and over all reptiles which creep on the earth" ... refers to the rule [τὸ ἀρχικόν] of humanity against the animals subjected to them. For one might marvel at how people catch with traps and nets both ordinary and wild beasts that are more powerful than they, that are naturally able to harm them, and that are of tremendous size. And this would not have happened had God not set a rule against them. For sometimes great herds of various animals are led by just a child or some other weak person, which clearly shows that some divine power is inherent in the rational animal, according to which these animals submit to them. Now rule is nothing other than a legal authority. Hence, none of the other animals rule over those of the same genus. And even if sometimes the so-called ram [κτίλος][200] rules outside the flock in accord with the fact that he is leader, it is not by rationality, like human shepherds, but by nature that he does this. But humanity was made "according to the image and likeness of God," in order that they might rule over the things mentioned.[201]

This passage suggests that rationality is implied in a human being created in the image of God. As such "man" (i.e., body and soul) takes on the divine characteristic of rule. It also suggests that people have the ability to rule over animals because something inherent in the animal recognizes their superiority.

A clear parallel may be located in Philo's *Opif.* 84–85. Philo writes, "For this reason the Father, when he brought him into existence as the living being who was by nature dominant, not only in fact but also by means of a pronouncment appointed him king of all the creatures in the sub-lunary realm, those on land and in the sea and borne on the air (84)."[202] Runia cites a parallel from the *Pesiqta Rabbati*, "And God had in mind to appoint

---

200. See LSJM supplement for this meaning.
201. *Comm. Gen.* 59.25–60.14 (trans. mine). The Greek reads, Τὸ δὲ « καὶ ἀρχέτωσαν τῶν ἰχθύων τῆς θαλάσσης καὶ τῶν πετεινῶν τοῦ οὐρανοῦ καὶ τῶν κτηνῶν καὶ πάσης τῆς γῆς [καὶ] πάντων τῶν ἑρπετῶν τῶν ἑρπόντων ἐπὶ τῆς γῆς » ... ἐμφαίνοι ἂν τὸ ἀρχικὸν τοῦ ἀνθρώπου κατὰ τῶν ὑποτεταγμένων αὐτῷ ζῴων. Θαυμάσαι γὰρ ἄν τις πῶς τὰ πάνυ ὑπὲρ τὴν δύναμιν αὐτοῦ τυγχάνοντα καὶ ἄγρια ἅμα καὶ βλάπτειν πεφυκότα καὶ προσέτι ὑπερμεγέθη πάγαις τισὶν καὶ δικτύοις ἀγρεύει· οὐκ ἂν δὲ τοῦτο οὕτως ἐγίνετο, εἰ μὴ ἀρχὴν κατ' αὐτῶν εἶχεν θεόθεν. Ἔσθ' ὅτε γὰρ καὶ ὑπὸ κομιδῇ παιδίου ἢ ἄλλως ἀνθρώπου ἀσθενοῦς ἀγέλαι πολυπληθεῖς διαφόρων ζῴων ἐλαύνονται, ὅπερ σαφῶς ἐπιδείκνυσιν θείαν τινὰ δύναμιν ἐνεῖναι τῷ λογικῷ ζῴῳ, καθ' ἣν αὐτῷ ταῦτα ὑποτέτακται. Ἀρχὴ δὲ οὐδὲν ἕτερόν ἐστι ἢ νόμιμος ἐπιστασία. Οὐδὲν γοῦν τῶν ἄλλων ἄρχει τοῦ ὁμογενοῦς· κἄν ποτε δὲ ὁ καλούμενος κτίλος πρόβατον ἐξάρχῃ ἀγέλης κατὰ τὸ προηγεῖσθαι, οὐ λογισμῷ κατὰ τοὺς ποιμένας ἀνθρώπους, φύσει δὲ τοῦτο δρᾷ. Γέγονεν δὲ ἄνθρωπος κατ' εἰκόνα καὶ ὁμοίωσιν Θεοῦ, ἵνα ἄρχῃ τῶν εἰρημένων.
202. The Greek reads, παρ' ἣν αἰτίαν καὶ γεννήσας αὐτόν ὁ πατὴρ ἡγεμονικὸν φύσει ζῷον οὐκ ἔργῳ μόνον ἀλλὰ καὶ τῇ διὰ λόγου χειροτονίᾳ καθίστη τῶν ὑπὸ σελήνην ἁπάντων βασιλέα χερσαίων καὶ ἐνύδρων καὶ ἀεροπόρων (trans. Runia, *On the Creation*, 69).

him ruler over this world, and king over all of his creatures, as he said, 'I am King of the upper world and man is the king of the lower world.'"[203]

Philo goes on, "It can happen that vast flocks of animals are led by a single ordinary human being, who does not wear armour or carry a weapon of iron or bear any other kind of defensive instrument" (84).[204] Instead, writes Philo, shepherds, goatherds, and cowherds are "men who are not so physically robust and energetic."[205] Yet, "the combined strength and power of so many well-armed creatures ... stand in awe of him like slaves before their master and carry out his commands" (85).[206] Philo closes his argument as follows: "The Maker thus proceeded to fashion the human being after all the others as a kind of charioteer and pilot, so that he could guide and steer earthly affairs, taking on the care of animals and plants like a governor acting on behalf of the first and great King" (88).[207]

Now Philo's arguments here are offered to explain why the human being is created last. Didymus is attempting to elucidate how it can be that humans are created in God's image. But the passages overlap in subject matter. Nautin notes that Didymus features "the same development and examples" as Philo.[208] While it does not appear that Didymus is quoting from Philo, he certainly has similar ideas in mind that are developed in a similar fashion. Both recognize that some innate or God-given quality must exist in animals to allow human beings to domesticate them. Not only does the order of creation reflect the human being's superiority, but also divine command (Gen 1:26). Utilizing examples from nature, both Philo and Didymus are able to celebrate the ruling principle granted to humankind.

---

203. Ibid, 255.
204. The Greek reads, θρεμμάτων ἔστιν ὅτε πλήθη μυρία πρὸς ἀνδρὸς ἑνὸς ἄγεται τοῦ τυχόντος οὔθ᾽ ὁπλοφοροῦντος οὔτε σίδηρον οὔτε τι τῶν ἀμυντηρίων ἐπιφερομένου, διφθέραν δ᾽ αὐτὸ μόνον ἔχοντος σκεπαστήριον καὶ βακτηρίαν ἕνεκα τοῦ διασημῆναί τε καὶ ἐν ταῖς ὁδοιπορίαις εἰ κάμοι στηρίσασθαι (trans. Runia, ibid, 69).
205. The Greek reads, ἄνθρωποι μηδὲ τοῖς σώμασιν ἐρρωμένοι καὶ σφριγῶντες (trans. Runia, loc. cit.)
206. The Greek reads, καὶ αἱ τοσαῦται τῶν τοσούτων ἀλκαί τε καὶ δυνάμεις εὐοπλούντων ἔχουσι ... καθάπερ δοῦλοι δεσπότην κατεπτήχασι καὶ τὰ προσταττόμενα δρῶσι (trans. Runia, loc. cit.).
207. The Greek reads, ἡνίοχον δή τινα καὶ κυβερνήτην ἐφ᾽ ἅπασιν ὁ ποιητὴς ἐδημιούργει τὸν ἄνθρωπον, ἵνα ἡνιοχῇ καὶ κυβερνᾷ τὰ περίγεια ζώων καὶ φυτῶν λαβὼν τὴν ἐπιμέλειαν οἷά τις ὕπαρχος τοῦ πρώτου καὶ μεγάλου βασιλέως (trans. Runia, On the Creation, 70).
208. Sur la Genèse 1:153 ("le même développement et les mêmes exemples").

CHAPTER 8

Creation in the Image of God

The discussion above makes clear that Didymus regards hegemony over animal creation to be one of the implications of being created in the image of God. But Didymus depends on Philo for much more information on this theme. The final section of this chapter will concern the discussion of creation in God's image in both Philo and in Didymus.

Didymus describes how a human being can be especially divine over animal creation, and defends God scripturally as "spirit" (John 4:24) and "light" (1 John 1:5), which "do not possess human form." Since humanity was made in the image of God, then the "man" of Gen 1 cannot be corporeal. Otherwise, God would be corporeal. He must be a noetic substance.[209] Then Didymus launches into an apologetic discussion of biblical anthropomorphism, which leads him to two Philonic conclusions regarding Gen 1:26.

The first is that the image symbolizes human authority over creation. This can be regarded as a borrowing of Philo's own comments in *Opif.* 69: "For it would seem that the same position that the Great director holds in the entire cosmos is held by the human intellect in the human being."[210] Didymus develops the thought differently than Philo since he wishes to pursue the theme of participation in the divine image. He first asserts, as does Philo, that the "man created rational" is the metaphorical "image" reflecting God's own hegemony over creation.[211]

Then Didymus launches into a discussion of the soul's participation in God: "We have said that 'man' is, properly speaking, mind and soul. Now when the soul participates in God it becomes his image by virtue of its own communion with him, just as we claim that the one who participates in virtue becomes an image of virtue."[212] This thread allows Didymus to pick up Origen's idea that Christ is the ultimate *imago dei*.[213] Our soul, then, can

---

209. The latter point is borrowed from Philo, who assigns far greater significance to the image, and is less prone to distinguish "image" from "likeness" as Clement and Origen do (Bayliss, *The Vision of Didymus*, 131).

210. The Greek reads, ὃν γὰρ ἔχει λόγον ὁ μέγας ἡγεμὼν ἐν ἅπαντι τῷ κόσμῳ, τοῦτον ὡς ἔοικε καὶ ὁ ἀνθρώπινος νοῦς ἐν ἀνθρώπῳ (trans. Runia, *On the Creation*, 64.).

211. *Comm. Gen.* 57.9–13.

212. *Comm. Gen.* 57.26–28 (trans. mine). The Greek reads, προείρηται κυρίως ἄνθρωπος εἶναι ὁ νοῦς καὶ ἡ ψυχή· αὕτη μετέχουσα Θεοῦ ἐξ αὐτῆς τῆς μετουσίας εἰκὼν αὐτοῦ γίνεται, καθὸ λέγομεν εἰκονίζ[ει]ν τὴν ἀρετὴν τὸν μετέχοντα αὐτῆς.

213. *Cels.* 6.66 is a nearly exact parallel to our passage here (cf. *Hom. Gen.* 1.13).

only at its best become an *imago imaginis*.[214] Didymus may have thought of this Origenian strand of interpretation because the Logos is, in Philo, the image of God.[215] Of course, thanks to John 1:1–5 any thought of the Logos would automatically be interpreted in reference to Christ.

David Runia sees a Didymean development of *Opif.* 69–71 in our section, in three particular areas: (1) the soul (or νοῦς as the highest part of the soul) is being described in Gen 1:26–27, and not the body-soul compound; (2) the term "image" is described in similar terms as a seal and its impression; (3) the term "likeness" is described as an explanation of the term "image."[216]

As for Runia's first point, Didymus makes clear that the "man" being created in Gen 1 is not the man composed of body and soul. He writes, "It was not in accord with the compound [τό συνθετόν] that God made man in his image, for God is not in human form."[217] Now, Runia refers to this passage as a direct quote from *Opif.* 69.[218] The only precise verbal parallel between the two texts is with the words ἀνθρωπόμορφος ὁ θεός, but it is clear that Didymus follows Philo's argument as well as his language here, as he continues to do throughout this section of the commentary.

The second point of comparison, as Runia shows, concerns the meaning of the term "image." Didymus writes, "Therefore God, having made the universe and being ruler and leader (for as Demiurge he was also ruler and king), having created the human being so as to rule over the things he created, namely beasts, cattle, and birds, he reveals that humanity is the 'image' in accord with his own rule."[219] Again, we can locate a parallel to this notion in Philo's *Opif.* 69, where νοῦς is placed in the role as ruler of humanity. Philo states, "For it would seem that the same position that the Great director holds in the entire cosmos is held by the human intellect in

---

214. See Origen, *Hom. Luc.* 8.2 for this exact expression. We cannot enter here into the probability that Origen's "image of the image" derives ultimately from Philo (see, e.g., *Spec.* 1.81; 3.83).
215. See, e.g., *Opif.* 25, 31; *Leg.* 3.96. On this see Tobin, *The Creation of Man*, 63–71.
216. See David Runia, "L'exégèse philosophique et l'influence de la pensée philonienne dans la tradition patristique," in *Philon d'Alexandrie et le langage de la philosophie*, 327–48 (on our passage, 336–42). For a summary, see Runia, *On the Creation*, 234.
217. *Comm. Gen.* 56.14–16 (trans. mine). The Greek reads, Οὐ κατὰ τὸν σύνθετον τοίνυν κατ' εἰκόνα Θεοῦ ὁ ἄνθρωπος γέγονεν· οὐ γὰρ ἀνθρωπόμορφος ὁ Θεός.
218. *On the Creation* 234.
219. *Comm. Gen.* 57.9–13 (trans. mine). The Greek reads, Ὁ Θεὸς οὖν πεποιηκὼς τὰ ὅλα πάντων τε ἄρχων καὶ προ<ηγ>ητὴς ὑπάρχων—ὡς γὰρ δημιουργὸς οὕτω καὶ ἄρχων καὶ βασιλεύς ἐστιν—ποιήσας τὸν ἄνθρωπον ὥστε καὶ ἄρχειν τῶν δι' αὐτὸν γενομένων θηρίων, κτηνῶν, πτηνῶν, δείκνυσιν εἰκόνα κατὰ τὸ ἄρχειν ἑαυτοῦ εἶναι τὸν ἄνθρωπον.

the human being."[220] While there is a difference in Didymus's application to the rule of animals, it seems that the basic conceptions he explicates are from Philo. A few lines after the passage above, Didymus clarifies that the "human being" to whom he is referring is "the human being created rational" (ὁ ἄνθρωπος λογικὸς γεγενημένος), which may bring us closer to the Philonic idea of νοῦς being the ruler.[221] Nevertheless, it would seem that Didymus is certainly borrowing Philonic ideas here, even if he does not adopt entirely all of the details.

Didymus goes on to flirt with the Philonic idea of the ruling mind but changes his course. He states, "It is possible to take the predominant principle [τὸ προκείμενον] in the sense of the leading mind. For 'man' is said to be, properly speaking, mind and soul. Now soul itself, having a share in God of its own participation, becomes his image, just as we claim that that which participates in virtue becomes the image of virtue."[222] There is clearly a difference here between Philo and Didymus. Philo applies the same logic to the mind and not to the soul.[223] At the beginning of his discussion, it seems that Didymus will follow the same route, but he suddenly switches from discussing the mind to the soul. It may be that Didymus could describe for the soul what also applies to the mind since the mind is the leading part of the soul. More probably, Didymus is influenced by Origen here, who interprets the image in terms of the soul rather than the mind.[224] In any case, it would seem that the basic conceptions go back to Philo whether directly or indirectly, through the mediation of Origen.

Didymus then turns to an explanation of the words "image" and "likeness." Having argued that Christ is the first image of God, he argues that the human being is created according to the image of Christ.[225] Thus the human being becomes *imago imaginis*.[226] Origen had already made this point, using the term λόγος with reference to Christ.[227] In Philo, the Logos

---

220. The Greek reads, ὃν γὰρ ἔχει λόγον ὁ μέγας ἡγεμὼν ἐν ἅπαντι τῷ κόσμῳ, τοῦτον ὡς ἔοικε καὶ ὁ ἀνθρώπινος νοῦς ἐν ἀνθρώπῳ (trans. Runia, *On the Creation*, 64).
221. *Comm. Gen.* 57.23.
222. *Comm. Gen.* 57.26–29 (trans. mine). The Greek reads, Ἔστιν δὲ μάλιστα κατὰ προηγουμένην διάνοιαν ἐκλαβεῖν τὸ προκείμενον· προείρηται κυρίως ἄνθρωπος εἶναι ὁ νοῦς καὶ ἡ ψυχή· αὕτη μετέχουσα Θεοῦ ἐξ αὐτῆς τῆς μετουσίας εἰκὼν αὐτοῦ γίνεται, καθὸ λέγομεν εἰκονίζ[ει]ν τὴν ἀρετὴν τὸν μετέχοντα αὐτῆς.
223. *Opif.* 69.
224. *Hom. Gen.* 1.13; *Hom. Lev.* 12.7; *Hom. Luc.* 8.2.
225. *Comm. Gen.* 58.3–15.
226. For this expression, see Origen, *Hom. Luc.* 8.2.
227. See *Cels.* 6.66 for a near exact parallel to the passage in Didymus (see also *Hom. Gen.* 1.13).

is the image of God, and thus one has a similar idea. He states, "But God's shadow is his word [λόγος], which he made use of like an instrument, and so made the world. But this shadow, and what we may describe as the representation, is the archetype for further creations. For just as God is the Pattern of the Image ... even so the Image becomes the pattern of other beings." Philo then cites Gen 1:27 and concludes that "the Image had been made such as representing God, but that the man was made after the Image when it had acquired the force of a pattern."[228]

With the help of the Johannine prologue (John 1:1–4), Christ becomes identified with the Logos through which God made the world. Although Didymus does not use the term Logos here with reference to Christ, he clearly is dependent upon a tradition of exegesis that goes back to Philo, personalizing the Logos by making it refer to Jesus. The result is something immensely personal for Christian expositors: humanity is made in the image of the preexistent Christ.

A third area of correspondence which Runia highlights between Philo and Didymus is in the term "likeness." Didymus states, "I think that term 'likeness' refers to an extraordinary similarity [ἐμφέρεια], image and likeness being indistinguishable, so that 'likeness' is the supreme degree of 'image.' The reason is that an image is not in every way so precise [ἀκριβόω] that it does not require a likeness to accompany it, which makes the image and the likeness perfectly indistinguishable."[229] Whereas modern readers might be inclined to regard "image" and "likeness" as synonyms in the biblical text, Didymus sees a further clarification of the biblical message. Philo, too, makes similar observations. He writes in *Opif.* 71, "Since, however, not every single image resembles its archetypal model, but many are dissimilar, he added to the words 'after the image' as an extra indication the words 'after the likeness,' in order to emphasize that it is an accurate and clearly marked casting."[230] It certainly seems that Didymus has borrowed from Philo again here.

Runia suggests that Didymus takes his point of departure from Philo.[231] This estimation is likely correct, especially when we compare the interpre-

---

228. *Leg.* 3.96 (trans. *PLCL* 1:365, 367).

229. *Comm. Gen.* 58.18–22 (trans. mine). The Greek reads, οἶμαι γὰρ ὅτι ἡ ὑπερβάλλουσα ἐμφέρεια ἀπαράλλακτος ὁμοιότητα ἐμφαίνει, ὡς εἶναι τὴν μὲν ὁμοιότητα καὶ εἰκόνος ὑπερβολήν, οὐ πάντως δὲ τὴν εἰκόνα οὕτως ἠκριβάσθαι ὡς ἀπαράλλακτον ἔχειν ὁμοιότητα (My translation is heavily dependent here on that of Nautin).

230. The Greek reads, ἐπεὶ δ' οὐ σύμπασα εἰκὼν ἐμφερὴς ἀρχετύπῳ παραδείγματι, πολλαὶ δ' εἰσὶν ἀνόμοιοι, προσεπεσημήνατο εἰπὼν τῷ κατ' εἰκόνα τὸ καθ' ὁμοίωσιν εἰς ἔμφασιν ἀκριβοῦς ἐκμαγείου τρανὸν τύπον ἔχοντος (trans. Runia, *On the Creation*, 64–65).

[231] Runia, "L'exégèse philosophique," 341.

tation of Clement. He argues that "according to the image" refers to what one receives at birth, and "according to the likeness" the ethical advancement that can characterize one's life.[232] Thus the two phrases convey meanings completely separate from one another. Nevertheless, in this case it seems that Didymus is directly dependent upon a very specific passage in Philo's writings, and that he has developed the exegesis of Philo to suit his own purposes. The "image" does not represent an inferior stage of advancement, and the "likeness" a superior one, but the latter is an elaboration of the former.

Conclusion

In this chapter we have examined general Philonic themes that appear to have influenced Didymus. We can see that, while Didymus does not always cite his source, he is never far from the Philonic thought world. Often Origen, and occasionally Clement, can be cited as mediating inspirations between Philo and Didymus, but it is abundantly clear that Didymus has read Philo on his own, and often develops Philonic themes to suit his own interests. Philo is present in nearly every aspect of his thought.

Didymus's psychology, theology, and soteriology are all constructed from a foundation laid by Philo, with bricks provided by Origen. But it is Didymus who supplies the mortar. His theories on education, and specifically the Hagar-Sarah allegory, are influenced by Philo and Origen, but Didymus has developed his own his understanding as well. The biblical Cherubim are interpreted in a clear Philonic way, but Didymus seeks Pauline proofs for the doctrine of the Powers as well. These examples show that Didymus is no mere parrot of Origen, as he is sometimes imagined to be. Nor does he repeat Philo uncritically. He is a dynamic thinker who does not mind using predecessors to develop his own thoughts toward a moral progress directed to the One in conformity with the divine image. While Didymus rarely quotes Philo directly, and while he does not feel bound to parrot the interpretations of his predecessors uncritically, we can state from our survey of the evidence that Didymus appears to owe more to Philo than to any other author, with the possible exception of Origen.

---

232. *Strom.* 2.131.5.

9

REVIEW AND CONCLUSION

In the preceding pages, we have examined the thought of a man who in his own time was almost universally recognized for his exegetical skill. His blindness does not appear to have hampered his acquisition of an excellent education in both the traditional philosophical and in the growing Christian curricula. His abilities in the classroom led to his appointment as a "teacher," if not the "director," of the prestigious Alexandrian School. From this position, Didymus was able to cast a long shadow, acquiring a reputation throughout the Christian world for his exegesis and pedagogy.

When we turn to the use of sources in Didymus, we find little direct information. Like most ancient writers, he rarely names his sources. But this does not prevent us from reconstructing his most significant influences. Most scholars would agree that Origen exercises a strong influence on the thought of Didymus, but the famous Alexandrian is mentioned only once by name in the Didymean corpus. With the author under consideration in this study, however, the situation is much better. Philo of Alexandria is mentioned by name nine times in the Tura commentaries of Didymus the Blind, and personally referenced (although not by name) two additional times. Seven of these can be located in the *Comm. Gen.*, which has served as our primary text in this study. Simply stated, the name of Philo appears more in the writings of Didymus than any other non-biblical author.

In addition to the nine occurrences of Philo's name, the *Comm. Gen.* alone contains close to three hundred possible passages with influence from the Jewish author. The distribution of these verbal and thought parallels indicates that Didymus had access to a range of treatises from the Philonic library. Based on references found in the current work, the borrowings include possible text-specific influences from *Opif.* (24), *Leg.* 1–3 (52), *Cher.* (13), *Sacr.* (12), *Det.* (13), *Post.* (8), *Gig.* (2), *Deus* (4), *Agr.* (16), *Plant.* (5), *Ebr.* (5), *Sobr.* (2), *Conf.* (5), *Migr.* (14), *Her.* (4), *Congr.* (19), *Fug.* (11), *Mut.* (10), *Somn.* (9), *Abr.* (17), *Ios.* (1), *Mos.* (12), *Dec.* (7), *Spec.* (13), *Virt.* (2), *Praem.* (3), *Prob.* (5), *Aet.* (3), *Flacc.* (2), *Legat.* (3), *Prov.* (1), *QG* (22), and *QE* (3).[1] Such a dispersion indicates that Didymus had a

---

1. Nautin provides just over eighty references to the works of Philo in the footnotes to his edition of the *Comm. Gen.* Now, admittedly, some of these references in both Nautin and

thorough acquaintance with the Philonic literature, even if some of the references might have come through the Alexandrian tradition.

In addition to the verbal and thought parallels, we can find evidence of specific borrowings from the works of Philo. The structure of Didymus' exegesis in the *Comm. Gen.* is very similar to that of the Philonic *Quaestiones*. In fact, the two-step procedure of literal and allegorical interpretations of the same passage may indeed derive inspiration from the Philonic material, although Origen too engaged the *quaestiones* form in his interpretation of Genesis.[2] Didymus sometimes offers additional levels of meaning to be sure, but the standard two-fold exegetical structure seems to dominate the *Comm. Gen.* in particular.

Beyond structural concerns, the exegetical tools used in Didymus are similar to those of Philo. Both authors make frequent use of etymologies as a springboard to allegorical interpretation. In fact, we saw that, of the twenty-six etymologies of proper names in *Comm. Gen.*, exactly half can be found in Philo. One might attribute the parallels to onomastic lists alone if it were not for two facts: (1) Didymus explicitly recommends that his readers go to Philo for "the interpretation of names" (*Comm. Gen.* 139.10–14), indicating that he was familiar with the etymological method of the Jewish author, and (2) Didymus, at least on two occasions, follows both the etymology and the allegorical interpretation found in Philo. On this basis, it seems appropriate to conclude that Didymus, just as Origen before him, was familiar with the art of Philonic etymology.

Another area of influence is arithmological exegesis. We saw that Origen rarely launches into lengthy discussions of number symbolism. But Didymus, like Philo, often devotes several paragraphs and, occasionally, several pages, to discussions of numbers. We also know that arithmological handbooks were in circulation at the time, and one might be tempted to suggest that Didymus simply depends on those, and did not use Philo at all. But as in the case of etymology, Didymus also recommends Philo explicitly for his numerological exegesis (*Comm. Gen.* 235.24–236.21). In addition, Didymus provides explanations of several numbers, including six, seven, and 120 that contain specific parallels to the Philonic explanations of the same numbers. Definitions of "perfect" numbers and "squared" and

---

in the present work are duplicates (i.e., same idea found in multiple Philonic passages, in which case Didymus needs to know only one). Also, some of the ideas represented in the works of Philo can also be located in works of Clement or Origen. In these cases, we cannot be certain that Didymus depends directly on Philo.

2. Five of the extant fragments of Origen's "Alexandrian" commentary on Genesis follow the *quaestiones et solutiones* format (see Heine, "Origen's Alexandrian Commentary on Genesis," *Origeniana Octava* 1:66).

"cubed" numbers, while certainly borrowed from the handbooks even in Philo, are repeated in Didymus in nearly the exact language and in similar exegetical contexts. Such information suggests that Didymus is both generally and specifically dependent on Philo for much of his arithmology.

A third area of influence can be located in the general philosophical and exegetical themes found in Didymus. While Philo's name is never cited in most of these sections, it is clear that Philonic thought is driving Didymus' exegesis. Didymus' doctrine of the soul, especially in the case of psychic pre-existence, can be attributed to Philo, as can his interpretation of the "tunics of skins," which is mediated through Origen as well. We spoke at length of Didymus' doctrine of virtue, and specifically the Sarah-Hagar allegory, which definitely depends on Philo. Even if Didymus knows the versions of Clement and Origen as well, there is sufficient evidence that he is in direct contact with Philo. We discussed Didymus' explanation of the biblical Cherubim as the "powers" of God, a quintessentially Philonic understanding not represented in the works of Origen. Finally we detailed select passages covering the biblical creation narrative in the *Comm. Gen.* It seems that in these texts Philo was the primary source for Didymus, although we can trace Origen's influence as well.

We have attempted to show in the preceding pages that Didymus the Blind knew and used the works of Philo of Alexandria. When we add together the direct citations and the clear borrowings, it seems impossible to deny that Didymus was indebted to the Jewish author. Since Philo's name is mentioned rather frequently, we may assume that Didymus' audience did not feel scandalized by the Jewish author at all, if they even cared about his ethnicity. There is no reason to suspect that Didymus attempted to conceal the ethnicity of his predecessor, even though he does not explicitly refer to it. The Jewishness of Philo was important neither for Didymus nor for any of the Alexandrian Christian authors before him. They appear to have viewed Philo not primarily as a Jew, but as a respected exegete who blazed the trail in combining Greek scholarship with biblical interpretation.

BIBLIOGRAPHY

Abel, Karlhans. "Die Propatheia-Theorem: Ein Beitrag zur stoischen Affektenlehre." *Hermes* 111 (1983): 78–97.

Afonasin, Eugene V. "The Pythagorean Way of Life in Clement of Alexandria and Iamblichus." Pages 13–36 in *Iamblichus and the Foundations of Late Platonism.* Edited by Eugene Afonasin, John M. Dillon, and John F. Finamore. Studies in Platonism, Neoplatonism, and the Platonic Tradition 13. Leiden: Brill, 2013.

Alexandre, Monique. "Le lexique des vertus: Vertus philosophiques et religieuses chez Philon: μετάνοια et εὐγένεια." Pages 17–46 in *Philon d'Alexandrie et le langage de la philosophie.* Edited by Carlos Lévy. Monothéismes et Philosophie. Turnhout: Brepols, 1998.

Amsler, Mark. *Etymology and Grammatical Discourse in Late Antiquity and the Early Middle Ages.* Amsterdam Studies in the Theory and History of Linguistic Science 3.44. Amsterdam: Benjamins, 1989.

Attridge, Harold W. "Philo and John: Two Riffs on one Logos." *SPhiloA* 17 (2005): 103–17.

Ax, Wolfram. "Quadripertita ratio: Bemerkungen zur Geschichte eines aktuellen Kategoriensystems (Adiectio–Detractio–Transmutatio–Immutatio)." Pages 17–40 in *The History of Linguistics in the Classical Period.* Edited by Daniel J. Taylor. Amsterdam Studies in the History of Linguistic Science 3.46. Amsterdam: Benjamins, 1987.

Ayres, Lewis. *Nicaea and its Legacy: An Approach to Fourth-Century Trinitarian Theology.* Oxford: Oxford University Press, 2004.

Baer, Richard A. *Philo's Use of the Categories Male and Female.* ALGHJ 3. Leiden: Brill, 1970.

Bammel, Caroline, "Adam in Origen." Pages 62–93 in *The Making of Orthodoxy: Essays in Honour of Henry Chadwick.* Edited by Rowan Williams. Cambridge: Cambridge University Press, 1989.

Baltussen, Han. "From Polemic to Exegesis: The Ancient Philosophical Commentary." *Poetics Today* 28 (2007): 247–81.

———. *Philosophy and Exegesis in Simplicius: The Methodology of a Commentator.* London: Bloomsbury, 2008.

Bardy, Gustave. "Aux origins de l'école d'Alexandrie." *RevScRel* 27 (1937): 64–90.

———. *Didyme l'Aveugle.* Paris: Beauchesne, 1910.

———. "Les traditions juives dans l'oeuvre d'Origène." *RB* 34 (1925): 217–52.

———. "Pour l' histoire de l'école d'Alexandrie." *Vivre et Penser* 2 (1942): 80–109).
Barnes, Timothy D. *Constantine and Eusebius*. Cambridge: Harvard, 1981.
Barthélemy, Dominique. "Est-ce Hoshaya Rabba qui censura le «Commentaire Allégorique»?" Pages 45–78 in *Philon d'Alexandrie: Colloques nationaux du centre national de la recherche scientifique, Lyons, 11–15 Septembre 1966*. Paris: Centre National de la recherche scientifique, 1967.
———. *Les Devanciers d'Aquila*. VTS 10. Leiden: Brill, 1963.
Bauer, Walter. *Orthodoxy and Heresy in Earliest Christianity*. Edited by Robert A. Kraft and Gerhard Krodel. Philadelphia: Fortress, 1971.
Bayliss, Grant. *The Vision of Didymus the Blind: A Fourth-Century Virtue-Origenism*. Oxford: Oxford University Press, 2016.
Beatrice, Pier Franco. "Didyme l'Aveugle et la tradition de l'allégorie." Pages 579–90 in *Origeniana Sexta: Origène et la Bible/Origen and the Bible*. Edited by Gilles Dorival and Alain Boulluec. Leuven: Leuven University Press, 1995.
———. "Le tuniche di pelle: Antiche letture di Gen. 3,21." Pages 433–82 in *La tradizione dell'Enkrateia: Motivazioni ontologiche e protologiche*. Edited by Ugo Bianchi. Rome: Edizioni dell'Ateneo, 1985.
Becker, Adam. *Sources for the Study of the School of Nisibis*. Liverpool: Liverpool University Press, 2008.
Bennett, Byard. "Didymus the Blind's Knowledge of Manichaeism." Pages 38–67 in *The Light and the Darkness: Studies in Manichaeism and its World*. Edited by Paul Mirecki and Jason Beduhn. Leiden: Brill, 2001.
Berchman, Richard. *From Philo to Origen: Middle Platonism in Transition*. Chico, Calif.: Scholar's, 1984.
Betz, Hans-Dieter. *Galatians*. Hermeneia. Philadelphia: Fortress, 1979.
Bienert, Wolfgang A. *"Allegoria" und "Anagoge" bei Didymos dem Blinden von Alexandria*. PTS 13. Berlin: de Gruyter, 1972.
Bigger, Charles P. *Participation: A Platonic Inquiry*. Baton Rouge, La: Louisiana State University Press, 1968.
Binder, Gerhard. *Didymos der Blinde. Kommentar zum Ecclesiastes (Tura-Papyrus). Teil 1,2: Kommentar zu Ecclesiastes (2.), Kapitel 1,1–2,14*. PTA 26. 1983.
Binder, Gerhard, and Leo Liesenborghs. *Didymos der Blinde: Kommentar zum Ecclesiastes (Tura-Papyrus), Teil I.1: Kommentar zu Eccl. Kap. 1, 1–2, 14*. PTA 25. Bonn: Habelt, 1979.

Binder, Gerhard, Leo Liesenborghs, and Ludwig Koenen. *Didymos der Blinde: Kommentar zum Ecclesiastes (Tura-Papyrus); Tl 6: Kommentar zu Ecclesiastes, Kapitel 11–12*. PTA 9. Bonn: Habelt, 1969.

Bloch, René. *Moses und der Mythos: Die Auseinandersetzung mit der griechischen Mythologie bei jüdisch-hellenistischen Autoren*. JSJSup 145. Leiden: Brill, 2011.

Blowers, Paul M. "Origen, the Rabbis, and the Bible: Toward a Picture of Judaism and Christianity in Third-Century Caesarea." Pages 96–116 in *Origen of Alexandria: His World and His Legacy*. Edited by Charles Kannengiesser and William L. Petersen. Notre Dame: University of Notre Dame Press, 1988.

Blumenthal, H. J. *Aristotle and Neoplatonism in Late Antiquity: Interpretations of the* De anima. Ithaca, NY: Cornell University Press, 1996.

Bos, Abraham P. "Philo of Alexandria: A Platonist in the Image and Likeness of Aristotle." *SPhiloA* 10 (1998): 66–86.

Bostock, Gerald. "Origen and the Pythagoreanism of Alexandria." Pages 465–78 in *Origeniana Octava: Origen and the Alexandrian tradition = Origene e la tradizione alessandrina*. Papers of the Eighth International Origen Congress, Pisa, 27–31, August 2001. Edited by Lorenzo Perrone. Leuven: Leuven University Press, 2003.

———. "The Sources of Origen's Doctrine of Pre-existence." Pages 259–64 in *Origeniana Quarta: Die Referate des 4. Internationalen Origenskongresses*. Edited by Lothar Lies. Innsbruck: Tyrolia, 1987.

Bovon, François. "Names and Numbers in Early Christianity." *NTS* 45 (2001): 267–88.

Bousset, Wilhelm. *Jüdisch-Christlicher Schulbetrieb in Alexandria und Rom*. Göttingen: Vandenhoek & Ruprecht, 1915.

Buffière, Felix. *Les mythes d'Homère et la pensée grecque*. Paris: Les Belles Lettres, 1956.

Burkert, Walter. *Lore and Science in Ancient Pythagoreanism*. Translated by Edwin L. Minar Jr. Cambridge, Mass.: Harvard University Press, 1972.

Cadiou, Réne. *Origen: His Life at Alexandria*. Translated by John A. Southwell. London: Herder, 1944.

Calleja, Joseph. "Gn 1,26s in Filone, nelle Omilie di Origene e nel Commentario in Genesim di Didimo il Cieco." *Melita Theologica* 39 (1988): 91–102.

Caner, Daniel F. "The Practice and Prohibition of Self-Castration in Early Christianity." *VC* 51 (1997): 396–415.

Carlini, Antonio. "La polemica di Porfirio contro l'esegesi 'tipologica' dei Cristiani." *SCO* 46 (1998): 385–94.

Carriker, Andrew James. *The Library of Eusebius of Caesarea*. VCSup 67. Leiden: Brill, 2003.

Cassel, J. David. "Patristic and Rabbinic Interpretation of Genesis 3: A Case Study in Contrasts." StPatr 39 (2006): 203–11.

Chadwick, Henry. *Early Christianity and the Classical Tradition*. Oxford: Clarendon, 1966.

Chapman, John. "Didymus the Blind." Page 784 in *The Catholic Encyclopedia*. Vol. 4. New York: Appleton, 1908.

Chin, Catherine M. "Origen and Christian Naming: Textual Exhaustion and the Boundaries of Gentility in Commentary on John 1." *JECS* 14 (2006): 407–36.

Clark, Elizabeth A. *The Origenist Controversy: The Cultural Construction of an Early Christian Debate*. Princeton: Princeton University Press, 1992.

Clements, Ruth A. "Epilogue: 70 CE After 135 CE—The Making of a Watershed?" Pages 517–36 in *Was 70 CE a Watershed in Jewish History? On Jews and Judaism before and after the Destruction of the Second Temple*. Edited by Daniel R. Schwartz and Zeev Weiss. AJEC 78. Leiden: Brill, 2012.

Conroy, John T., Jr. "Philo's 'Death of the Soul:' Is This Only a Metaphor?" *SPhiloA* 23 (2011): 23–40.

Crouzel, Henri. *Théologie de l'image de Dieu chez Origène*. Théologie 34. Paris: Aubier-Montaigne, 1956.

Culpepper, R. Alan. "Designs for the Church in the Imagery of John 21:1–14." Pages 369–402 in *Imagery in the Gospel of John*. Edited by Jörg Frey, Jan G. van der Watt, and Ruben Zimmermann. WUNT 200. Tübingen: Mohr Siebeck, 2006.

———. *The Johannine School: An Evaluation of the Johannine-School Hypothesis Based on an Investigation of the Nature of Ancient Schools*. SBL Dissertation Series 26. Missoula, Mont.: Scholars, 1975.

Daley, Brian E. "What Did 'Origenism' Mean in the Sixth Century?" Pages 627–38 in *Origeniana Sexta: Origène et la Bible/Origen and the Bible*. Edited by Gilles Dorival and Allain Le Boulluec. Leuven: Leuven University Press, 1995.

Daniélou, Jean. *Origen*. Translated by Walter Mitchell. New York: Sheed & Ward, 1955.

Dawson, David. *Allegorical Readers and Cultural Revision in Ancient Alexandria*. Berkeley: University of California Press, 1992.

Denis, Albert-Marie. *Introduction à la littérature religieuse judéo-hellénistique*. 2 vols. Turnhout: Brepols, 2000.

DeVore, David J. "Eusebius' Un-Josephan History: Two Portraits of Philo of Alexandria and the Sources of Ecclesiastical Historiography." StPatr 66 (2013): 161–79.

De Longe, Nicholas. *Origen and the Jews: Studies in Jewish-Christian Relations in Third-Century Palestine.* Cambridge: Cambridge University Press, 1976.

De Faye, Eugène. *Origen and His Work.* Translated by Fred Rothwell. London: Allen & Unwin, 1926.

de Lubac, Henri. *Medieval Exegesis: The Four Senses of Scripture.* 4 vols. Translated by M. Sebanc. Grand Rapids: Eerdmans, 1988.

———. "Typology and Allegorization." Pages 129–64 in *Theological Fragments.* Translated by R.H. Balinski. San Francisco: Ignatius, 1984.

De Vogel, Cornelia. "Platonism and Christianity: A Mere Antagonism or a Profound Common Ground?" *VC* 39 (1985): 1–62.

de Vries, Hent. "Philosophia Ancilla Theologiae." Translated by Jack Ben-Levi. *The Bible and Critical Theory* 5 (2009): 41.1–41.19.

DelCogliano, Mark. "Basil of Caesarea, Didymus the Blind, and the Anti-Pneumatomachian Exegesis of Amos 4:13 and John 1:3." *JTS* 61 (2010): 644–58.

Demura, Miyako. "Origen and the Exegetical Tradition of the Sarah-Hagar Motif in Alexandria." StPatr 56 (2013): 73–81

Diekamp, Franz. *Die origenischen Streitigkeiten im sechsten Jahrhundert und das fünfte allgemeine Concil.* Münster: Aschendorff, 1899.

Dillon, John. "Metriopatheia and Apatheia: Some Reflections on a Controversy in Later Greek Ethics." Pages 508–517 in vol. 1 of *Essays in Ancient Greek Philosophy.* Edited by John P. Anton and Anthony Preus. Albany: SUNY, 1983.

———. *The Middle Platonists: 80 CE to AD 220.* Ithaca, N.Y.: Cornell University Press, 1977.

———. "Philo of Alexandria and Platonist Psychology." Pages 17–24 in *The Afterlife of the Platonic Soul: Reflections of Platonic Psychology in the Monotheistic Religions.* Edited by Maha Elkaisy-Friemuth and John M. Dillon. Studies in Platonism, Neoplatonism, and the Platonic Tradition 9. Leiden: Brill, 2009.

———. "Plotinus, Philo and Origen on the Grades of Virtue." Pages 92–105 in *Platonismus und Christentum: Festschrift für Heinrich Dörrie.* Edited by Horst-Dieter Blume and Friedhelm Mann. JAC 10. Münster: Aschendorffshe Verlagsbuchhandlung, 1983.

———. "Pythagoreanism in the Academic Tradition." Pages 250–73 in *A History of Pythagoreanism*. Edited by Carl A. Huffman. Cambridge: Cambridge University Press, 2014.

———. "Ocellus." Page 1030 in *The Oxford Classical Dictionary*. Edited by Simon Hornblower and Anthony Spawforth. 4th edition. Oxford: Oxford University Press, 2012.

Dinan, Andrew. "Another Citation of Philo in Clement of Alexandria's *Protrepticus* (10.93.1–2)." *VC* 64 (2010): 435–44.

———. "The Mystery of Play: Clement of Alexandria's Appropriation of Philo in the *Paedagogus* (1.5.21.3–22.1)." *SPhiloA* 19 (2007): 59–80.

Dörrie, Heinrich. "Ammonios, der Lehre Plotins." *Hermes* 83 (1955): 439–78.

Dorival, Gilles. "Origen." Pages 605–28 in *The New Cambridge History of the Bible: From the Beginnings to 600*. Edited by James Carleton Paget and Joachim Schaper. Cambridge: Cambridge University Press, 2013.

Doutreleau, Louis. *Didyme l'Aveugle: Sur Zacharie*. Vol. 1. SC 83. Paris: Cerf, 1962.

———. "Que Savons-nous aujourd-hui des Papyrus de Toura?" *RSR* 43 (1955): 161–76.

Doutreleau, Louis, Adolphe Gesché, and Michael Gronewald. *Didymos der Blinde: Psalmenkommentar (Tura-Papyrus); Teil 1: Kommentar zu Psalm 20–21*. PTA 7. Bonn: Habelt, 1969.

Drake, Susanna. *Slandering the Jew: Sexuality and Difference in Early Christian Texts*. Philadelphia: University of Pennsylvania Press, 2013.

Droge, Arthur J. *Homer or Moses? Early Christian Interpretations of the History of Culture*. HUT 26. Tübingen: Mohr Siebeck, 1989.

Edwards, Mark. "Ammonius, Teacher of Origen." *JEH* 44 (1993): 168–81.

———. *Origen Against Plato*. Ashgate Studies in Philosophy and Theology in Late Antiquity. Aldershot: Ashgate, 2002.

Endo, Masanobu. *Creation and Christology: A Study on the Johannine Prologue in the Light of Early Jewish Accounts*. WUNT 2/149. Tübingen: Mohr Siebeck, 2002.

Erler, Michael. "Interpretieren als Gottesdienst: Proklos' Hymnen vor dem Hintergrund seines Kratyloskommentars." Pages 179–217 in *Proclus et son influence: Actes du colloque de Neuchâtel juin 1985*. Edited by Gilbert Boss and Gerhard Seel. Zürich: GMB Éditions du Grand Midi, 1987.

Fernández-Marcos, Natalio. *The Septuagint in Context: Introduction to the Greek Versions of the Bible*. Translated by Wilfred G. E. Watson. Leiden: Brill, 2000.

Field, Frederick. *Origenis Hexaplorum quae supersunt.* Oxford: Clarendon, 1875.
Frede, Michael. "Principles of Stoic Grammar." Pages 27–75 in *The Stoics.* Edited by John M. Rist. Berkeley: University of California Press, 1978.
Frick, Peter. *Divine Providence in Philo of Alexandria.* TSAJ 77. Tübingen: Mohr: Siebeck, 1999.
Friedländer, Moritz. *Der vorchristliche jüdische Gnosticismus.* Göttingen: Vandenhoek & Ruprecht, 1898.
Friedl, Alfred. "St. Jerome's Dissertation on the Letter to Philemon." Pages 289–316 in *Philemon in Perspective: Interpreting a Pauline Letter.* Edited by D. Francois Tolmie. Berlin: de Gruyter, 2010.
Furst, Alfons. "Origen: Exegesis and Philosophy in Early Christian Alexandria." Pages 13–32 in *Interpreting the Bible and Aristotle in Late Antiquity: The Alexandrian Commentary Tradition between Rome and Baghdad.* Edited by Josef Lössel and John W. Watt. Surrey: Ashgate, 2011.
Gaca, Kathy L. "Philo's Principles of Sexual Conduct and their Influence on Christian Platonist Sexual Principles." *SPhiloA* 8 (1996): 21–39.
Gaster, Moses. "The Hebrew Text of one of the Testaments of the Twelve Patriarchs." *The Proceedings of the Society of Biblical Archaeology* 16 (1893–1894): 33–49, 109–117.
Geljon, Albert C. "Philonic Elements in Didymus the Blind's Exegesis of the Story of Cain and Abel." *VC* 61 (2007): 282–312.
———. "Philo's Influence on Didymus the Blind." Pages 357–72 in *Philon d'Alexandrie: Un penseur à l'intersection des cultures Gréco-Romaine, Orientale, Juive et Chrétienne.* Edited by Sabrina Inowlocki and Baudouin Decharneux. Monothéismes et Philosophie. Turnhout: Brepols, 2011.
Geljon, Albert C., and David T. Runia. *Philo of Alexandria: On Cultivation.* PACS 4. Leiden: Brill, 2012.
Ghattas, Michael. "Didymus der Blinde von Alexandrien in der Auseinandersetzung mit Apollinaris von Laodicea und seinen Lehren." Pages 45–49 *in Patristica et Oecumenica: Festschrift für Wolfgang A. Bienert zum 65. Geburtstag.* Edited by Peter Gemeinhardt and Uwe Kühneweg. Marburg: Elwert, 2004.
———. *Die Christologie Didymos' den Blinden von Alexandria in den Schriften von Tura: Zur Entwicklung der alexandrinischen Theologie des 4. Jahrhunderts.* Studien zur Orientalischen Kirchengeschichte 7. Munster: Lit, 2002.
Ginzberg, Louis. *The Legends of the Jews.* 6 vols. Philadelphia: The Jewish Publication Society of America, 1909–1938.

Gnilka, Christian. *ΧΡΗΣΙΣ, Die Methode der Kirchenväter im Umgang mit der antiken Kultur.* Vol. 1: *Der Begriff des "Rechten Gebrauchs."* Basel: Schwabe, 1984.
Grabbe, Lester L. "Eschatology in Philo and Josephus." Pages 163–86 in *Judaism in Late Antiquity: Death, Life-After-Death, Resurrection, and the World-to Come in the Judaisms of Antiquity.* Edited by Alan J. Avery-Peck and Jacob Neusner. HO 1.49. Leiden: Brill, 2000.
———. *Etymology in Early Jewish Interpretation.* BJS 115. Atlanta: Scholars Press, 1988.
Grant, Robert M. *The Letter and the Spirit.* London: Macmillan, 1957.
Graver, Margaret. *Stoicism and Emotion.* Chicago: University of Chicago Press, 2007.
Greenstone, J. H. "Philo of Alexandria and the Origins of the Stoic ΠΡΟΠΑΘΕΙΑΙ." Pages 197–221 in *Philo of Alexandria and Post-Aristotelian Philosophy.* Edited by Francesca Alesse. Studies in Philo of Alexandria 5. Leiden: Brill, 2008.
———. "Polygamy." Pages 120–22 in the *Jewish Encyclopedia.* Vol. 10. New York: Funk & Wagnalls, 1905.
Gregg, Robert, and Dennis E. Groh. *Early Arianism: A View of Salvation.* Philadelphia: Fortress, 1981.
Griggs, C. Wilfred. *Early Egyptian Christianity from Its Origins to 451 CE.* Leiden: Brill, 2000.
Gronewald, Michael. *Didymos der Blinde: Kommentar zum Ecclesiastes (Tura-Papyrus); Teil 2: Kommentar zu Ecclesiastes, Kapitel 3–4,12.* PTA 22. Bonn: Habelt, 1977.
———. *Didymos der Blinde: Kommentar zum Ecclesiastes (Tura-Papyrus); Tl 5: Kommentar zu Ecclesiastes, Kapitel 9,8–10,20.* PTA 24. Bonn: Habelt, 1979.
———. *Didymos der Blinde: Psalmenkommentar (Tura-Papyrus); Teil 2: Kommentar zu Psalm 22–26,10.* PTA 4. Bonn: Habelt, 1968.
———. *Didymos der Blinde: Psalmenkommentar (Tura-Papyrus); Teil 4: Kommentar zu Psalm 35–39.* PTA 6. Bonn: Habelt, 1969.
———. *Psalmenkommentar (Tura-Papyrus); Teil 5: Kommentar zu Psalm 40–44,4.* PTA 12. Bonn: Habelt, 1970.
Gronewald, Michael, and Adolphe Gesché. *Didymos der Blinde: Psalmenkommentar (Tura-Papyrus); Teil 3: Kommentar zu Psalm 29–34.* PTA 8. Bonn: Habelt, 1969.
Gustafsson, B. "Eusebius' Principles in Handling His Sources, as Found in His Church History, Books I–VII." StPatr 24 (1961): 429–441.

Haas, Christopher. *Alexandria in Late Antiquity: Topography and Social Conflict.* Baltimore: Johns Hopkins University Press, 1997.

———. "Hellenism and Opposition to Christianity in Alexandria." Pages 217–29 in *Ancient Alexandria between Egypt and Greece.* Edited by W.V. Harris and Giovanni Ruffini. Columbia Studies in the Classical Tradition 26. Leiden: Brill, 2004.

Hagedorn, Dieter, and Ursula Hagedorn. "Kritisches zum Hiobkommentar Didymos des Blinden." *ZPE* 67 (1987): 59–78.

———. *Didymos der Blinde. Kommentar zu Hiob (Tura-Papyrus); Teil 4.1: Kommentar zu Hiob Kapitel 12,1–16,8a. Einleitung, Text, Übersetzung.* PTA 33.1. Bonn: Habelt, 1985.

Hadot, Ilsetraut. "Der fortlaufende philosophische Kommentar." Pages 183–99 in *Der Kommentar in Antike und Mittelalter: Beiträge zu seiner Erforschung.* Edited by Wilhelm Geerlings and Christian Schulze. Clavis Commentariorum Antiquitatis et Medii Aevi 2. Leiden: Brill, 2002.

———. "Le Commentaire philosophique continu dans l'antiquité." *Antiquité Tardive* 5 (1997): 169–76.

———. "Les introductions aux commentaires exégétiques chez les auteurs néoplatoniciens et les auteurs chrétiens." Pages 99–122 in *Les règles de l'interprétation.* Edited by Michel Tardieu. Paris: Cerf, 1987.

Hadot, Pierre. "Théologie, exégèse, revelation, écriture, dans la philosophie grecque." Pages 13–34 in *Les règles de l'interprétation.* Edited by Michel Tardieu. Paris: Cerf, 1987.

Hahn, Johannes. "The Conversion of the Cult Statues: The Destruction of the Serapeum 392 A.D. and the Transformation of Alexandria into the 'Christ-Loving' City." Pages 335–65 in *From Temple to Church: Destruction and Renewal of Local Cultic Topography in Late Antiquity.* Edited by Ulrich Gotter, Stephen Emmel, and Johannes Hahn. Leiden: Brill, 2008.

———. *Gewalt und religiöser Konflikt: Studien zu den Auseinandersetzungen zwischen Christen, Heiden und Juden im Osten des Römischen Reiches (von Konstantin bis Theodosius II.).* KLIO ns 8. Berlin: de Gruyter, 2004.

Hall, Robert G. "Isaiah, Ascension of." Pages 772–74 in *The Eerdmans Dictionary of Early Judaism.* Edited by John J. Collins and Daniel C. Harlow. Grand Rapids: Eerdmans, 2010.

Hanson, R.P.C. "Interpretations of Hebrew Names in Origen." *VC* 10 (1956): 103–23.

———. *The Search for the Christian Doctrine of God.* Edinburgh: T&T Clark, 1988.

Hardwick, Michael E. *Josephus as an Historical Source in Patristic Literature through Eusebius.* BJS 128. Atlanta: Scholars Press, 1989.

Harl, Marguerite. "La preexistence des ames dans l'oeuvre d'Origène." Pages 238–58 in *Origeniana Quarta: Die Referate des 4. Internationalen Origenskongresses*. Edited by Lothar Lies. Innsbruck: Tyrolia, 1987.

———. "Origène et la sémantique du langage biblique." *VC* 26 (1972): 161–87.

———. *Philon d'Alexandrie: Quis rerum divinarum heres sit*. Les oeuvres de Philon d'Alexandrie 15. Paris: Éditions du Cerf, 1966.

———. *Sur les Écritures*. SC 302. Paris: Cerf, 1983.

Hay, David H. "Philo of Alexandria." Pages 357–80 in *Justification and Variegated Nomism*. Vol. 1. Edited by Donald A. Carson, Peter T. O'Brien, and Mark A. Seifrid. Grand Rapids: Baker Academic, 2001.

———. "Philo's Treatise on the Logos-Cutter." *SPhiloA* 2 (1973): 9–22.

———. "References to Other Exegetes." Pages 81–97 in *Both Literal and Allegorical: Studies in Philo of Alexandria's Questions and Answers on Genesis and Exodus*. Edited by David H. Hay. BJS 232. Atlanta: Scholar's Press, 1991.

Hayes, Walter M. "Didymus the Blind is the author of Adversus Eunomium IV/V." StPatr 17 (1982): 1108–14.

Heimann, Peter. *Erwähltes Schicksal: Präexistenz der Seele und christlicher Glaube im Denkmodell des Origenes*. Theologische Beiträge und Forschungen 5. Tübingen: Katzmann, 1998.

Heine, Ronald E. "The Introduction to Origen's Commentary on John Compared with the Introductions to the Ancient Philosophical Commentaries on Aristotle." Pages 3–12 in *Origeniana Sexta*. Edited by Gilles Dorival and Allain le Boulleuc. BETL 118. Leuven: Leuven University Press, 1995.

———. *Origen: Commentary on the Gospel According to John Books 1–10*. FC 80. Washington, D.C.: The Catholic University of America Press, 1989.

———. *Origen: Homilies on Genesis and Exodus*. FC 71. Washington, D.C.: Catholic University of America Press, 1982.

———. *Origen: Scholarship in the Service of the Church*. Christian Theology in Context. Oxford: Oxford University Press, 2010.

———. "Origen's Alexandrian Commentary on Genesis." Pages 63–73 in *Origeniana Octava: Origen and the Alexandrian tradition = Origene e la tradizione alessandrina*. Papers of the Eighth International Origen Congress, Pisa, 27–31, August 2001. Vol. 1. Edited by Lorenzo Perrone. Leuven: Leuven University Press, 2003.

Helleman, Wendy. "Philo of Alexandria on Deification and Assimilation to God." *SPhiloA* 2 (1990): 51–71.

Helmbold, William C., and Edward N. O'Neil. *Plutarch's Quotations.* American Philological Association Monographs 19. Baltimore: American Philological Association, 1959.

Henrichs, Albert. *Didymos der Blinde: Kommentar zu Hiob (Tura-Papyrus); Teil 1: Kommentar zu Hiob Kapitel 1–4.* PTA 1. Bonn: Habelt, 1968.

———. *Didymos der Blinde: Kommentar zu Hiob (Tura-Papyrus); Teil 2: Kommentar zu Hiob Kapitel 5,1–6,29.* PTA 2. Bonn: Habelt, 1968.

———. "Philosophy, the Handmaiden of Theology." *GRBS* 9 (1968): 437–50.

Heron, Alasdair. "Studies in the Trinitarian Writings of Didymus the Blind: his Authorship of the *Adversus Eunomium* IV–V." Ph.D. diss., Tübingen, 1972.

Hicks, Benjamin. "Roman *Religio* as a Framework at Tacitus' *Histories* 4.83–84." *Journal of Ancient History* 1 (2013): 70–82.

Hill, Robert. *Didymus the Blind: Commentary on Zechariah.* FC 111. Washington D.C.: Catholic University of America Press, 2006.

———. *Reading the Old Testament in Antioch.* The Bible in Ancient Christianity 5. Leiden: Brill, 2005.

Hollerich, Michael J. *Eusebius of Caesarea's* Commentary on Isaiah*: Christian Exegesis in the Age of Constantine.* OECS. Oxford: Oxford University Press, 1999.

Hornschuh, Manfred. "Das Leben des Origenes und die Entstehung der alexandrinischen Schule." *ZKG* 71 (1960): 1–25.

Inowlocki, Sabrina. *Eusebius and the Jewish Authors: His Citation Technique in an Apologetic Context.* AGAJU 64; Leiden: Brill, 2006.

———. Eusebius of Caesarea's *Interpretatio Christiana* of Philo's *De vita contemplativa.*" *VC* 97 (2004): 305–28.

———. "The Reception of Philo's *Legatio ad Gaium* in Eusebius of Caesarea's Works." *SPhA* 16 (2004): 30–49.

Inwood, Brad. *Ethics and Human Action in Early Stoicism.* Oxford: Oxford University Press, 1985.

———. *Reading Seneca: Stoic Philosophy at Rome.* Oxford: Oxford University Press, 2005.

Jacobs, Andrew. *Remains of the Jews: The Holy Land and Christian Empire in Late Antiquity.* Divinations: Rereading Late Ancient Religion. Stanford: Stanford University Press, 2004.

Jakab, Attila. *Ecclesia alexandrina: Evolution sociale et institutionnelle du christianisme alexandrine.* Wien: Peter Lang, 2001.

Jakobovits, Immanuel. "Celibacy." Page 537 in vol. 4 of *The Encyclopedia Judaica.* 2nd ed. Detroit: Macmillan, 2007.

Johnson, William A. *Readers and Reading Culture in the High Roman Empire.* Oxford: Oxford University Press, 2010.

Kahn, Charles H. *Pythagoras and the Pythagoreans: A Brief History.* Indianapolis: Hackett, 2001.

Kalvesmaki, Joel. *The Theology of Arithmetic: Number Symbolism in Platonism and Early Christianity.* Hellenic Studies 59. Cambridge, Mass.: Center for Hellenic Studies, 2013.

Kamesar, Adam. "Biblical Interpretation in Philo." Pages 65–91 in *The Cambridge Companion to Philo.* Edited by Adam Kamesar. Cambridge: Cambridge University Press, 2010.

———. "The Evaluation of the Narrative Aggadah in Greek and Latin Patristic Literature." *JTS* 45 (1994): 37–75.

———. "The *Logos Endiathetos* and the *Logos Prophorikos* in Allegorical Interpretation: Philo and the D-Scholia to the *Iliad*." *GRBS* 44 (2004): 163–81.

———. "Philo, the Presence of 'Paideuctic' Myth in the Pentateuch, and the 'Principles' or Kephalaia of Mosaic Discourse." *SPhiloA* 10 (1998): 34–65.

———. "San Basilio, Filone, e la tradizione ebraica." *Hen* 17 (1995): 129–40.

Knibb, Michael A. "Martyrdom and Ascension of Isaiah." Pages 143–76 in *The Old Testament Pseudepigrapha.* Vol. 2. Edited by James H. Charlesworth. ABRL. New York: Doubleday, 1985.

Koenen, Ludwig, and W. Müller-Wiener. "Zu den Papyri aus dem Arsenios Kloster bei Tura." *ZPE* 2 (1968): 41–63.

Kramer, Bärbel, and Johannes Kramer. "Les éléments linguistiques hébreux chez Didyme l'Aveugle." Pages 313–23 in Ἀλεξανδρῖνα: *Hellénisme, judaïsme, et christianisme à Alexandrie. Mélanges offerts au P. Claude Mondésert.* Paris: Éditions du Cerf, 1987.

Kramer, Johannes, and Ludwig Koenen. *Didymos der Blinde: Kommentar zum Ecclesiastes (Tura-Papyrus); Teil 3: Kommentar zu Ecclesiastes, Kapitel 5 und 6.* PTA 13. Bonn: Habelt, 1970.

Kramer, Johannes, and Bärbel Krebber. *Didymos der Blinde: Kommentar zum Ecclesiastes (Tura-Papyrus); Teil 4: Kommentar zu Ecclesiastes, Kapitel 7– 8,8.* PTA 16. Bonn: Habelt, 1972.

Lamberton, Robert. *Homer the Theologian: Neoplatonist Allegorical Reading and the Growth of the Epic Tradition.* Berkeley: University of California Press, 1986.

Lamirande, Emilien. "Le masculin et le feminin dans la tradition alexandrine: le commentaire de Didyme l'Aveugle sur la 'Genèse.'" *Science et Esprit* 41 (1989): 137–65.

Lampe, G. W. H. *A Patristic Greek Lexicon*. Oxford: Oxford University Press.

Lauro, Elizabeth Dively. *The Soul and Spirit within Origen's Exegesis*. The Bible in Ancient Christianity 3. Leiden: Brill, 2005.

Lawson, R.P. *Origen: The Song of Songs: Commentary and Homilies*. Ancient Christian Writers 26. London: Longmans, Green and Co., 1957.

Layton, Richard. *Didymus the Blind and His Circle in Late-Antique Alexandria*. Urbana, IL: University of Illinois Press, 2004.

———. "Didymus the Blind and the Philistores: A Contest over Historia in Early Christian Exegetical Argument." Pages 243–67 in *Studies on the Texts of the Desert of Judah: New Approaches to the Study of Biblical Interpretation in Judaism of the Second Temple Period and in Early Christianity*. Edited by Gary Anderson, Ruth Clements, and David Satran. Leiden: Brill, 2013.

———. "Judas Yields a Place to the Devil: The Appropriation of Origen's Commentary on Ephesians by Didymus of Alexandria." Pages 531–41 in *Origeniana Septima: Origenes in den Auseinandersetzungen des 4. Jahrhunderts*. BETL 137. Edited by Wolfgang A. Bienert and U. Kühneweg. Leuven: Peeters, 1999.

———. "Propatheia: The Origins of the Passions in the Exegesis of Origen and Didymus." *VC* 54 (2000): 242–62.

Leemans, Johann. "After Philo and Paul: Hagar in the Writings of the Church Fathers." Pages 435–47 in *Abraham, the Nations, and the Hagarites: Jewish, Christian, and Islamic Perspectives on Kinship with Abraham*. Themes in Biblical Narrative 13. Edited by Martin Goodman, George H. van Kooten, and J. van Ruiten. Leiden: Brill, 2010.

Leonhardt, Jutta. *Jewish Worship in Philo of Alexandria*. Texts and Studies in Ancient Judaism 84. Tübingen: Mohr Siebeck, 2001.

Leipoldt, Johannes. *Didymus der Blinde*. Texte und Untersuchungen zur geschichte der altchristlichen literature 29. Leipzig: Hinrichs, 1905.

Lévy, Carlos. "Philo's Ethics." Pages 146–71 in *The Cambridge Companion to Philo*. Edited by Adam Kamesar. Cambridge: Cambridge University Press, 2010.

Levine, Lee. *The Ancient Synagogue: The First Thousand Years*. 2nd ed. New Haven: Yale University Press, 2005.

Lewy, Hans. "Julian the Apostate and the Building of the Temple." *The Jerusalem Cathedra* 3 (1983): 70–96.

Lilla, Salvatore. *Clement of Alexandria: A Study in Christian Platonism and Gnosticism.* Oxford Theological Monographs; Oxford: Oxford University Press, 1971.

Lloyd, A. C. "Grammar and Metaphysics in the Stoa." Pages 58–71 in *Problems in Stoicism.* Edited by A.A. Long. London: Athlone, 1971.

Lloyd, G. E. R. "Pythagoras." Pages 24–45 in *A History of Pythagoreanism.* Edited by Carl A. Huffman. Cambridge: Cambridge University Press, 2016.

———. *Science, Folklore and Ideology: Studies in the Life Sciences in Ancient Greece.* Cambridge: Cambridge University Press, 1983.

Long, A. A. *Hellenistic Philosophy.* 2nd edition. Berkeley: University of California Press, 1986.

Long, A. A., and David Sedley. *The Hellenistic Philosophers.* 2 vols. Cambridge: Cambridge University Press, 1987.

Lührmann, Dieter. "Alttestamentliche Pseudepigraphen bei Didymos von Alexandrien." *ZAW* 104 (1992): 231–49.

Mach, Michael. *Entwicklungsstadien des jüdischen Engelglaubens in vorrabinischer Zeit.* TSAJ 34. Tübingen: Mohr Siebeck, 1992.

Mackie, Scott D. "Seeing God in Philo of Alexandria: The Logos, the Powers or the Existent One?" *SPhiloA* 21 (2009): 25–47.

Maltby, Robert. Etymology." Pages 542–43 in *The Oxford Classical Dictionary.* 4th edition. Edited by Simon Hornblower and Anthony Spawforth. Oxford: Oxford University Press, 2012.

Mansfeld, Jaap. *Prolegomena: Questions to be Settled Before the Study of an Author, or a Text.* PhA 61. Leiden: Brill, 1994.

Marcovich, Miroslav. *Pseudo-Iustinus: Cohortatio ad Graecos, De monarchia, Oratio ad Graecos.* PTS 32. Berlin: de Gruyter, 1990.

Markschies, Christoph. "Origenes und die Kommentierung des paulinischen Römerbriefs." Pages 66–94 in *Commentaries–Kommentare.* Edited by Glenn W. Most. Aporemata: Kritische Studien zur Philologiegeschichte 4. Göttingen: Vandenhoeck and Ruprecht, 1999.

Marmorstein, Arthur. "Philo and the Names of God." *JQR* 22 (1931): 295–306.

Martens, Peter. "A Fitting Portrait of God: Origen's Interpretations of the 'Garments of Skins' (Gen 3:21)." Pages 55–84 in *Hidden Truths from Eden: Esoteric Readings of Genesis 1–3.* Edited by Caroline Vander Stichele and Susanne Scholz. Atlanta: SBL Press, 2014.

———. "Origen's Doctrine of Pre-Existence and the Opening Chapters of Genesis." *ZAC* 16 (2013): 516–49.

Martyn, J. Louis. *Galatians.* AB 33A. New York: Doubleday, 1979.

McGill, Scott. *Plagiarism in Latin Literature*. Cambridge: Cambridge University Press, 2012.

McGuckin, John. "Origen on the Jews." Pages 1–13 in *Christianity and Judaism Papers Read at the 1991 Summer Reading and the 1992 Winter Meeting of the Ecclesiastical Historical Society*. Edited by Diana Wood. SCH 29. Oxford: Oxford University Press, 1992.

———. *St. Gregory of Nazianzus: An Intellectual Biography*. Crestwood, N.Y.: SVS Press, 2001.

McLeod, Frederick G. *Theodore of Mopsuestia*. The Early Church Fathers. New York: Routledge, 2010.

Méasson, Anita. *Du char ailé de Zeus à l'Arche d'Alliance: Images et mythes platoniciens chez Philon d'Alexandrie*. Paris: Études augustiniennes, 1986.

Mélèze-Modrzejewski, Joseph. *The Jews of Egypt from Rameses II to Emperor Hadrian*. Translated by Robert Cornman. Philadelphia: Jewish Publication Society, 1997.

Mendelson, Alan. *Secular Education in Philo of Alexandria*. Cincinnati: Hebrew Union College Press, 1982.

Metzler, Karin. *Origenes: Werke mit deutscher Übersetzung 1/1. Die Kommentierung des Buches Genesis*. Berlin: de Gruyter, 2010.

———. *Prokop von Gaza: Eclogarum in libros historicos Veteris Testamenti epitome*. GCS n.s 22. Berlin: de Gruyter, 2015.

Miller, Hannah. "Cyril of Alexandria's Treatment of Sources in His Commentary on the Twelve Prophets." StPatr 68 (2013): 85–93.

Mohring, Horst. "Arithmology as an Exegetical Tool in the Writings of Philo of Alexandria." *SBLSP* 1 (1978): 191–227.

———. "Arithmology as an Exegetical Tool in the Writings of Philo of Alexandria." Pages 141–76 in *The School of Moses: Studies in Philo and Hellenistic Religion in Memory of Horst R. Moehring*. Edited by J.P. Kenney. BJS 304; SPhiloM 1. Atlanta: Scholar's Press, 1995.

Monaci, A. Costagno. "L'idea della preesistenza delle anime e l'esegesi di Rm 9,9–2." Pages 69–78 in *Origeniana Secunda: Second colloque international des études origéniennes (Bari, 20–23 septembre 1977)*. Edited by Henri Crouzel and Antonio Quacquarelli. Quaderni di *Vetera Christianorum* 15. Rome: Edizioni dell'Ateneo, 1980.

Montes-Peral, Luis Angel. *Akataleptos Theos: der unfassbare Gott*. ALGHJ 16. Leiden: Brill, 1987.

Morlet, Sébastien. "L'Écriture image des vertus: La transformation d'un theme philoniene dans l'apologétique d'Eusèbe de Césarée." StPatr 42 (2006): 187–92.

Morris, Jenny. "The Jewish Philosopher Philo." Pages 809–89 in Emil Schürer, *The History of the Jewish People in the Age of Jesus Christ*. Vol. 3.2. Revised and edited by Geza Vermes, Fergus Millar, and Martin Goodman. Edinburgh: T&T Clark, 1987.

Mortley, Raoul. *Connaissance religieuse et herméneutique chez Clément d'Alexandrie*. Leiden: Brill, 1973.

Most, Glenn W. "Cornutus and Stoic Allegoresis." *ANRW* 2.36.3 (1989): 2014–65.

———. "Preface." Pages VII–XV in *Commentaries–Kommentare*. Edited by Glenn W. Most. Aporemata: Kritische Studien zur Philologiegeschichte 4. Göttingen: Vandenhoeck and Ruprecht, 1999.

Mühl, M. "Der λόγος ἐνδιάθετος und προφορικός von der älteren Stoa bis zur Synode von Sirmium 351." *Archiv für Begriffsgeschichte* 7 (1962): 7–56.

Müller-Wiener, W. "Zu den Papyri aus dem Arsenios Kloster bei Tura." *ZPE* 2 (1968): 41–63.

Nautin, Pierre. *Didyme l'Aveugle: Sur la Genèse*. Vol. 1. SC 233. Paris: Cerf, 1976.

———. *Didyme l'Aveugle: Sur la Genèse*. Vol. 2. SC 244. Paris: Cerf, 1978.

———. "La date des commentaires de Jérôme sur les épîtres pauliniennes." *RHE* 74 (1979): 5–12.

———. *Origène: Sa vie et son oeuvre*. Christianisme antique 1. Paris: Beauchesne, 1977.

Nelson, Anne Browning. "The Classroom of Didymus the Blind." Ph.D. diss., The University of Michigan, 1995.

Neuschäfer, Bernard. *Origenes als Philologe*. 2 vols. Schweizerische Beiträge zur Altertumswissenschaft 18.1–2. Basel: Friedrich Reinhardt, 1987.

Nielsen, Dave. "The History, Provenance, and Importance of BYU's Didymus Papyri." http://scholarsarchive.byu.edu/cgi/viewcontent.cgi?article=1083&context=studentpub.

Nielsen, Donald. "Civilizational Encounters in the Development of Early Christianity." Pages 267–90 in *Handbook of Early Christianity: Social Science Approaches*. Edited by Anthony J. Blasi, Paul Andre Turcotte, and Jean Duhaime. Walnut Creek, CA: AltaMira, 2002.

Nikiprowetzky, Valentin. *Le Commentaire de l'Écriture chez Philon d'Alexandrie: son caractère et sa portée, observations philologiques*. ALGHJ 11. Leiden: Brill, 1977.

———. "Rébecca, vertu de constance et constance de vertu chez Philon d'Alexandrie." *Sem* 26 (1976): 109–36.

Nippel, Wilfried. *Fußnoten, Zitate, Plagiate: Wissenschaftsgeschichtliche Streifzüge*. Karl-Christ-Preis für Alte Geschichte 1. Heidelberg: Verlag Antike, 2014.

O'Meara, Dominic J. *Pythagoras Revived: Mathematics and Philosophy in Late Antiquity*. Oxford: Clarendon, 1989.

Osborn, Eric. *Clement of Alexandria*. Cambridge: Cambridge University Press, 2005.

———. "Philo and Clement." *Prudentia* 19 (1987): 35–49.

———. "Philo and Clement: Citation and Influence," Pages 228–43 in *Lebendige Überlieferung: Prozesse der Annäherung und Auslegung; Festschrift für Hermann-Josef Vogt zum 60. Geburtstag*. Edited by Nabil el-Khoury. Beirut: Rückert; Ostfildern: Schwaben, 1992.

———. "Philo and Clement: Quiet Conversion and Noetic Exegesis." *SPhiloA* 10 (1998): 108–124.

———. Review of Annewies Van den Hoek, *Clement of Alexandria and His Use of Philo in the Stromateis*. *JTS* 41 (1990): 653–56.

Otto, Jennifer. "Philo, Judaeus? A Re-evaluation of Why Clement Calls Philo 'the Pythagorean.'" *SPhiloA* 25 (2013): 115–38.

Pancerz, Roland Marcin. "Didimo il Cieco e gli antropomorfismi biblici." Pages 751–63 in *Origeniana Decima: Origen as Writer*. Edited by Henryk Pietras and Sylwia Kaczmarek. BETL 244. Leuven: Peeters, 2011.

Parvis, Sarah. "Justin Martyr and the Apologetic Tradition." Pages 115–27 in *Justin Martyr and his Worlds*. Edited by Sara Parvis and Paul Foster. Minneapolis: Fortress, 2007.

Pearce, Sarah J. K. *The Land of the Body: Studies in Philo's Representation of Egypt*. WUNT 208. Tübingen: Mohr Siebeck, 2007.

Pearson, Birger A. *Ancient Gnosticism: Traditions and Literature*. Philadelphia: Fortress, 2007.

———. *Gnosticism, Judaism, and Egyptian Christianity*. Philadelphia: Fortress, 1990.

Pépin, Jean. "A propos de l'histoire de l'exégèse allégorique: l'absurdité, signe de l'allégorie." StPatr 1 (1955): 395–413.

———. *Mythe et Allégorie: Les origins grecques et les contestations judéo-chétiennes*. 2nd edition. Paris: Études augustiniennes, 1976.

Peraki-Kyriakidou, Helen. "Aspects of Ancient Etymologizing." *CQ* ns 52 (2002): 473–98.

Perrone, Lorenzo. "Continuité et innovation dans les commentaires d'Origène: un essai de comparaison entre le Commentaire sur Jean et le Commentaire sur Matthieu." Pages 183–97 in *Le Commentaire entre tradition et innovation*. Edited by Marie-Odile Goulet-Cazé. Bibliotèque d'histoire de la philosophie. Paris: J. Vrin, 2000.

———. "*Origenes pro domo sua*: Self-Quotations and the (Re)construction of a Literary *Oeuvre*." Pages 3–38 in *Origeniana Decima: Origen as Writer*. Edited by Henryk Pietras and Sylwia Kaczmarek. Leuven: Peeters, 2011.

Petit, Alain. "Philon et le pythagorisme: un usage problématique." Pages 471–82 in *Philon d'Alexandrie et le langage de la philosophie*. Edited by Carlos Lévy. Monothéismes et Philosophie. Turnhout: Brepols, 1998.

Petit, Françoise. *L'ancienne version latine des Questions sur la Genèse de Philon d'Alexandrie*. 2 vols. TU 113–114. Berlin: Akademie Verlag, 1973.

Pfeiffer, Rudolph. *History of Classical Scholarship from the Beginnings to the End of the Hellenistic Age*. Oxford: Clarendon, 1968.

Pohlenz, Max. *Die Stoa: Geschichte einer geistigen Bewegung*. 2 vols. Göttingen: Vandenhoeck & Ruprecht, 1949.

———. *Philo von Alexandria*. NAWG. Philologisch-historische Klasse 5. Göttingen: Vandenhoeck & Ruprecht, 1942.

Prinzivalli, Emanuela. *Didimo il Cieco e l'interpretazione dei Salmi: Quaderni di studi e materiali di storia delle religioni*. Rome: Japadre, 1988.

———. *Didimo il Cieco: Lezioni sui Salmi. Il Commento ai Salmi scoperto a Tura*. Milan: Paoline, 2005.

———. "Le metamorfosi della scuola alessandrina da Eracala a Didimo il Cieco." Pages 911–37 in *Origeniana Octava: Origen and the Alexandrian tradition = Origene e la tradizione alessandrina*. Papers of the Eighth International Origen Congress, Pisa, 27–31, August 2001. Edited by Lorenzo Perrone. Leuven: Leuven University Press, 2003.

———. *Magister Ecclesiae: Il Dibattito su Origene fra III e IV Siecolo*. SEAug 82. Rome: Institutum Patristicum Augustinianum, 2002.

———. "A Rediscovered Author and Origen's Heritage: Didymus the Blind." Pages 779–90 in *Origeniana Decima: Origen as Writer*. Edited by Henryk Pietras and Sylwia Kaczmarek. Leuven: Peeters, 2011.

Puech, Henri-Charles. "Les nouveaux écrits d'Origène et de Didyme découverts à Toura." *RHPR* 31 (1951): 293–329.

Pouderon, Bernard. "Athénagore chef d'école: A propos du témoignage de Philippe de Side." StPatr 26 (1993): 167–76.

———. *D'Athènes à Alexandrie: études sur Athénagore et les origines de la philosophie chrétienne*. Leuven: Peeters, 1997.

Quandt, Kenneth. "Αἱ γὰρ τῶν ἐναντίων εἰσίν: Philosophical Program and Expository Practice in Aristotle " *Classical Antiquity* 2 (1983): 279–98.

Quasten, Johannes. *Patrology*. Vol. 3: *The Golden Age of Patristic Literature*. Utrecht: Spectrum, 1963.

Quispel, Gilles. "Origen and the Valentinian Gnosis." *VC* 28 (1974): 29–42.

Radde-Gallwitz, Andrew, and Lewis Ayres. *Works on the Holy Spirit: Athanasius the Great and Didymus the Blind*. Popular Patristics Series 43. Yonkers, NY: SVS Press, 2011.

Radice, Roberto. "Commentario a La creazione del mondo." Pages 231–313 in *Filone di Alessandria: La filosofia mosaica*. Edited by Roberto Radice and Giovanni Reale. Milan: Rusconi, 1987.

———. "Observations on the Theory of the Ideas as the Thoughts of God in Philo of Alexandria." *SPhA* 3 (1991): 126–34.

Ramelli, Ilaria. "Origen, Patristic Philosophy, and Christian Platonism: Rethinking the Christianization of Hellenism." *VC* 63 (2009): 217–63.

———. "Philo as Origen's Declared Model: Allegorical an Historical Exegesis of Scripture." *Studies in Christian-Jewish Relations* 7 (2012): 1–17.

Rankin, David. *Athenagoras: Philosopher and Theologian*. London: Ashgate: 2009.

Reale, Giovanni. *A History of Ancient Philosophy: The Schools of the Imperial Age*. Edited and translated by John R. Catan. Albany: SUNY Press, 1990.

Reuling, Hanneke. *After Eden: Church Fathers and Rabbis on Genesis 3,16–21*. Leiden: Brill, 2006.

Reydams-Schils, Gretchen. "Stoicized Readings of Plato's Timaeus in Philo of Alexandria." *SPhiloA* 7 (1995): 85–102.

Riedweg, Christoph. *Ps.-Justin (Markell von Ankyra?), Ad Graecos De Vera Religione: Einleitung und Kommentar*. Schweizerische Beiträge zur Altertumswissenschaft 25. Basel: Reinhardt, 1994.

———. *Pythagoras: His Life, Teaching, and Influence*. Translated by Steven Rendall. Ithaca, NY: Cornell University Press, 2005.

Robbins, Frank Egleston. "Arithmetic in Philo Judaeus." *CP* 26 (1931): 345–61.

———. "Posidonius and the Sources of Pythagorean Arithmology." *CP* 15 (1920): 309–322.

———. "The Tradition of Greek Arithmology." *CP* 16 (1921): 97–123.

Roberts, Colin H. *Manuscript, Society, and Belief in Early Christian Egypt*. Schweich Lectures on Biblical Archaeology. Oxford: Oxford University Press, 1985.

Robertson, David G. "Mind and Language in Philo." *JHI* 67 (2006): 423–41.

Rogers, Justin M. "Origen in the Likeness of Philo: Eusebius of Caesarea's Portrait of the Model Scholar." *Studies in Christian-Jewish Relations* 12 (2017): 1–13.

———. "Origen's Use of Philo Judeaus." In *The Oxford Handbook of Origen*. Editd by Ronald Heine and Katherine Jo Torjesen. Oxford: Oxford University Press, *forthcoming*.

———. "The Philonic and the Pauline: Hagar and Sarah in the Exegesis of Didymus the Blind." *SPhiloA* 26 (2014): 57–77.

Rokeah, David. "A New Onomasticon Fragment from Oxyrhyncus and Philo's Etymologies." *JTS* 19 (1968): 70–82.

Rönsch, Hermann. *Das Buch der Jubiläen, oder die Kleine Genesis*. Leipzig: Fues, 1874.

Rose, Martha L. *The Staff of Oedpius: Transforming Disability in Ancient Greece*. Ann Arbor: University of Michigan Press, 2003.

Roskam, Geert. *On the Path to Virtue: The Stoic Doctrine of Moral Progress and its Reception in (Middle-)Platonism*. Ancient and Medieval Philosophy 1. Leuven: Leuven University Press, 2005.

Royse, James. "Cain's Expulsion from Paradise: The Text of Philo's *Congr*. 71." *JQR* 79 (1989): 219–25.

———. "Did Philo Publish His Works?" *SPhiloA* 25 (2013): 75–100.

———. *The Spurious Texts of Philo of Alexandria: A Study of Textual Transmission and Corruption with Indexes to the Major Collections of Greek Fragments*. ALGHJ 22. Leiden: Brill, 1991.

Runia, David T. "Caesarea Maritima and the Survival of Hellenistic-Jewish Literature." Pages 476–95 in *Caesarea Maritima: A Retrospective After Two Millennia*. Edited by A. Raban and K. G. Holum. DMOA 21. Leiden: Brill, 1996.

———. "Clement of Alexandria and the Philonic Doctrine of the Divine Power(s)." *VC* 5 (2004): 256–276.

———. "Etymology as an Allegorical Technique in Philo of Alexandria." *SPhiloA* 16 (2004): 101–21.

———. "Festugière Revisited: Aristotle in the Greek Patres." *VC* 43 (1989): 1–34.

———. "L'exégèse philosophique et l'influence de la penseé philonienne dans la tradition patristique." Pages 327–48 in *Philon d'Alexandrie et le langage de la philosophie*. Edited by Carlos Lévy. Monothéismes et Philosophie. Turnhout: Brepols, 1998.

———. "A Neglected Text of Philo of Alexandria: First Translation into a Modern Language." Pages 199–207 in *Things Revealed: Studies in Early Jewish and Christian Literature in Honor of Michael E. Stone*. Edited by

Esther G. Chazon, David Satran, and Ruth A. Clements. JSJSup 89. Leiden: Brill, 2004.

———. *On The Creation Of The Cosmos According To Moses.* PACS 1. Leiden: Brill, 2001.

———. "Philo and the Early Christian Fathers." Pages 210–30 in *The Cambridge Companion to Philo.* Edited by Adam Kamesar. Cambridge: Cambridge University Press, 2010.

———. *Philo in Early Christian Literature: A Survey.* CRINT 3.3. Assen: Van Gorcum; Minneapolis: Fortress, 1993.

———. "Philo in the Patristic Tradition: A List of Direct References." Pages 268–86 in *Reading Philo: A Handbook to Philo of Alexandria.* Edited by Torrey Seland. Grand Rapids: Eerdmans, 2014.

———. "The Text of the Platonic Citations in Philo of Alexandria." Pages 261–91 in *Studies in Plato and the Platonic Tradition: Essays Presented to John Whittaker.* Edited by Mark Joyal. Aldershot: Ashgate, 1997.

———. "Why Does Clement of Alexandria Call Philo 'The Pythagorean?'" *VC* 49 (1995): 1–22.

Russell, D. S. *Criticism in Antiquity.* Berkeley: University of California Press, 1981.

Russell, Norman. *Cyril of Alexandria.* Early Church Fathers. London: Routledge, 2000.

———. *The Doctrine of Deification in the Greek Patristic Tradition.* Oxford: Oxford University Press, 2005.

Ruwet, Jean. "Origène et l'Apocalpyse d'Élie: À propos de 1 Cor 2:9." *Bib* 30 (1949): 517–19.

Saffrey, H. D. "Quelques aspects de la spiritualité des philosophes néoplatoniciens de Jamblique à Proclus et Damascius." *RSPT* 68 (1984): 169–82.

Schereschewsky, B.-Z., and M. Elon. "Bigamy and Polygamy." Pages 691–94 in vol. 2 of *The Encyclopedia Judaica.* 2nd ed. Detroit: Macmillan, 2007.

Schäublin, Christoph. *Untersuchungen zu Methode und Herkunft der antiochenischen Exegese.* Theophania 23. Cologne-Bonn: Hanstein, 1974.

Scheck, Thomas P. *Origen, Commentary on the Epistle to the Romans, Books 1–5.* FC 103. Washington, D.C.: Catholic University of America Press, 2001.

Schenkeveld, Dirk M. "Language." Pages 177–225 in *The Cambridge History of Hellenistic Philosophy.* Edited by Keimpe Algra, Jonathan Barnes, Jaap Mansfeld, and Malcom Schofield. Cambridge: Cambridge University Press, 1999.

Schibli, Hermann. "Origen, Didymus, and the Vehicle of the Soul." Pages 381–91 in *Origeniana Quinta: Historica, Text and Method, Biblica, Philoso-*

phica, Theologica, Origenism and Later Developments. Edited by R.J. Daly. BETL 105. Leuven: Peeters, 1992.

Scholten, Clemens. "Die alexandrinische Katechetenschule." *JAC* 38 (1995): 16–37.

Schreckenberg, Hans, and Kurt Schubert, *Jewish Historiography and Iconography in Early and Medieval Christianity*. CRINT 3.2. Assen: Van Gorcum; Minneapolis: Fortress, 1992.

Scott, Alan B. "Opposition and Concession: Origen's Relationship to Valentinianism." Pages 79–84 in *Origeniana Quinta: Historica, Text and Method, Biblica, Philosophica, Theologica, Origenism and Later Developments*. Edited by R. J. Daly. BETL 105. Leuven: Peeters, 1992.

Sedley, David N. "The Etymologies in Plato's Cratylus." *JHS* 118 (1998): 140–54.

Segal, Alan. *Two Powers in Heaven: Early Rabbinic Reports about Christianity and Gnosticism* (Leiden: Brill, 2002).

Sellew, Philip. "Achilles or Christ? Porphyry and Didymus in Debate over Allegorical Interpretation." *HTR* 82 (1989): 79–100.

Serra, Aristide. "La 'spada:' simbolo della 'parola di Dio,' nell'Antico Testamento biblica-guidaico e nel Nuono Testamento." *Marianum* 63 (2001): 17–89.

Shroyer, Montgomery J. "Alexandrian Jewish Literalists." *JBL* 55 (1936): 261–84.

Simonetti, Manlio. *Biblical Interpretation in the Early Church: An Introduction to Patristic Exegesis*. Translated by John A. Hughes. Edinburgh: T&T Clark, 1994.

———. "Didymiana." *Vetera Christianorum* 21 (1984): 129–55.

———. *Lettera e/o allegoria: Un contributo alla storia dell'esegesi patristica*. SEAug 23. Rome: Institutum Patristicum Augustinianum, 1985.

Skeb, Matthias. *Exegese und Lebensform: Die Proömien der antiken griechischen Bibelkommentare*. Clavis commentariorum, Antiquitatis et Medii Aevi 5. Leiden: Brill, 2007.

Sluiter, Ineke. "Commentaries and the Didactic Tradition." Pages 173–205 in *Commentaries–Kommentare*. Edited by Glenn W. Most. Aporemata: Kritische Studien zur Philologiegeschichte 4. Göttingen: Vandenhoeck & Ruprecht, 1999.

Solari, Placid. "Christ as Virtue in Didymus the Blind." Pages 67–88 in *Purity of Heart in Early Ascetic and Monastic Literature: Essays in Honor of Juana Raasch*. Edited by Harriet A. Luckman and Linda Kulzer. Collegeville: Minn.: Liturgical Press, 1999.

Sorabji, Richard. "Chrysippus-Posidonius-Seneca: A High-Level Debate on Emotion." Pages 149–70 in *The Emotions in Hellenistic Philosophy*. Edited by Juha Sihvola and Troels Engberg-Pederson. The New Synthese Historical Library 46. Dordrecht: Kluwer, 1998.

Staehle, Karl. *Die Zahlenmystik bei Philon von Alexandreia.* Leipzig: Teubner, 1931.

Stefaniw, Blossom. *Mind, Text and Commentary: Noetic Exegesis in Origen of Alexandria, Didymus the Blind and Evagrius Ponticus.* Early Christianity in the Context of Antiquity 6. Frankfurt and New York: Peter Lang, 2010.

——. "Reading Revelation: Allegorical Exegesis in Late Antique Alexandria." *RHR* 224 (2007): 231–51.

Steiger, Peter D. "The Image of God in the Commentary On Genesis of Didymus the Blind." StPatr 42 (2006): 243–47.

Stemplinger, Eduard. *Der Plagiat in der Griechischen Literatur.* Leizig: Teubner, 1912.

Strutwolf, Holger. *Gnosis als System: Zur Rezeption der valentinianischen Gnosis bei Origenes.* Göttingen: Vandenhoek & Ruprecht, 1993.

Sterling, Gregory. "Did Josephus Know the Writings of Philo?" *SPhiloA* 25 (2013): 101–13.

——. "Philo's School: The Social Setting of Ancient Commentaries." Pages 123–42 in *Sophisten im Hellenismus und Kaiserzeit: Orte, Methoden und Personen der Bildungsvermittlung.* Edited by Beatrice Wyss, Rainer Hirsch-Leupold, and Solmeng- Jonas Hirschi. STAC 101. Tübingen: Mohr Siebeck, 2017.

——. "'The Queen of the Virtues:' Piety in Philo of Alexandria." *SPhiloA* 18 (2006): 103–23.

——. "Recherché or Representative? What Is the Relationship between Philo's Treatises and Greek-Speaking Judaism?" *SPhiloA* 11 (1999): 1–30.

——. "'The School of Sacred Laws': The Social Setting of Philo's Treatises." *VC* 53 (1999): 148–64.

Stückelberger, Alfred. *Senecas 88. Brief: Über Wert und Unwert der Freien Künste.* Heidelberg: Winter, 1965.

Tarrant, Harold. "Must Commentators Know Their Sources? Proclus *in Timaeum* and Numenius." Pages 175–90 in vol. 1 of *Philosophy, Science and Exegesis in Greek, Arabic and Latin Commentaries.* Edited by Peter Adamson, Han Baltussen, and M. W. F. Stone. BICS Supplement 83.1. London: Institute of Classical Studies, 2004.

Tcherikover, Victor. "The Decline of the Jewish Diaspora in Egypt in the Roman Period." *JJS* 14 (1963): 1–32.

Terian, Abraham. "A Philonic Fragment on the Decad." Pages 173–82 in *Nourished with Peace: Studies in Hellenistic Judaism in Memory of Samuel Sandmel.* Edited by Frederick E. Greenspahn et al. Chico, Calif.: Scholars Press, 1984.
Termini, Christina. *Le potenze di Dio: Studio su δύναμις in Filone d Alessandria.* SEAug 71. Rome: Institutum Patristicum Augustinianum, 2000.
———. "Philo's Thought within the Context of Middle Judaism." Pages 95–123 in *The Cambridge Companion to Philo.* Edited by Adam Kamesar. Cambridge: Cambridge University Press, 2010.
Theiler, Willy. *Poseidonios: Die Fragmente.* 2 vols. TK 10. Berlin: de Gruyter, 1982.
Thesleff, Holger. *The Pythagorean Texts of the Hellenistic Period.* Acta Academiae Aboensis 30. Åbo: Akademi, 1965.
Thümmel, Hans Georg. "Philon und Origenes." Pages 275–86 in *Origeniana Octava: Origen and the Alexandrian tradition = Origene e la tradizione alessandrina.* Papers of the Eighth International Origen Congress, Pisa, 27-31, August 2001. Edited by Lorenzo Perrone. Leuven: Leuven University Press, 2003.
Tigcheler, Jo. *Didyme l'Aveugle et l'exégèse allégorique: Étude sémantique de quelques termes exégètiques importants de son commentaire sur Zacharie.* Graecitas Christianorum Primaeva 6. Nijmegen: Dekker & Van de Vegt, 1977.
Tobin, Thomas. *The Creation of Man: Philo and the History of Interpretation.* CBQMS 14. Washington, D.C.: Catholic University of America Press, 1983.
———. "The Prologue of John and Hellenistic Jewish Speculation." *CBQ* 52 (1990): 252–69.
Torjesen, Katherine Jo. *Hermeneutical Procedure and Theological Method in Origen's Exegesis.* PTS 28. Berlin: de Gruyter, 1985.
Trigg, Joseph. *Origen: The Bible and Philosophy in the Third-century Church.* London: SCM, 1983.
Tzvetkova-Glaser, Anna. *Pentateuchauslegung bei Origenes und den frühen Rabbinen.* Early Christianity in the Context of Antiquity 7. Frankfurt am Main: Lang, 2010.
Ulrich, Jorg. *Euseb und die Juden: Studien zur Rolle der Juden in der Theologie des Eusebius von Caesarea.* PTS 149. Berlin: de Gruyter, 1999.
Van den Hoek, Annewies. "Assessing Philo's Influence in Christian Alexandria: The Case of Origen." Pages 223–39 in *Shem in the Tents of Japheth: Essays on the Encounter of Judaism and Hellenism.* Edited by James L. Kugel. JSJSup 74. Leiden: Brill, 2002.

———. "The 'Catechetical' School of Early Christian Alexandria and Its Philonic Heritage." *HTR* 90 (1997): 59–87.

———. *Clement of Alexandria and His Use of Philo in the Stromateis: An Early Christian Reshaping of a Jewish Model*. VCSup 3. Leiden: Brill, 1988.

———. "Clement of Alexandria and the Book of Proverbs," Pages 197–216 in *Clement's Biblical Exegesis: Proceedings of the Second Colloquium on Clement of Alexandria*. Edited by Veronika Černušková, Judith L. Kovacs, and Jana Plátová. VCSup 139. Leiden: Brill, 2016.

———. "Philo and Origen: A Descriptive Catalogue of Their Relationship." *SPhiloA* 12 (2000): 44–121.

———. "Origen and the Intellectual Heritage of Alexandria: Continuity or Disjunction?" Pages 40–50 in *Origeniana Quinta: Historica, Text and Method, Biblica, Philosophica, Theologica, Origenism and Later Developments*. Edited by R.J. Daly. BETL 105. Leuven: Peeters, 1992.

———. "Techniques of Quotation in Clement of Alexandria: A View of Ancient Literary Working Methods." *VC* 50 (1996): 223–43.

Van Geytenbach, A. C. *Musonius Rufus and Greek Diatribe*. Assen: Van Gorcum, 1962.

Van Winden, J. C. M. "Quotations from Philo in Clement of Alexandria's Protrepticus." *VC* 32 (1978): 208–13.

VanderKam, James C., and William Adler, eds. *The Jewish Apocalyptic Heritage in Early Christianity*. CRINT 3.4. Assen: Van Gorcum; Minneapolis: Fortress, 1996.

Vesey, M. "Jerome's Origen: The Making of a Christian Literary Persona." StPatr 28 (1993]) 135–45.

Vian, Giovanni M. "Le *Quaestiones* di Filone." *Annali di Storia dell'Esegesi* 9 (1992): 365–88.

Völker, Walther. *Fortschritt und Vollendung bei Philo von Alexandrien*. TUGAL 4.49.1. Leipzig: Henrichs, 1938.

Vööbus, Arthur. *History of the School of Nisibis*. Leuven: Peeters, 1965.

Von Rompay, Lucas. *Théodore de Mopsueste: Fragments syriaques du Commentaire des Psaumes (Psaume 118 et Psaumes 138–148)*. CSCO 190. Leuven: Peeters, 1982.

Walter, Nikolaus. *Der Toraausleger Aristobulos*. TU 86. Berlin: Akademie-Verlag, 1964.

Watts, Edward J. *City and School in Late Antique Athens and Alexandria*. Berkeley: University of California Press, 2006.

———. "Translating the Personal Aspect of Late Platonism in the Commentary Tradition." Pages 137–50 in *Interpreting the Bible and Aristotle in Late Antiquity: The Alexandrian Commentary Tradition between*

Rome and Baghdad. Edited by Josef Lössel and John W. Watt. London: Ashgate, 2011.

Wellhausen, Julius. *Prolegomena to the History of Israel.* Translated by John Sutherland Black and Allan Menzies. Edinburgh: Black, 1885.

Weisser, Sharon. "Why Does Philo Criticize the Stoic Ideal of Apatheia in *On Abraham* 257? Philo and Consolatory Literature." *CQ* 62 (2012): 242–59.

Westermann, Claus. *Genesis 12–36.* Translated by John J. Scullion Jr. A Continental Commentary. Minneapolis: Fortress, 1995.

Wilson, Walter T. *Philo of Alexandria On Virtues: Introduction, Translation and Commentary.* PACS 3. Leiden: Brill, 2011.

Williams, Megan Hale. *The Monk and the Book: Jerome and the Making of Christian Scholarship.* Chicago: University of Chicago Press, 2006.

Williams, Robert Lee. *Bishop Lists: Formation of Apostolic Succession of Bishops in Ecclesiastical Crises.* Piscataway, NJ: Gorgias, 2005.

Williams, Rowan. *Arius: Heresy and Tradition.* Revised ed. Grand Rapids: Eerdmans, 2003.

Wilken, Robert L. *John Chrysostom and the Jews: Rhetoric and Reality in the Late Fourth Century.* The Transformation of the Classical Heritage 4. Berkeley: University of California Press, 1983.

Winston, David. "Aspects of Philo's Linguistic Theory." *SPhiloA* 3 (1991): 109–25.

———. *Logos and Mystical Theology in Philo of Alexandria.* Cincinnati: Hebrew Union College Press, 1985.

———. "Philo and the Rabbis on Sex and the Body." *Poetics Today* 19 (1998): 41–62.

———. "Philo and Rabbinic Literature." Pages 231–53 in *The Cambridge Companion to Philo.* Edited by Adam Kamesar. Cambridge: Cambridge University Press, 2010.

———. "Philo's Ethical Theory.' *ANRW* 2.21.1 (1984): 372–416.

Wintermute, O. S. "Jubilees." Pages 35–142 in *The Old Testament Pseudepigrapha.* Edited by James H. Charlesworth. ABRL. New York: Doubleday, 1985.

Wolfson, Harry Austryn. *Philo: Foundations of Religious Philosophy in Judaism, Christianity, and Islam.* 2 vols. Cambridge: Harvard University Press, 1962.

———. *The Philosophy of the Church Fathers: Faith, Trinity, Incarnation.* 3rd ed. Cambridge: Harvard 1970.

Wutz, Franz. *Onomastica Sacra: Untersuchungen zum Liber interpretationis nominum hebraicorum des hl. Hieronymus*. 2 vols. TU 41. Leipzig: Hinrichs, 1914.

Wyrwa, Dietmar. "Religiöses Lernen im zweiten Jahrhundert und die Anfänge der alexandrinischen Katechetenschule." Pages 271–305 in *Religiöses Lernen in der biblischen, frühjüdischen und frühchristlichen Überlieferung*. Edited by Beate Ego and Helmut Merkel. WUNT 180. Tübingen: Mohr Siebeck, 2005.

Wyss, Beatrice. "Philo und die Pentas: Arithmologie als exegetische Methode." Pages 361–79 in *Alexandria*. Edited by Reinhard Feldmeier, Tobias Georges, and Felix Albrecht. COMES 1. Tübingen: Mohr Siebeck, 2013.

Yarbro Collins, Adela. "Numerical Symbolism in Apocalyptic Literature." *ANRW* 2.21.2 (1984): 1221–87.

Yli-Karjanmaa, Sami. *Reincarnation in Philo of Alexandria*. SPhiloM 7. Atlanta: SBL Press, 2015.

INDICES

1. *Septuagint*

Genesis		15:6	100
Entire book	113, 165, 167, 168, 169, 196, 199	16:1–2	82, 99, 100
		16:1–4	98
1	160, 161, 169, 204, 205	16:4	113
		16:1–6	103, 112
1–2	199	16:6	112
1:1–2:3	199	16:7–8	109, 188
1–3	167	16:9	109
1:14–19	160	17:5	122, 129
1:21	195	17:10–14	100
1:23	200	18	190, 194, 196
1:26–27	205	20	116
1:26	169, 171, 173–176, 184, 194, 196, 199, 201, 203–205	20:5	116
		20:6	116
		23	116
1:27	187, 207	23:2	179
1:28	100, 187	23:3	179
2	171, 199	23:6	80
2:2	172	25:1	115
2:3	199	25:6	115
2:5–25	199	25:23	84
2:5	91	25:24	84
2:7	98, 108, 169, 171, 173–177	26:8	117
		26:18	129
2:8	176	27	130
2:19–20	128	28:15	170
2:23	168	30:1	97–98
3	171	32:28	122, 129
3:7	176	47:24	151
3:15	188		
3:19	175, 186	Exodus	
3:20	140, 175	19:6	80
3:21	5, 166, 168, 169, 171, 173–177, 187	25:17	152
3:24	137, 196	Leviticus	
4	113	Entire book	1
4:1–2	82	19:25	201
4:2	82, 90, 91		
4:18	82, 93, 94	Numbers	
4:26	178	Entire book	132
5:3–5	82, 95, 156	13:16	129
6:3	157, 159	17	81
6:18	73	35	192
9:20	88		
11:7	194, 196	Deuteronomy	
11:14	61	14:4–5	149
12:1–3	78	34:7	96
12:4–5	138		
14:14	143		

1 Kings
   19:18　　　　　158

Psalms
   Entire book　　177
   1:3　　　　　　136
   4:5　　　　　　179–180
   23:9–10　　　　193
   49:13　　　　　98
   82:6　　　　　　136
   94:5　　　　　　174
   103:4　　　　　174
   127:3–4　　　　98

Proverbs
   Entire book　　1, 30, 106–107, 117
   1:6　　　　　　60, 73, 74
   5:18　　　　　　78, 106
   5:20　　　　　　112
   10:23　　　　　98
   16:12　　　　　197

Ecclesiastes
   Entire book　　1, 7, 78
   1:9–10　　　　　172
   9:9　　　　　　78, 106
   10:7　　　　　　79
   11:2　　　　　　159–160
   11:7　　　　　　136
   12:3　　　　　　67–68
   12:5　　　　　　80

Song of Songs/Canticles
   Entire book　　1

Job
   Entire book　　1, 24, 177
   3:3–5　　　　　172
   5:19　　　　　　158
   5:26　　　　　　136
   6:17–24　　　　63
   10:11　　　　　175
   19:25–26　　　175

Wisdom
   Entire book　　23, 114
   8:9　　　　　　114
   11:20　　　　　144
   9:15　　　　　　173

Isaiah
   Entire book　　1
   1:1　　　　　　133
   1:8　　　　　　67
   1:11　　　　　　109
   6　　　　　　　71
   6:1　　　　　　71–72
   22:13　　　　　88

Jeremiah
   Entire book　　1
   1:5　　　　　　166, 172
   12:7　　　　　　67

Daniel
   Entire book　　1

Hosea
   Entire book　　1

Amos
   1:1　　　　　　71–72
   8:11　　　　　　102

Zechariah
   Entire book　　1, 76
   4:8–9　　　　　133
   6:12　　　　　　76
   8:16–17　　　　57
   8:19　　　　　　110
   10:5–7　　　　　76
   11:17　　　　　77, 134
   12:1–3　　　　　70
   12:2　　　　　　70
   12:10　　　　　73
   14:5　　　　　　71

2. Old Testament Pseudepigrapha

The "Book of the Covenant"
   Entire book   61–65

Coptic Apocalypse of Elijah
   Entire book   65–67
   4:2   66
   4:7–19   66

Enoch and Elijah Apocryphon
   Entire book   60

Ascension of Isaiah
   Entire book   63–65

Jubilees
   Entire book   61–63
   4:31   62

3. New Testament

Matthew
   Entire book   1
   25:30   33
   19:12   54
   23:38   67
   26:37   180–181

Mark
   14:33   182

Luke
   Entire book   1
   1:15   167
   1:44   172
   15:4–5   151
   16:19–31   65
   16:22–23   66

John
   Entire book   1
   1:1–5   205
   1:1–4   207
   1:1   56
   1:3   131
   1:6   167
   2:6   153
   2:20   151
   4:24   204
   8:23   112
   8:26   158
   10:35–36   136
   15:19   158
   19:37   73
   20:26   160
   21:11   143

Acts
   Entire book   1
   14:22   198

Romans
   Entire book   1
   4   100
   4:19   114
   9:8–23   166
   9:13   172
   11:4   158
   12:2   112

1 Corinthians
   2:9   65
   10:31   88
   15:32   88
   16:17–18   2, 81, 111

2 Corinthians
   Entire book   1
   2:15   114
   3:6   106, 108
   4:4   112
   4:7   131

Galatians
   Entire book   1, 102
   3:1–4:31   101
   3   100
   3:24–25   109
   4:22–31   79
   4:22–26   102
   4:23   102
   4:24   98

Ephesians
   Entire book   1
   1:4   166
   6:19   57

Colossians
  Entire book   131
  1:16   196–197
  3:5   114

1 Timothy
  2:5   131, 153

2 Timothy
  3:16–17   119
  3:16   121

Hebrews
  Entire book   1
  1:7   174
  4:15   180–181
  11:5   66
  12:2   182

1 John
  1:5   204
  3:2   187

Revelation
  Entire book   1, 143

4. Philonic Texts

Abr. (De Abrahamo)
  Entire text   209
  8   140
  12   140
  34   115
  52–53   184
  52   85, 92
  72   139, 141
  99   105, 141
  107–132   194
  113   108
  119   198
  121   191
  217   92
  245   116
  248–254   100
  248–252   101
  256–257   185
  257   183
  258   170
  269   86

Aet. (De aeternitate mundi)
  Entire text   27, 209
  12   145
  86   108
  125   108

Agr. (De agricultura)
  Entire text   209
  1–2   128
  4   92
  21   92
  25   86
  29   90
  41   89
  48   90

  51   44–45, 46
  59   107
  66   89
  67–76   77
  72–76   90
  97   120
  101   86
  146–168   185
  159–161   184–185
  160   86, 115
  161   185

Cher. (De cherubim)
  Entire text   209
  3   130
  4   129
  5   116
  7   105, 116, 141
  12   139, 140
  20   198
  27–28   194
  28   198
  41   114, 141, 201
  46   108
  49   107
  52   140
  56   128

Conf. (De confusione linguarum)
  Entire text   209
  36   170
  62–63   76
  77–78   170
  146   46
  168–182   194

Congr. (*De congressu eruditionis gratia*)
Entire text	103, 104, 105, 111, 117, 209
2	105, 112, 116
2–4	130
4	86
6	108, 141
9–12	104, 183
12	104
19	112
20	105, 112
20–21	105
23	183
24	86
25	114
44	128
49–50	104
59	170
71	83
77–79	107
79	111
96–97	90
153–154	112

Contempl. (*De vita contemplativa*)
Entire text	10, 41

Det. (*Quod deterius potiori insidiari soleat*)
Entire text	54, 209
9	141
32	140
47–48	92
53	90
59	107, 108
63–64	154
109	91
118	133
119	139
138	140
140	139
170	86
176	54

Deus (*Quod Deus sit immutabilis*)
Entire text	209
11	148
26	86
83	134
154	86

Ebr. (*De ebrietate*)
Entire text	209
58	107
94	104
101	170
152	185
199	91

In Flaccum
Entire text	27, 40, 118, 209
43	11
48–52	11
48	11

Fug. (*De fuga et inventione*)
Entire text	209
24	86, 130
45	139
54	119
63	177
81	92
94–95	192
95	198
166–167	184
183	86
188	141, 201
196	140
213	140

Gig. (*De gigantibus*)
Entire text	209
55–57	96
137	96

Her. (*Quis rerum divinarum heres sit*)
Entire text	191, 209
79	133
156	145
242	108
247	86

Hypoth. (*Hypothetica*)
Entire text	26, 44, 118

Ios. (*De Iosepho*)
Entire text	209
2	90
2–3	89

Leg. 1–3 (*Legum allegoriae*)
Entire text	209
1.2–3	160
1.3	149
1.15	145
1.20	160
1.31–32	169
1.32–33	171
1.43–47	176
1.54	91
1.61	140

1.73	90	89–93	34, 109
1.89	185	142	86
1.90	91, 96	168–175	185
1.105	170	177–187	104
2.8	86, 185	188	139
2.14–15	128	195	104
2.19–24	120	200	140
2.23–24	201	203–204	152
2.23	201	204	149
2.24	130	221	141
2.34	140		
2.48	86, 108	*Mos.* 1–2 (*De vita Mosis*)	
2.60	86	Entire text	36, 117, 145, 209
2.61	108	1.5	36
2.77	105	1.48	86
2.82	141	1.60	89
2.86	133	1.75	36
2.89	140, 142, 184	2.2	79
2.100–101	86	2.29–40	36
2.104	77	2.37–40	127
3.2	83, 107	2.97	197
3.15	140	2.98	141
3.25	141	2.99	198
3.81	92	2.115	147
3.93	140	2.186	80
3.96	205, 207	2.216	11
3.109	90		
3.111	90	*Mut.* (*De mutatione nominum*)	
3.118	90	Entire text	209
3.125	115	12	85
3.129	184	15–24	185
3.132	184	18	127
3.135	187	70	129
3.140	86	77	105, 116, 141
3.147	119	88	85
3.160	91	121–122	129
3.162	91	193	141
3.168	91	209	140
3.180	140	263	86
3.223–224	91		
3.239	108	*Opif.* (*De opificio mundi*)	
3.244	107	Entire text	36, 147, 161, 209
		13	149, 160, 161
Legat. (*Legatio ad Gaium*)		15	147
Entire text	27, 40, 209	17	39
44	90	20–25	39
132–139	11	20	135
311–313	11	25	205
		28	160
Migr. (*De migratione Abrahami*)		31	205
Entire text	209	33	163
2	78	46	91
53	83	52	147
60	91	62	201
67	90, 107	67	108

69–71	205	*Prov.* (*De providentia*)	
69	169, 173, 204, 205, 206	Entire text	209
		2.3	45
71	207		
72–75	194	*QE* (*Quaestiones et solutiones in Exodum*)	
84–85	202	Entire text	83, 209
91–101	162	2.61	194
91–92	145	2.62	197, 198
91	163	2.68	191–192
92	164		
93–94	162	*QG* (*Quaestiones et solutiones in Genesim*)	
99	163	Entire text	83, 117, 209
100	145	1.6	176
102	145	1.17	145
134	169	1.53	171, 176
146	39	1.57	198
154	120	1.59	88
		1.78	83
Plant. (*De plantatione*)		1.79	178
Entire text	209	1.81	96
34	96	1.91	96, 159, 160
46	91	1.99	145
114	86	2.3	108
133	201	2.62	34
169	117	3.10	170
		3.11	170
Post. (*De posteritate Caini*)		3.16	145
Entire text	94, 96, 209	3.20	100
10	96	3.49	145
32	194	4.1	171
62	105	4.26	100
66–75	94	4.73	116, 179, 183
67	11	4.110	147, 148, 201
124	96	4.194	129
130	107		
124	141	*Sacr.* (*De sacrificiis Abelis et Caini*)	
174	185	Entire text	209
		1–4	83–84, 93, 117
Praem. (*De praemiis et poenis*)		2–5	93
Entire text	209	2–3	129
14	140	2	140
48	108	4	83
63–65	86	5	85
63	83	11–49	85
		11	84
Prob. (*Quod omnis probus liber sit*)		17	83
Entire text	107, 209	35–36	187
2	146	42	140
19	145	43	114, 115
31	90	45	90
107	107	48	105
154	91	51	140
		134	140

246 INDICES

Sobr. (*De sobrietate*)
  Entire text   209
  44   141
  52   141

Somn. (*De somniis*)
  Entire text   209
  1.41   141
  1.53   104
  1.141   170
  1.180–181   169
  1.201   86
  1.215   46
  1.168   85
  2.127   11
  2.235   86

Spec. (*De specialibus legibus*)
  Entire text   209
  1.20   45
  1.81   205
  1.252   115
  2.47   184
  2.62   11
  2.163   90
  2.200   147
  3.34   100
  3.83   205
  3.313   100
  4.105   149
  4.123   39
  4.147   116

Virt. (*De virtutibus*)
  Entire text   109
  67   115
  127   91

5. Other Ancient Authors

ARISTOBULUS
  Fragment 2.1   120
  Fragment 2.5   120
  Fragment 3   144
  Fragment 5   146

ARISTOTLE
Eth. nic.
  5.4.7   77

Int.
  16a3–5   123
  16a26   123

Metaph.
  985b22–986a3   149

Poet.
  1460b–1461b   99

Rhet.
  1404b   176
  1408a   176
  1414a   176

CLEMENT OF ALEXANDRIA
Ecl.
  56.2   13

Paed.
  1.6   189

Strom.
  1.5.28   110
  1.15.72   25
  1.20   71
  1.30.1–2   111
  1.22.150   149
  1.30.3–4   111
  1.30.4   112
  1.31.1   27, 107, 112
  1.72.4   27, 28
  1.151.2   27
  1.153.2–3   179
  1.165–166   47
  2.18   109
  2.19.97   186
  2.100.3   27, 28
  2.131.5   208
  3.95.2   169
  5.11.69   43
  5.14.97   28
  6.85   143
  7.87.2   154

CYRIL OF ALEXANDRIA
Comm. Is.
  Praef.   51

DIOGENES LAERTIUS
Vit. phil.

1.13	144
7.57	126
7.59	127
7.110	177
7.147	194
8.1	144
8.17	146

EUSEBIUS OF CAESAREA
Dem. ev.

6.18.34–37	71, 72
6.18.36	71
8.2.123	44
390.5	44

Hist. eccl.

1.11.3–9	43
2.4.2–3	41
2.5.1	40
2.16–17	10, 34
2.17.1	41
2.17.2	43
2.17.12	43
2.16	11
2.18	27, 79, 147
2.18.7	97, 142
2.24	14
3.8.4–8	68
3.21	14
4.1	14
4.4	14
4.5.2	44
4.5.5	14
4.11.6	14
4.19	14
4.20	14
5.8.11	20
5.9	14
5.10–11	13
5.10.1	14
6.3.1–3	19
6.6.1	19
6.17	72
6.17.1	43
6.19.6–7	150
6.19.8	150
6.19.13	17
6.20.2	87
6.24.2	113
6.26	19
7.24.1	43
7.32.16	34

Praep. ev.

Entire text	44
1.9.20	44
7.12.14–13.7	44
7.13.1–2	44
7.13.3	44
7.13.4–6	44
7.13.6	46
7.17.4–18.3	44
7.18.1–2	44
7.20.9–21.5	44
7.21.1–4	44
8.6.1–7.20	44
8.8	47
8.8.56–57	94
8.9.38	94
8.10.18	46, 94
8.10.19–12.20	44
8.10.19	45
8.11.1–18	44
8.12.1–19	44
8.12.21–14.72	44
8.13.1–6	44
8.14.1	44
8.14.2–42	44
8.14.43–72	44
8.15.11–7.21	44
11.9.5	36
11.14.10–15.7	44
11.15.1	44
11.15.2–4	44
11.15.5–6	44
11.16.1–2	47
11.23.12–24.12	44
11.24.1–6	44
11.24.7–110	44
11.24.11–12	44
13.12.1–2	46
13.12.1	144
13.12.3	149
13.18.12–16	44, 47
13.18.12–15	44
13.18.15	45
13.18.16	44, 45

HOMER
Il.

1.263	90

Od.

1.55	122
1.62	122
2.243	90
7.259–260	103

INDICES

IRENAEUS
Haer.
1.5.5	169
1.11.1	15
1.24.7	15
2.31.1	15
1.27.1–2	15
1.28.1	15
2.25.1	143
3.30.5	72

JEROME
Chron.
246e	3

Comm. Am.
1	71

Comm. Gal.
Praef.	4

Comm. Zach
Praef.	76

Did. Spir.
Praef.	5

Epist.
33.4	113
36.4	5
51.5	168
68.2	2

Nom. Hebr.
Praef.	96, 142

Ruf.
1.6	5, 173
2.16	5, 173

Vir. ill.
1	2
36	15
54.4	19
89.6	132
109	2, 3, 7, 76
120	5
135	2

JOSEPHUS
Ant.
9.225	71
18.63	43
18.116–117	43
18.259	41

C. Ap.
2.256–257	46

B.J.
2.489–97	11
6.293–302	68–69

JUSTIN MARTYR
1 Apol. 44.8	47

ORIGEN
Cels.
1.24	124, 126
2.31	46
4.39	121
4.40	166, 168
4.50	121
4.51	32, 33
4.71	79
4.87	106
5.45	140
5.55	33
6.2	79
6.19	47
6.21	32, 33
6.43	166
6.66	204
7.20	33

Comm. Cant.
1	133
2.8	130
3.9	131

Comm. Gen.
Entire text	5, 82, 113, 210

Comm. Matt.
10.22	32, 33
11	141
12.43	131
14.2	33
14.5	153
14.16	171
15.3	32, 33, 54
16.2	121
17.17	33
27.9	65
Ser. 92	180

Comm. Jo.
1.1	140
1.15	131
1.89	56
1.119	152
2.21	93
2.33	96

2.34	196	13.1	127
2.180	168	14.3	33
2.181	168	15.3–4	133
2.182–184	168	16.5	151
2.182	166	16.6	149
2.196	131		
2.220	153	*Hom. Ex.*	
6.25	32, 142	2.1–2	33
6.217	33	7.5	133
10.1	153	8.2	33
10.26	108	9.4	33
10.39	196	13.3	33
10.261–262	151		
13.8	108	*Hom. Ezek.*	
13.62	140	Entire text	4
13.408	153		
19.149–150	166	*Hom. Is.*	
20.10	140	9.4	133
28.1–5	149		
		Hom. Jer.	
Comm. Rom.		Entire text	4
Entire text	31	1.10	166, 168
1.1	33	5.6	90
1.3	143	14.5	33
2.6	121	17.1–2	132
2.6.4	33	20.1–7	93
2.13.19	32, 33		
3.2.9	32, 33	*Hom. Jes. Nav.*	
3.6.4	32	3.4	140
3.8.4	152–153	16.1	33
8.73–4	158	20	140
		20.4	121
Ep. Greg.		23.4	138
1	116		
		Hom. Judic.	
Fr. Col.		8.4	31
?	131		
		Hom. Lev.	
Fr. Exod.		6.2	168
12:22	33	8.6	33
		12.7	206
Fr. Luc.			
212	152	*Hom. Luc.*	
		8.2	205, 206
Fr. Matt.		10.30–37	93
25:30	33		
		Hom. Num.	
Hom. Gen.		5.3	141, 197
1.13	171, 204, 206	9.5	33
2.5	151	11.4	133, 140
6.2	116	13.1	127
7.2–4	102	14.2	121
7.6	102	19	140
11.1–2	113–114	20.3	96
11.3	127	22.4	33

26.4	33	**PLATO**	
27.5	131	*Crat.*	
		384C	123
Orat.		397B–C	122
24.2	132, 138	397D	122
		398B	122
Philoc.		398E–399C	122
4	130	434C	125
4.1	131	435D	123
		437C	123
Princ.		439B	123
Entire text	5		
1.1	131, 135	*Phaedr.*	
1.1.6	152	245–249	167
1.5.2	196	246B–C	168
1.6.2	167	274B	176
1.7.4	173		
1.8.4	167	*Resp.*	
2.1.1	167	473D	80
2.6.3–6	167		
2.8.1	201	*Theaet.*	
2.8.3–4	167	176B	8
2.9.1–2	167		
2.9.5–6	167	**PLINY**	
2.9.7	166	*Hist. nat.*	
2.11.1	189	*Praef.* 17	50
3.1.22	166	*Praef.* 21–22	50
3.5.4	166	*Praef.* 23	50
3.6.1	186		
4.2.1–4	83	**PORPHYRY**	
4.2–3	120	*Antr. nymph.*	
4.3.1	176	789.12–19	189–190
4.3.5	93		
4.3.15	130	*Marc.*	
4.12	153	17	43
Sel. Gen.		*Quaest. hom.*	
2.2	33	1.12–14	138–139
3:21	168, 169, 175, 176		
16:4–5	33, 113	**PROCLUS**	
40:20	33	*El. Theol.*	
		129	43
Sel. Lev.		135	43
8.6	32	153	43
Sel. Ps.		*In Parm.*	
?	151	617	127
4:5	180		
50	154	**PS-IAMBLICHUS**	
		Theol. Arith.	
PALLADIUS		34.5–6	200
Hist. Laus.		54.13–55.1	145, 163
4.1	3	54.18	163
4.4	6		

Vit. Pyth.
  3–4   144
  14   144, 149

PS-JUSTIN
Coh.
  9.2   35
  10.1   35
  13.1–4   36
  13.4   35, 36
  21.2   36
  22.2   36

QUINTILIAN
Inst.
  1.8.10–12   53

RUFINUS
Apol. Hier.
  2.15   18
  2.28   5

H.E.
  2.7   6
  11.7   2, 3, 18, 22–23, 38
  11.23   21

SENECA
Epist.
  42.1   186
  75   115
  75.9   185
  88.2   104
  88.20   104
  88.21–23   105

SOCRATES (church historian)
H.E.
  4.25   3, 4
  4.25.7   5

SOZOMEN
H.E.
  3.15.1   17, 155
  3.15.2   3, 22
  3.15.3   4
  3.15.4   4

TERTULLIAN
Marc.
  5.4.8   102

Mon.
  6   100

Praesc.
  7   25

Res.
  7   169

Val.
  4   15

THEODORE OF MOPSUESTIA
Comm. Cant.
  Praef.   52

Treatise against the Allegorists
  ad. Ps 118   13

THEODORET
H.E.
  3.30.3   155

Quaest. Gen.
  68   100

6. Topical Index

Aaron	81, 184	Etymology	94, 96, 107, 112, 114, 116, 119–164, 197
Abraham	36, 63, 77, 80, 85, 97–117, 129, 132, 137–138, 143, 145, 179–180, 184–185, 190–91	Eunomius	2, 5, 6
Ascension of Isaiah	63–65	Eusebius of Caesarea	10, 14–17, 39–47, 68, 71–72 117, 50, 166
Adam	91, 95–97, 98, 128, 129, 137, 139, 156, 168, 170, 175–176, 196	Eve	130, 140, 168, 176
		Gregory of Nazianzus	3, 4, 87
Apocalypse of Elijah	65–67	Gregory of Nyssa	6, 78, 106
Apostolic Fathers	59 (references to *Barn.*, *Did.*, *Ign.*, and *Herm.*)	Hagar	29, 78–79, 86, 97–117, 177, 183, 188, 208, 211
		Heresy, Heretical	15, 23, 37, 59, 173
Aquila	72–74	Iamblichus	55, 155–156
Arianism	2, 6, 37, 38, 39, 78, 102	Image	95, 135, 171, 173, 184, 187, 198, 199, 202, 204–208
Arithmology	26, 96, 119, 143–164		
Arius	25, 35, 37–39, 59		
Aristobulus	25, 28, 46, 94, 120, 127, 144, 146	Isaac	85, 112, 117, 129, 130, 145, 184
Aristotle, Aristotelians	7, 20, 22, 47, 59, 77, 99, 103, 123–124, 144, 149, 156, 176	Jacob	83–85, 97–98, 100, 101, 112, 137, 138, 145, 166, 172, 184
Athanasius	2, 6, 18–20, 25, 35, 38–39, 87, 102	Jesus	34, 43, 54, 64, 68, 131, 143, 153, 157, 180, 182, 207
Barhadbeshabba	12–14	Jewish Tradition	71–72
Basil of Caesarea	4, 5, 87	Josephus	11, 16, 34, 35, 36, 40, 41, 42, 43, 45, 46, 60, 67–71, 72, 74, 87, 94, 170
Basilides	15		
Book of the Covenant	61–63	Likeness	187, 202, 204–208
Cain	93–95, 139, 195	Logos	34, 37–38, 45–46, 60, 131–136, 152, 184, 191–192, 194, 198, 205, 206, 207
Cain and Abel	62, 82–84, 84–87, 88–93, 129		
Catechetical School	1, 2, 10, 14, 17–20, 38	Manicheanism	2, 6, 59
Clement of Alexandria	9, 11, 12, 15, 16, 22, 26–30, 32, 33, 40, 54, 59, 71, 81, 103, 107, 109–113, 117, 143, 148, 156, 183, 189, 196, 199, 207, 208, 211	Moses	29, 35, 36, 76, 78, 80, 96, 102, 120, 128–129, 131–132, 149, 166, 185, 193
		Origen	2, 5, 9, 10–16, 19, 22, 23, 25, 26, 30–34, 37, 39, 46, 47, 48, 54–57, 60, 65, 67, 72, 73, 76, 79, 81–83, 87, 90, 93, 94, 95, 96, 97, 102, 103, 108–117, 120–121, 124, 130–133, 135–138, 140–142, 148–149, 150–154, 157, 164, 165, 166–169, 171–177, 179–180, 181, 183, 189, 196,
Creation	36, 38, 39, 151–153, 158, 161, 169, 172, 174, 184, 190, 199–208		
Education	3, 21–22, 97–117, 121, 155, 183–186		
Esau	83–84, 166, 172		

	199, 201, 204, 205, 206, 208, 210–211	Powers	190–199
		Progress	183–190
Origenism	1–5, 19, 35	Ps-Justin	35–36
Philip of Side	2, 13–14, 16–17, 19–20	Pythagoras,	
Philokalos	70, 85–87, 90, 93, 117	Pythagoreans	28–29, 41–42, 47, 59, 100, 101, 144–148, 149, 150–154, 157, 194, 200, 201
Philosopher-king	79–80		
Plagiarism	50–52		
Plato,		Seth	95–97, 185
Platonists	8, 28, 29, 31, 36, 43, 56, 59, 90, 91, 93, 136, 144, 145, 146, 148, 150, 166, 167, 168, 170, 177, 178, 184, 189, 190, 192, 195, 200	Symmachus	72–74
		Theodore of Mopsuestia	13, 52
		Theodotion	72–74
		Tura	1–2, 6–9
		Valentinus	15, 25, 26, 31
Plotinus	134–135, 136, 150, 189	Virtue	8, 42, 77, 78, 79, 85, 86, 90, 91, 92, 98, 101, 103–117, 129, 130, 137, 139, 165, 167, 177–183, 184–190, 197–198, 199, 204, 206, 211
Porphyry	7, 8, 43, 59, 119, 138, 150, 156, 189, 190		
Pre-passions	177–183		
Pre-existence of souls	165–177		
Procreation	97–101		

7. *Index of Modern Authors*

Abel, Karlhans	177, 178	Beatrice, Pier Franco	7, 168
Adler, William	61		
Afonasin, Eugene	148–149	Becker, Adam	12
Alexandre, Monique	187	Bennett, Byard	6, 18
		Berchman, Richard	31
Amir, Jehoshua	97		
Amsler, Mark	123, 124	Betz, Hans-Dieter	102
Attridge, Harold W.	46	Bienert, Wolfgang	8, 18, 93–94, 119, 136, 181
Ax, Wolfram	126	Bigger, Charles P.	43
Ayres, Lewis	6, 69	Binder, Gerhard	24, 79
		Bloch, René	120
Baer, Richard A.	100, 169	Blowers, Paul	31
Bammel, Caroline	174	Blumenthal, H.J.	8
Baltussen, Han	49, 52, 54, 55	Bos, Abraham P.	194
Bardy, Gustav	2, 10, 14, 16, 18, 31, 82, 93, 155, 156	Bostock, Gerald	144, 149, 150, 152, 166
		Bovon, François	143
Barnes, Timothy	37	Bousset, Wilhelm	11–12, 28
Barthélemy, Dominique	16, 40, 46, 60, 73	Buffière, Felix	103
		Burkert, Walter	145, 161
Bauer, Walter	14	Butterworth, G.W.	130, 131, 167
Bayless, Grant D.	75, 77, 82, 87, 90, 91, 93, 106, 119, 159, 165, 171, 172, 173, 174, 177, 181–183, 187, 198, 199, 204		
		Cadiou, Réne	166
		Calleja, Joseph	95
		Caner, Daniel	54
		Carlini, Antionio	119

Carriker, Andrew	27, 39, 41	Moritz	15
Cassel, J. David	75–76	Friedl, Alfred	4
Chadwick, Henry	25, 31, 46, 121, 168, 174	Fürst, Alfons	56
Chapman, John	5	Gaca, Kathy L.	100, 101, 145
Chin, Catherine M.	130	Gaster, Moses	61–62
Clark, Elizabeth A.	6, 166	Geljon, Albert C.	75, 76, 84, 90, 91, 94, 120
Clements, Ruth A.	69, 176, 192	Ghattas, Michael	6, 181
Conroy Jr., John T.	170	Ginzberg, Louis	71–72
Crouzel, Henri	47	Gnilka, Christian	25
Culpepper, R. Alan	12, 143	Grabbe, Lester L.	96, 97, 127, 130, 170
		Grant, Robert M.	93
		Graver, Margaret	177, 178, 179
		Greenstone, J.H.	100
Daley, Brian E.	165	Gregg, Robert	37
Daniélou, Jean	166	Griggs, C. Wilfred	10
Dawson, David	120, 124, 125, 129, 170	Groh, Dennis	37
Denis, Albert-Marie	61, 62, 64, 65	Gronewald, Michael	79, 106
DeVore, David	41	Gustafsson, B.	41
De Longe, Nicholas	31, 132	Haas, Christopher	2, 11, 21
De Faye, Eugène	166	Hagedorn, Dieter	62
de Lubac, Henri	83, 94	Hagedorn, Ursula	62
De Vogel, Cornelia	39	Hadot, Ilsetraut	47, 49, 56
de Vries, Hent	105	Hadot, Pierre	56
DelCogliano, Mark	5, 6	Hahn, Johannes	21
Demura, Miyako	183	Hall, Robert G.	64
Diekamp, Franz	6	Hanson, R.P.C.	26, 37, 130
Dillon, John	115, 144, 145, 146, 169, 178, 192, 194	Hardwick, Michael E.	67
Dinan, Andrew	25	Harl, Marguerite	26, 44, 87, 121, 130, 131, 132, 166
Dörrie, Heinrich	150	Hay, David	8, 109–110, 186, 198
Dorival, Gilles	26	Hayes, Walter	5
Doutreleau, Louis	1, 78, 93, 133, 155–156	Heimann, Peter	166
Drake, Susanna	34	Heine, Ronald E.	32, 56, 83, 102, 113, 114, 116, 151, 152, 153, 168, 210
Droge, Arthur J.	47	Helleman, Wendy	184
		Helmbold, William C.	53
Edwards, Mark	31, 150, 167	Henrichs, Albert	62, 100, 103, 105, 106, 111, 113, 116, 132, 183, 185
Elon, M.	100		
Endo, Masanobu	46		
Erler, Michael	56	Heron, Alasdair	6
		Hicks, Benjamin	20
Fernandez-Marcos, Natalio	73	Hill, Robert	1, 4, 57, 66, 70, 76, 77, 81, 133
Field, Frederick	73, 74	Hollerich, Michael J.	47
Frede, Michael	125, 127	Hornschuh, Manfred	14
Frick, Peter	190		
Friedländer,			

Inowlocki, Sabrina	10, 40, 41, 42, 43–45, 67, 68, 75	Marcovich, Miroslav	35
Inwood, Brad	178	Markschies, Christoph	8
Jacobs, Andrew	61, 69	Marmorstein, Arthur	193
Jakab, Attila	10	Martens, Peter	166, 167, 168, 169, 171, 174
Jakobovits, Immanuel	101	Martyn, J. Louis	102
Johnson, William A.	135	McGill, Scott	51
		McGuckin, John	3, 31
Kahn, Charles H.	146	McLeod, Frederick	9, 13
Kalvesmaki, Joel	26, 143, 146, 152, 156	Méasson, Anita	91
Kamesar, Adam	39, 71, 92, 119, 120, 121, 127, 134, 191	Mélèze-Modrzejewski, Joseph	11
Knibb, Michael A.	63, 64	Mendelson, Alan	104
Koenen, Ludwig	1	Metzler, Karin	89, 168, 179
Kramer, Bärbel	97, 137	Miller, Hannah	51
Kramer, Johannes	97, 137	Mohring, Horst	147
Kehl, Aloys	24	Monaci, A. Costagno	166
Lake, Kirsopp	14, 41, 42, 43	Mondésert, Claude	27, 97
Lamberton, Robert	134, 135, 189, 190	Montes-Peral, Luis Angel	190
Lamirande, Emilien	75, 201	Morlet, Sébastien	47
Lampe, G.W.H.	42, 43, 87, 106, 108, 162	Morris, Jenny	44
		Mortley, Raoul	37–38
Lauro, Elizabeth Dively	83, 120	Most, Glenn W.	8, 49, 124
Lawson, R.P.	130, 131	Mühl, M.	134
Layton, Richard	1–2, 7, 18–20, 21–22, 24, 77, 78, 93, 136, 176, 180, 181, 182, 186, 187, 188	Müller-Wiener, W.	1
		Nautin, Pierre	4, 9, 30, 40, 62–63, 78, 81, 83, 84, 85, 94, 95, 96, 97, 109, 142, 159, 161, 162, 199, 201, 203, 207, 209
Leemans, Johann	183		
Leonhardt, Jutta	11	Nelson, Anne Browning	24, 138, 154–155, 157, 161
Leipoldt, Johannes	2, 18		
Lévy, Carlos	42, 184, 185	Neuschäfer, Bernard	26, 54, 56, 119, 139
Levine, Lee	11	Nielsen, Dave	1
Lewy, Hans	69	Nielsen, Donald	152
Lilla, Salvatore	8, 184, 186	Nikiprowetzky, Valentin	11, 26, 130
Lloyd, A.C.	125		
Lloyd, G.E.R.	50, 51	Nippel, Wilfried	53
Long, A.A.	115, 125, 200		
Lührmann, Dieter	60, 62–64, 65–66	O'Meara, Dominic J.	156
		O'Neil, Edward N.	53
Mach, Michael	195	Osborn, Eric	25, 28, 29, 110
Mackie, Scott D.	185	Otto, Jennifer	29
Maltby, Robert	122		
Mansfeld, Jaap	52, 124		

Pancerz, Roland
  Marcin 8
Parvis, Sarah 69
Pearce, Sarah J.K. 105
Pearson, Birger 14, 15
Pépin, Jean 46, 120
Peraki-Kyriakidou,
  Helen 128
Perrone, Lorenzo 8, 16, 31, 44, 144, 149
Petit, Alain 42
Petit, Françoise 40, 147
Pfeiffer, Rudolph 20, 138
Pohlenz, Max 105, 134, 179
Prinzivalli,
  Emanuela 2, 5, 6, 16–17, 18, 20, 24, 75
Puech, Henri-
  Charles 1
Pouderon,
  Bernard 13, 14

Quandt, Kenneth 50
Quasten,
  Johannes 5, 19
Quispel, Gilles 31

Radde-Gallwitz,
  Andrew 6
Radice, Roberto 145, 146
Ramelli, Ilaria 31–32, 150
Rankin, David 13
Reale, Giovanni 134, 135, 136
Reuling, Hanneke 76, 168, 201
Reydams-Schils,
  Gretchen 200
Riedweg,
  Christoph 35–36, 144
Robbins, Frank
  Egleston 147, 148, 163
Roberts, Colin 14
Robertson,
  David G. 135
Rogers, Justin 15, 32, 34, 41, 79, 97, 101, 103, 183
Rokeah, David 97
Rönsch,
  Hermann 61
Rose, Martha 22
Roskam, Geert 177
Royse, James 12, 16, 83–84
Runia, David 7, 9, 13, 16, 22, 25, 26, 27, 28–29, 31–33, 36, 37, 38, 39, 40, 41, 44, 45, 75, 78, 79, 80, 82, 83, 90, 96, 101, 108, 120, 129, 130, 145, 147, 148, 156, 161, 163, 164, 173, 192, 193, 196, 201, 202–203, 204, 205, 206, 207
Russell, D.S. 53, 121
Russell, Norman 42, 43, 51
Ruwet, Jean 65

Saffrey, H.D. 56
Schereschewsky,
  B.-Z. 100
Schäublin,
  Christoph 54
Scheck,
  Thomas P. 153
Schenkeveld,
  Dirk M. 124
Schibli, Hermann 174
Scholten, Clemens 14
Schreckenberg,
  Hans 67
Schubert, Kurt 67
Scott, Alan 31
Sedley, David N. 115, 123, 200
Segal, Alan 193
Sellew, Philip 7, 156
Serra, Aristide 198
Shroyer,
  Montgomery J. 109
Simonetti, Manlio 5, 7, 26, 95, 101, 165
Skeb, Matthias 56
Sluiter, Ineke 49
Solari, Placid 8, 60
Sorabji, Richard 177
Staehle, Karl 145, 147, 148, 163
Stählin, Otto 26, 27
Stefaniw, Blossom 56, 119, 136, 189
Steiger, Peter D. 75
Stemplinger,
  Eduard 49
Strutwolf, Holger 31
Sterling, Gregory 11–13, 15–16, 116
Stückelberger,
  Alfred 104, 105, 113

Tarrant, Harold 55
Tcherikover,
  Victor 11, 102
Terian, Abraham 40, 147
Termini,
  Christina 190
Theiler, Willy 103, 104
Thesleff, Holger 144
Thümmel, Hans

Georg	31	Lucas	13
Tigcheler, Jo	8, 93	Walter, Nikolaus	146
Tobin, Thomas	46, 169, 205	Watts, Edward	21, 55
Torjesen, Katherine Jo	32, 131	Wellhausen, Julius	191
Trigg, Joseph	31	Weisser, Sharon	183, 185
Tzvetkova-Glaser, Anna	31, 168	Westermann, Claus	143
		Wilson, Walter	7
Ulrich, Jorg	40	Williams, Megan Hale	76
Van den Hoek, Annewies	12, 15–16, 25, 27, 28–30, 31, 32–33, 34, 54, 55, 90, 107, 109, 111, 112–113, 117, 132, 139, 142, 183	Williams, Robert Lee	14
		Williams, Rowan	37–39, 174
		Wilken, Robert L.	69
		Winston, David	46, 101, 127, 134, 170, 184, 191, 192, 194
Van Geytenbach, A.C.	101	Wintermute, O.S.	61, 65
Van Winden, J.C.M.	25, 27	Wolfson, Harry Austryn	11, 37–38, 46, 97, 193
VanderKam, James C.	61	Wutz, Franz	114, 132, 140, 141
Vesey, M.	132–133	Wyrwa, Dietmar	14
Vian, Giovanni M.	120	Wyss, Beatrice	15, 147, 200
Völker, Walther	185		
Vööbus, Arthur	12–13	Yarbro Collins, Adela	143
Von Rompay,		Yli-Karjanmaa, Sami	169, 170

www.ingramcontent.com/pod-product-compliance
Lightning Source LLC
Chambersburg PA
CBHW021659230426
43668CB00008B/669